Yearbook of Type II

Edited by Slanted

Content

Yearbook of Type II
Introduction

The task of picking the right fonts (whatever that means!) is a mystifying process. Putting the right font forward can help readability, emotionalize the design, give character. There seem to be endless choices—from normal, classical-looking fonts and workhorse typefaces to brand new candy cane fonts. Selecting the right typeface is a mixture of loose intuition and firm rules. Though it is an old saying that the first thing one learns about typography and type design is that these rules are made to be broken. And that "breaking the rules" has always been just another rule.

Typography is important because it can make—not break—the image you want to portray. Like everything else, the proper usage of typography manifests through knowledge; selecting the desired typeface requires a combination of understanding and intuition, and—as with any skill—demands practice. As an alternative you may grab a flowchart like the one we published in the first Yearbook of Type—*You Need A Typeface?* by Julian Hansen—something serious lies at the heart of every joke!

Typefaces play an essential role in establishing identities which later become a visual footprint. Some fonts are diamonds (buy them!). Every designer has a few favorite fonts like this—expressive personal favorites that we hold onto and wait for the perfect festive occasion to use. Some opt for the strategy of picking one favorite typeface and using it over and over for months and excluding all the others. Like a song on continuous loop.

As the organizers of *ISType 2015* said "Metal letters were strong and solid enough to lift the weight of grand ideologies that unified cultures across bridges. Today's technologies endow letters with swiftness, adaptable to new needs and complex functions. They can shift forms swiftly, respond directly, and embrace plurality." Aside from their mass appearance in print, advertising, corporate identity, and user interfaces brought about new opportunities through new technologies to overthink type design not as a ballet of beautiful curves but as a mission with cultural significance. The challenges are to think "out of the box," especially for less linear writing systems such as Arabic.

Just like the first edition, the second edition of the Yearbook of Type offers a high-quality selection of numerous recently published digital typefaces in the form of a clear, comprehensive compendium of great practical value. The emotional and informative presentation of these typefaces will serve designers and agencies as a source of inspiration and will help others select the desired typeface.

A variety of blogs and Internet portals provide regular information about new fonts and foundries, but there is still not yet a high-quality, independent print publication that provides an overview of the field. This is the main goal of the Yearbook of Type: to present typefaces which were created in the last few years all the way from large and small typefoundries to independent typographers.

In the Yearbook of Type each typeface or typeface family is presented on a spread. The typographic composition on the left page features each type designer's personal take on presenting their own typeface. On the right side more detailed background information of the typeface is provided as an overview of the typeface's various additional features. The catalogue is followed by an index of all the typefaces arranged by category. Short texts provide information on individual type designers and an essay section offers sketches, background knowledge, technical information, instructions and descriptions from the world of typography.

We would like to thank all those involved in helping make this volume possible where we featured typeface designers and labels. We wish readers inspiration and joy in exploring this publication.

Yours sincerely,
Slanted Editorial Staff

Typefaces A

...in a rush as usual?

Get a pencil and take your time to play*

A is for giraffe
B is for computer
C is for yeti
D is for apple
E **is for rocket**
F **is for light**
G **is for whale**
H ***is for umbrella***
I ***is for igloo***
J ***is for sun***
K *is for jacket*
L *is for kangaroo*
M *is for mouse*
N *is for xylophone*
O is for nose
P is for orange
Q is for elephant
R is for penguin
S is for fish
T **is for queen**
U **is for tulip**
V **is for beaver**
W **is for viking**
X **is for zebra**
Y is for dinosaur
Z is for house

*or let your children do it! ☺

also works in German except from Q, U and V

About

ABeZeh was designed for children learning to read. Far too often, children's literature and school books are set in typefaces mirroring "b," "d," "p" and "q" and hardly differentiate between capital "I" and small "l."

None of that! ABeZeh's distinguished, open and friendly shapes simplify the reading process—and by the way, the same goes for adults with reading difficulties.

Design
Anja Meiners
2015

Foundry
Carrois Type Design, Germany
www.carrois.com

Styles / Weights
Family of two styles (Regular, Slab), each with seven weights (Thin, ExtraLight, Light, Regular, Medium, Bold, ExtraBold) and Regular style with Italics

Language support
Latin, Cyrillic, Greek

OpenType options
Tabular and Proportional Lining, Standard Ligatures, All Caps, Small Caps, Capitals to Small Caps, Superscript, Subscript, Fractions, Numerator, Denominator, Arrows, Slashed Zero

Optimized for web
No

REGULAR 18PT

abcdefghijklmnopqrstuvwxyzæfjåçéñöûß
ABCDEFGHIJKLMNOPQRSTUVWXYZÆÇØ
01234567890@.,-:;!?')]§*""«»/–€$&⅓☺↗

SLAB REGULAR 18PT

aabcdefghijklmnopqrstuvwxyzæfjåçéñöûß
ABCDEFGHIJKLMNOPQRSTUVWXYZÆÇØ
01234567890@.,-:;!?')]§*""«»/–€$&⅓☺↗

BOLD & SLAB BOLD 36PT

aejgGQR7
aejgGQR7

REGULAR, ALL WEIGHTS 7PT

Thin
ThinItalic
ExtraLight
ExtraLightItalic
Light
LightItalic
Regular
RegularItalic
Medium
MediumItalic
Bold
BoldItalic
ExtraBold
ExtraBoldItalic

SLAB, ALL WEIGHTS 8PT

Thin
ExtraLight
Light
Regular
Medium
Bold
ExtraBold

ABeZeh

ADRIA SLAB

Voix ambiguë d'un cœur qui au zéphyr préfère les jattes de kiwi. Quizdeltagerne spiste jordbær med fløde, mens cirkusklovnen Walther spillede på xylofon. Fix problem with galvanized jets. **Jove xef, porti whisky amb quinze glaçons d'hidrogen, coi! Nechť již hříšné saxofony ďáblů rozezvučí síň úděsnými tóny waltzu**

Miles High
Kalkulation
Ποσειδώνας
Xylophones

Bernardiño
Μυθολογία
Rum Runner
Mültiļịngûåļ

Voix ambiguë d'un cœur qui au zéphyr préfère les jattes de kiwi. Quizdeltagerne spiste jordbær med fløde, mens cirkusklovnen Walther spillede på xylofon. Fix problem with galvanized jets. **Jove xef, porti whisky amb quinze glaçons d'hidrogen, coi! Nechť již hříšné saxofony ďáblů rozezvučí síň úděsnými tóny waltzu**

Adria Slab

About

Adria Slab is a smooth slab serif typeface that comes in seven weights and charming upright Italics. Try combining it with its super friendly family member Adria Grotesk.

Enjoy making great typography with a vast choice of lining, tabular and old style figures, numerators, denominators, tabular figures, fractions, ligatures, some sweet symbols and even alternate arrows.

Design
Marcus Sterz
2014

Foundry
FaceType, Austria
www.facetype.org

Styles / Weights
Thin, ExtraLight, Light, Regular, Medium, Bold, Black, each with upright Italics

Language support
Latin, Greek

OpenType options
Proportional Oldstyle, Tabular and Proportional Lining, Tabular Oldstyle, Standard Ligatures, Discretionary Ligatures, Superscript, Subscript, Ordinals, Numerator, Denominator, Ornaments, Arrows, Stylistic Alternates, Stylistic Sets, Slashed Zero, Justification Alternates

Optimized for web
Yes

REGULAR 18PT

abcdefghijklmnopqrstuvwxyzæfjåçéñöûß
ABCDEFGHIJKLMNOPQRSTUVWXYZÆÇØ
01234567890@.,-:;!?')]§*""«»/–€$& ↗

BLACK & LIGHT 30PT

aejgGQR7
aejgGQR7

BOLD & LIGHT 16PT

Typographers want amazing, exquisite
& clever justified text in books

BOLD & REGULAR 9PT

→ **com·pen·dium** / noun / (pl. com·pen·dia / or com·pen·diums) a collection of facts, drawings and photographs on a particular subject, especially in a book: "a compendium of typography."

ALL WEIGHTS 7PT

Thin
ExtraLight
Light
Regular
Medium
Bold
Black

UPRIGHT ITALICS 7PT

Thin UprightItalic
ExtraLight UprightItalic
Light UprightItalic
Regular UprightItalic
Medium UprightItalic
Bold UprightItalic
Black UprightItalic

FS Albert Arabic

اف اس ألبرت
خط جذاب

Thin

برّاق دافئ ودي

Light

حساس حيوي

Regular

قوي يُعتمد عليه

Bold

مدوِّر ثري ريّان

ExtraBold

جمال ديناميكي

FS Albert Arabic

About
To create a truly global font family, FS Albert needed a W script sibling. Emanuela Conidi set about the delicate task of creating an alphabet to harmonize visually with its Latin sans serif counterpart so that the two could be used side-by-side in bilingual publications. Working with the Kufic style of script, with its simpler, geometric forms, Emanuela sculpted letters with a similar optical size, weight and rhythm as FS Albert, with open counters and monolinear strokes. To match Albert's cheery, charming character, FS Albert Arabic needed an injection of warmth and informality. Emanuela incorporated some of the more expressive, calligraphic shapes of the Naskh script style, which lent the letterforms a looser, softer, more handwritten quality, while remaining functional and structured.

The end result is an Arabic script that's the perfect partner to FS Albert: open counters, monolinear strokes and a friendly, rounded appearance.

Design
Emanuela Conidi
2014

Foundry
Fontsmith, Great Britain
www.fontsmith.com

Styles / Weights
Thin, Light, Regular, Bold

Language support
Latin, Arabic

OpenType options
Mark Positioning

Optimized for web
Yes

REGULAR 18PT

ء آ آ أ أ ؤ ؤ إ إ ى ئ ئئ ا ا ب ببب ت تتت ث ثثث ج ججج ح ححح خ خخخ
د ـد ذ ـذ ر ـر ز ـز س سسس ش ششش ص صصص ض ضضض
ط ططط ظ ظظظ ع ععع غ غغغ ف ففف ق ققق ك ككك ل للل
م ممم ن ننن ه ههه و ـو ى ـى ي ييي ٱ ـٱ ٹ ٹٹٹ پ پپپ چ چچچ
ڈ ـڈ ڑ ـڑ ژ ـژ ڤ ڤڤڤ ک ککک گ گگگ ں ـں ھ ھھھ ۀ ـۀ ہ ہہہ ۂ ـۂ ۃ ـۃ
ی ییی ے ـے ۓ ـۓ ە ـە

BOLD 30PT

ض گ ههه س

BOLD & REGULAR 14PT

أبجد هوز حطي كلمن
سعفص قرشت ثخذ ضظغ
الثعلب البني السريع يقفز من
فوق الكلب الكسول

REGULAR 30PT

ض گ ههه س

BOLD & REGULAR 9PT

أبجد هوز حطي كلمن
سعفص قرشت ثخذ ضظغ
الثعلب البني السريع يقفز من
فوق الكلب الكسول

LAND ART BY NATURE

Algo FY

sculptural, rustic & primitive

About
Algo FY is a singular font family with broken ductus and blackletter aspect. Clearly inspired by calligraphic shapes, each of the three weights has been especially designed as if the tool has changed. With its special articulations and its differentiated instrokes and outstrokes, Algo FY is a sculptural, rustic, primitive and dynamic font family. The alternating game between concave and convex shapes gives this typeface a spontaneous and unpredictable style with a strong personality. Each weight shows finest details on each part of the letters. Light and Regular are for text setting, while the Black style should be used for titling and headlines.

Algo FY will fit with every project you want to give a strong and singular personality. Algo FY received a Typeface Creation award at Club des Directeurs Artistiques in Paris.

Design
Michel Derre, Jérémie Hornus, Alisa Nowak, Julien Priez
2014

Foundry
Fontyou, France
www.fontyou.com

Styles / Weights
Light, Regular, Black

Language support
Latin

OpenType options
Proportional Oldstyle, Tabular and Proportional Lining, Tabular Oldstyle, Standard Ligatures, All Caps, Superscript, Subscript, Ordinals, Fractions, Numerator, Denominator, Slashed Zero

Optimized for web
Yes

REGULAR 17PT

abcdefghijklmnopqrstuvwxyzæfjåçéñöûß
ABCDEFGHIJKLMNOPQRSTUVWXYZÆÇØ
0123456789@.,-:;!?')]§*"""«»/-€$&⅓

BLACK 36PT

aejgGQR7

LIGHT 16PT

Typographers want amazing, exquisite & clever justified text in books

LIGHT 36PT

aejgGQR7

REGULAR 13PT

The Yearbook of Type compendium works well as a tool in vexed typography questions for polarizing job

Alverata

Latin, Greek & Cyrillic

High legibility in print & screen

Inspired by the shapes of ROMANESQUE capitals in inscriptions of the eleventh and twelfth centuries • • • • • • • • •

CONTEMPORARY TYPEFACE
WITH ROOTS IN EARLY EUROPE

РОМАНСКАЯ

Κεφτέδες γαλοπούλας με καρότο ϗ πάπρικα

καφές ϗ ζάχαρη

A	a	a	a	a	a
A	e	e	e	e	e
x	x	u	u	u	u

About
Gerard Unger's new typeface Alverata is a 21st century typeface inspired by the shapes of Romanesque capitals in inscriptions from the eleventh and twelfth centuries, without being a close imitation of them. It is additionally based on the early twentieth century model, but tweaked so as to prevent blandness and monotony.

Alverata performs beautifully both on screen and paper, delivering excellent legibility. Its letters are open and friendly in small sizes and lively and attractive in large sizes. They are robust, and show refinement in their detail. Unger's Alverata is an extensive type family, with versions for both formal and informal applications, and with Greek and Cyrillic relatives. Alverata consists of three different fonts: Alverata, Alverata Informal and Alverata Irregular, these vary in form and width, but maintain the same spirit.

Design
Gerard Unger
2014

Foundry
TypeTogether, Czech Republic
www.type-together.com

Styles / Weights
Family of three styles (Alverata, Alverata Informal and Alverata Irregular), each with six weights (Light, Regular, Medium, Semibold, Bold, Black), Alverata with Italics

Language support
Latin, Cyrillic, Greek

OpenType options
Proportional Oldstyle, Tabular and Proportional Lining, Tabular Oldstyle, Standard Ligatures, All Caps, Small Caps, Capitals to Small Caps, Superscript, Subscript, Ordinals, Fractions, Numerator, Denominator, Stylistic Alternates, Stylistic Sets, Localized Forms

Optimized for web
Yes

REGULAR 18PT

abcdefghijklmnopqrstuvwxyzæfjåçéñöûß
ABCDEFGHIJKLMNOPQRSTUVWXYZÆÇØ
0123456789@.,-:;!?')]§*“”«»/–€$&½

INFORMAL BOLD 35PT

aejgGQR7

IRREGULAR BLACK & MEDIUM 14PT

Typographers want amazing, exquisite
& clever justified text in books

SEMIBOLD & REGULAR 8PT

over·view / *noun* / a brief summary of something: *in the index of the Yearbook of Type the reader can find an overview of all typefaces presented in the book sorted by classification*

BLACK & MEDIUM 14PT

Typographers want *amazing, exquisite*
& clever justified text *in books*

AM SANS ONE

Alois Menacher trained as a lead typesetter. Since his apprenticeship, he has worked intensively with typography and type design. His artistic focus was always on Logo and Corporate Design. His knowledge in the field of graphic design and Mac computers is all self-taught.

designed in

2013

Early in 2012 Alois Menacher fulfilled a long-desired wish: To develop his own font. Even if the development of a font course is done nowadays with the computer, the first ideas and designs were initially still on paper.

ALOIS MENACHER

Sugar Maple

Maple leaves are used as a food plant for the larvae of a number of Lepidoptera species. Aphids are also very common sap-feeders on maples. In horticultural applications a dimethoate spray will solve this.

STRAND BOARDS

In printing and typography, hot metal typesetting refers to technologies for typesetting text in letterpress printing.

cue shafts

Leather tips of varying curvature and degrees of hardness are glued to (or in some cases screwed into) the ferrule.

WOODWIND INSTRUMENTS

When designing "AM Sans One" it was a great challenge for me to develop a modern sans serif, which, despite the large number of existing fonts in this sector, has its own unique character. The starting point for the design concept was the cap O, designed as a rectangle with rounded corners, and not as a circle or an oval. The O should form the basis for the whole alphabet. Another feature is the characters with oblique starting and end strokes such as "A, V, W". These don't have exactly straight lines, but rather a slight curvature. Thus, these letters do not look too geometric. Also the cap K deviates slightly from the usual shape which makes AM Sans One different from other already existing fonts. I could well imagine applying this font to areas such as engineering or architecture.

LIGHT REGULAR **SEMIBOLD**

AM Sans One

About

When designing AM Sans One "it was a great challenge for me to develop a modern sans serif, which, despite the large number of existing fonts in this sector, has its own unique character. The starting point for the design concept was the cap 'O,' designed as a rectangle with rounded corners, and not as a circle or an oval. The 'O' should form the basis for the whole alphabet. Another feature are the characters with oblique starting and end strokes such as 'A, V, W.' These don't have exactly straight, diagonal lines, but a slight curvature. Thus, these letters do not look too geometric. Also the cap K deviates slightly from the usual shape which makes AM Sans One different from other already existing fonts. I could well imagine applying this font to areas such as engineering or architecture."

Design
Alois Menacher
2013

Foundry
URW++, Germany
www.urwpp.com

Styles / Weights
Light, Regular, SemiBold

Language support
Latin

OpenType options
Tabular and Proportional Lining, Standard Ligatures, Discretionary Ligatures, Superscript, Subscript, Ordinals, Fractions

Optimized for web
Yes

REGULAR 18PT

abcdefghijklmnopqrstuvwxyzæfjåçéñöûß
ABCDEFGHIJKLMNOPQRSTUVWXYZÆÇØ
0123456789@.,-:;!?')]§*""«»/–€$&½

REGULAR 43PT

aejgGQR7

SEMIBOLD & LIGHT 16PT

Typographers want amazing, exquisite
& clever justified text in books

SEMIBOLD 43PT

aejgGQR7

SEMIBOLD & REGULAR 15PT

Typographers want amazing, exquisite
& clever justified text in books

El amor fue inventado una tarde de abril de 1134 en el sur de Francia. ¶ La humanidad no siempre ha estado de acuerdo en que lo más importante en la vida de un hombre sea enamorarse de una mujer y viceversa. Aunque el impulso del amor es antiguo, no lo es el valor que se asigna al fenómeno del enamoramiento. Sus efectos fueron considerados durante siglos una pura estupidez. Solo desde el siglo XII fue el amor escalando posiciones en el *ranking* de valores hasta alcanzar su prestigioso puesto actual. ¶ ¡Grandes inventos de la humanidad! La juventud es otro. Jóvenes ha habido siempre, pero la juventud solo aparece en el siglo XVIII. Antes hubo niños, adultos y viejos. [...] Desde su invención, la juventud no dejará de acumular derechos. Con el tiempo exigirá por su dinero productos a su gusto; nacerán así el *Rock & Roll* y otras industrias que definirán su identidad. La juventud se ha instalado sólidamente, y está a punto de hacerse obligatoria. ¶ **Y hay más. La educación, por ejemplo, fue inventada en Inglaterra en septiembre de 1802. El acto de educar es viejo como el hombre, pero el que los niños deban ir al colegio no lo es. [...] No por inventos son menos verdaderos, pero ni el amor, ni la juventud, ni la educación, ni la locura, ni la libertad deben tener necesariamente la forma que hoy les damos. Jóvenes sí, pero, ¿por qué juventud? Educación sí, ¿por qué colegios? ¶ Es el viejo error de confundir las causas con los efectos.**

Beltrán Mena { Amster Blanca, Fina, Gris, Negra y SúperNegra | 9/12 pt }

ÀÊÏŐŮ ABCDEFGHIJKLMNOPQRST UVWXYZß ÀÊÏŐŮ ABCDEFGHIJKLM NOPQRSTUVWXYZß àêïőů abcdefgh ijklmnopqrstuvwxyzß;1234567890 mchmctmffmffimfimfimfjmflmftmgymstmshmrrm

GRÜßEN

§ $ @ ℓ ® % Ⓐ

Ratispone Anno Dommini Domini mense decembri mclv kronica Baudolini apelido de Aulario · Ego io Baudolino de Galiaudio de los Aulari con ena cabeza ke semblat uno lione alleluja sien dadas Gratias al sinior ke me perdone

[$ ¢ £ ¤ ¥ ₢ ₣ ₤ ₥ ₦ ₧ ₩ ₪ ₫ € ₭ ₮ ₱ ₵]

1234567890 1234567890 1234567890

AMSTER VERSAL ILUMINADA | 90 PT

ÀÊÏŐŮ ABCDEFGHIJKLMNOPQR STUVWXYZß ÀÊÏŐŮ ABCDEFGHIJ KLMNOPQRSTUVWXYZß àêïőů abcde fghijklmnopqrstuvwxyzß;1234567890 mchmctmffmffimfimfimfijmfimfjmflmftmstmstmshmrrm

Hamburgo › Santiago

Bruselas › ***Munich*** › ***Tokyo***

Reykjavík › Buenos Aires › Mauduguri

Amster Pro

About
Amster is an energetic and refined type created by Francisco Gálvez, with a powerful concept on how refinement and austerity can meet harmoniously. Amster can build a text that is highly readable and friendly. It has five roman and cursive weights. Amster Pro (only available at *PampaType.com*) is fully equipped with all OpenType sorts such as roman and cursive small caps, two kinds of swashes, smart ornaments, and more. There is also a wonderful set of illuminated initials, Amster Versal Iluminada. All Amster fonts include diacritics coverage for more than 200 languages. Its style makes Amster a very versatile family, allowing for a wide range of uses: screen to print, small text to display, science to poetry. Amster was prized at two different editions of the Tipos Latinos biennale (2008, 2014) and it is a Typographica favorite of 2014.

Design
Francisco Gálvez Pizarro
2014

Foundry
PampaType, Argentina
www.pampatype.com

Styles / Weights
Blanca, Fina, Gris, Negra, SuperNegra, Amster Versal Iluminada, each with Italics

Language support
Latin

OpenType options
Proportional Oldstyle, Tabular and Proportional Lining, Tabular Oldstyle, Standard Ligatures, Discretionary Lig., Historical Lig., All Caps, Small Caps, Capitals to Small Caps, Superscript, Subscript, Ordinals, Swashes, Contextual Swashes, All Alternates, Contextual Alt., Contextual Lig., Fractions, Alternative Fractions, Numerator, Denominator, Ornaments, Arrows, Stylistic Alt., Stylistic Sets, Historical Forms, Slashed Zero, Localized Forms, Required Lig.

Optimized for web
Yes

BLANCA 16PT

abcdefgghijklmnopqrstuvwxyzæfjåçéñöûß
ABCDEFGHIJJKLLMNOPQQRRSTUVWXYZÆÇØ
01234567890@.,-:;!?')]§*“”«»/–€$&⅓→

SUPERNEGRA 36PT

aejgGQR7

NEGRA & GRIS 14PT

Typographers want
amazing, exquisite
& clever justified text
in books

FINA 36PT

aejgGQR7

ALL WEIGHTS 10PT

Blanca
Fina
Gris
Negra
SuperNegra

ITALICS 10PT

Blanca Italica
Fina Italica
Gris Italica
Negra Italica
SuperNegra Italica

ANISETTE

About
Anisette, built around the idea of capitals in two widths, can be described as a geometric sans serif typeface influenced by the 30s and the Art Deco movement. Its design relies on multiple sources, from Banjo through Cassandre posters, but especially the lettering of Paul Iribe. In France, at that time, the Art Deco spirit is mainly capitals.

Anisette reinforces the initial idea by adding an outfit set of connected capitals, contextual forms and small caps. Because of the benefit of OpenType features, the Anisette advanced typography is easy to use in any graphic design. Indeed, the three capitals widths and lowercases (from Anisette Petite) can alternatively be used alone or mixed. Today, the resulting mixture is provided by various context functionnalities, providing alternative settings. With Anisette, typography becomes a game, as to design any title page as flamboyant as if it has been specially drawn for it.

Design
Jean François Porchez
2014

Foundry
Typofonderie, France
www.typofonderie.com

Styles / Weights
Thin, ExLight, Light, Regular, Demi, Bold, ExBold, Heavy, Black

Language support
Latin

OpenType options
Tabular and Proportional Oldstyle, Tabular and Proportional Lining, Standard, Discretionary, Contextual and Historical Ligatures, All Caps, Small Caps, Capitals to Small Caps, Superscript, Subscript, Ordinals, Titling Alternates, Swashes, Contextual Swashes, All Alt., Contextual Alt., Fractions, Numerator, Denominator, Ornaments, Arrows, Stylistic Alt., Stylistic Sets, Historical Forms, Slashed Zero, Justification Alt., Petite Caps, Capitals to Petite Caps

Optimized for web
No

REGULAR 13PT
ABCDEFGHIJKLMNOPQRSTUVWXYZÆFJÅÇÉÑÖÛSS
ABCDEFGHIJKLMNOPQRSTUVWXYZÆÇØ
01234567890@.,-:;!?')]§*"" «»/–€$&½ →

EXBOLD 28PT
AEJGGQR7

EXLIGHT 16PT
TYPOGRAPHERS WANT AMAZING, EXQUISITE & CLEVER JUSTIFIED TEXT IN BOOKS

BLACK & DEMI 10PT
THE YEARBOOK OF TYPE COMPENDIUM WORKS WELL AS A TOOL IN VEXED TYPOGRAPHY QUESTIONS FOR POLARIZING JOBS

BLACK 13PT
TYPOGRAPHERS WANT AMAZING, EXQUISITE & CLEVER JUSTIFIED TEXT IN BOOKS

Aniuk

Since

you are walking on thin ice, You MIGHT as well Dance!

About
Aniuk is an original display type family designed and optimized for the use in large sizes. With five robust weights—Regular, Medium, Bold, Heavy and Black—it is perfectly suited for editorial, posters or logo design. A perfect balance of characteristic curves and edgy details make this a strong but playful typeface; a solid partner for your creative adventures.

Design
Thomas Gabriel
2011

Foundry
Typejockeys, Austria
www.typejockeys.com

Styles / Weights
Regular, Medium, Bold, Heavy, Black

Language support
Latin

OpenType options
Proportional Oldstyle, Tabular and Proportional Lining, Tabular Oldstyle, Superscript, Subscript, Contextual Ligatures, Stylistic Alternates, Stylistic Sets

Optimized for web
Yes

REGULAR 18PT
abcdefghijklmnopqrstuvwxyyzæfjåçéñöûß
ABCDEFGHIJKLMNOPQRSTUVWXYZÆÇØ
0123456789@.,-:;!?')]§*""«»/–€$&½

BOLD 30PT
aejgGQR7

BLACK & REGULAR 14PT
Typographers want amazing, exquisite
& clever justified text in books

MEDIUM 30PT
aejgGQR7

BOLD & MEDIUM 13PT
The Yearbook of Type compendium works well as
a tool in vexed typography questions for polarizing jobs

ali
coupé
izocel
aleph
abF
NDEBELE
abF
Octobre
poudre
ABF
Apeloig Type Library

About
The Apeloig Type Library is a compilation of ten typefaces created by Philippe Apeloig during the past twenty years of the designer's outstanding typographic creations. Wih this library, Apeloig's distinctive approach to letters and type is made visible. Apeloig conceives the process of type design as a research project and play between legibility and forms. His designs aim to defeat legibility but remain accessible for the viewer. A rich typographic expression and an impressive variety of shapes have emerged from his creations. Originating from orders of posters, book covers or corporate and visual identities, those fonts initially came to life as a few letters designed especially for the project. For Philippe Apeloig, Nouvelle Noire has undertaken the development of typefaces from those existing letters. From 2011–2013, Nouvelle Noire developed the designs into ten full working fonts. All library fonts support a wide range of western European languages and have embedded OTF.

Design
Philippe Apeloig
2013

Foundry
Nouvelle Noire, Switzerland
www.nouvellenoire.ch

Styles / Weights
ABF Lineaire Thin, ABF Lineaire Light, ABF Lineaire Book, ABF Lineaire Regular, ABF Lineaire Medium, ABF Lineaire Bold, ABF Petit, ABF Silhouette, Aleph, Ali, Coupé Izocel, Ndebele Half, Ndebele Plain, Ndebele Quater, Octobre, Poudre (zero–six)

Language support
Latin

OpenType options
Proportional Oldstyle, Tabular Lining, Proportional Lining, Tabular Oldstyle, Standard Ligatures, Superscript, Subscript, Contextual Ligatures, Fractions, Denominator, Arrows, Stylistic Alternates, Stylistic Sets, Slashed Zero, Unicase

Optimized for web
Yes

ABF LINEAIRE 13PT

AAABCDEFGHIJKLMNOPQRSTUVWXYZÆFJÅÇÉÑÖÛß
ABCDEFGHIJKLMNOPQRSTUVWXYZÆÇØ
0123456789@.,-:;!?'"]§*""«»/–€$&½↗

ABF PETIT 36PT

IZOCEL 16PT

TYPOGRAPHERS WANT AMAZING, EXQUISITE & CLEVER JUSTIFIED TEXT IN BOOKS

NDEBELE PLAIN 16PT

TYPOGRAPHERS WANT AMAZING, EXQUISITE & CLEVER JUSTIFIED TEXT IN BOOKS

ALL WEIGHTS 6PT

ABF Lineaire Thin
ABF Lineaire Light
ABF Lineaire Book
ABF Lineaire Regular
ABF Lineaire Medium
ABF Lineaire Bold
abf petit
abf silhouette
aleph
ali
coupé
izocel

ALL WEIGHTS 6PT

Ndebele Half
Ndebele Plain
Ndebele Quater
Octobre
poudre six
poudre five
poudre four
poudre three
poudre two
poudre one
poudre zero

Signals intelligence

Signals intelligence (often abbreviated as SIGINT) is intelligence-gathering by interception of signals, whether between people («communications intelligence» —COMINT) or from electronic signals not directly used in communication («electronic intelligence» —ELINT), or a combination of the two. As sensitive information is often encrypted, signals intelligence often involves the use of cryptanalysis. Also, traffic analysis—the study of who is signaling whom and in what quantity—can often produce valuable information, even when the messages themselves cannot be decrypted.

As a means of collecting intelligence, signals intelligence is a subset of intelligence collection management, which, in turn, is a subset of intelligence cycle management.

Contents

About

In autumn 2014, Zurich University of the Arts and Zurich University of Applied Sciences moved to the Toni-Areal (a former dairy production site). Bivgrafik collaborated with Hi—Visuelle Gestaltung to design the complete signage for the campus. The Areal BL typeface is a further development of the original developed signage typeface with the focus to set body text.

Design

Design Partnership Areal BL
2014

Foundry

Binnenland, Switzerland
www.binnenland.ch

Styles / Weights

Book, Book Italic, Medium, Medium Italic, Black

Language support

Latin

OpenType options

Superscript, Subscript, Fractions, Numerator, Denominator, Stylistic Alternates, Arrows

Optimized for web

Yes

BOOK 18PT

aabcdefghijklmnopqrstuvwxyzæfjåçéñöûß
ABCDEFGHIJKLMNOPQRSTUVWXYZÆÇØ
0123456789@.,-:;!?')]§*“”«»/–€$&⅓↗

MEDIUM 36PT

aejgGQR7

MEDIUM & BOOK 16PT

Typographers want
amazing, exquisite
& clever justified text
in books

BLACK & BOOK 8PT

→ **ar·chive** / *noun* / a collection of documents such as letters, photographs or other material: *the Yearbook of Type is an archive of contemporary typefaces from all over the world*

ALL WEIGHTS 12PT

Book
Medium
Black

ITALICS 12PT

Book Italic
Medium Italic

The three grades of Aria Text.

Each style has three grades: G1, G2 and G3. With these variants, the color of the text can be matched across different point sizes.

Grade 1

At vero eos et accusamus et iusto odio dignissimos ducimus qui blanditiis *praesentium voluptatum* deleniti atque corrupti quos dolores et quas molestias excepturi sint occaecati **cupiditate non provident**, similique sunt in culpa qui officia deserunt mollitia animi, id est laborum et dolorum fuga. Et harum quidem rerum facilis est et expedita distinctio. Nam libero tempore, cum soluta

Grade 2

At vero eos et accusamus et iusto odio dignissimos ducimus qui blanditiis *praesentium voluptatum* deleniti atque corrupti quos dolores et quas molestias excepturi sint occaecati **cupiditate non provident**, similique sunt in culpa qui officia deserunt mollitia animi, id est laborum et dolorum fuga. Et harum quidem rerum facilis est et expedita distinctio. Nam libero tempore, cum soluta

Grade 3

At vero eos et accusamus et iusto odio dignissimos ducimus qui blanditiis *praesentium voluptatum* deleniti atque corrupti quos dolores et quas molestias excepturi sint occaecati **cupiditate non provident**, similique sunt in culpa qui officia deserunt mollitia animi, id est laborum et dolorum fuga. Et harum quidem rerum facilis est et expedita distinctio. Nam libero tempore, cum soluta

Aria Text

About
Aria Text is the new text version of the lyric Aria Pro. More sober and rational, Aria Text was designed for books. The decoration mannerisms, extreme contrast, the italics angle, among other attributes of the original display typeface, were now tamed and re-thought towards readability and transparency.

The new text fonts were designed to perform well on a page with different point sizes. The family comes with three grades for each one of the six main styles. That way, the color of headlines, subheads, text and captions can be matched.

Aria Text is a fully featured family of 18 OpenType fonts in total, with small caps for all the weights, different figure styles including old-style and tabular sets, full Latin language support, stylistic options, ligature sets and more.

Design
Rui Abreu
2013

Foundry
R-typography, Portugal
www.r-typography.com

Styles / Weights
Family of three styles (G1, G2, G3), each with three weights (Regular, Semi Bold, Bold), each with Italics

Language support
Latin

OpenType options
Proportional Oldstyle, Tabular and Proportional Lining, Tabular Oldstyle, Standard Ligatures, Discretionary Ligatures, All Caps, Small Caps, Superscript, Subscript, Fractions, Numerator, Denominator, Arrows, Stylistic Alternates, Stylistic Sets, Historical Forms, Slashed Zero

Optimized for web
No

G1 REGULAR 17PT

abcdefghijklmnopqrstuvwxyzæfjåçéñöûß
ABCDEFGHIJKLMNOPQRSTUVWXYZÆÇØ
01234567890@.,-:;!?’)]§*“”«»/–€$&½✽↗

G2 SEMIBOLD 36PT

aejgGQR7

G3 BOLD & REGULAR 16PT

Typographers want
amazing, exquisite
& clever justified text
in books ✽

G2 BOLD & REGULAR 8PT

Year·book of Type / *noun* / book published every second year, giving details on typefaces of the previous two years and also about general current typographic topics—*e.g. OpenType features, font editors like Glyphs etc.*

G1 BOLD & REGULAR 16PT

Typographers want
amazing, exquisite
& clever justified text
in books ✽

Aa Bb Cc Dd Ee Ff Gg Hh Ii Jj Kk Ll Mm Nn Ññ Oo Pp
Qq Rr Ss Tt Uu Vv Ww Xx Yy Zz 1 2 3 4 5 6 7 8 9 0

GLYPHS · MEDIUM, 21 PTS

Sebastián Pérez works at *Millenium Nucleus for Protoplanetary Disk Research* (MAD) at Alma, chaired by Simon Casassus, astronomer at the Astronomy department in the University of Chile. This team made an important discovery published by Nature magazine, they observed gas fluids channelled by giant planets in formation of the star HG 142 527, located more than 450 light-years away from the Earth. The finding was possible thanks to the joined work of the 16 radio telescopes of the Atacama Large

PARAGRAPH · BOOK, 14 PTS

Observatorio Alma

THIN · 66 PTS

Nicolaus Copernicus

HEAVY · 31 PTS

The Wonder of Deep Space

BOLD · 55 PTS

Introduction to Celestial Mechanics

MEDIUM · 50 PTS

Vanhauwaert-Bustamante

BLACK · 45 PTS

IMPRESIONISTAS	DESARROLLADO	CIGARRETES
AU REVOIR LEA	REPUBLICANO	AUTOMOBILE
BRANDS	HORSES	FRANCE
JEAN	CERA	KIDS
THIN	**BOLD**	**BLACK**

Nn REGULAR — *Nn* REGULAR ITALIC — **Nn** BLACK — ***Nn*** BLACK ITALIC
Nn BOOK — *Nn* BOOK ITALIC — **Nn** HEAVY — ***Nn*** HEAVY ITALIC
Nn LIGHT — *Nn* LIGHT ITALIC — **Nn** BOLD — ***Nn*** BOLD ITALIC
Nn THIN — *Nn* THIN ITALIC — **Nn** MEDIUM — ***Nn*** MEDIUM ITALIC

£31.99
€85.70
$94.26

NUMBERS · 58 PTS

AMPERSAND COMPARISION · 128 PTS

LOWERCASE AMPERSAND · 258 PTS

THIN · 165 PTS

HAN
PSR

GLYPHS · BLACK, 72 PTS

About
Arquitecta. The humanist typography as a rational project.

From the first experiments by Bauhaus and through modern sans history, we looked for a new mix to construct a rational geometric typeface with humanist proportions suitable for text layout and continuous reading.

Inspired by American and European hand lettering from the first half of the last century, Arquitecta finds its own space as a great alternative for paragraphs in front of classics like Futura, Kabel or Avant Garde.

The family contains eight upright romans and eight italics with the following features: European accents, Oldstyle numbers, Numerators and Fractions; Ink traps to avoid press impressing spots and hinting optimized; small x-height with accentuated ascenders and descenders.

Design
Daniel Hernández, Miguel Hernández
2014

Foundry
Latinotype, Chile
www.latinotype.com

Styles / Weights
Thin, Thin Italic, Light, Light Italic, Regular, Italic, Book, Book Italic, Medium, Medium Italic, Bold, Bold Italic, Heavy, Heavy Italic, Black, Black Italic

Language support
Latin

OpenType options
Proportional Oldstyle, Tabular Lining, Proportional Lining, Tabular Oldstyle, Standard Ligatures, Superscript, Subscript, Ordinals, Fractions

Optimized for web
No

REGULAR 18PT

abcdefghijklmnopqrstuvwxyzæfjåçéñöûß
ABCDEFGHIJKLMNOPQRSTUVWXYZÆÇØ
0123456789@.,–:;!?')]§*“”«»/–€$&⅓

HEAVY & LIGHT 36PT

aejgGQR7
aejgGQR7

BLACK & REGULAR 18PT

Typographers want
amazing, exquisite
& clever justified text
in books

BOLD & REGULAR 10PT

com·pen·dium / *noun* / (pl. com·pen·dia / or com·pen·diums) a collection of facts, drawings and photographs on a particular subject, especially in a book: *“a compendium of typography.”*

ALL WEIGHTS 10PT

Thin
Light
Book
Regular
Medium
Bold
Heavy
Black

ITALICS 12PT

Thin Italic
Light Italic
Book Italic
Italic
Medium Italic
Bold Italic
Heavy Italic
Black Italic

Asterism

Asterism embraces all things handmade. She is the perfect addition to any project that needs a decorative touch.

About
Asterism is a calligraphy style font with a moving baseline and lots of shining personality.

This hand-written style font is based on one of Molly's signature calligraphy styles and pairs beautifully with Frosted, Icing, and Saint Agnes.

Design
Great Lakes Lettering, Dathan Boardman & Molly Jacques Erickson
2013

Foundry
Great Lakes Lettering, USA
www.greatlakeslettering.com

Styles / Weights
Regular

Language support
Latin

OpenType options
Standard Ligatures, Fractions

Optimized for web
Yes

REGULAR 18PT

abcdefghijklmnopqrstuvwxyzæffiåçéñõüßß
ABCDEFGHIJKLMNOPQRSTUVWXYZÆÇØ
0123456789@.,–:;!?()[]*“”«»/-£$€½

REGULAR 36PT

aefgJQR7

SEMI BOLD & REGULAR 16PT

Typographers want
amazing, exquisite
& clever justified text
in books

FIVE RELATED SUPERFAMILIES

BLACK SYMBOLS

SANS

Motorcycle Reviews

SLAB

CHRYSALIS Hubspot

UNIVERSAL

Moon LANDING

INLINE

Multivitamins

ROUND

Best show on Amazon

SANS

About
Bague Sans is a versatile monoline typeface with a distinct and eye-catching personality. Drawing inspiration from early 20th century geometrics, it diverts from the mechanical rigidity of those typefaces by incorporating humanist characteristics, such as subtle variations in stroke width and open counter shapes with vertical endings. One of its most remarkable features is a vast array of uppercase alternates and ligatures which truly shine when set at display sizes. This typeface is automatically transformed into a flexible, charming and stylish typeface with strong modern aesthetics. Bague Sans is part of an enhanced type system which includes four more related families such as Slab with semiwedge serifs, Round with sharp diagonals, Universal with minimalistic forms, and Inline with four distinct weights.

Design
Panos Vassiliou
2014

Foundry
Parachute, Greece
www.parachute.gr

Styles / Weights
Extra Thin, Hairline, Thin, Light, Regular, Medium, Bold, Black, Ultra Black, each with Italics

Language support
Latin, Cyrillic, Greek

OpenType options
Proportional Oldstyle, Tabular and Proportional Lining, Tab. Oldstyle, Standard Ligatures, Discretionary Lig., All Caps, Small Caps, Capitals to Small Caps, Superscript, Subscript, Ordinals, Contextual Lig., Fractions, Numerator, Denominator, Stylistic Alternates, Stylistic Sets, Historical Forms, Localized Forms

Optimized for web
Yes

REGULAR 18PT

aabcdefgghijklmnopqrstuvwxyzæfjåçéñöûß
ABCDEFGHIJKLMNOPQRSTUVWXYZÆÇØ
0123456789@.,-:;!?')]§*“”«»/–€$&⅓

BOLD & HAIRLINE 36PT

BLACK & REGULAR 16PT

Typographers want
amazing, exquisite
& clever justified text
in books

BOLD & REGULAR 9PT

ex·am·ple/*noun*/an illustration that supports or provides more information: *by showing examples the Yearbook of Type presents each font in different sizes and weights*

ALL WEIGHTS 8PT

Hairline
Extra Thin
Light
Regular
Medium
Bold
Black
Ultra Black

ITALICS 8PT

Hairline Italic
Extra Thin Italic
Light Italic
Italic
Medium Italic
Bold Italic
Black Italic
Ultra Black Italic

"when you have ELIMINATED ALL WHICH IS IMPOSSIBLE THEN WHATEVER REMAINS, HOWEVER IMPROBABLE MUST BE THE TRUTH"

SHERLOCK HOLMES

About
Baker Street was inspired by the streets of London, particularly the signage of a pub that paid tribute to the famous detective, Sherlock Holmes. The family includes Black, Italic, Inline and Rough and delivers a multitude of OpenType features. Primarily, the type family includes hundreds of discretionary ligatures that connect letter pairs through varying flourishes. These distinct ligatures are used in combinations between capital, lowercase and number combinations. For selected capital and lowercase letters, large swashes expand above and below the characters. Stylistic Alternatives offer variations to leading capital letters and Titling Alternatives provide more traditional letter proportions to the alphabet. Tabular Lining and Oldstyle figures are included for numerical alternatives. Lastly, the family also includes two sets of ornaments created specially to work with Baker Street's style. Overall, the innumerable OpenType features give every user the tools to solve their own case. The game is on!

Design
Kimmy Kirkwood
2015

Foundry
Kimmy Design, United States
www.kimmydesign.com

Styles / Weights
Black, Oblique, Inline, Rough, Flourishes, Swashes

Language support
Latin

OpenType options
Tabular Lining, Tabular Oldstyle, Standard Ligatures, Discretionary Ligatures, All Caps, Small Caps, Capitals to Small Caps, Titling Alternates, Swashes, Contextual Swashes, Contextual Alternates, Contextual Ligatures, Numerator, Denominator, Ornaments, Stylistic Alternates, Stylistic Sets

Optimized for web
Yes

BLACK 18PT

abcdefghijklmnopqrstuvwxyzæfjåçéñöûß
ABCDEFGHIJKLMNOPQRSTUVWXYZÆÇØ
0123456789@.,-:;!?')]§*"" «»/-€$&

BLACK & INLINE 30PT

aejgGQR7
aejgGQR7

OBLIQUE 16PT

Typographers want amazing, exquisite & clever justified text in books

ROUGH 11PT

The Yearbook of Type compendium works well as a tool in vexed typography questions for polarizing jobs

SWASH & FLOURISH 24PT

Con+
fœde+
ratio
Base+
tica

www.nonpareille.net

www.openswitzerland.org

About
Basetica has been designed for the project *Open Switzerland*. The Geneva-based GVA Studio wanted to celebrate its entrance into the Base group: three graphic agencies in Europe (Brussels) and America (New York, Santiago). They wanted to show their commitment to "Swiss" graphic design, with all its qualities of precision and rigor. And at the same time, to present Switzerland far from its common stereotypes.

So, Basetica wants to be a "Helvetica for 2013," open minded, neat and modern. Sometimes a bit raw, but always clean and discrete, Basetica ironically recalls the "Swiss International Style" of the 50s and 60s.

A basic version of the Medium weight is available for free on the website *www.openswitzerland.org*

Design
Matthieu Cortat
2013

Foundry
Nonpareille, France
www.nonpareille.net

Styles / Weights
Thin, Thin Italic, Light, Light Italic, Regular, Italic, Medium, Medium Italic, Bold, Bold Italic, Black, Black Italic

Language support
Latin

OpenType options
Proportional Oldstyle, Tabular and Proportional Lining, Tabular Oldstyle, Standard Ligatures, All Caps, Superscript, Subscript, Fractions, Numerator, Denominator, Localized forms

Optimized for web
Yes

REGULAR 18PT

abcdefghijklmnopqrstuvwxyzæfjåçéñöûß
ABCDEFGHIJKLMNOPQRSTUVWXYZÆÇØ
0123456789@.,-:;!?')]§*“”«»/–€$&1/3

BOLD 35PT

aejgGQR7

BLACK & MEDIUM 14PT

Typographers want
amazing, exquisite
& clever justified text
in books

BOLD & LIGHT 9PT

cata·logue / *noun* / a complete list of things that people can look at or buy: *a catalogue of typefaces (a book showing the newest fonts, to help people choose the right typeface)*

ALL WEIGHTS 12PT

Thin
Light
Regular
Medium
Bold
Black

ITALICS 12PT

Thin Italic
Light Italic
Italic
Medium Italic
Bold Italic
Black Italic

★ ALTONA VALENCIA ★

1ère tablette de chocolate

type specimen book

HAMBURGER HAFEN

3£ fresh herring salad

ÜBERIRDISCHE KRÄFTE

MONACO'S GRAND PRIX

affinity of temperament

Schifffahrtsrouten

FF Bauer Grotesk

About
FF Bauer Grotesk is a revival of the metal type Friedrich Bauer Grotesk, released between 1933 and 1934 by the foundry Trennert & Sohn in Hamburg Altona, Germany. The geometric construction of the typeface, infused with the Art Deco zeitgeist of that era, is closely related to such famous German designs as Futura, Erbar, Kabel and Super Grotesk that debuted a few years earlier.

However, Bauer Grotesk stands out because it is not so dogmatic with geometry, lending the design a warmer, more homogenous feeling. The oval "O" is a good example of that, as well as characteristic shapes like the capital "M" or the unconventionally differing endings of "c" and "s" which make for a less constructed look.

FF Bauer Grotesk 2015 consists of six weights with accompanying Italics. Condensed weights and a decorative inline version are being worked on.

Find a detailed portrait of FF Bauer Grotesk and its history here: *www.fontshop.com / content / friedrich-bauer-grotesk-reloaded*

Design
Felix Bonge, Thomas Ackermann
2014

Foundry
FontFont, Germany
www.fontfont.com

Styles / Weights
Light, Light Italic, Regular, Italic, Book, Book Italic, Medium, Medium Italic, Demibold, Demibold Italic, Bold, Bold Italic

Language support
Latin

OpenType options
Proportional Oldstyle, Tabular and Proportional Lining, Standard Ligatures, Small Caps, Capitals to Small Caps, Superscript, Subscript, Ordinals, Titling Alternates, Contextual Alternates, Fractions, Alternative Fractions, Numerator, Denominator, Ornaments, Arrows, Stylistic Sets, Initial Form, Isolated Form, Alternate Annotation Forms, Symbols, Scientific Inferiors

Optimized for web
Yes

REGULAR 18PT

abcdefghijklmnopqrstuvwxyzæfjåçéñöûß
ABCDEFGHIJKLMNOPQRSTUVWXYZÆÇØ
0123456789@.,-:;!?')]§*"" «»/–€$&⅓☂↗

BOLD 36PT

aejgGQR7

DEMIBOLD & LIGHT 16PT

Typographers want
amazing, exquisite
& clever justified text
in books

BOLD & BOOK 10PT

☛ **Year·book of Type** / *noun* / book published every second year, giving details on typefaces of the previous two years and also about general current typographic topics—*e.g. OpenType features, font editors like Glyphs etc.*

ALL WEIGHTS 10PT

Light
Regular
Book
Medium
Demibold
Bold

ITALICS 10PT

Light Italic
Italic
Book Italic
Medium Italic
Demibold Italic
Bold Italic

REGIONAL
Fédéralisme

BEATS & RHYMES
Hardcore Battle Rap

MAN VS MACHINE
The Never Ending Story

SLY & THE FAMILY STONE
Psychedelic Funk from California

LA NEUVEVILLE AT LAKE BIENNE
Medieval Town Surrounded by Vineyards

About
Beausite marries the trend of the 20s to 40s for high contrast sans with the classic Swiss Grotesk models, in a contemporary design. By applying contrast onto a Grotesk skeleton, it adds a new dimension to Frutiger's revolutionary Univers program for weights and widths. Starting from the simple idea of a stylish high-contrast sans serif font, this project has evolved organically to a less decorative principle that would generate many styles. All styles come with a full character set.

Design
Yassin Baggar
2014

Foundry
Fatype, Germany / Switzerland
www.fatype.com

Styles / Weights
Family of three styles (Grotesk, Grand, Slick), each with six weights (Thin, Light, Regular, Medium, Bold, Black)

Language support
Latin

OpenType options
Proportional Oldstyle, Tabular Oldstyle, Discretionary Ligatures, Ordinals, Fractions, Numerator, Denominator, Stylistic Sets

Optimized for web
Yes

GROTESK REGULAR 16PT

aabcdefgghijklmnopqrstuvwxyzæfjåçéñöûß
AABCDEFGHIJKLMNOPQRSTUVVWXYZÆÇØ
0123456789@.,-:;!?')]§*“”«»/–€$&½

GRAND BLACK 36PT

aejgGQR7

GROTESK BOLD & LIGHT 14PT

Typographers want amazing, exquisite
& clever justified text in books

SLICK REGULAR 36PT

aejgGQR7

SLICK MEDIUM & LIGHT 14PT

Typographers want amazing, exquisite
& clever justified text in books

About
Begum is a Latin display serif typeface with contrast. With an ultra-contemporary appearance, its characters share DNA with classic Anglo-Dutch types like Caslon, Fleischmann or Times. The family shines in shorter length texts, multi-line article introductions, and even on packaging. Begum is part of a larger family that also supports Devanagari and Tamil scripts.

Design
Manushi Parikh
2015

Foundry
Indian Type Foundry, India
www.indiantypefoundry.com

Styles / Weights
Light, Regular, Medium, Semi Bold, Bold

Language support
Latin

OpenType options
Proportional Lining, Standard Ligatures, Superscript, Fractions

Optimized for web
Yes

REGULAR 16PT

abcdefghijklmnopqrstuvwxyzæfjåçéñöûß
ABCDEFGHIJKLMNOPQRSTUVWXYZÆÇØ
0123456789@.,-:;!?')]§*“”«»/–€$&½

SEMIBOLD 30PT

aejgGQR7

BOLD & MEDIUM 14PT

Typographers want amazing, exquisite
& clever justified text in books

LIGHT 30PT

aejgGQR7

SEMIBOLD & LIGHT 12PT

The Yearbook of Type compendium works well as
a tool in vexed typography questions for polarizing jobs

Begum

BERENJENA

Północy z Rosją

BERENJENA PRO NEGRA 44 PTS

Bb

John Baskerville

BERENJENA PRO FINA ITÁLICA 43 PTS

Ff

Col·lectiu d'especialistes

BERENJENA PRO BLANCA 31 PTS

DARKSIDE

BERENJENA PRO GRIS 60 PTS

Kk

Isidore Lucien Ducasse † 24·11·1870

BERENJENA PRO FINA ITÁLICA 20 PTS

Los Detectives Salvajes

BERENJENA PRO NEGRA 30 PTS

Sś

60 PTS

Hagx13

BERENJENA PRO BLANCA 48 PTS

Hagx13

BERENJENA PRO FINA 48 PTS

Hagx13

BERENJENA PRO GRIS 48 PTS

Hagx13

BERENJENA PRO NEGRA 48 PTS

ITRO FIL MOGEN is the centre of our philosophy, and its significance is *'totality without exclusion'* — the unfragmented integrity of all life, and all living things, that which contemporary Western culture often refers to as 'biodiversity'. We are merely a small part of the universe — but one more aspect of nature, of the earth, from where we derive our words. Just one small part, an existence implicitly dependent on reciprocity. The elders say that this is why we must take of the earth only that which we truly need for survival. ***We have no utilitarian purpose for the earth. We each take what we need during our brief existence, just as the earth takes back from us, bit by bit, as we are converted back into water, air, fire and verdure.***

10,4/16,4 PTS

— *Elicura Chihuailaf*

About
Berenjena is a friendly type designed by Javier Quintana Godoy in Santiago de Chile. It has the right combination of comfort in reading and a lyric spirit. This helps keep readers in the delicate atmosphere in which novels and tales can display all their charm. Berenjena (Spanish for aubergine or eggplant) gives your text that spicy environment in which word shapes are easy to read while letterforms maintain their capricious feeling. It comes in roman and cursive declined in four weights: Blanca, Fina, Gris, and Negra. All Berenjena character sets include extensive diacritics coverage for more than 200 languages. Berenjena Pro (only available at *PampaType.com*) includes small caps, elegant ligatures, cute swashes, every kind of figures, and all contextual sorts. Berenjena will give your design a very individual character. It wears captivating details of calligraphic poetry which link subtlety to vernacular sign painting from Santiago de Chile. Berenjena was prized at the Tipos Latinos 2012.

Design
Javier Quintana Godoy
2014

Foundry
PampaType, Argentina
www.pampatype.com

Styles / Weights
Blanca, Blanca Italica, Fina, Fina Italica, Gris, Gris Italica, Negra, Negra Italica

Language support
Latin

OpenType options
Proportional Oldstyle, Tabular and Prop. Lining, Tab. Oldstyle, Standard Ligatures, Discretionary Lig., Historical Lig., All Caps, Small Caps, Capitals to Small Caps, Superscript, Subscript, Ordinals, Swashes, All Alternates, Contextual Alt., Contextual Lig., Fractions, Alternative Fractions, Numerator, Denominator, Stylistic Alternates, Stylistic Sets, Historical Forms, Localized Forms

Optimized for web
Yes

BLANCA 17PT

abcdefghijklmnopqrstuvwxyzæfjåçéñöûß
ABCDEFGHIJKLMNOPQRSTUVWXYZÆÇØ
0123456789@.,-:;!?')]§*“”«»/–€$&⅓

GRIS 36PT

aejgGQR7

NEGRA & FINA 16PT

Typographers want
amazing, exquisite
& clever justified text
in books

NEGRA & FINA 9PT

com·pen·dium / noun / (pl. com·pen·dia / or com·pen·diums) a collection of facts, drawings and photographs on a particular subject, especially in a book: *“a compendium of typography.”*

ALL WEIGHTS 13PT

Blanca
Fina
Gris
Negra

ITALICS 13PT

Blanca Italica
Fina Italica
Gris Italica
Negra Italica

Berlingske Family: Sans, Sans Round, Serif, Serif Text, Serif Stencil, Typewriter, Slab, Slab Display, Slab Stencil

bb bb bb bb bb bb bb bb

bb bb bb bb

bb bb bb bb bb bb bb bb bb bb bb bb

bb bb bb bb bb bb bb bb bb b b bb bb bb bb bb bb

bb bb bb bb bb bb bb bb bb bb bb bb bb

bb bb bb bb bb bb bb bb bb bb bb bb bb bb bb

bb bb bb bb bb bb bb bb bb bb bb bb bb bb bb

bb bb bb bb bb bb bb bb bb bb bb bb bb bb bb

bb bb bb bb bb bb bb bb bb bb bb bb bb bb bb bb bb

b bb bb bb

About

The Berlingske typeface was originally designed by Jonas Hecksher in 2010 for the Danish newspaper Berlingske. After four years of development with extended styles, language and weights, it represents a wide-ranging family that delivers freedom to play around and give any section or subject area a specific tonality, without sacrificing consistency.

The resulting font family comes in 227 more weights, contains almost half a million different glyphs and is compatible with 170 different languages.

Berlingske has its origin in newspaper typography, where the difference in height between capitals and lowercase characters must be significant, in order for the text to be immediately decodable.

The design is carefully balanced to deliver significant modernization while paying homage to a unique heritage, and is crafted to give a smooth and exclusive look that optimizes visual experience, providing clear and sharp readability, while remaining aesthetically pleasing.

Design

Jonas Hecksher
2014

Foundry

Playtype, Denmark
www.playtype.com

Styles / Weights

Four families in one to three widths, six to ten weights, each with Italics, Round, Stencil, Text and Display versions

Language support

Latin, Cyrillic, Greek

OpenType options

Proportional Oldstyle, Tabular and Prop. Lining, Tab. Oldstyle, Standard Ligatures, Discretionary Lig., Historical Lig., All Caps, Small Caps, Capitals to Small Caps, Superscript, Subscript, Ordinals, Titling Alternates, All Alt., Contextual Alt., Contextual Lig., Fractions, Numerator, Denominator, Ornaments, Arrows, Stylistic Alternates, Stylistic Sets, Historical Forms, Justification Alternates

Optimized for web

Yes

REGULAR 18PT

abcdefghijklmnopqrstuvwxyzæfjåçéñöûß
ABCDEFGHIJKLMNOPQRSTUVWXYZÆÇØ
0123456789@.,-:;!?')]§*“”«»/–€$&⅓≣➻

SERIF BLACK & SLAB POSTER 30PT

aejgGQR7
aejgGQR7

SANS ROUND BOLD & LIGHT 16PT

Typographers want
amazing, exquisite
& clever justified text
in books ✿

SANS BOLD & SERIF TX REGULAR 9PT

➻ **ref·er·ence book** / *noun* / a book that contains facts and information that you look at when you need to find out sth. particular— *“I am looking for the right typeface for my project, so I use the Yearbook of Type as a reference book.”*

SERIF STENCIL EXTRABOLD & MEDIUM 16PT

Typographers want
amazing, exquisite
& clever justified text
in books

NOVO

WOOD IS THE NEW MODERNISM

NOVO TYPO

PROUDLY PRESENTS

'BIXA'

A TYPEWOOD PRODUCTION

LAYERING
IS THE NEW
CONCEPT
AVAILABLE
IN WOOD
FOR LETTERPRESS
OR DIGITAL .OTF FILE

BIXA COMES IN ELEVEN
DIFFERENT LAYERS

MAXIMAL
TYPO
GRAPHY

DESIGNED IN
AMSTERDAM
THE NETHERLANDS
WWW.NOVOTYPO.NL

TYPOGRAPHIC

DECONSTRUCTED

DECONSTRUCTED

TYPOGRAPHIC

NOVO

TYPO

TYPO

NT Bixa

About

Bixa is originally designed for the Woodtype project. An experiment to translate digital files based on bezier curves into woodtype for letterpress. Bixa is based on the principle of multi-layering. Every style represents a different-colored-layer which can be placed upon another. Bixa will challenge the traditional black and white approach in typeface design. Color is the new black. Bixa is available for letterpress in wood and as a digital .otf or .woff file.

Design

Mark van Wageningen
2014

Foundry

Novo Typo, The Netherlands
www.novotypo.nl

Styles / Weights

Thin, Contra, Deconstruct, Shadow, Stencil, Stripe, Medium Left, Medium Right, Regular, Black, Black Left, Right

Language support

Latin

OpenType options

All Caps, Multi-layered, Multi-colored

Optimized for web

Yes

REGULAR 18PT

ABCDEFGHIJKLMNOPQRSTUVWXYZ
0123456789

SHADOW 30PT

MEDIUM LEFT & MEDIUM RIGHT 14PT

TYPOGRAPHERS WANT AMAZING EXQUISITE AND CLEVER JUSTIFIED TEXT IN BOOKS

BLACK 30PT

AEJGQR7

STENCIL 10PT

THE YEARBOOK OF TYPE COMPENDIUM WORKS WELL AS A TOOL IN VEXED TYPOGRAPHY QUESTIONS FOR POLARIZING JOBS

UltraThinUltra

ThinThinItalic

LightLightItalic

RegularRegul

BoldBoldItalic

AB BDot, the skeleton for AB BLine.

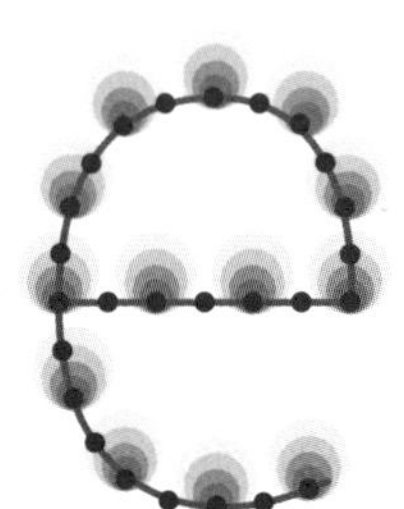

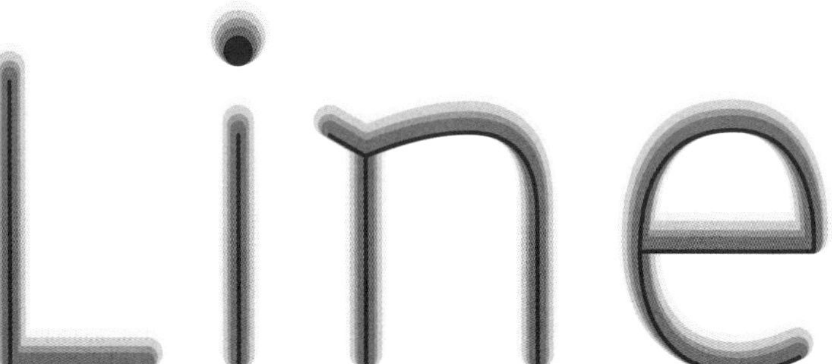

N0123456789 Nabcdefghijklmnopqrstuvwxyz NABCDEFGHIJKLMNOPQRSTUVWXYZ.:;,!?«»''"",,

0123456789 01234 0123, Hello «BLine!», Hi «Euclid!»

ABCDEFGHIJKLMNOPQRSTUVWXYZ

The notion of line or straight line was introduced by ancient mathematicians to represent straight objects with negligible width and depth. Lines are an idealization of such objects. Thus, until the seventeenth century, lines were defined like this: *"The line is the first species of quantity, which has only one dimension, namely length, without any width or depth, and is nothing else than the flow or run of the point which [...] will leave from its imaginary moving some vestige in length, exempt of any width. [...] The straight line is that which is equally extended between its points".* Euclid described a line as *"breadthless length"*, and introduced several postulates as basic unprovable properties from which he constructed the geometry, which is now called Euclidean geometry to avoid confusion with other geometries which have been introduced since the end of nineteenth century, such as non-Euclidean geometry and projective geometry. Source: Wikipedia...

AB BLine

About
AB BLine has been created to complement AB BDot. It took the skeleton and connected the points as closely as possible. It was necessary to first create the AB BDot type in essence more prescriptive. AB BLine can be used completely independently. However, it is most interesting when used in conjunction with the AB BDot. The family has further declinations with the AB BLine-Mono and the AB BLineSans which we use for the new sign system of the Les Halles district in the heart of Paris. Its very large x-height is not only interesting for sign systems, it also allows small and economic text use while remaining very comfortable to read.

Design
André Baldinger
2012

Foundry
AB Type Foundry, France
www.abtypefoundry.com

Styles / Weights
UltraThin, Thin, Light, Regular, Bold, each with Italics

Language support
Latin

OpenType options
Proportional Oldstyle, Tabular Lining, Standard Ligatures, Superscript, Ordinals, Fractions, Numerator, Arrows, Slashed Zero

Optimized for web
Yes

REGULAR 18PT

abcdefghijklmnopqrstuvwxyzæfjåçéñöûß
ABCDEFGHIJKLMNOPQRSTUVWXYZÆÇØ
0123456789Ø@.,-:;!?')]§*""«»/–€$&½→

BOLD 36PT

aejgGQR7

BOLD & THIN 14PT

Typographers want
amazing, exquisite
& clever justified text
in books

BOLD & REGULAR 9PT

→ ex·am·ple / *noun* / an illustration that supports or provides more information: *by showing examples the Yearbook of Type presents each font in different sizes and weights*

ALL WEIGHTS 12PT

UltraThin
Thin
Light
Regular
Bold

ITALICS 12PT

UltraThin Italic
Thin Italic
Light Italic
Regular Italic
Bold Italic

Brahmos

Indian Type Foundry
www.indiantypefoundry.com

About
Brahmos is a display typeface family in five upright styles. Modular methods of letter construction are common, but Brahmos' referencing of the broad nib pen is a refreshing twist. The typeface's most striking feature is the appearance of its characters, which seem "written" by a pen held at a typically Devanagari angle. Letterforms have also been simplified where possible; curves are eschewed in favor of straight lines and (usually) right angles. Diagonals are still present.

Design
Satya Rajpurohit
2015

Foundry
Indian Type Foundry, India
www.indiantypefoundry.com

Styles / Weights
Light, Regular, Medium, Semibold, Bold

Language support
Latin

OpenType options
Proportional Lining, Standard Ligatures, Superscript, Fractions

Optimized for web
Yes

REGULAR 18PT

abcdefghijklmnopqrstuvwxyzœfjåçéñöûß
ABCDEFGHIJKLMNOPQRSTUVWXYZÆÇØ
0123456789@.,-:;!?')]§*'"" «»/–€$&½

SEMIBOLD & LIGHT 30PT

aejgGQR7
aejgGQR7

MEDIUM & LIGHT 16PT

Typographers want amazing, exquisite
& clever justified text in books

BOLD & REGULAR 9PT

over·view / noun / a brief summary of something: in the index of the Yearbook of Type the reader can find an overview of all typefaces presented in the book sorted by classification

BOLD & REGULAR 16PT

Typographers want amazing, exquisite
& clever justified text in books

Endstation Sehnsucht

I'm a chicken—What do I know about bombs?

Mørkets hjerte

CRISTÓBAL COLÓN: EL DESCUBRIMIENTO

Stanislavski System

Brando, mi amor y mi desgarro

Les Révoltés

3 de abril de 1924 – 1 de julio de 2004

Een rebelse levensstijl

Belgian river station on the Congo River, 1889

DARKNESS

Une nouvelle façon d'interpréter les rôles

MLÁDÍ A JINÉ POVÍDKY

About
Brando is a contemporary serif with humanist proportions, exploring the balance between mechanical and Egyptian forms. The careful interaction of rigid and fluid strokes give Brando its modern appeal and sturdiness. The light styles of Brando assume the shape of an elegant slab serif with open letterforms, while the heavier weights feature just the right amount of contrast to give it an even and comfortable texture in text. The distinctive Italics strike a harmonious balance between true Italics and Oblique with letterforms that are supple and vigorous alike.

Design
Mike Abbink
2014

Foundry
Bold Monday, The Netherlands
www.boldmonday.com

Styles / Weights
Hairline, Hairline Italic, ExtraLight, ExtraLight Italic, Light, Light Italic, Regular, Italic, Book, Book Italic, SemiBold, SemiBold Italic, Bold, Bold Italic, Black, Black Italic

Language support
Latin

OpenType options
Proportional Oldstyle, Tabular and Proportional Lining, Tabular Oldstyle, Standard Ligatures, Small Caps, Capitals to Small Caps, Superscript, Subscript, Ordinals, Contextual Alternates, Fractions, Numerator, Denominator, Stylistic Alternates, Stylistic Sets, Slashed Zero

Optimized for web
Yes

REGULAR 18PT

abcdefgghijklmnopqrstuvwxyzæfjåçéñöûß
ABCDEFGHIJKLMNOPQRSTUVWXYZÆÇØ
01234567890@.,-:;!?')]§*“”«»/–€$&⅓

BOLD 30PT

aejgGQR7

BLACK & SEMIBOLD 14PT

Typographers want
amazing, exquisite
& clever justified text
in books

BOLD & LIGHT 9PT

ar·chive / *noun* / a collection of documents such as letters, photographs or other material: *the Yearbook of Type is an archive of contemporary typefaces from all over the world*

ALL WEIGHTS 11PT

Hairline
ExtraLight
Light
Regular
Text
SemiBold
Bold
Black

ITALICS 11PT

Hairline Italic
ExtraLight Italic
Light Italic
Italic
Text Italic
SemiBold Italic
Bold Italic
Black Italic

BRANDON PRINTED

BASED ON THE FAMOUS BRANDON GROTESQUE

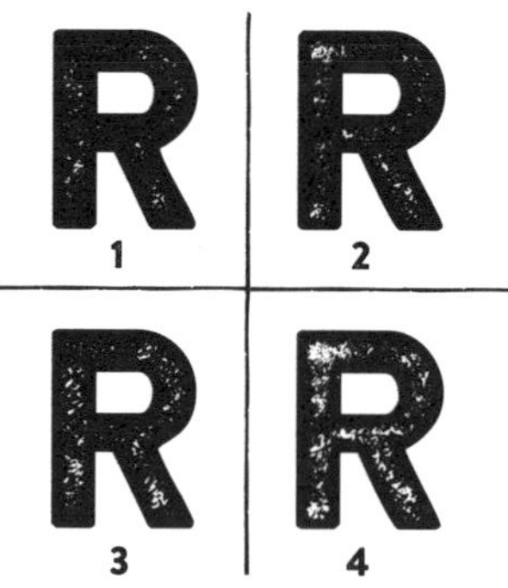

DIFFERENT SETS OF
ERODED ALTERNATES

★ 95 ★

EXTRAS

STARS, ARROWS, EMBLEMS,
ORNAMENTS, CATCHWORDS,
TEXTURES, NUMBERS & LINES

For ALL TYPELOVERS!
the CATCHWORDS
ARE MADE with LOVE
AND FUN.

Brandon Printed

About
Brandon Printed is based on the famous Brandon Grotesque typeface. It has an eroded, printed look with four variations of every letter. With several different styles such as a shadowed version, an inline version and a double printed version, you can create a lot of lovely combinations. The Brandon Printed package also contains a set with 95 extras such as arrows, catchwords, stars, emblems, numbers and lines.

Brandon Printed has a high level of detail, so it may process more slowly in some applications.

Design
Hannes von Döhren
2014

Foundry
HVD Fonts, Germany
www.hvdfonts.com

Styles / Weights
One, Two, One Shadow, Two Shadow, Inline, Double, Shadow, Extras

Language support
Latin

OpenType options
Fractions

Optimized for web
No

ONE 14PT

ABCDEFGHIJKLMNOPQRSTUVWXYZÆÅÇÉÑÖÛ
0123456789@.,-:;!?')*“”«»/–€$&½

ONE SHADOW 28PT

AEJGQR7

INLINE & TWO SHADOW 14PT

TYPOGRAPHERS WANT
AMAZING, EXQUISITE
& CLEVER JUSTIFIED
TEXT IN BOOKS

EXTRAS 34PT

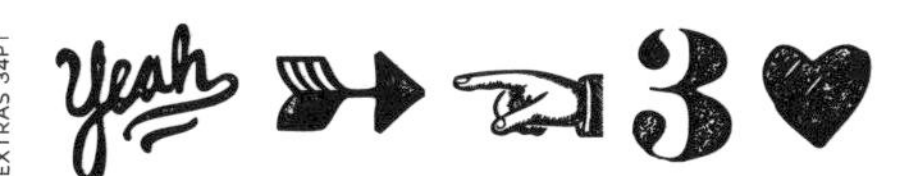

DOUBLE & SHADOW 14PT

TYPOGRAPHERS WANT
AMAZING, EXQUISITE
& CLEVER JUSTIFIED
TEXT IN BOOKS

upright italic

A SLAB SERIF WITH A HI

Bree Serif

in, light, **regular, semibold, bold and extral**

handwriting flavou

1 IN 3 MILLION

Energetic & charming

*in, light, **italic, semibold, bold and extrab***

ow much? 31.740!

*he perfect companion for **Bree***

Aconcagua

About
Bree Serif is a young and energetic upright italic that approaches readers with hip and somewhat elegant charm. It has a range of styles that can perform as counterparts to the original Bree fonts. At the same time though they bring a whole range of new and individual features that make Bree Serif a separate type family in its own right.

The characters in Bree Serif maintain the original flavor of handwriting, but have a more subtle appearance to support optimal editorial usage. The slab-like nature of its shapes, particularly in the heavier weights, makes for a strong impression.

Some of the characteristic features of its sans serif cousin are present in Bree Serif too, such as the single-story "a," the cursive "e" and the rhythmical "k" and "y." Alternate letters of these are also available when a more neutral look is desired.

Bree Serif offers a mixture of fluid and attractive forms that convey a contemporary and vivid aspect.

Design
Veronika Burian, José Scaglione
2013

Foundry
TypeTogether, Czech Republic
www.type-together.com

Styles / Weights
Thin, Thin Italic, Light, Light Italic, Regular, Italic, SemiBold, SemiBold Italic, Bold, Bold Italic, ExtraBold, ExtraBold Italic

Language support
Latin

OpenType options
Proportional Oldstyle, Tabular and Proportional Lining, Tabular Oldstyle, Standard Ligatures, All Caps, Ordinals, Numerator, Denominator, Stylistic Alternates, Stylistic Sets, Arbitrary Fractions, Superior, Inferior

Optimized for web
Yes

REGULAR 17PT

aabcdefgghijklmnopqrstuvwxyyzœfjåçéñöûß
ABCDEFGHIJKLMNOPQRSTUVWXYZÆÇØ
0123456789@.,-:;!?')]§*“”«»/–€$&⅓

EXTRA BOLD 36PT

aejgGQR7

SEMIBOLD & REGULAR 16PT

Typographers want
amazing, exquisite
& clever justified text
in books

EXTRABOLD & LIGHT 10PT

over·view / *noun* / a brief summary of something: *in the index of the Yearbook of Type the reader can find an overview of all typefaces presented in the book sorted by classification*

ALL WEIGHTS 9PT

Thin
Light
Regular
SemiBold
Bold
ExtraBold

ITALICS 9PT

Thin Italic
Light Italic
Italic
SemiBold Italic
Bold Italic
ExtraBold Italic

Anywhere,
n'importe où.
Soleil et pluie,
je t'aime aussi
Comme l'ombre
de ton ombre.
Anywhere,
partout.

From *Dilindam* by Stereo Total (Françoise Cactus & Brezel Göring)

Brezel Grotesk

About
Brezel Grotesk is a sans serif typeface, an unpretentious type, inspired by the character of classic 19th century Grotesques. And by the regular, yet organic shape of a Bavarian pretzel. Readable in small point sizes, yet remarkable at larger sizes, the letters have distinctive terminals.

Brezel Grotesk was originally designed by Stefanie Preis in four weights and later refined and further developed by Milieu Grotesque and Björn Gogalla until 2014. Meant to function in all text settings, Brezel Grotesk is suited for a wide range of applications. The family now comes in eight styles (four weights with corresponding Italics), each style comprising an extended Latin character set.

Design
Stefanie Preis
2015

Foundry
Milieu Grotesque, Switzerland
www.milieugrotesque.com

Styles / Weights
Light, Light Italic, Regular, Italic, Medium, Medium Italic, Bold, Bold Italic

Language support
Latin

OpenType options
Standard Ligatures, Fractions, Stylistic Alternates

Optimized for web
Yes

REGULAR 18PT

abcdefghijklmnopqrstuvwxyzæfjåçéñöûß
ABCDEFGHIJKLMNOPQRSTUVWXYZÆÇØ
0123456789@.,-:;!?')]§*""«»/–€$&⅓

BOLD 36PT

aejgGQR7

BOLD & REGULAR 14PT

Typographers want
amazing, exquisite
& clever justified text
in books

LIGHT 36PT

aejgGQR7

ALL WEIGHTS 12PT

Light
Regular
Medium
Bold

ITALICS 12PT

Light Italic
Italic
Medium Italic
Bold Italic

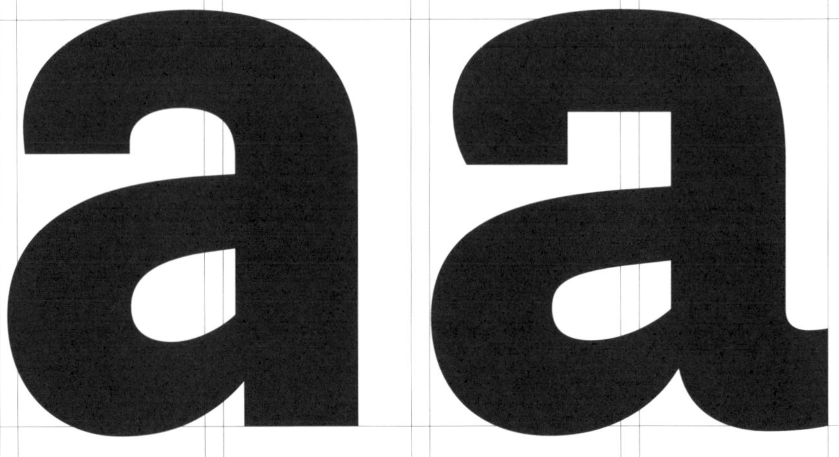

Brix Sans

Brix Slab

Editorial Design

Precise Type Engineering

Different Characteristics – One Family

It took Hannes von Döhren and Livius Dietzel almost two years to develop and complete the Brix Sans family – the companion of the well-known Brix Slab. The approach was to design an independent type family following the rules of the "Sans-Serif" genre, harmonizing with its older sister Brix Slab from the "Slab-Serif" genre.

Brix Sans & Slab

About
It took Hannes von Döhren and Livius Dietzel two years to develop and complete the Brix Sans family—the companion of the well-known Brix Slab. The approach was to design an independent type family following the rules of the sans serif "genre," harmonizing with its older sister Brix Slab from the slab serif "genre." The result is a family of six weights with matching Italics, which works perfectly for corporate design and editorial design. Combined with Brix Slab, high and complex typographical challenges can be solved.

Design
Livius Dietzel, Hannes von Döhren
2014

Foundry
HVD Fonts, Germany
www.hvdfonts.com

Styles / Weights
Family of two styles (Sans, Slab), each in six weights (ExtraLight, Light, Regular, Medium, Bold, Black), each with Italics

Language support
Latin

OpenType options
Proportional Oldstyle, Tabular and Proportional Lining, Tabular Oldstyle, Standard Ligatures, All Caps, Small Caps, Superscript, Subscript, Ordinals, Fractions, Numerator, Denominator, Arrows, Stylistic Alternates, Stylistic Sets, Localized Forms

Optimized for web
Yes

SANS REGULAR 18PT

aabcdefgghijklmnopqrstuvwxyzæfjåçéñöûß
ABCDEFGHIJKLMNOPQRSTUVWXYZÆÇØ
0123456789@.,-:;!?')]§*""«»/–€$&⅓↗

SLAB REGULAR 18PT

aabcdefgghijklmnopqrstuvwxyzæfjåçéñöûß
ABCDEFGHIJKLMNOPQRSTUVWXYZÆÇØ
0123456789@.,-:;!?')]§*""«»/–€$&⅓↗

SANS BLACK & REGULAR 9PT

Year·book of Type / *noun* / book published every second year, giving details on typefaces of the previous two years and also about general current typographic topics—*e.g. OpenType features, font editors like Glyphs etc.*

SANS, ALL WEIGHTS 8PT

ExtraLight
ExtraLight Italic
Light
Light Italic
Regular
Regular Italic
Medium
Medium Italic
Bold
Bold Italic
Black
Black Italic

SLAB, ALL WEIGHTS 8PT

ExtraLight
ExtraLight Italic
Light
Light Italic
Regular
Regular Italic
Medium
Medium Italic
Bold
Bold Italic
Black
Black Italic

OMOO

ADVENTURES IN THE SOUTH SEAS

HERMAN MELVILLE

About
Originally painted on paper with swift brush strokes, Brush Up waited patiently a couple of years before being translated to this dynamic font.

Packed with alternates for letters, numbers and punctuation marks, Brush Up counts with a nice OpenType programming—and an extra-careful kerning table—to manage all these glyphs. Its Contextual Alternates feature instantly substitutes glyphs for their alternative forms, resulting in striking compositions.

Surprisingly versatile, Brush Up is available in two styles: upright and oblique. Released less than two years ago, these have been widely used for quite diverse purposes, from as massive and physical as billboards to as airy and digital as websites. Brush Up is always right over there, in bus adverts, t-shirts, bottle labels, magazine headlines, book covers, just to name a few. It has been playing really great, and nicely enough, always looks fresh.

Design
Erica Jung, Ricardo Marcin
2013

Foundry
PintassilgoPrints, Brazil
www.pintassilgoprints.com

Styles / Weights
Brush Up, Brush Up Too

Language support
Latin

OpenType options
All Alternates, Contextual Alternates, Ornaments, Stylistic Alternates, Stylistic Sets

Optimized for web
Yes

BRUSH UP REGULAR 17PT

AABCDEFGHIJJKLMNOoPQRSTUVWXYYZÆÅÇÉÑÖÛ
0123456789@.,-:;!?')*""«»/-€$&½

BRUSH UP REGULAR 28PT

AEJGQR7

BRUSH UP REGULAR 16PT

TYPOGRAPHERS WANT AMAZING, EXQUISITE & CLEVER JUSTIFIED TEXT IN BOOKS

BRUSH UP TOO REGULAR 28PT

AEJGQR7

BRUSH UP TOO 16PT

TYPOGRAPHERS WANT AMAZING, EXQUISITE & CLEVER JUSTIFIED TEXT IN BOOKS

BTP,
Building
Typing
Publishing

un vertigineux chaos
de pierres de taille
éparpillées comme
les blocs d'un jeu de
construction. Le pré

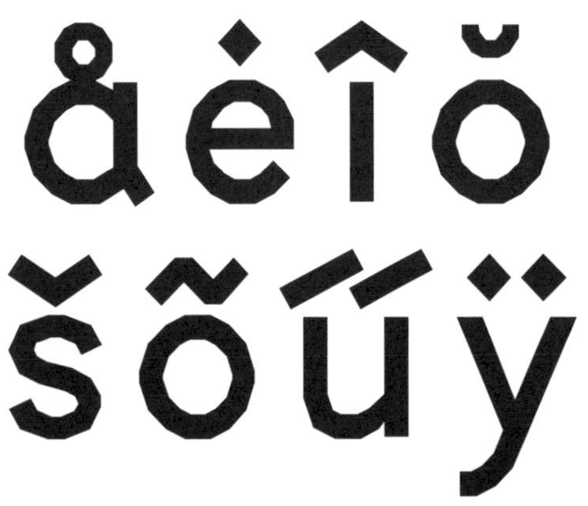

→ **BTP regular**
→ ***BTP rotated***
→ BTP light
→ *BTP light rotated*

About
In August 2011, the #195 issue of *Étapes* French magazine, "Somewhere between graphic design and architecture ...," became the experimental field for the creation and use of the typeface BTP (by the Équipe type, art direction by Guillaume Grall and Étienne Hervy). The design of BTP is freely inspired by the default typeface used in the computer-assisted design software AutoCAD, mainly used by architects for the conception of graphic documents (plans, elevations, etc.).

Since the issue was published, Jeremy Perrodeau and Guillaume Grall have been working together to enhance the typeface. After several months of construction, BTP, a font with angular curves, gained an autonomous life in 2013, released in one multifunction weight.

But that wasn't the end of the story. In February 2015, Emilie Rigaud designed a new light weight, as well as rotated versions for both the regular and the light.

Design
Guillaume Grall, Jeremy Perrodeau, Émilie Rigaud
2015

Foundry
A is for..., France
www.aisforapple.fr

Styles / Weights
Light, Light Rotated, Normal, Rotated

Language support
Latin

OpenType options
Superscript, Subscript, Ordinals, Fractions, Numerator, Ornaments, Arrows, Stylistic Sets

Optimized for web
Yes

REGULAR 16PT
abcdefghijklmnopqrstuvwxyzæfjåçéñöûß
ABCDEFGHIJKLMNOPQRSTUVWXYZÆÇØ
0123456789@.,-:;!?')]§*“”«»/–€$&½↗

LIGHT 30PT
aejgGQR7

NORMAL & ROTATED 14PT
Typographers want
amazing, exquisite
& clever justified text
in books

ROTATED 30PT
aejgGQR7

NORMAL 24PT

BURFORD

THE PURE & SIMPLE TRUTH IS RARELY PURE AND NEVER SIMPLE

-OSCAR WILDE-

About
Burford is a font family that I sketched while traveling through Europe. I was mesmerized by all the unique typography that was showcased throughout the five countries I visited. Inspired by all that I had seen, I found myself spending four–five hours per day in Amsterdam's Vondelpark drawing characters. Once back in the states I digitalized Burford, deciding it would make for a beautiful layer-based font.

It comes with all 18 layering fonts including five base layers, three top layers, five bottom layers and two sets of graphic elements. They are strategically made to build on top of each other, creating a cohesive and easy to use layer-based family. Each font also comes with a set of Stylistic Alternatives for the letters "A, C, E, F, G, H, P, Q, R."

Design
Kimmy Kirkwood
2015

Foundry
Kimmy Design, USA
www.kimmydesign.com

Styles / Weights
Base, Dots, DropShadow, DropShadow Solo, Extrude A, Extrude A Shadow, Extrude B, Extrude B Solo, Extrude C, Extrude C Solo, Inline, Line, Marquee, Outline, Stripes A, Stripes B

Language support
Latin, Cyrillic, Greek

OpenType options
Tabular Lining, All Caps, Fractions, Ornaments, Stylistic Alternates

Optimized for web
Yes

BASE 17PT

ABCDEFGHIJKLMNOPQRSTUVWXYZÆÅÇÑÖÛ
0123456789@.,-:;!?')*"" «»/-€$&½

DOTS 42PT

A E J G Q R 7

DROPSHADOW & STRIPES A 16PT

TYPOGRAPHERS WANT
AMAZING, EXQUISITE
& CLEVER JUSTIFIED
TEXT IN BOOKS

EXTRAS 30PT

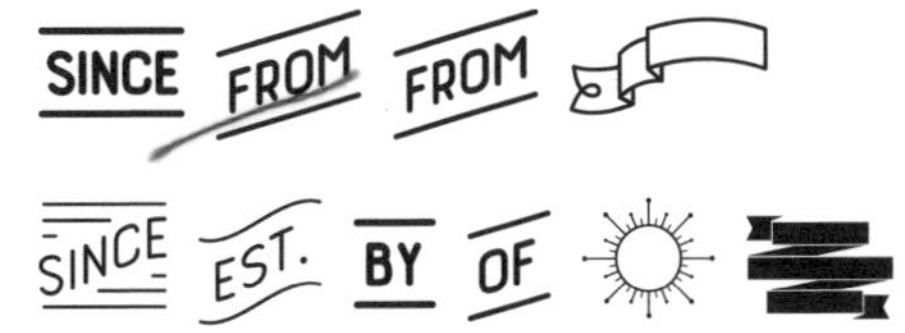

ALL WEIGHTS 9PT

BASE
DOTS
DROPSHADOW
DROPSHADOW SOLO
EXTRUDE A
EXTRUDE A SHADOW
EXTRUDE B
EXTRUDE B SOLO
EXTRUDE C
EXTRUDE C SOLO

ALL WEIGHTS 9PT

INLINE
LINE
MARQUEE
OUTLINE
STRIPES A
STRIPES B

con
SIDER
EVERY
THING
an
EXPERI
MENT.

FROM
Sister Corita's
10 RULES FOR
STUDENTS
AND **Teachers**

About
Burg Grotesk is the official typeface of Burg Giebichenstein University of Art and Design Halle, specifically designed for the new visual identity of the institution. Burg Grotesk is a sans serif typeface combining functionality and playfulness with many refined details. The typeface is characterized by a mixture of rather modest capitals with a slightly smaller proportion and more vivid lowercase letters with a slightly wider proportion, adding fluidity and rhythm to the text. Burg Grotesk currently consists of three weights—Regular, Medium and Bold—as well as a Bold Condensed and a regular monospaced version; more fonts and matching italics are in the making. The OpenType fonts include many advanced layout features with various figure sets, Small Caps, alternate characters, ligatures as well as geometric symbols and Arrows. Burg Grotesk also comes with a symbol font offering a wide range of geometric composites and a logotype font called "Burg Letters."

Design
Andrea Tinnes
2014

Foundry
typecuts, Germany
www.typecuts.com

Styles / Weights
Regular, Medium, Bold, Bold Condensed, Mono Regular, Mono Regular Italic, Symbols

Language support
Latin

OpenType options
Proportional Oldstyle, Tabular and Proportional Lining, Tabular Oldstyle, Standard Ligatures, Discretionary Ligatures, All Caps, Small Caps, Superscript, Subscript, Ordinals, Fractions, Numerator, Denominator, Ornaments, Arrows, Stylistic Alternates, Stylistic Sets, Slashed Zero

Optimized for web
Yes

REGULAR 16PT

aabcdefgghijklmnopqrstuvwxyyzæfjåçéñöûß
ABCDEFGHIJKLMNOPQRSTUVWXYZÆÇØ
0123456789ø@.,-:;!?')]§*“”«»/–€$&¼▦↗

BOLD 30PT

aejgGQR7

BOLD REGULAR 14PT

Typographers want amazing, exquisite
& clever justified text in books

BOLD CONDENSED 30PT

aejgGQR7

MONO & MONO ITALIC 9PT

ar·chive / *noun* / a collection of documents such as letters, photographs or other material: *the Yearbook of Type is an archive of contemporary typefaces from all over the world*

abcdefghijklmn ***ABCDEFGHI***

Lesbarkeit **Videospeletjie**

0123456789 ¼½¾ **$¢£¥€**

Thin Light Regular Medium

Flat Tips on *Sharp Counters*

Näyttö *Jednoduché tvary*

A B C D E F G H I J K L M N O P Q R S
T U V W X Y Z a b c d e f g h i j k l
m n o p q r s t u v w x y z Æ Á Ă Â Ä
À Ā Ą Å Ã Ć Č Ç Ĉ Ċ Ď Đ É Ĕ Ě Ê Ë Ė È
Ē Ę Ğ Ĝ Ģ Ġ Ħ Ĥ Í Ĭ Î Ï İ Ì Ī Į Ĩ Ĳ Ĵ
Ķ Ĺ Ľ Ļ Ŀ Ł Ń Ň Ņ Ñ Ŋ Ó Ŏ Ô Ö Ò Ő Ō Ø
Õ Œ Ŕ Ř Ŗ Ś Š Ş Ŝ Ș Ŧ Ť Ţ Þ Ú Ŭ Û Ü Ù
Ű Ū Ų Ů Ũ Ẃ Ŵ Ẅ Ẁ Ý Ŷ Ÿ Ỳ Ź Ž Ż á ă â
ä æ à ā ą å ã ć č ç ĉ ċ ď đ ı ȷ é ĕ ě
ê ë ė è ē ę ð ğ ĝ ģ ġ ß ħ ĥ í ĭ î ï ì
ī į ĩ ĳ ĵ ķ ĸ ĺ ľ ļ ŀ ł µ ń ŉ ň ņ ñ ŋ
ó ŏ ô ö ò ő ō ø õ œ ŕ ř ŗ ś š ş ŝ ș ŧ
ť þ ú ŭ û ü ù ű ū ţ ų ů ũ ẃ ŵ ẅ ẁ ý ŷ
ÿ ỳ ź ž ż ff ffi ffl fi fl 0 1 2 3 4 5 6 7 8
9 0 1 2 3 4 5 6 7 8 9 ⁄ 0 1 2 3 4 5 6
7 8 9 ½ ¼ ¾ . … : , ; • · ! ¡ ? ¿ / \
_ - – — { } [ ] « » ‹ › ‚ „ “ ” ‘ “ ’
, * # $ € ƒ £ ₹ ₺ ¥ ¢ ¤ & @ § © ® ℮ ™
ℓ † ‡ ¶ | ¦ ^ ◊ ° + ± − ÷ × · = ≠ ≈ ~
< > ≤ ≥ % ‰ / ¬ ∞ √ ∫ ∂ ∏ ∑ Ω ∆ μ π

About
Burlingame is a multi-purpose font family that started out as a single typeface with a more specialized purpose. Originally intended for a game identity, it has found a wider purpose following pioneering investigations by Monotype into the legibility of vehicle displays. The research revealed a set of optimum criteria for dashboard display fonts: large counters and x-heights, simple shapes and a loose spacing of characters. With its open, clear shapes, it is a family of faces that could meet the high-performance demands. Carl's refinements, increasing the x-height, loosening the spacing and paring down the corners, improved the clarity and led to a design in two widths and nine fine weight grades, suited to a wide range of uses.

Design
Carl Crossgrove
2014

Foundry
Monotype, USA
www.monotype.com

Styles / Weights
Thin, Thin Italic, Light, Light Italic, Regular, Italic, Medium, Medium Italic, Semi Bold, Semi Bold Italic, Bold, Bold Italic, Black, Black Italic, Extra Black, Extra Black Italic, each with condensed width

Language support
Latin

OpenType options
Standard Ligatures, Superscript, Subscript, Fractions, Numerator, Denominator, Stylistic Alternates, Stylistic Sets, Localized Forms

Optimized for web
Yes

REGULAR 16PT

abcdefghijklmnopqrstuvwxyzæfjåçéñöûß
ABCDEFGHIJKLMNOPQRSTUVWXYZÆÇØ
0123456789@.,-:;!?')]§*“”«»/–€$&½

BOLD & LIGHT 8PT

cata·logue / noun / a complete list of things that people can look at or buy: *a catalogue of typefaces (a book showing the newest fonts, to help people choose the right typeface)*

BLACK & REGULAR 13PT

Typographers want amazing, exquisite
& clever justified text in books

SEMI BOLD & CONDENSED SEMI BOLD 32PT

aejgGQR7
aejgGQR7

ALL WEIGHTS 6PT

Thin
Thin Italic
Light
Light Italic
Regular
Italic
Medium
Medium Italic
Semi Bold
Semi Bold Italic
Bold
Bold Italic
Black
Black Italic
Extra Black
Extra Black Italic

CONDENSED WEIGHTS 8PT

Condensed Thin
Condensed Thin Italic
Condensed Light
Condensed Light Italic
Condensed
Condensed Italic
Condensed Medium
Condensed Medium Italic
Condensed Semi Bold
Condensed Semi Bold Italic
Condensed Bold
Condensed Bold Italic
Condensed Black
Condensed Black Italic
Condensed Extra Black
Condensed Extra Black Italic

Burlingame

Type
in Elegant
Calligraphy
Style
filled with Nifty Swash
and some Script
Flair

Caligo

Caligo is a typeface based on calligraphy done with a parallel pen. It's classic and elegant with a modern twist, featuring flared serifs, lots of ligatures and swashes. It's great for book cover and signage design where beauty and tradition are important. The font can be used for fashion, jewelries, novels, magazines, and many more.

Q&A ‘Z, G C B

About
Caligo is a typeface based on calligraphy done with a parallel pen. It's classic and elegant with a modern twist, featuring flared serifs and lots of ligatures and swashes. It's great for book covers and signage design where beauty and tradition are important. The font can be used for fashion, jewelry, novels, magazines, and much more.

Design
Áron Jancsó
2013

Foundry
Gestalten, Germany
www.gestaltenfonts.com

Styles / Weights
Text, Text Italic, Poster, Poster Italic

Language support
Latin

OpenType options
Proportional Oldstyle, Standard Ligatures, Discretionary Ligatures, Ordinals, Swashes, Stylistic Alternates

Optimized for web
No

TEXT 16PT

aabcdefgghijklmnopqrstuvwxyyzzæfjåçéñöûß
ABCDEFGHIJKLMNOPQRSTUVWXYZÆÇØ
0123456789@.,-:;!?')]§*“”«»/–€$&½

POSTER ITALIC 16PT

abcdefghijklmnopqrstuvwxyyzæfjåçéñöûß
ABCDEFGHIJKLMNOPQRSTUVWXYZÆÇØ
0123456789@.,-:;!?')]§“”«»/–€$&½*

POSTER 36PT

aejgGQR7

TEXT 9PT

hand·book/*noun*/a book giving instructions on how to use sth. or information about a particular subject like typefaces—*compare manual or Yearbook of Type*

Caligo

CAMPTON —
A GEOMETRIC
FONTFAMILY
OF 10 WEIGHTS
PLUS MATCHING
ITALICS, INCLUDING
OPENTYPE
FEATURES LIKE
ALTERNATIVE
GLYPHS, OLDSTYLE
FIGURES,
FRACTIONS AND
MANY MORE.

About
Campton is a simple sans serif with a geometric skeleton. Campton tries to find its niche in the field of geometric typefaces by combining simplicity with a subtle friendliness. It is perfectly suited for graphic design application ranging from editorial and corporate design via web and interaction design through to product design.

Design
René Bieder
2014

Foundry
Rene Bieder / Design and Direction, Germany
www.renebieder.com

Styles / Weights
Thin, Thin Italic, Extralight, Extralight Italic, Light, Light Italic, Book, Book Italic, Medium, Medium Italic, Semi Bold, Semi Bold Italic, Bold, Bold Italic, ExtraBold, ExtraBold Italic, Black, Black Italic

Language support
Latin

OpenType options
Proportional Oldstyle, Tabular and Proportional Lining, Standard Ligatures, Superscript, Subscript, Ordinals, Contextual Alternates, Fractions, Numerator, Denominator, Arrows, Stylistic Alternates, Stylistic Sets, Slashed Zero, Localized Forms

Optimized for web
Yes

LIGHT 17PT
aabcdefghijklmnopqrstuvwxyyzæfjåçéñöûß
ABCDEFGHIJKLMNOPQRSTUVWXYZÆÇØ
01234567890@.,-:;!?')]§*“”«»/–€$&⅛↗

BOLD 34PT
aejgGQR7

BLACK & MEDIUM 14PT
Typographers want
amazing, exquisite
& clever justified text
in books

THIN 34PT
aejgGQR7

ALL WEIGHTS 10PT
Thin
Extralight
Light
Book
Medium
Semi Bold
Bold
ExtraBold
Black

ITALICS 10PT
Thin Italic
Extralight Italic
Light Italic
Book Italic
Medium Italic
Semi Bold Italic
Bold Italic
ExtraBold Italic
Black Italic

FONTFARM.DE

Caput: Superfamily.

Ein typisches »Workhorse« für die meisten typografischen Aufgaben, bestehend aus einer Sans- und einer Slabserif Schriftfamilie.

Smallcaps Styles with tabular 1627384950 **OLDSTYLE FIGURES** *and proportional* **1627384950** *OLDSTYLE FIGURES ...*

Anus ging alsbald zu Bett, weil er nicht schlafen konnte. »Cäsar« beäugte ihn ängstlich — doch ohne den erwünschten Erfolg. Fymosa, die Gattin von Horfis, ging ihm nach, die Insula vergessend, derer sie nicht habhaft werden konnten. Jocus! — dachte er sich, denn Kenko roch sehr gut im Land der platten Malmen. Nihil geht mehr, versprach Onadero dem Pfaffen. *Die Quellen sind* QUICKE REIGEN *und ich muss noch rasch die Steuererklärung machen.* »Trump« ist das Nogo der Vervielfältigung im Wechsel mit stetigen Ursachen.

Anus ging alsbald zu Bett, weil er nun nicht schlafen konnte. »Cäsar« beäugte ihn ängstlich — doch ohne den erwarteten Erfolg. Fymosa, die Gattin von Horfis, ging ihm nach, die Insula vergessend, derer sie nicht habhaft werden konnten. Jocus! dachte er sich, denn Kenko roch sehr gut im Land der platten Malmen. NIHIL GEHT MEHR, VERSPRACH ONADERO DEM PFAFFEN.

Aag Aag

¥$€£ 1362704895

¥$€£ 136204895

NILE

Anus ging alsbald zu Bett, weil er nicht schlafen konnte. »CÄSAR« BEÄUGTE IHN ÄNGSTLICH — doch ohne den erwünschten Erfolg. Fymosa, die Gattin von Horfis, ging ihm nach, die Insula vergessend, derer sie nicht habhaft werden konnten. *Jocus! dachte er sich,* denn Kenko roch sehr gut im Land der platten Malmen. Nihil geht mehr, versprach Onadero dem Pfaffen in unglaublicher Weise.

About
The Caput (Sans) type family—designed in 2008—is a legible, dynamic contemporary Sans Serif with a moderate but visible "square character." The glyph (width) contrast is low, the appearance of the font is a bit more narrow (space saving) than in usual humanistic sans serif fonts.

During 2012 and 2013 we designed a (Slab-) Serif font family, based on the formal appearance and architecture of the Caput Sans Styles. The result is a super family (SF: sans and slab) which is a workhorse for all common design issues, even for the usage in longer text passages and in small sizes on screen.

There is a titling style for the usage in large display sizes and in the sans family you can choose between different glyph forms (style sets) in the letter "a" and "g": open and closed.

Design
Natascha Dell, K.-F. (Kai) Oetzbach
2013

Foundry
Fontfarm.de, Germany
www.fontfarm.de

Styles / Weights
Family of two styles (Sans, Serif), each with four weights (Light, Regular, Bold, Heavy), each with Italics and Small Caps

Language support
Latin

OpenType options
Proportional Oldstyle, Tabular and Proportional Lining, Tabular Oldstyle, Standard Ligatures, Small Caps, Capitals to Small Caps, Superscript, Subscript, Titling Alternates, Fractions, Stylistic Alternates, Stylistic Sets, Optical size

Optimized for web
Yes

SANS REGULAR 18PT

aabcdefgghijklmnopqrstuvwxyzæfjåçéñöûß
ABCDEFGHIJKLMNOPQRSTUVWXYZÆÇØ
0123456789@.,-:;!?')]§*""«»/–€$&⅓

SERIF REGULAR 18PT

abcdefghijklmnopqrstuvwxyzæfjåçéñöûß
ABCDEFGHIJKLMNOPQRSTUVWXYZÆÇØ
0123456789@.,-:;!?')]§*""«»/–€$&⅓

SERIF BOLD & REGULAR 9PT

Year·book of Type / noun / book published every second year, giving details on typefaces of the previous two years and also about general current typographic topics—*e.g. OpenType features, font editors like Glyphs etc.*

SANS, ALL WEIGHTS 10PT

Light
Light Italic
Regular
Italic
Bold
Bold Italic
Heavy
Heavy Italic

SERIF, ALL WEIGHTS 10PT

Light
Light Italic
Regular
Italic
Bold
Bold Italic
Heavy
Heavy Italic

CARAVEL
Frank J. Hecker,
St. Clair, Michigan
Sideways Launch
Lake Freighter
04.10
1905
Openings to the water
I stopped; I searched
for cracks and the
wanting parts I fixed:
Three sari of bitumen
I poured over the out
side; To the gods I
caused oxen to be
sacrificed.

About
Caravel is a Latin grotesk sans typeface family. An original contribution to a well-known style, Caravel distinguishes itself from similar typefaces by adding in extra character where it can; several lowercase letters and non-alphabetic glyphs are livelier than average. The typeface's design is both space-saving and friendly—everything an international audience requires, including many accents, multiple currency symbols, optional oldstyle figures, and five separate weights.

Design
Jonny Pinhorn
2015

Foundry
Indian Type Foundry, India
www.indiantypefoundry.com

Styles / Weights
Light, Regular, Medium, Semi Bold, Bold

Language support
Latin

OpenType options
Proportional Lining, Standard Ligatures, Superscript, Subscript, Fractions, Stylistic Sets

Optimized for web
Yes

REGULAR 18PT

abcdefghijklmnopqrstuvwxyzæfjåçéñöûß
ABCDEFGHIJKLMNOPQRSTUVWXYZÆÇØ
0123456789@.,-:;!?')]§*"″«»/–€$&½

BOLD 30PT

aejgGQR7

SEMIBOLD & REGULAR 14PT

Typographers want amazing, exquisite
& clever justified text in books

LIGHT 30PT

aejgGQR7

BOLD & LIGHT 8PT

ex·am·ple / noun / an illustration that supports or provides more information: by showing examples the Yearbook of Type presents each font in different sizes and weights

CARROSSERIE

ORIENTAL LUXUS -LINER ! RETRO TYPE EINE SCHÖNE WANDERUNG INMITTEN UNBEKANNTER BERGE | NATIONAL PARK
MONTENEGRO FAHRZEUG (KENYA-SAFARI) VANCOUVER TRIP SAFARI @ COMPANION
PASSAGIER KONDUKTEUR-KONTROLLE EISCRÈME → GOOD LUCK! DELHI BAZAAR NAIROBI
WWW·DOMAIN·COM EXOTIC LANDSCAPES! ISTANBUL GLÜCK KOMMT OFT ÜBERRASCHEND

DISPLAY USE

POSTCARD CAPE VERDE THE BELLE VOYAGE 1930 NORTH BRITISH COMPANY PALACE ON WHEELS | CAFÉ SEATTLE
«SILIGURI BOILS THE CURRY» CALCUTTA MADE FOR DISPLAY USE € DELUX
MOVIE THEATER & ROYAL BEST PRICE! KAKAOBOHNE PARIS ↦ MANUFACTURER NO. 1270 ·CH CAPS...
CAPPUCCINO CUP BOARDING AT: PLATTFORM 1 EXPRESS EUROPA CÔTE D'AZURE | DARJEELING TEA JANUAR LETTERWERK FRIEND

WWW·EXAMPLE·COM

About
Carrosserie is based on the kind of straightforward capitals you may find in hand-rendered signs or book covers from the 1930s. It's an all-caps sans serif, strictly meant for display use. It comes with some alternate letter shapes that you can play around with, such as an "A" with rounded top or an "M" with diverging legs. There are also some alternate ampersands for creating company logos. The typeface has been updated for the internet age by adding a set of www domain symbols.

Design
Fabian Widmer
2011

Foundry
Letterwerk, Switzerland
www.letterwerk.ch

Styles / Weights
Thin, Extralight, Light, Regular, Medium, Bold, Fat

Language support
Latin

OpenType options
Stylistic Alternates, Domainsymbols

Optimized for web
No

REGULAR 18PT

AABCDEFGHIJKLMMNOPQRSTUVWXYZÆÅÇÉÑÖÛ
0123456789@.,-:;!?')*""«»/–€$&½

BOLD & LIGHT 9PT

→ **CATA·LOGUE** / NOUN / A COMPLETE LIST OF THINGS THAT PEOPLE CAN LOOK AT OR BUY: A CATALOGUE OF TYPEFACES (A BOOK SHOWING THE NEWEST FONTS, TO HELP PEOPLE CHOOSE THE RIGHT TYPEFACE)

FAT & THIN 16PT

TYPOGRAPHERS WANT AMAZING, EXQUISITE & CLEVER JUSTIFIED TEXT IN BOOKS

MEDIUM & EXTRA LIGHT 36PT

AEJGQR7
AEJGQR7

REGULAR 13PT

THE YEARBOOK OF TYPE COMPENDIUM WORKS WELL AS A TOOL IN VEXED TYPOGRAPHY QUESTIONS FOR POLARIZING JOBS

Enjoy some delicious
flourishes, frames, borders,
arrows and banners too!

CLEMENTE
Upright & *Italic* in a geometric retro style

ANACAPA
SLAB & SANS
TALL AND SKINNY WITH 3 WEIGHTS

AVALON
SANS & SLAB
3 HIGH CONTRASTING WEIGHTS

Upright & *Italics*
A hand-drawn family inspired by vintage typewriters

upright and
italics
Script
made in three
weights

YOU ARE
the cream
TO MY
COFFEE

Catalina Family

About
I recently visited a charming bakery in Newport Beach, CA, decorated with hand-drawn menus, table cards, chalkboards, and wall quotes. I was inspired to create a new font family based on the combination of hand-drawn fonts made to go with each other. Included in this package are five font families, with two graphic ornament fonts. So here is a breakdown of what's cookin' at Catalina's Bakery:

Catalina Anacapa is tall and skinny in both sans and slab serif styles. Avalon is similar to Anacapa but with high contrasting line weight and including an inline alternative for both sans and slab serif styles. Clemente is a more standard sans serif geometric family that can be used for paragraph text as well as headlines. Catalina Script rounds out the package with its hand-drawn cursive flair while Catalina Typewriter's expanded serifs add another family for both display and paragraph type. The Extras set includes borders, frames, arrows, banners, flourishes and more.

Design
Kimmy Kirkwood
2014

Foundry
Kimmy Design, USA
www.kimmydesign.com

Styles / Weights
Family of five styles (Typewriter, Script, Clemente, Avalon, Anacapa), each in four weights (Light, Regular, Bold, Inline), each with Italics

Language support
Latin

OpenType options
All Caps, Small Caps, Capitals to Small Caps, Titling Alternates, Fractions, Stylistic Alternates

Optimized for web
Yes

CLEMENTE REGULAR 18PT

AVALON SANS INLINE 36PT

AEJGQR7

TYPEWRITER BOLD & LIGHT 14PT

Typographers want amazing, exquisite
& clever justified text in books

ANACAPA SANS BOLD 42PT

AEJGQR7

SCRIPT BOLD & REGULAR 10PT

Year·book of Type / noun / book published every second year, giving details of typefaces of the previous two years and about general current typographic topics—e.g. OpenType features, font editors like Glyphs etc.

ALL'UOVO

κουταλιές της σούπας ζάχαρη

ΕΓΚΥΚΛΙΟΣ ① ❽

❞Яйцата се смесват добре❝

QUICHE

№ 36.74 ↔ Trave

ΚΥΡΓΑ ₮ 28,9

με έναν υπαινιγμό του 10° rotali

fèves fraîches au

About
After Adrian Frutiger reinvented Paul Renner's all-time classic Futura with the kind Avenir, Hoefler and Frere-Jones worked out the powerful Gotham, Christian Schwartz did the fashionable Neutraface and Mark Simonson hit the nail with the Proxima Nova as the new kid on the block, Cera is just another but distinctive geometric sans serif.

Nevertheless, the pan-European typeface supports pure geometry plus Latin, Cyrillic, and Greek script. With over 990 glyphs per weight, Cera includes localized letter shapes plus ordinals and provides matching OpenType features.

Equipped with six precise weights, a clean Italic—carefully slanted to 10 degrees—and useful dingbats plus Arrows, Cera is a good companion for setting clean text and headlines for print and screen in multiple languages and all its facets.

For the upright shapes there is a stencil version available as well.

Design
Jakob Runge
2014

Foundry
type me! fonts, Germany
www.typemefonts.com

Styles / Weights
Thin, Thin Italic, Light, Light Italic, Regular, Italic, Medium, Medium Italic, Bold, Bold Italic, Black, Black Italic plus Stencil version of upright weights

Language support
Latin, Cyrillic, Greek

OpenType options
Proportional Oldstyle, Tabular and Proportional Lining, Tabular Oldstyle, All Caps, Superscript, Subscript, Ordinals, All Alternates, Fractions, Numerator, Denominator, Ornaments, Arrows, Stylistic Alternates, Stylistic Sets, Slashed Zero, Localized Forms

Optimized for web
No

REGULAR 17PT

aabcdefghijklmnopqrstuvwxyyzæfjåçéñöûß
ABCDEFGHIJKLMNOPQRSTUVWXYZÆÇØ
0123456789⌀@.,-:;!?')]§*"'"«»/–€$&⅓♡↗

BLACK 36PT

aejgGQR7

BLACK & MEDIUM 16PT

Typographers want
amazing, exquisite
& clever justified text
in books

BOLD & REGULAR 9PT

☞ **over·view** / *noun* / a brief summary of something: *in the index of the Yearbook of Type the reader can find an overview of all typefaces presented in the book sorted by classification*

ALL WEIGHTS 8PT

Thin
Thin Italic
Light
Light Italic
Regular
Regular Italic
Medium
Medium Italic
Bold
Bold Italic
Black
Black Italic

STENCIL WEIGHTS 8PT

Thin
Light
Regular
Medium
Bold
Black

eliminating the stockpile

50 miles south

"FALLING BEHIND (SCHEDULE) IS ACTUALLY RELATIVELY EASY."

PUEBLO

By January 2012, troops had completed 90 percent of the job

You never get a second chance to make a first impression

uudisrakennustöitä

....

Colón Mono THE PHRASE began appearing in typing and stenography.

Colón Mono Alt THE PHRASE began appearing in typing and stenography.

About
Colón is a slab serif typeface, influenced by the nostalgia for the aesthetics of a typewriter. Colón extended family consists of two subfamilies: Colón Mono with monospaced glyphs sets, and Colón (proportional characters sets). The typeface is ideal for use in display sizes, though is quite legible in text.

Colón is released in OpenType format with extended support for most Latin languages, and includes some OpenType features—such as Proportional / Tabular Figures, Slashed Zero, Ligatures, Fractions, etc.

Design
Ramiz Guseynov
2013

Foundry
TipogafiaRamis, USA
www.tipografiaramis.com

Styles / Weights
Family of two styles (proportional, monospaced), each three weights (Light, Regular, Bold), each with Italics

Language support
Latin

OpenType options
Proportional Oldstyle, Tabular and Proportional Lining, Tabular Oldstyle, Standard Ligatures, Discretionary Ligatures, Superscript, Subscript, Fractions, Numerator, Denominator, Slashed Zero

Optimized for web
Yes

REGULAR 16PT

abcdefghijklmnopqrstuvwxyzæfjåçéñöûß
ABCDEFGHIJKLMNOPQRSTUVWXYZÆÇØ
01234567890@.,-:;!?')]§*“”«»/–€$&½

BOLD 35PT

aejgGQR7

MONO ALT REGULAR & LIGHT 14PT

Typographers want
amazing, exquisite
& clever justified
text in books

REGULAR & LIGHT 9PT

ex·am·ple / *noun* / an illustration that supports or provides more information: *by showing examples the Yearbook of Type presents each font in different sizes and weights*

ALL WEIGHTS 6PT

Light
Light Italic
Regular
Italic
Bold
Bold Italic

ALL WEIGHTS MONO 6PT

Mono Light
Mono Alt Light
Mono Alt Light Italic
Mono Regular
Mono Italic
Mono Alt Regular
Mono Italic

You say ↙

Slab Serif?

↘ I say

«COLROY!»

You say ↙

„Why?“

↘ I say

Because it’s Beautiful!

About
Colroy is a superbly and subtly crafted contemporary Clarendon—like typeface. Some of its many advantages are perfect suitability for body text usage, marvelous italics and the coverage of up to 86 languages. Furthermore, it supports Small Caps and various OpenType features. Compared to existing Clarendon—like typefaces, it is slightly more geometricized but still has the vividness which you have come to appreciate in traditional Clarendon typefaces. After Hermann Eidenbenz redrew the original Clarendon for the Haas'sche Schriftgiesserei in Münchenstein in the early 1950s, it took more than 60 years until Marc Droz (dreh gmbh) created a modern and thoroughly crafted and clarendon-like slab serif that stands in the Swiss tradition of strong and somehow understated typefaces: the Colroy.

The creation of Colroy started in 2009 during the CAS Typedesign at the Zurich University of the Arts and was completed as a font family with six cuts by 2014.

Design
Marc Droz
2014

Foundry
Nouvelle Noire, Switzerland
www.nouvellenoire.ch

Styles / Weights
Regular, Italic, Medium, Medium Italic, Bold, Bold Italic

Language support
Latin

OpenType options
Proportional Oldstyle, Tabular and Proportional Lining, Tabular Oldstyle, Standard Ligatures, Discretionary Ligatures, All Caps, Small Caps, Superscript, Subscript, Contextual Alternates, Contextual Ligatures, Fractions, Numerator, Denominator, Ornaments, Arrows, Stylistic Alternates, Stylistic Sets, Required Ligatures

Optimized for web
Yes

REGULAR 18PT

abcdefghijklmnopqrstuvwxyzæfjåçéñöûß
ABCDEFGHIJKLMNOPQRSTUVWXYZÆÇØ
0123456789@.,-:;!?')]§*“”«»/–€$&½ ↗

MEDIUM 36PT

aejgGQR7

BOLD & REGULAR 16PT

Typographers want
amazing, exquisite
& clever justified text
in books

REGULAR ITALIC 36PT

aejgGQR7

BOLD & REGULAR 8PT

ar·chive / *noun* / a collection of documents such as letters, photographs or other material: *the Yearbook of Type is an archive of contemporary typefaces from all over the world*

COLUMBIA TITLING BY TYPETANIC FONTS

LIGHT STANDARD **MEDIUM BOLD**

401 EUCLID AVENUE

ZOOPRAXISCOPE

QUEEN CITY OF THE GREAT LAKES

BLATZ

CINCINNATI SUBWAY

KALAMAZOO

1893 COLUMBIAN EXHIBITION

NIAGARA

20TH CENTURY LIMITED

EST. 1875

McSORLEY'S OLD ALE HOUSE

FRANK E. KIRBY

NEW YORK CENTRAL (J-1) #5270

Columbia Titling

About
Columbia Titling is a titling-caps display family based on wide Clarendon-style wood type and industrial signage design from the late 19th and early 20th century.

Columbia Titling includes a small set of OpenType features, including both tabular and proportional figures, special superscript ordinal suffixes, underlined superscript alternate letters, and OpenType fractions. Columbia Titling can have a 'period feel' depending on its use, but is fresh enough to use in contemporary designs, like magazine headlines, invitations, or stationery.

The typeface—released in four weights—takes its name from the historic SS Columbia, a steamboat launched in 1903. Lettering found on the ship's wheelhouse provided initial inspiration for Columbia Titling.

Design
Gregory Shutters
2013

Foundry
Typetanic Fonts, USA
www.typetanicfonts.com

Styles / Weights
Light, Standard, Medium, Bold

Language support
Latin

OpenType options
Tabular and Proportional Lining, All Caps, Ordinals, Fractions, Numerator, Denominator, Arrows

Optimized for web
No

REGULAR 13PT

ABCDEFGHIJKLMNOPQRSTUVWXYZ
ÆÅÇÉÑÖÛ
0123456789@.,-:;!?')*“”«»/–€$&½»→

BOLD 23PT

AEJGQR7

BOLD & LIGHT 10PT

TYPOGRAPHERS WANT AMAZING, EXQUISITE & CLEVER JUSTIFIED TEXT IN BOOKS

STANDARD 23PT

AEJGQR7

MEDIUM & LIGHT 9PT

THE YEARBOOK OF TYPE COMPENDIUM WORKS WELL AS A TOOL IN VEXED TYPOGRAPHY QUESTIONS FOR POLARIZING JOBS

NOVA
OBJETIVIDADE
BRASILEIRA
- 2015 NEW BRAZILIAN OBJECTIVITY EXHIBITION -
MUSEU DE ARTE MODERNA
RIO DE JANEIRO
6 A 30 DE ABRIL
2015

About
Daft Brush is a stylish contemporary brush font. And it's not just a rad face! It's quite skillful, with four alternates for each letter, two alternates for numbers and yet variations for punctuation marks. Its ingenious OpenType Contextual Alternates feature is programmed to instantly cycle all these folks and deliver an amazing organic feel (OpenType savvy software is needed, but these days even the pretty basic Windows Notepad will do!). It's only rock and roll (and we like it). Play it loud!

Design
Erica Jung, Ricardo Marcin
2014

Foundry
PintassilgoPrints, Brazil
www.pintassilgoprints.com

Styles / Weights
Regular

Language support
Latin

OpenType options
All Alternates, Contextual Alternates, Fractions, Ornaments, Stylistic Alternates, Stylistic Sets, Randomize

Optimized for web
Yes

REGULAR 18PT

AAAABCDEFGHIJKLMNOPQRSTUVWXYZÆÅÇÉÑÖÛ
0123456789@.,-:;!?')*“”«»/–€$&½

REGULAR 30PT

AEJG8QR7

REGULAR 14PT

TYPOGRAPHERS WANT AMAZING, EXQUISITE & CLEVER JUSTIFIED TEXT IN BOOKS ★

Mm Ññ Oo Pp Qq Rr Ss Tt Uu Vv
Ww Xx Yy Zz 1 2 3 4 5 6 7 8 9 0

REGULAR 28 PTS

In 1837, the Scottish scientist Thomas Dick had a big idea. A really, really big idea: Build *"a huge triangle or ellipsis of many miles in extent, in Siberia or any other country."* He figured that because there are some 22 trillion aliens living in our solar system, 4.2 billion of which are on the moon, even if they don't have telescope technology to spy the triangle, surely some would have eyes powerful enough to see it unaided. Perhaps realizing just what a big idea this was, he added, *"Schemes far more foolish and preposterous than the above have been contrived and acted upon in every age of the world."*

LIGHT + LIGHT ITALIC 12/17 PTS

@

Categories

BLACK ALT 100 PTS

Q A

Typefaces

BOLD ITALIC 104 PTS

Q A

Extension

REGULAR 112 PTS

£52,78

¥34,90

Packages

LIGHT 115 PTS

$25,60

Winning

EXTRALIGHT ITALIC 135 PTS

Nº1

BOURBON
INFINITE
WHICH

EXTRALIGHT

ESCOCÉS
WHISKY
THINK

REGULAR ITALIC ALT

THOUGHT
SUNSET
EVERY

BLACK

¡Si!

Darwin

About
Darwin font family is an eclectic assembly of grotesque, geometric and humanistic styles, includes 20 fonts, ten normal and ten alt sub family, the alt variant gives spice to the compositions. The font family is good for headlines, small text, posters and logos.

Design
Luciano Vergara
Mendoza Vergara Studio
2014

Foundry
Los Andes Type, Chile
www.behance.net/losandestype

Styles / Weights
Family of two styles (Normal, Alt Sub), each in five weights (ExtraLight, Light, Regular, Bold, Black), each with Italics

Language support
Latin

OpenType options
Fractions

Optimized for web
No

REGULAR 18PT

abcdefghijklmnopqrstuvwxyzæfjåçéñöûß
ABCDEFGHIJKLMNOPQRSTUVWXYZÆÇØ
0123456789@.,-:;!?')]§*"" ‹ › /–$&⅓

BLACK & ALT BLACK 30PT

aejgGQR7
aejgGQR7

BOLD & LIGHT 14PT

Typographers want
amazing, exquisite
& clever justified text
in books

EXTRALIGHT & ALT EXTRALIGHT 30PT

aejgGQR7
aejgGQR7

ALT BLACK & ALT LIGHT 14PT

Typographers want
amazing, exquisite
& clever justified text
in books

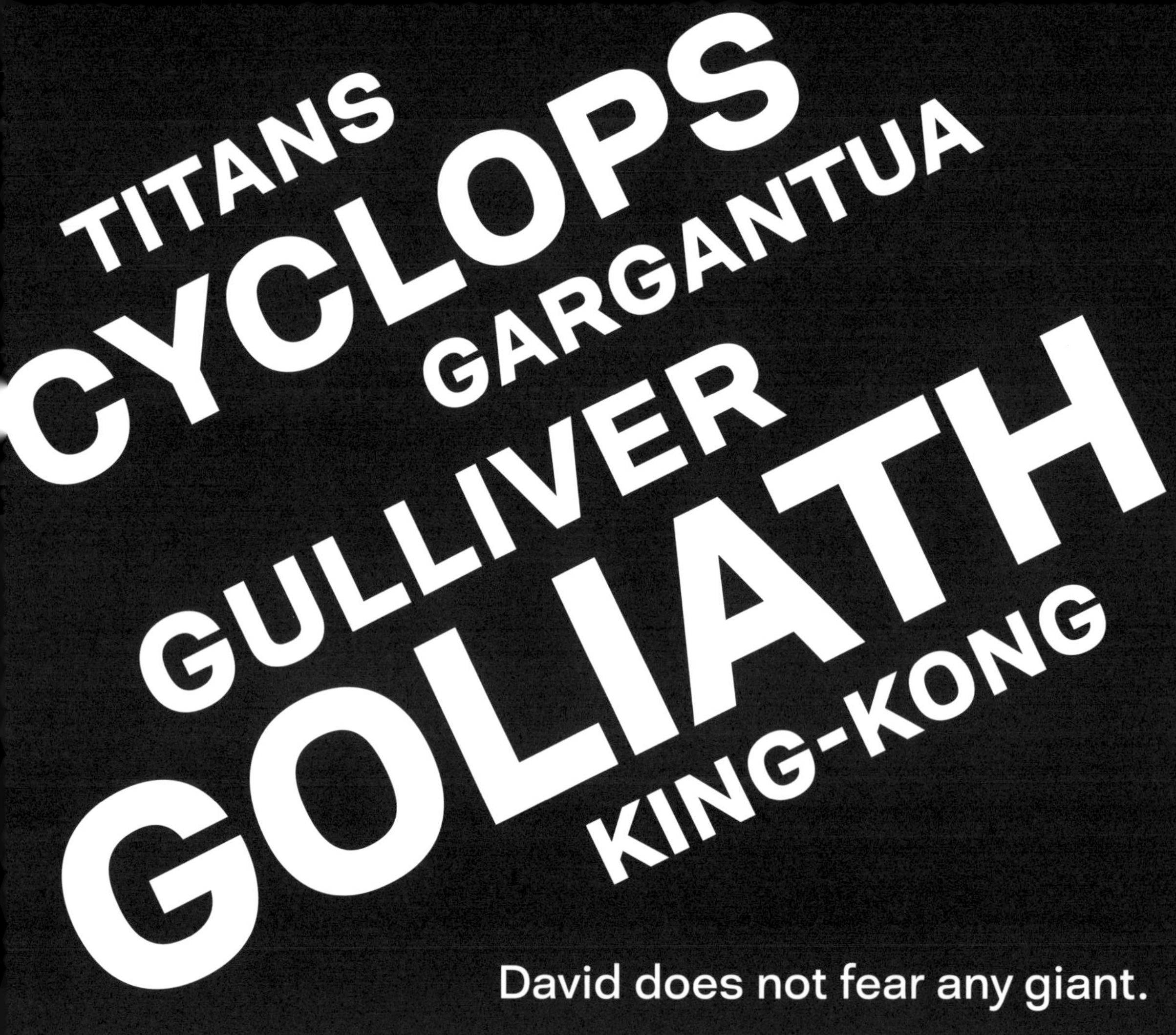

David is a sans-serif typeface that looks sturdy and stable but maintains a swinging spirit, that fits with its foundry companions. *It does not fear the difficulties and has therefore equipped itself with a proper italic.*

At the forefront of all the various fonts on offer, David is a homonymous statue sculpted by *Michelangelo* in a block of marble rejected by other people because of its flaws. This statue had been placed in front of the *palazzo Vecchio* to symbolize the determination of the young Florentine republic facing surrounding tyrants.

Supported by an extended family of six weights, standing firm, of a generous width, the David typeface stands up to merciless giants and philistines of all kinds.

DAVID COMES IN SIX WEIGHTS & ITALICS :

obtuse philistine	*obtuse philistine*
obtuse philistine	*obtuse philistine*
obtuse philistine	*obtuse philistine*
obtuse philistins	***obtuse philistine***
obtuse philistine	***obtuse philistine***
obtuse philistine	***obtuse philistine***

About
David is a sans-serif typeface that looks sturdy and stable but maintains a swinging spirit, that fits with its foundry companions. It does not fear the difficulties and has therefore equipped itself with a proper italic.

At the forefront of all the various fonts on offer, David is a homonymous statue sculpted by Michelangelo in a block of marble rejected by other people because of its flaws. This statue had been placed in front of the palazzo Vecchio to symbolize the determination of the young Florentine republic facing surrounding tyrants.

Supported by an extended family of six weights, standing firm, of a generous width, the David typeface stands up to merciless giants and philistines of all kinds.

Design
Émilie Rigaud
2014

Foundry
A is for..., France
www.aisforapple.fr

Styles / Weights
ExtraLight, ExtraLight Italic, Light, Light Italic, Regular, Italic, Medium, Medium Italic, Bold, Bold Italic, Heavy, Heavy Italic

Language support
Latin

OpenType options
Proportional Oldstyle, Tabular and Proportional Lining, Tabular Oldstyle, All Caps, Small Caps, Capitals to Small Caps, Superscript, Subscript, Ordinals, Fractions, Numerator, Denominator, Stylistic Sets

Optimized for web
Yes

REGULAR 16PT

abcdefghijklmnopqrstuvwxyzæfjåçéñöûß
ABCDEFGHIJKLMNOPQRSTUVWXYZÆÇØ
0123456789@.,-:;!?')]§*'""«»/-€$&½

BOLD 30PT

aejgGQR7

HEAVY & EXTRALIGHT 14PT

Typographers want
amazing, exquisite
& clever justified text
in books

BOLD & REGULAR 8PT

ref·er·ence book/*noun*/a book that contains facts and information that you look at when you need to find out sth. particular—*"I am looking for the right typeface for my project, so I use the Yearbook of Type as a reference book."*

ALL WEIGHTS 10PT

ExtraLight
Light
Regular
Medium
Bold
Heavy

ITALICS 10PT

ExtraLight Italic
Light Italic
Italic
Medium Italic
Bold Italic
Heavy Italic

THE CENTIMETRE REMAINS

Decimeter

A PRACTICAL UNIT OF LENGTH FOR

(des-uh-mee-ter)

MANY EVERYDAY MEASUREMENTS.

from deci+meter, noun.

CENTIMETRE IS APPROXIMATELY

A unit of length equal

THE WIDTH OF THE FINGERNAIL OF

to 1/10 (0.1) meter.

ADULT PERSON.

Abbreviation: dm.

Decima

Decima Mono

Though for many physical quantities, SI prefixes for factors of 10^3 like milli- and kilo- often preferred by technicians the **CENTIMETRE** remains a practical unit of length for many everyday measurements.
Centimetre is approximately the width of the fingernail of adult person between 3/8″ and 7/16″ on an ***English inch ruler***.

About
Decima—a condensed geometric sans serif typeface, was first released back in 2008 and quite successful ever since (MyFonts Rising Star, February 2009).

Decima Pro and Decima Mono X are upgraded versions of their older counterparts, with careful refinements to glyph shapes and extension of character set—which enabled support of more Latin languages, as well as Cyrillic. Some alternate styles have been added to the original styles. The typeface is released in OpenType format with some OpenType features.

Design
Ramiz Guseynov
2014

Foundry
TipografiaRamis, USA
www.tipografiaramis.com

Styles / Weights
Family of two styles (Pro, Mono X), each in three weights (Light, Regular, Bold), Pro with Obliques, Mono X with Italics

Language support
Latin, Cyrillic

OpenType options
Tabular Lining and Proportional Lining, Standard Ligatures, Superscript, Subscript, Contextual Ligatures, Fractions, Numerator, Denominator, Slashed Zero

Optimized for web
Yes

DECIMA A REGULAR 18PT

abcdefghijklmnopqrstuvwxyzæﬁåçéñöûß
ABCDEFGHIJKLMNOPQRSTUVWXYZÆÇÜØ
01234567890@.,-:;!?')]§*""«»/–€$&⅓

MONO X BOLD & REGULAR 10PT

The Yearbook of Type
compendium works well as
a tool in vexed typography
questions for polarizing jobs

A BOLD & REGULAR 16PT

Typographers want
amazing, exquisite
& clever justified text
in books

BOLD & ITALIC 36PT

aejgGQR7
aejgGQR7

ALL WEIGHTS 8PT

Light
Light Oblique
A Light
A Light Oblique
Regular
Italic
A Regular
A Oblique
Bold
Bold Oblique
A Bold
A Bold Oblique

ALL WEIGHTS MONO X 8PT

Light
Light Italic
Regular
Italic
Bold
Bold Italic

Fun fun auf der autobahn! Tellers en noemers

A COMMANDING PRESENCE

Fremstillet til maskiner, finpudset til mennesker

Right up your Straße *Efficienza teutonica*

Institut für Normung *1234567890*

Vienodo pločio senamadiški skaitmenys

Not so square **Alternatiewe**

Fresco e frizzante Spokojna i świeża

About
Like a new concrete bridge crossing the autobahn, DIN Next™ Slab brings a sturdy, square serif to the font family that has its roots in the German road sign system. With 14 new fonts, all inspired by the classic German DIN 1451 typefaces, its industrial heritage makes it surprisingly versatile for a wide range of design applications. See more at: *www.monotype.com / libraries / din-next-slab / #sthash.AXHooyjQ.dpuf*

Design
Tom Grace, Akira Kobayashi, Sandra Winter
2014

Foundry
Monotype, USA
www.monotype.com

Styles / Weights
UltraLight, UltraLight Italic, Light, Light Italic, Regular, Italic, Medium, Medium Italic, Bold, Bold Italic, Heavy, Heavy Italic, Black, Black Italic

Language support
Latin

OpenType options
Proportional Oldstyle, Tabular and Proportional Lining, Tabular Oldstyle, Standard Ligatures, Discretionary Ligatures, Small Caps, Capitals to Small Caps, Superscript, Subscript, Fractions, Numerator, Denominator, Stylistic Alternates, Stylistic Sets, Localized Forms

Optimized for web
Yes

REGULAR 18PT

aαbcdefghijklmnopqrstuvwxyzæfjåçéñöûß
ABCDEFGHIJKLMNOPQRSTUVWXYZÆÇØ
01234567890@.,-:;!?')]§*"" «»/–€$&½

BLACK 36PT

aejgGQR7

BOLD & LIGHT 16PT

Typographers want amazing, exquisite
& clever justified text in books

BLACK & LIGHT 8PT

Year·book of Type / *noun* / book published every second year, giving details on typefaces of the previous two years and also about general current typographic topics—*e.g. OpenType features, font editors like Glyphs etc.*

ALL WEIGHTS 8PT

UltraLight
Light
Regular
Medium
Bold
Heavy
Black

ITALICS 8PT

UltraLight Italic
Light Italic
Italic
Medium Italic
Bold Italic
Heavy Italic
Black Italic

Monotype

DIN Next Slab

»Aren't you ashamed, you who walk backward along the whole path of existence, and blame me for walking backward along the path of the promenade?«

When people laughed at Diogenes because he walked backward beneath the portico.

About
Diogenes is an elegant and crisp text typeface. While the skeletons of the individual characters are distinct and strong, the serifs are fine and sharp. This is especially true for the capitals with their comparatively strong horizontal strokes. The graceful appearance of Diogenes makes it an ideal choice for books, newspapers, and magazines, both at small text sizes and display sizes. Diogenes comes in five weights from Light to Black, each with Italic and Small Caps.

Design
Ludwig Übele
2014

Foundry
LudwigType, Germany
www.ludwigtype.de

Styles / Weights
Light, Light Italic, Regular, Italic, Medium, Medium Italic, Bold, Bold Italic, Black, Black Italic

Language support
Latin

OpenType options
Proportional Oldstyle, Tabular Lining, Proportional Lining, Tabular Oldstyle, Standard Ligatures, Discretionary Ligatures, All Caps, Small Caps, Capitals to Small Caps, Superscript, Subscript, Ordinals, Contextual Alternates, Fractions, Numerator, Denominator, Stylistic Alternates, Stylistic Sets, Slashed Zero

Optimized for web
Yes

REGULAR 18PT

abcdefghijklmnopqrstuvwxyzæfjåçéñöûß
ABCDEFGHIJKLMNOPQRSTUVWXYZÆÇØ
01234567890@.,-:;!?')]§*“”«»/–€$&½

BOLD & LIGHT 34PT

aejgGQR7
aejgGQR7

BLACK & LIGHT 16PT

Typographers want
amazing, exquisite
& clever justified text
in books

BOLD & REGULAR 8PT

ar·chive / *noun* / a collection of documents such as letters, photographs or other material: *the Yearbook of Type is an archive of contemporary typefaces from all over the world*

ALL WEIGHTS 12PT

Light
Regular
Medium
Bold
Black

ITALICS 12PT

Light Italic
Italic
Medium Italic
Bold Italic
Black Italic

written

Ebüzziya

Mehmet Tevfik Bey*

Türkiye'de "matbaacılığı sanat hâline getiren kişi" olarak kabul edilir.

№28 TASVİR-İ EFKAR

Nevsal-i Marifet

1880'de Salname-i Kamerî

Ebuzziya Tevfik & Ahmet Mithat Efendi

script

About
Duru Sans is low contrast and classic 20th century style sans design. The project aimed to harmonize the humanist urge with the modernist one. It was created particularly to perform well on printed continuous text projects while retaining its legibility on the screen. The typefaces consist of nine weights with accompanying Italics. Its extreme weights such as Hariline were created to complement running texts by enabling the setting of large headlines. The localization features allow correct orthographic setting for Turkish text. It also offers various stylistic alternates such as the double- and single-story "a" and "g" variations for certain typesetting tasks.

Design
Onur Yazıcıgil
2014

Foundry
Sorkin Type, USA
www.sorkintype.com

Styles / Weights
Hairline, UltraLight, ExtraLight, Light, SemiLight, Book, Medium, SemiBold, Bold, each with Italics

Language support
Latin

OpenType options
Proportional Oldstyle, Tabular Oldstyle, Tabular Lining, Standard Ligatures, Discretionary Ligatures, Small Caps, Capitals to Small Caps, Contexual Alternates, Arrows, Stylistic Sets, Slashed Zero

Optimized for web
Yes

BOOK 16PT

aabcdefgghijklmnopqrstuvwxyzæfjåçéñöûß
ABCDEFGHIJKLMNOPQRSTUVWXYZÆÇØ
01234567890@.,-:;!?')]§*""«»/–€$&↗

BOLD & MEDIUM 31PT

aejgGQR7
aejgGQR7

SEMIBOLD & SEMILIGHT 15PT

Typographers want
amazing, exquisite
& clever justified text
in books

BOLD & LIGHT 9PT

ref·er·ence book / *noun* / a book that contains facts and information that you look at when you need to find out sth. particular—*"I am looking for the right typeface for my project, so I use the Yearbook of Type as a reference book."*

ALL WEIGHTS 10PT

Hairline
UltraLight
ExtraLight
Light
SemiLight
Book
Medium
SemiBold
Bold

ITALICS 10PT

Hairline Italic
UltraLight Italic
ExtraLight Italic
Light Italic
SemiLight Italic
Book Italic
Medium Italic
SemiBold Italic
Bold Italic

Today I *made* nothing *as* ***usual***
except *type* design.

*
&
@
Á
0
1
2
3
4
5
6
7
8
9

About
The careful balance between the emotional swings and shapes set in strong contrast such as the burly, deliberately constructed and emphasized design of the serifs, or generally vertical and orderly appearance within the Duwal Pro determine the special look of this Antiqua typeface. All characters of the Duwal Pro are designed to be open, accessible and detailed, so it is suitable for use in small font sizes as well as for headlines and work marks.

Design
Dennis Dünnwald
2014

Foundry
VolcanoType, Germany
www.volcano-type.de

Styles / Weights
Regular, Italic, Bold, Bold Italic

Language support
Latin

OpenType options
Proportional Oldstyle, Tabular and Proportional Lining, Tabular Oldstyle, Standard Ligatures, Discretionary Ligatures, All Caps, Small Caps, Capitals to Small Caps, Superscript, Subscript, Swashes, Contextual Ligatures, Alternative Fractions, Numerator, Denominator, Arrows, Stylistic Alternates

Optimized for web
Yes

REGULAR 18PT

abcdefghijklmnopqrstuvwxyzæfjåçéñöûß
ABCDEFGHIJKLMNOPQRSTUVWXYZÆÇØ
0123456789@.,-:;!?')]§*“”«»/–€$&⅓↗

BOLD 30PT

aejgGQR7

BOLD & REGULAR 16PT

Typographers want
amazing, exquisite
& clever justified text
in books

ITALIC 30PT

aejgGQR7

BOLD & REGULAR 8PT

over·view / *noun* / a brief summary of something: *in the index of the Yearbook of Type the reader can find an overview of all typefaces presented in the book sorted by classification*

Echo Pro

Fine quality workhorse type available in five weights across Latin, Cyrillic and Greek scripts. Echo takes a restrained approach that contrasts the distinct warmth of the humanist sans genre.
Available exclusively from typotheque.com

California Chrome Native Da
ked Strong Close Hatches Bay
alacer **Moreno** *Old Rosebud*
et Reason Main Sequence ***Ziv***
Shared Belief Tapiture **Imp**
Ar Speaker *Fantastic Light* **S**
at Red ***Seabiscuit*** Secretaria
Ring Weekend Bold Ruler Se
Silver Charm ***Best Pal*** Rose
ance in the Mood *Sunday Sile*
er Perfect Drift **Moon Ballad**

About
Echo, a sans serif counterpart to the previously published Charlie typeface, designed by Ross Milne, with the Cyrillic by Gayaneh Bagdasaryan and Greek by Natasha Raissaki. Echo is clear and direct, with subtle influences from the broad nib pen. The two typefaces were developed more-or-less simultaneously, learning from the other.

Design
Ross Milne
2014

Foundry
Typotheque, The Netherlands
www.typotheque.com

Styles / Weights
Regular, Italic, Medium, Medium Italic, Semibold, Semibold Italic, Bold, Bold Italic, Black, Black Italic

Language support
Latin, Cyrillic, Greek

OpenType options
Proportional Oldstyle, Tabular and Proportional Lining, Tabular Oldstyle, Standard Ligatures, Discretionary Ligatures, All Caps, Small Caps, Capitals to Small Caps, Superscript, Subscript, Ordinals, All Alternates, Contextual Ligatures, Fractions, Numerator, Denominator, Ornaments, Arrows, Stylistic Alternates, Stylistic Sets, Slashed Zero

Optimized for web
Yes

REGULAR 18PT

abcdefghijklmnopqrstuvwxyzæfjåçéñöûß
ABCDEFGHIJKLMNOPQRSTUVWXYZÆÇØ
0123456789ø@.,-:;!?')]§*""«»/–€$&⅓ ↗

BOLD 30PT

aejgGQR7

BLACK & REGULAR 14PT

Typographers want
amazing, exquisite
& clever justified text
in books

BOLD & REGULAR 9PT

cata·logue / *noun* / a complete list of things that people can look at or buy: *a catalogue of typefaces (a book showing the newest fonts, to help people choose the right typeface)*

ALL WEIGHTS 12PT

Regular
Medium
Semibold
Bold
Black

ITALICS 12PT

Regular Italic
Medium Italic
Semibold Italic
Bold Italic
Black Italic

↖ Pilier Nord

↖ Pilier Nord

↖ Pilier Nord

La tour Eiffel, initialement nommée tour de 300 m, était construite par Eiffel et ses collaborateurs pour l'exposition universelle de 1889.

Ce monument parisien, symbole de la capitale française, est le premier monument payant visité au monde avec 6,893 millions de visiteurs en 2007.

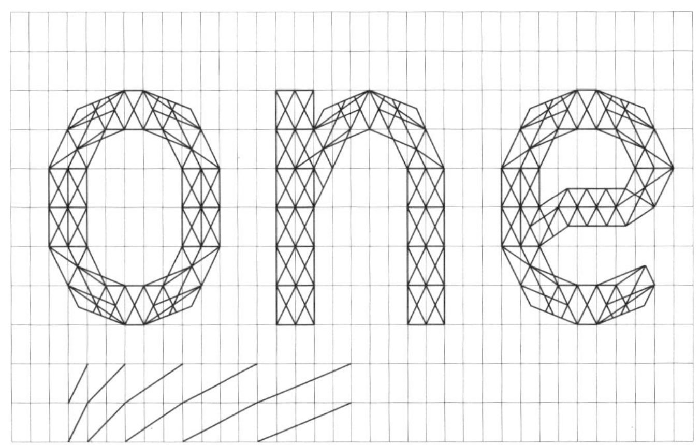

Elevateur ↗

3. Étage Sud

Escallier N° 4

Pillier Nord →

Billetterie

Collaborator on the AB EiffelSolid-Bold & Regular: Anton Studer

About
The trigger for the development of this font was a design competition for a new signage project of the Eiffel Tower in Paris, to which I was invited by Ruedi Baur to create and contribute the typeface. It was required to serve two very different purposes: a large display variant for signs, and a text variant for printed matter.

During research, it quickly became evident that it is less the shape of the tower as such, but rather its structure elements which offered an interesting starting point for the type design. The characteristics of the structure are the square, the double square and a series of struts at different angles. This geometric form language was the starting point for the construction and design process.

There were hardly any models which could have served as orientation. With a defined design principle, you have less leeway than in free drawing. It was a tricky task with formal, aesthetic and technical problems to be solved mainly for the three display variants.

Design
André Baldinger
2013

Foundry
AB Type Foundry, France
www.abtypefoundry.com

Styles / Weights
Regular, Bold, Level1, Level2, Level3 for the Display variants

Language support
Latin

OpenType options
Proportional Oldstyle, Tabular and Proportional Lining, Tabular Oldstyle, Standard Ligatures, Contextual Ligatures, Alternative Fractions, Arrows, Slashed Zero

Optimized for web
Yes

REGULAR 16PT

abcdefghijklmnopqrstuvwxyzæfjåçéñöûß
ABCDEFGHIJKLMNOPQRSTUVWXYZÆÇØ
01234567890@.,-:;!?')]§*“”«»/–€$&½↗

LEVEL 2 42PT

aegjGQR7

BOLD & REGULAR 16PT

Typographers want amazing, exquisite
& clever justified text in books

BOLD 42PT

aejgGQR7

LEVEL 2 20PT

Typographers want amazing, exquisite & clever justified text in books

MODERN
DURABILITY
RESEARCH
UNIT
BRUNSWICK
GREEN
INDUSTRY
STANDARD
ELEGANT
SIMPLICITY

About
Elliot Pro is an enduring type. A future-proof, 21st Century, open and harmonious sans serif design. Rooted in '60s Brit modernism but re-born with neo-modernist vigour. Elliot's clear fluid shapes lend words a distinctive and optimistic bounce.

Design
Nick Job
2012

Foundry
Fontsmith, Great Britian
www.fontsmith.com

Styles / Weights
Thin, Thin Italic, Light, Light Italic, Regular, Italic, Bold, Bold Italic, Heavy, Heavy Italic

Language support
Latin, Cyrillic, Greek

OpenType options
Proportional Oldstyle, Proportional Lining, Tabular Oldstyle, All Caps, Small Caps, Capitals to Small Caps, Superscript, Subscript, Ordinals, Fractions, Numerator, Denominator, Arrows, Localized Forms

Optimized for web
Yes

REGULAR 16PT

abcdefghijklmnopqrstuvwxyzæfjåçéñöûß
ABCDEFGHIJKLMNOPQRSTUVWXYZÆÇØ
0123456789@.,-:;!?')]*""«»/–€$&⅓↗

HEAVY & THIN 31PT

aejgGQR7
aejgGQR7

BOLD & LIGHT 15PT

Typographers want
amazing, exquisite
& clever justified text
in books

BOLD & REGULAR 9PT

ref·er·ence book / *noun* / a book that contains facts and information that you look at when you need to find out sth. particular—*"I am looking for the right typeface for my project, so I use the Yearbook of Type as a reference book."*

ALL WEIGHTS 10PT

Thin
Light
Regular
Bold
Heavy

ITALICS 10PT

Thin Italic
Light Italic
Italic
Bold Italic
Heavy Italic

Bibliothèque Binding Bitmap ABC

— *Clearly Optimistic Measure* —

Olympik Linear Play Byline ABC

— *Form ± Function Swatch* —

Förmographic Arctic* Layout ABC

— *Quantic Calligraphy Dash* —

Berlin Straße Trilogy Die Folio ABC

— *Speed of Life Display Face* —

Omnicrom Reproduction A1 ABC

— *Litho Prepress Foil Pass* —

NB: One Hundred Core Unit ABC

— *Printed Matter {-hyphen}* —

Pentagonål «project» Play ABC

— *Monochromatic Offset* —

Build Bureau Exploration ABC

— ***Swipe File Substitution*** —

“Atelier” Graph Rotterdam ABC

— ***Post-Objective Colophon*** —

Duotone Ephemera Footer ABC

— ***Analogue Clipping Error*** —

Thinking+Doing=Progress ABC

— ***Complementary Colours.*** —

About
FS Emeric is about what is happening right now: A sharper aesthetic that cuts across design disciplines—graphic, fashion, product, automotive. A reflection of the present that is accepting and open to whatever shape the future might take.

There was a feeling among Fontsmith's clients that the principles of modernism needed to find fresh voices. In response to this, Phil asked whether the time might be right to move away from the deliberate neutrality of the classic fonts of the '30s and '50s, towards something with a visibly more contemporary and human character. Throughout the design process, two central ideas competed for attention: Firstly, Jan Tschichold's contention that a good letter is "one that expresses itself, speaking with the utmost distinctiveness and clarity." And secondly, the belief that a font can be personally expressive without compromising its functionality. This underlying tension became the fuel that drove the project to its conclusion.

Design
Phil Garnham
2013

Foundry
Fontsmith, Great Britain
www.fontsmith.com

Styles / Weights
Thin, Thin Italic, Extralight, Extralight Italic, Light, Light Italic, Book, Book Italic, Regular, Italic, Core, Core Italic, Medium, Medium Italic, Semi Bold, Semi Bold Italic, Bold, Bold Italic, Extra Bold, Extra Bold Italic, Heavy, Heavy Italic

Language support
Latin

OpenType options
Proportional Oldstyle, Tabular and Proportional Lining, Tabular Oldstyle, Standard Ligatures, All Caps, Arrows

Optimized for web
Yes

REGULAR 17PT

abcdefghijklmnopqrstuvwxyzæfjåçéñöûß
ABCDEFGHIJKLMNOPQRSTUVWXYZÆÇØ
0123456789@.,-:;!?')]§*""«»/–€$&↗

EXTRA BOLD 35PT

aejgGQR7

SEMI BOLD & REGULAR 16PT

Typographers want
amazing, exquisite
& clever justified text
in books

BOLD & LIGHT 10PT

Year·book of Type / *noun* / book published every second year, giving details on typefaces of the previous two years and also about general current typographic topics—e.g. *OpenType features, font editors like Glyphs etc.*

ALL WEIGHTS 8PT

Thin
Extralight
Light
Book
Regular
Core
Medium
Semi Bold
Bold
Extra Bold
Heavy

ITALICS 8PT

Thin Italic
Extralight Italic
Light Italic
Book Italic
Italic
Core Italic
Medium Italic
Semi Bold Italic
Bold Italic
Extra Bold Italic
Heavy Italic

Elegant Serif Typeface

INTENDED FOR SETTING BOOKS

½ teaspoon ground ginger & ⅓ cup maple syrup

How much? 58,912,476?!

Oh the quart pot, pint pot & half a pint

Möbius function μ(n) = 1

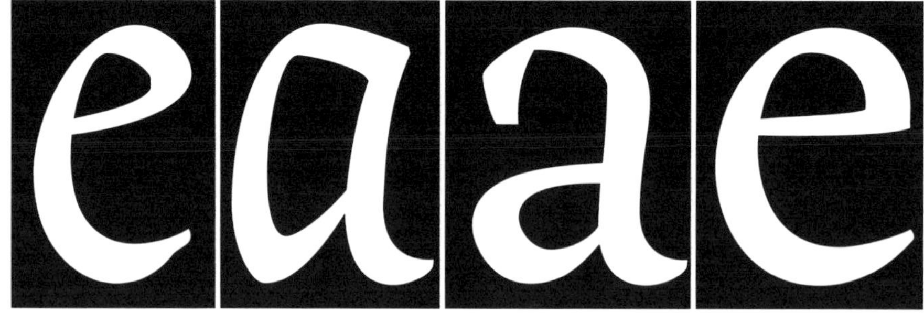

"organic strokes & counters"

FRENCH RENAISSANCE

—*with many stylistic alternates & other* typographic *goodies*—

Includes Regular & *Italic*

Essay Text

About
Essay is an elegant serif typeface intended for setting books, with many stylistic alternates and other typographic goodies, designed by Ellmer Stefan.

It is a highly legible text face with a natural flow of reading. This is enhanced by a slight slant of the roman, the combination of open and closed apertures and the amalgamation of organic strokes and counters with a static, fully straight baseline.

Essay Text Regular looks back at the spirit of the French Renaissance, when the roman typographic letterforms came to full emancipation. Departing from that historical reference, Essay Text gets rid of all sentimental antiquity and becomes a contemporary interpretation of the "archetypes" of that period.

Essay Text Italic refers to that more vaguely, resulting in a formalized look with fairly upright and open shapes and little cursiveness. As in the Renaissance, before the mating of roman and italic, Essay Text Italic works as a separate text face and a perfect secondary type.

Design
Ellmer Stefan
2014

Foundry
TypeTogether, Czech Republic
www.type-together.com

Styles / Weights
Regular, Italic

Language support
Latin

OpenType options
Proportional Oldstyle, Tabular and Proportional Lining, Tabular Oldstyle, Standard Ligatures, Discretionary Ligatures, Historical Ligatures, All Caps, Small Caps, Capitals to Small Caps, Superscript, Ordinals, Alternative Fractions, Numerator, Denominator, Ornaments, Arrows, Stylistic Alternates, Stylistic Sets, Historical Forms, Slashed Zero, Superior, Inferior

Optimized for web
Yes

REGULAR 17PT

aabcdefghijklmnopqrstuvwxyyzæfjåçéñöûß
ABCDEFGHIJKLMNOPQRSTUVWXYZÆÇØ
0123456789o@.,-:;!?')]§*"«»/–€$&⅓⁂↗

REGULAR 30PT

aejgGQR7

REGULAR & ITALIC 14PT

Typographers want
amazing, exquisite
& clever justified text
in books

ITALIC 30PT

aejgGQR7

REGULAR 9PT

ar·chive / *noun* / a collection of documents such as letters, photographs or other material: *the Yearbook of Type is an archive of contemporary typefaces from all over the world*

Amor Amor
Amor AMOR Amor
AMOR Amor

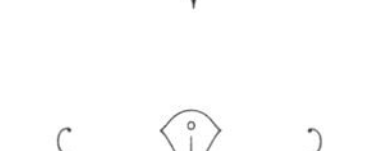

I COULD STAY LOST

IN THIS MOMENT

Forever

Letters
NEED A TOUCH OF
MAGIC

Fantasy

LOMBARDIC
INITIALS

CAPS & ORNAMENTS

Imagine
THERE IS NO
Heaven

Tale as old as time
STORY & LEGEND
FANTASTIC WORLD
imagination unrestricted by reality
Get Fantasy and Build a Lovely World
Once upon a time
You may say I'm a dreamer, but I'm
not the only one. I hope some day...

About
As Typesenses believes that "Letters need a touch of magic," Sabrina Lopez presents her new creation, a burst of innovation: Fantasy. This display font arises from the mix between Roman Style and Lombardic Decorations, with a little air of the medieval age.

Fantasy works perfectly in book covers, greeting cards, invitations, weddings, posters, magazines, fashion world, logos, packaging, letterpress, etc.

Let your imagination fly and let's play with all its Alternates, Ornaments, Frames, Caps and the exclusive set of Decorated Lombardic Initials. The Pro version has more than 1,400 glyphs! Ornaments (Fantasy Ornaments), Caps (Fantasy Caps1) and Lombardic Initials (Fantasy Caps2) are sold in separate versions, too. Additionally, there is a Standard Version (Fantasy Std) designed to be used in lines of text and smaller sizes.

To make the most of the alternatives proposed, use applications that support OpenType.

Get Fantasy and build a lovely world of imagination!

Design
Sabrina Lopez
2014

Foundry
Typesenses, Argentina
www.typesenses.tumblr.com

Styles / Weights
Std, Pro, Ornaments, Caps1, Caps2

Language support
Latin

OpenType options
Standard Ligatures, Discretionary Ligatures, Capitals to Small Caps, Titling Alternates, Swashes, Contextual Alternates, Contextual Ligatures, Ornaments, Stylistic Alternates, Stylistic Sets, Slashed Zero, Terminal Form, Initial Form

Optimized for web
Yes

STD 18PT

abcdefghijklmnopqrstuvwxyzæfjåçéñöûß
ABCDEFGHIJKLMNOPQRSTUVWXYZÆÇØ
0123456789Ø@.,-:;!?')]§*"" « » / –€$&½

STD 16PT

Typographers want
amazing, exquisite
& clever justified text
in books

PRO 16PT

Typographers want
amazing, exquisite
& clever justified text
in books

CAPS 1 & 2 20PT

ORNAMENTS 24PT

the Jazz Factory in the Louisville→

die geschriebene und offizielle Sprache in den Schulen bleibt Schriftdeutsch

La víctima, de 56 años

golfový rezort!

BARACK OBAMA & VLADIMIR PUTIN

miło cię spotkać

Organe d'expression de la Société Française d'Opthalmologie

KEPPNISBORÐ

to protect their citizens but do a lot to infringe on civil liberties. In Paris, a dozen interior ministers from European Union countries including France, Britain and Germany issued a statement earlier this week calling on Internet service providers to identify and take down online content *that aims to incite hatred and terror*. The ministers also want the European Union to start monitoring and storing information about the itineraries of air travelers. And in Britain, Prime Minister DAVID CAMERON suggested the country should ban Internet services that did not give the government the ability to monitor all encrypted chats and calls. Even before the CHARLIE HEBDO attack, European leaders were proposing or enacting harsh mea-

they believed intended to join foreign terrorist organizations. And this week, French officials said they had *arrested 54 people* for hate speech, including a controversial comic. Appealing as these measures may sound in the aftermath of a tragedy, they are deeply flawed. Countries like France and Germany have long had stricter controls on speech than the United States. For example, their governments have in the past forced Internet firms like Yahoo and Twitter to take down Nazi propaganda. But those decisions are generally made by government officials or judges, not technology companies. Internet service providers do not have the staff or the skill to determine what content is likely to lead to terrorist attacks. That is why a

About
Fazeta is a modern static Antiqua, but distant from the festive and rigid look of this type category. Inspiration was the Czechoslovakian type production in the 60s—J. Týfa, V. Preissig, J. Linzboth or A. Krátky. These typefaces are characterized by a vivid and sharp design with stable serifs and tend to construction rather than calligraphy; some sophisticated small details vitalized general impression. In this case, the facetted asymmetrical arches. To provide that traditional text feeling, there are alternative glyphs for "a, c, f, j, k, r, y, K, R," finished with typical serif. The typeface is graded by optical size into three variants—caption (suitable for size 6–9 pt), text (ordinary text about 10pt) and display (for 20 pt and higher). Every variant has five weights with italics. The typeface with its naked cold expression is suitable for neutral text without emotional feelings. In contrast to most antique typefaces, this one is intended for modern glossy white papers where crisp details can be excelled. Every font has 1,140 glyphs.

Design
Andrej Dieneš
2014

Foundry
ADTypo, Slovakia
www.adtypo.com

Styles / Weights
Family of three styles (Text, Display, Caption), each with five weights (Light, Regular, Medium, Bold, Black), each with Italics

Language support
Latin

OpenType options
Proportional Oldstyle, Tabular and Proportional Lining, Tabular Oldstyle, Standard Ligatures, Discretionary Ligatures, All Caps, Small Caps, Capitals to Small Caps, Superscript, Subscript, Ordinals, Fractions, Numerator, Denominator, Ornaments, Arrows, Stylistic Sets, Slashed Zero, Alternate Annotation, Localized Forms, Optical size

Optimized for web
Yes

REGULAR TEXT 17PT

aabccdefghijjkklmnopqrrstuvwxyyzzæfjåçéñöûß
ABCDEFGHIJKKLMNOPQRRSTUVWXYZÆÇØ
01234567890@.,-:;!?')]§*""«»/–€$&⅓☆↗

BLACK CAPTION 30PT

aejgGQR7

BOLD & REGULAR DISPLAY 14PT

Typographers want
amazing, exquisite
& clever justified text
in books

LIGHT DISPLAY 30PT

aejgGQR7

BOLD & REGULAR TEXT 9PT

⇒ **ref·er·ence book** / *noun* / a book that contains facts and information that you look at when you need to find out sth. particular—*"I am looking for the right typeface for my project, so I use the Yearbook of Type as a reference book."*

FLANDERS ART

SERIF & SANS SERIF FONT FAMILY

---

conceptual, visionary & future-oriented

cutting edge

DESIGN CULTURE

innovative concepts

rigourous research **attitude** & **thorough** investigations

ARTISTIC MIND-SET

in harmony with latest technologies

“harmonious”

FASHION FORWARD

* respectful of Flemish heritage *

CONTEMPORARY & TIMELESS

About
The Flanders Art typeface was designed and developed by Jo De Baerdemaeker uniquely and exclusively for the new visual identity of the Organization of the Flemish Authorities (Vlaamse Overheid). Since this custom typeface will be used to typeset a variety of information (from bus timetables to billboard texts and long paragraphs in books, magazines and newsletters) in different environments and platforms (from printed works to digital communication on different screen resolutions), the font concept was conceived as a family with a sans serif and serif style, each executed in four different weights (light, regular, medium and bold). The new visual identity for Flanders was conceptualized to create unity within the more than one hundred logos and styles that were currently in use by the different departments and services. It is the first typeface created in Belgium for a government organization. The Flanders Art font family is at present being expanded to 24 weights.

Design
Jo De Baerdemaeker
2014

Foundry
studio type, Belgium
www.studiotype.be

Styles / Weights
Family of two styles (Sans Serif, Serif), each in seven weights (Thin, Light, Regular, Medium, Bold, Black, Extra Black), each with Italics

Language support
Latin

OpenType options
Proportional Oldstyle, Tabular and Proportional Lining, Tabular Oldstyle, Standard Ligatures, Contextual Alternates

Optimized for web
Yes

SANS REGULAR 18PT

abcdefggghijklmnopqrstuvwxyzæfjåçéñöûß
ABCDEFGHIJKLMNOPQRSTUVWXYZÆÇØ
0123456789@.,-:;!?')]§*“”«»/–€$&

SERIF REGULAR 18PT

abcdefggghijklmnopqrstuvwxyzæçéñößABCDEFGHIJKLMNOPQRSTUVWXYZÆÇØ
0123456789@.,-:;!?')]§*“”«»/–€$&

SANS BOLD & SERIF REGULAR 10PT

ex·am·ple / noun / an illustration that supports or provides more information: by showing examples the Yearbook of Type presents each font in different sizes and weights

SANS, ALL WEIGHTS 12PT

Light
Regular
Medium
Bold

SERIF, ALL WEIGHTS 12PT

Light
Regular
Medium
Bold

“SIBIR” — NEWSPAPER KIRENSK, JULY 2, 1908:

F

“It was hot and dry.

L Y

The cloud began emitting flames

0 0

1 2 8 9

3 4 5 of uncertain shapes... 5 6 7

6 7 8 9 all villagers were stricken 1 2 3 4

with panic and took to

the streets, women cried,

N T

thinking it was the end

of the world.”

About
Flynt is essentially based on the "Halbfette Renaissance" released by the German type foundry Flinsch in 1908. In this modified grotesque, the emphasis is on the velvety aesthetics of the original printed image. In this sense, Flynt was carefully redesigned for books and posters. The type specimen was designed by Simone Vollenweider.

Design
Reymund Schroeder
2015

Foundry
Zeugler, Germany
www.zeugler.de

Styles / Weights
Bold

Language support
Latin

OpenType options
Standard Ligatures

Optimized for web
No

BOLD 18PT

abcdefghijklmnopqrstuvwxyzfjöß
ABCDEFGHIJKLMNOPQRSTUVWXYZ
0123456789@.,-:;!?')|*""/–&

BOLD 36PT

aejgGQR7

BOLD 14PT

Typographers want amazing, exquisite & clever justified text in books

Formular & F. Mono

About
If you were a grotesque in mid-20th-century Switzerland, you were expected to be serious and proper, if a little dull. Unlike its dogmatic Modernist predecessors, Formular is a hip Swiss sans serif of the new generation. Inspired by the utilitarian 19th century grotesques, its precision and versatility are combined with a slightly eccentric character. A child of its time, it scoffs at the ideology of "ideal" forms, yet it is every bit as functional for all its idiosyncrasies, as any self-respecting Swiss sans.

Formular comes in five weights with corresponding Italics and a monospace companion to the regular weight. Each weight includes special extra-light punctuation, lining tabular and old style figures, case-sensitive punctuation, and stylistic alternates.

Design
Gayaneh Bagdasaryan, Vyacheslav Kirilenko
2014

Foundry
Brownfox, Russia
www.brownfox.org

Styles / Weights
Light, Light Italic, Regular, Italic, Medium, Medium Italic, Bold, Bold Italic, Black, Black Italic plus Mono Regular

Language support
Latin, Cyrillic

OpenType options
Proportional Oldstyle, Tabular and Proportional Lining, Standard Ligatures, All Caps, Ordinals, Fractions, Numerator, Denominator, Arrows, Stylistic Alternates, Stylistic Sets, Thin Punctuation

Optimized for web
Yes

REGULAR 16PT

aabcdefghijklmnopqrsttuvwxyzæfjåçéñöûß
ABCDEFGHIJKLMNOPQRSTUVWXYYZÆÇØ
01234567890@.,-:;!?')]§*""«»/–€$&½↗

MONO REGULAR 28PT

aejGQR7

LIGHT & BOLD 12PT

Typographers want
amazing, exquisite
& clever justified text
in books →

REGULAR 28PT

aejGQR7

ALL WEIGHTS 10PT

Light
Regular
Medium
Bold
Black
Mono

ITALICS 10PT

Light Italic
Italic
Medium Italic
Bold Italic
Black Italic

Entertainment

relatively inexpensive

NEWSPAPERS

subscription revenue

Crowdsourcing

6,580–7,132 daily titles

International

egocentric teamplayer

About
Started as a master thesis at Muthesius Academy of Fine Arts and Design in Kiel (Germany) under the guidance of Albert-Jan Pool and Prof. André Heers in 2012, FF Franziska is a robust serif type family for setting body copy as well as headlines using Hairline and Black. The typeface has been conceived as a hybrid of a serif and slab serif which becomes evident when comparing the weights from Hairline to Black. It has a generous x-height and short descenders. The italics have a rather slight angle of slope and playful shapes derived from handwriting. A range of icons including various arrows and signs like thumb up and down complement the usual figure sets, small caps and stylistic alternates.

For more design information visit FF Franziska's microsite *www.fffranziska.com*

Design
Jakob Runge
2014

Foundry
FontFont, Germany
www.fontfont.com

Styles / Weights
Hairline, Hairline, Thin, Thin, Light, Light, Regular, Book, Medium, Demibold, Bold, Extrabold, Black, each with Italics

Language support
Latin

OpenType options
Proportional Oldstyle, Tabular and Proportional Lining, Standard Ligatures, Discretionary Ligatures, Small Caps, Capitals to Small Caps, Superscript, Subscript, Ordinals, Contextual Alternates, Contextual Ligatures, Fractions, Numerator, Denominator, Ornaments, Arrows, Stylistic Sets, Slashed Zero, Alternate Annotation, Case Sensitive Forms, Capital Spacing

Optimized for web
Yes

REGULAR 16PT

abcdefghiijklmnopqrstuvwxyzæfjåçéñöûß
ABCDEFGHIJKLMNOPQRSTUVWXYZÆÇØ
01234567890@.,-:;!?')]§*""«»/–€$&⅓♡↗

BOLD 30PT

aejgGQR7

BOLD & MEDIUM 14PT

Typographers want
amazing, exquisite
& clever justified text
in books

DEMIBOLD & REGULAR 9PT

☞ **cata·logue** / *noun* / a complete list of things that people can look at or buy: *a catalogue of typefaces (a book showing the newest fonts, to help people choose the right typeface)*

ALL WEIGHTS 8PT

Hairline
Thin
Light
Regular
Book
Medium
Demibold
Bold
Extrabold
Black

ITALICS 8PT

Hairline Italic
Thin Italic
Light Italic
Italic
Book Italic
Medium Italic
Demibold Italic
Bold Italic
Extrabold Italic
Black Italic

GALANO CLASSIC —
A GEOMETRIC
FONTFAMILY OF
10 WEIGHTS PLUS
MATCHING ITALICS,
INCLUDING OPENTYPE
FEATURES LIKE
ALTERNATIVE GLYPHS,
OLDSTYLE FIGURES,
FRACTIONS AND
MANY MORE.

About
Galano Classic is the display companion of the Galano Grotesque family.

It pays tribute to the geometric shapes of Futura, Avant Garde, Avenir and the like. However, instead of resulting in a modern interpretation of the geometric genre, Galano Classic prefers to stay in the past, characterized by a moderate x-height and details like the long stretched leg of the uppercase "R," as well as the traditional shaped lowercase "g," to mention only a few. Galano Classic, compared to Galano Grotesque, includes lots of redesigned glyphs and consequently adjusted kerning pairs, an extended number of alternative characters, ligatures and OpenType features to match a great amount of design applications. It comes in ten different weights with matching Italics containing 555 glyphs per font.

Design
René Bieder
2014

Foundry
Rene Bieder / Design and Direction, Germany
www.renebieder.com

Styles / Weights
Thin, Extralight, Light, Regular, Medium, SemiBold, Bold, ExtraBold, Heavy, Black, Alt Thin, Alt ExtraLight, Alt Light, Alt Regular, Alt Medium, Alt SemiBold, Alt Bold, Alt ExtraBold, Alt Heavy, Alt Black, each with Italics

Language support
Latin

OpenType options
Proportional Oldstyle, Tabular and Prop. Lining, Standard Ligatures, Discretionary Lig., Superscript, Subscript, Ordinals, Contextual Lig., Fractions, Numerator, Denominator, Arrows, Stylistic Alternates, Stylistic Sets, Slashed Zero, Localized Forms

Optimized for web
Yes

REGULAR 15PT

aabcdefgghijklmnopqrstuvwxyyzæfjåçéñöûß
ABCDEFGHIJKLMNOPQRSTUVWXYZÆÇØ
0123456789ø@.,-:;!?')]§*""«»/–€$&½↗

BLACK 30PT

aejgGQR7

BOLD & REGULAR 12PT

The Yearbook of Type
compendium works well as
a tool in vexed typography
questions for polarizing jobs

BOLD & REGULAR 9PT

ref·er·ence book / *noun* a book that contains facts and information that you look at when you need to find out sth. particular—*"I am looking for the right typeface for my project, so I use the Yearbook of Type as a reference book."*

ALL WEIGHTS 8PT

Thin
ExtraLight
Light
Regular
Medium
SemiBold
Bold
ExtraBold
Heavy
Black

ITALICS 8PT

Thin Italic
ExtraLight Italic
Light Italic
Italic
Medium Italic
SemiBold Italic
Bold Italic
ExtraBold Italic
Heavy Italic
Black Italic

CATCHWORDS · 290 PTS

QUINOTO

ITALIC · 54 PTS

GOURMET TRENDS and TIPS

SLAB · 56 PTS

Huerta Orgánica

SWASH ALT · 70 PTS

Superstizioni

SWASH ITALIC · 60 PTS

WILLIAMSBURG

SLAB · 56 PTS

now for free

CATCHWORDS · 72 PTS

Violette Parfums

PRO ITALIC · 72 PTS

James Trevor, *Jamie Oliver* MBE, es un *cocinero* inglés nacido en *Essex*, condado al sureste de *Reino Unido*. Presentado por la *BBC*, se convirtió en uno de los cocineros más influyentes del mundo. Sus platos generalmente son una mezcla de cocina italiana y cocina oriental, y en ellos, tienen un importante papel las hierbas aromáticas y las especias, generalmente chile.

PARAGRAPH · 14/20 PTS

ORNAMENTS

DINGBATS · 58 PTS

verde

CATCHWORDS · 72 PTS

€46,30
$58,19
¥27,43

FIGURES & CURRENCY SIGN

About

Last year, we visited Brazil and we were totally captivated by its cheerful and warm people. Its wild nature is absolutely amazing and very noticeable in textile printing as well as in floral design. That was precisely what inspired us to create some ornaments and dingbats, which we then turned into a single typographic work. The resulting typeface is called Garden, a serif display handmade font with a playful and spontaneous feel.

The Garden family offers a font with a set of original "catchwords" ("Garden Catchwords," based on brush calligraphy), floral dingbats and botanical ornaments. Please be aware, "Garden Catchwords" is a "Catchwords" font, and does not offer standard AlphaNumeric characters.

The OpenType version provides a wide range of creative options. Garden is well-suited for text composition, posters, headlines, label design and handmade-style items. Garden is inspiration, nature and joy!

Design

Guisela Mendoza, Luciano Vergara
Mendoza Vergara Studio
2014

Foundry

Los Andes Type, Chile
www.behance.net/losandestype

Styles / Weights

Pro Regular, Pro Italic, Essential, Essential Italic, Essential Alt, Essential Alt Italic, Swash Regular, Swash Italic, Swash Alt Regular, Swash Alt Italic, Slab, Catchwords, Ornaments, Dingbats

Language support

Latin

OpenType options

Swashes, Contextual Alternates, Terminal Form, Fractions

Optimized for web

No

PRO 18PT

aabcdefgghijklmnopqrstuvwxyyzæfjåçéñöûß
ABCDEFGHIJKLMNOPQRSTUVWXYZÆÇØ
0123456789@.,-:;!?')]§*""«»/–€$&⅓

SWASH 36PT

aejgGQR7

ESSENTIAL ALT 14PT

Typographers want amazing, exquisite & clever justified text in books

DINGBATS 36PT

SLAB 14PT

TYPOGRAPHERS WANT AMAZING, EXQUISITE & CLEVER JUSTIFIED TEXT IN BOOKS

GarySans is clearly a text sans serif. During the design period text was one big testing area.

123456789

P A Ō D

Artwork: christianschaefer.de

It does not need to follow a serif model and therefore can use all sans serif advantages.

In modern hybrid families the sans serif follows the serif as a companion. ***Not in GarySans.***

abgABG

Reading sans serifs, most of the time, have a clear model in a classic serif.

About
GarySans is clearly a text sans serif. During the design period, text was one big testing area. Text sans serifs usually have a clear model in a classic serif. In modern hybrid families, the sans serif follows the serif as a companion. Not so in GarySans. It does not need to follow a serif model and therefore can use all sans serif advantages. Like an even stroke thickness that can easily be scaled. The weight system starts with bodycopy: Light, Book, Regular and Medium. Semibold, Bold and Heavy are made for text-size headlines. They are still open enough to work in small sizes. Extrabold and Ultrabold supply the warm dark display range for bigger headlines.

Design
Hubert Jocham
2014

Foundry
Hubert Jocham, Germany
www.hubertjocham.de

Styles / Weights
Fine, Fine Italic, Light, Light Italic, Book, Book Italic, Regular, Italic, Medium, Medium Italic, Semibold, Semibold Italic, Bold, Bold Italic, Extrabold, Extrabold Italic, Heavy, Heavy Italic, Ultrabold, Ultrabold Italic

Language support
Latin

OpenType options
Proportional Oldstyle, Tabular Lining, Standard Ligatures, Discretionary Ligatures, Fractions

Optimized for web
Yes

REGULAR 18PT

abcdefghijklmnopqrstuvwxyzæfjåçéñöûß
ABCDEFGHIJKLMNOPQRSTUVWXYZÆÇØ
0123456789@.,-:;!?')]§*“”«»/–€$&½

BOLD 30PT

aejgGQR7

BOLD & REGULAR 14PT

Typographers want
amazing, exquisite
& clever justified text
in books

BOLD & REGULAR 9PT

ex·am·ple / *noun* / an illustration that supports or provides more information: *by showing examples the Yearbook of Type presents each font in different sizes and weights*

ALL WEIGHTS 9PT

Fine
Light
Book
Regular
Medium
Semibold
Bold
Extrabold
Heavy
Ultrabold

ITALICS 9PT

Fine Italic
Light Italic
Book Italic
Regular Italic
Medium Italic
Semibold Italic
Bold Italic
Extrabold Italic
Heavy Italic
Ultrabold Italic

INVESTING $17 MILLION IN A NEW PLANT IN FLORENCE, TO RECYCLE

LA TECNOLOGÍA

EL CANAL DE ISABEL II PRODUCE 192.000 M^3/DÍA AGUA

Advanced Manufacturing

MINING PROCESS

verdens sværeste problemer

INVESTING $17 MILLION IN A NEW PLANT IN FLORENCE, TO RECYCLE HELIUM

Monitoring & Diagnostic

product life cycle management or reduced lead times

Präzisionsmeßgerät

von 0,25 bis 9,5 MW können sowohl mit Erdgas als

DE L'ÉNERGIE

CETTE ALLIANCE VA RENFORCER LA PRÉSENCE DE LA FRANCE DANS LE SECTEUR

De réseaux basée en France

SI DEDICANO AD ANTICIPARE E SODDISFARE LE NECESSITÀ, IN PERENNE

flights into usable information

GE Inspira Sans & Serif

About
GE Inspira Sans and Serif were commissioned by General Electric Company in 2013. The Sans companion is a contemporary design. With open apertures, subtle curved parts, and slightly rounded corners. Its four styles (Regular, Italic, Bold, Bold Italic) work great in small sizes, and have been optimized to perform in low-resolution environments. The Serif companion follows the structure of the Sans, yet takes inspiration from the Clarendons of the 19th century. Featuring a moderate contrast, sturdy slabs, and prominent ball terminals. The slightly rounded corners help to tie the family together, and simultaneously ensure a refined appearance.

Design
Mike Abbink, Paul van der Laan, Pieter van Rosmalen
2014

Foundry
Bold Monday, The Netherlands
www.boldmonday.com

Styles / Weights
Family of two styles (Sans, Serif), each with two weights (Regular, Bold), each with Italics

Language support
Latin

OpenType options
Standard Ligatures, Superscript, Ordinals, Fractions, Slashed Zero

Optimized for web
Yes

SANS REGULAR 18PT

abcdefghijklmnopqrstuvwxyzæfjåçéñöûß
ABCDEFGHIJKLMNOPQRSTUVWXYZÆÇØ
0123456789 0@.,-:;!?')]§*“”«»/–€$&½

SERIF REGULAR 18PT

abcdefghijklmnopqrstuvwxyzæfjåçéñöûß
ABCDEFGHIJKLMNOPQRSTUVWXYZÆÇØ
01234567890@.,-:;!?')]§*“”«»/–€$&½

SANS BOLD & SERIF BOLD 36PT

aejgGQR7
aejgGQR7

SANS, ALL WEIGHTS 11PT

Regular
Italic
Bold
Bold Italic

SERIF, ALL WEIGHTS 11PT

Regular
Italic
Bold
Bold Italic

Fontfarm: Gedau Gothic

A little more »GOTHIC« and with a slightly improved readability, the Format Set 01 has **a differentiation in the glyphs: a, t, and u.**

You can use *Gedau Gothic* with a touch of a typewriter in the **pseudomono style.** This style has a »vivid« appearance.

Standard Glyph-Set
as it appears without choosing a Format Set:

Dieser Blindtext ist eigens für die Gedau Gothic entworfen worden und besteht ausschließlich aus Glyphen, welche in dieser Schrift besonders toll aussehen. **Klar, man muss hier und da Abstriche machen, da einige Buchstaben nicht auftauchen, aber diesen Text liest sowieso kein Mensch und deshalb fällt es auch nicht auf.**

Format Set 01 — a bit more classic gothic style with improved legibility:

Dieser Blindtext ist eigens für die Gedau Gothic entworfen worden und besteht ausschließlich aus Glyphen, welche in dieser Schrift besonders toll aussehen. **Klar, man muss hier und da Abstriche machen, da einige Buchstaben nicht auftauchen, aber diesen Text liest sowieso kein Mensch und deshalb fällt es auch nicht auf.**

Format Set 02
the monostyle-lookalike-feature ...

Dieser Blindtext ist eigens für die Gedau Gothic entworfen worden und besteht ausschließlich aus Glyphen, welche in dieser Schrift besonders toll aussehen. **Klar, man muss hier und da Abstriche machen, da einige Buchstaben nicht auftauchen, aber diesen Text liest sowieso keiner und deshalb fällt es auch nicht auf.**

Format Set 03 — the purest glyphstyle combination with a round »a« and a one-story »g«.

Dieser Blindtext ist eigens für die Gedau Gothic entworfen worden und besteht ausschließlich aus Glyphen, welche in dieser Schrift besonders toll aussehen. **Klar, man muss hier und da Abstriche machen, da einige Buchstaben nicht auftauchen, aber diesen Text liest sowieso kein Mensch und deshalb fällt es auch nicht auf.**

lIJjaflrtug

lIJjaflrtug

IiJjaflrtug

lIJjaflrtug

About
The naming of Gedau Gothic is an acknowledgement to the valley of Gedau (German: Gedautal), where we lived for tow years (2010–2012).

While we were designing Gedau Gothic, we came up with our own contemporary interpretation of the so-called GOTHIC Fonts (like Franklin, News or Trade Gothic—German: Amerikanische Grotesk), combined them with more closed counters (in the glyphs a, c, e, s ...) and spiced it up with a mild new school square sans touch.

In 2013, we thought about this font family and decided to play a little with different glyph styles and corresponding OpenType format (style) sets in this typeface. The result is a four-in-one font family which allows you to choose between several flavors: The former (still standard) glyph set; a very pure style set with a "closed-a" and a "one-story-g;" a bit more legible style set with variants of the lowercase glyphs "a," "t" and "u;" and a funky monospace look-alike format set.

Design
Natascha Dell, K.-F. (Kai) Oetzbach
2013

Foundry
Fontfarm.de, Germany
www.fontfarm.de

Styles / Weights
Light, Light Oblique, Book, Book Oblique, Roman, Roman Oblique, Medium, Medium Oblique, Bold, Bold Oblique, Black, Black Oblique

Language support
Latin

OpenType options
Tabular Lining, Proportional Lining, Standard Ligatures, Fractions, Stylistic Alternates, Stylistic Sets

Optimized for web
Yes

ROMAN 18PT

aabcdefgghijjklmnopqrsttuvwxyzæfjåçéñöûß
ABCDEFGHIJKLMNOPQRSTUVWXYZÆÇØ
0123456789@.,-:;!?')]§*""«»/–€$&½

BLACK 36PT

aejgGQR7

BOLD & BOOK 16PT

Typographers want
amazing, exquisite
& clever justified text
in books

BOLD & BOOK 9PT

over·view / *noun* / a brief summary of something: *in the index of the Yearbook of Type the reader can find an overview of all typefaces presented in the book sorted by classification*

ALL WEIGHTS 10PT

Light
Book
Roman
Medium
Bold
Black

ITALICS 10PT

Light Oblique
Book Oblique
Roman Oblique
Medium Oblique
Bold Oblique
Black Oblique

GERBERA INVITING AND DISTINCTIVE

Designed by Brownfox

14.12.2014

Light Regular **Medium**

Bold Black

Latin Кириллица

Small Caps

Stylistic Alternates

Old Style Figures

About
Gerbera is a new sans serif with a distinct personality that fuses geometric and organic elements. It is at once hip and quaint, clear yet idiosyncratic, restrained but sensual. Its deliberately varied classical capital proportions and geometric structure are balanced by slightly reversed stress and pinched terminals on curved strokes. This versatile font comes in five weights and offers a variety of Open Type features, including small caps, alternate characters and punctuation, five sets of figures, and CE, Baltic, and Cyrillic support.

Design
Gayaneh Bagdasaryan, Vyacheslav Kirilenko
2014

Foundry
Brownfox, Russia
www.brownfox.org

Styles / Weights
Light, Regular, Medium, Bold, Black

Language support
Latin, Cyrillic

OpenType options
Proportional Oldstyle, Tabular and Proportional Lining, Tabular Oldstyle, Standard Ligatures, Discretionary Ligatures, All Caps, Small Caps, Superscript, Subscript, Ordinals, Fractions, Numerator, Denominator, Ornaments, Arrows, Stylistic Alternates, Stylistic Sets

Optimized for web
Yes

REGULAR 16PT

aabcdefghijklmnopqrstuvwxyzæfjåçéñöûß
ABCDEFGHIJKLMNOPQRSTUVWXYZÆÇØ
01234567890@.,-:;!?')]§*“”«»/–€$&⅓⁂↗

BOLD 35PT

aejgGQR7

BOLD & LIGHT 16PT

Typographers want amazing, exquisite
& clever justified text in books

BOLD & REGULAR 9PT

→ **com·pen·dium** / noun / (pl. com·pen·dia / or com·pen·diums) a collection of facts, drawings and photographs on a particular subject, especially in a book: “a compendium of typography.”

BLACK & REGULAR 16PT

Typographers want amazing, exquisite
& clever justified text in books

Gerbera

Gibbs by Typetanic Fonts

Thin *Italic* Light *Italic* Book *Italic* **Medium *Italic* Bold *Italic* Black *Italic***

Chart Room & Navigation Bridge

NEW YORK · HAVRE · SOUTHAMPTON · BREMERHAVEN

Restoration and curatorial development aboard the historic ocean liner SS *United States*

SWIMMING POOL →

LET'S LOOK INSIDE THE WORLD'S FASTEST LUXURY LINER

Largest Wine Cellar Afloat!

Rye Whiskey, Sweet Vermouth, and Angostura Bitters

4TH OF JULY

Bargain Rates on Staterooms (from $183.50)

COMPLETELY AIR-CONDITIONED

↖ TO BOATS ↗

Europe is only five dinner parties away

The world's smartest resort is the world's fastest ship!

Midnight Buffet

Dancing Under the Stars (Weather Permitting)

TOURIST CHILDRENS PLAYROOM →

About
Gibbs is a tough, sophisticated sans, named for prolific maritime architect William Francis Gibbs and inspired by his greatest design, the record-breaking mid-century luxury liner SS United States. Taking various cues from the unique cast aluminum signs found on board, the result is truly transatlantic—somewhere in between industrial American vernacular lettering and the English humanist styles of Gill or Johnston. Both stylish and comfortable to read, and with an extensive list of OpenType features, Gibbs allows you to set quality type with ease at both text and display sizes.

Built in 1952, the beautiful SS United States was the most revolutionary ship in the world when new. After a flawless 17-year career, she now sits unused and is in danger of scrapping. Her current owner, the non-profit SS United States Conservancy, wishes to restore the ship as a vibrant waterfront development and museum for future generations to enjoy for decades to come.

Design
Gregory Shutters
2014

Foundry
Typetanic Fonts, USA
www.typetanicfonts.com

Styles / Weights
Thin, Thin Italic, Light, Light Italic, Book, Book Italic, Medium, Medium Italic, Bold, Bold Italic, Black, Black Italic

Language support
Latin

OpenType options
Proportional Oldstyle, Tabular Lining, Proportional Lining, Tabular Oldstyle, Standard Ligatures, Discretionary Ligatures, All Caps, Small Caps, Capitals to Small Caps, Superscript, Subscript, Ordinals, Fractions, Numerator, Denominator, Stylistic Alternates

Optimized for web
Yes

BOOK 17PT

abcdefghijklmnopqrstuvwxyzæfjåçéñöûß
ABCDEFGHIJKLMNOPQRSTUVWXYZÆÇØ
0123456789@.,-:;!?')]§*""«»/–€$&⅓

BLACK 36PT

aejgGQR7

BOLD & THIN 16PT

Typographers want
amazing, exquisite
& clever justified text
in books

BLACK & BOOK 8PT

ref·er·ence book/*noun*/a book that contains facts and information that you look at when you need to find out sth. particular—*"I am looking for the right typeface for my project, so I use the Yearbook of Type as a reference book."*

ALL WEIGHTS 8PT

Thin
Light
Book
Medium
Bold
Black

ITALICS 8PT

Thin Italic
Light Italic
Book Italic
Medium Italic
Bold Italic
Black Italic

PACEY
RAIDER
BEANO
HUNK
CLEDGY
GOAL
JUNIOR
GUESS
SUPERB

Glober

Fontfabric

About
The Glober font family includes 18 weights—nine uprights with nine italics. It is characterized by excellent legibility in both web and print design areas, well-finished geometric designs, optimized kerning, excellent web font performance and legibility etc.

Inspired by the classic grotesque typefaces, Glober has its own unique style in expressed perfectly softened geometric forms. The font family is most suitable for headlines of all sizes, as well as for text blocks that come in both maximum and minimum variations.

Glober was awarded by diploma for excellence in typeface design at the international competition Modern Cyrillic in 2014.

Design
Ivan Petrov
2014

Foundry
Fontfabric, Bulgaria
www.fontfabric.com

Styles / Weights
Thin, Thin Italic, Light, Light Italic, Book, Book Italic, Regular, Italic, SemiBold, SemiBold Italic, Bold, Bold Italic, xBold, xBold Italic, Heavy, Heavy Italic, Black, Black Italic

Language support
Latin, Cyrillic

OpenType options
Standard Ligatures, Superscript, Subscript, Numerator, Denominator, Fractions, Arrows, Stylistic Alternates, Stylistic Sets

Optimized for web
Yes

REGULAR 18PT

abcdefgghijklmnopqrstuvwxyzæfjåçéñöûß
ABCDEFGHIJKLMNOPQRSTUVWXYZÆÇØ
0123456789@.,-:;!?')]§*“”«»/–€$&⅓↗

BLACK 36PT

aejgGQR7

HEAVY & LIGHT 16PT

Typographers want
amazing, exquisite
& clever justified text
in books

BOLD & REGULAR 10PT

ar·chive / *noun* / a collection of documents such as letters, photographs or other material: *the Yearbook of Type is an archive of contemporary typefaces from all over the world.*

ALL WEIGHTS 8PT

Thin
Light
Book
Regular
SemiBold
Bold
xBold
Heavy
Black

ITALICS 8PT

Thin Italic
Light Italic
Book Italic
Regular Italic
SemiBold Italic
Bold Italic
xBold
Heavy
Black

A B C D E F

LTC Goudy Initials

About
LTC Goudy Initials has been a bestseller since it was reformatted to font format by P22 in 2005. We decided that while it works very well in medium sizes, when it was used extra large, the outlines were not as true to Frederic Goudy's 1917 drawings as they could be.

We decided to redraw from the ground up—and here we have the NEW LTC Goudy Initials! Meticulously redrawn by Miranda Roth, these ornaments referenced original proofs of large sizes of Cloister Initials. In our quest for artwork for this project, we even arranged a quickly sold out recasting of the 120 point size and have produced a limited edition letter-press print from this casting. This new digital version features two additional layers to allow for quick colorizing of the central letter and/or the floral background.

Design
Miranda Roth
2014

Foundry
Lanston Type Co. (P22 Type Foundry), USA
www.p22.com/ltc

Styles / Weights
Regular, Fill, Flora

Language support
Latin

OpenType options
Not available

Optimized for web
No

FLORA 20PT

REGULAR 20PT

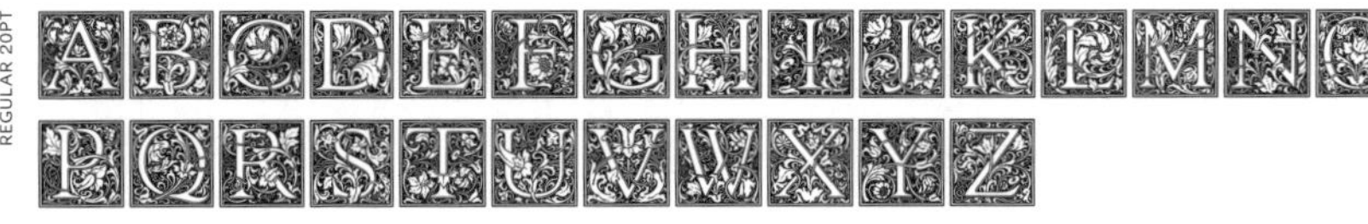

REGULAR 36PT

FLORA 36PT

GRAPHIQUE PRO NEXT

ЯЗЫКОВАЯ
SWISS TYPE DESIGN
LAYERED
HERMANN+EIDENBENZ
PROFONTS

THE NEXT LEVEL DESIGNED BY JÖRN OELSNER

About
The original Graphique Pro was designed by the famous Swiss designer Hermann Eidenbenz in 1945 and included one outline shadow style. His idea of a very narrow, very economic headline font has become increasingly popular over the last few decades and since the recent trend of layered fonts, his idea is more up-to-date than ever. profonts studio has now taken the idea of the Graphique Pro to its next level: Graphique Pro Next. This layered type family consists of eight styles which can be combined in plenty of ways to create unique designs. The fonts thereby preserve the outstanding and timeless drawings of the original Graphique Pro font and will add an aesthetic and fresh look to every project.

Design
Jörn Oelsner
2014

Foundry
profonts type foundry, Germany
www.profonts.de

Styles / Weights
Solid, Solid Lines, Shadow, Shadow Lines, Outline, Inline, 3D, Combination

Language support
Latin, Cyrillic, Greek

OpenType options
Proportional Lining, Standard Ligatures, All Caps, Superscript, Ordinals, Fractions

Optimized for web
No

COMP 22PT

ABCDEFGHIJKLMNOPQRSTUVWXYZÆÅÇÉÑÖÛ
0123456789@.,-:;!?')*""«»/-€$&½

SOLID LN 36PT

AEJGGQR7

OUTLINE & INLINE 16PT

TYPOGRAPHERS WANT
AMAZING, EXQUISITE
& CLEVER JUSTIFIED TEXT
IN BOOKS

3D 36PT

AEJGGQR7

SOLID & SOLID LN 16PT

TYPOGRAPHERS WANT
AMAZING, EXQUISITE
& CLEVER JUSTIFIED TEXT
IN BOOKS

Service Route*

(30/N55) HACKNEY

Marble Arch → King's Cross → Highbury → **Hackney → Hackney Wick.**

Exploring Squareness.

{it doesn't have to be like this}

Super-elliptical skeleton.

{unprecedented graft}

Hackney Carriages.

{compelling lines, alluring simplicity}

Measured Tone.

{refined, assured and versatile}

About
It was the Hackney carriage—the London black cab—that gave this font its name, not the north London neighborhood. Solid, dependable, effective and built to last, FS Hackney was honed to perform in all conditions. Cool, compelling lines and a satisfying overall simplicity lend FS Hackney its assertive air. Assured, versatile and effective; just like a black cab (but without the grumbling).

The squareness of curves and vertical terminals create a gentle, soft sans serif, with a little bit of magic. A momentary thought—"It doesn't have to be like this"—provided the spur to explore the verticals and skeletons of letterforms beyond conventional type design limits.

Design
Nick Job
2013

Foundry
Fontsmith, Great Britain
www.fontsmith.com

Styles / Weights
Thin, Thin Italic, Light, Light Italic, Regular, Italic, Bold, Bold Italic, Heavy, Heavy Italic

Language support
Latin

OpenType options
Proportional Oldstyle, Tabular and Proportional Lining, Tabular Oldstyle, Standard Ligatures, All Caps, Small Caps, Capitals to Small Caps, Superscript, Subscript, Ordinals, Fractions, Numerator, Denominator, Arrows

Optimized for web
Yes

REGULAR 18PT

abcdefghijklmnopqrstuvwxyzæfjåçéñöûß
ABCDEFGHIJKLMNOPQRSTUVWXYZÆÇØ
0123456789@.,-:;!?')]§*""«»/–€$&⅓↗

BOLD & THIN 30PT

aejgGQR7
aejgGQR7

BOLD & LIGHT 16PT

Typographers want
amazing, exquisite
& clever justified text
in books

BOLD & REGULAR 9PT

→ com·pen·dium / *noun* / (pl. com·pen·dia / or com·pen·diums) a collection of facts, drawings and photographs on a particular subject, especially in a book: *"a compendium of typography."*

ALL WEIGHTS 12PT

Thin
Light
Regular
Bold
Heavy

ITALICS 12PT

Thin Italic
Light Italic
Italic
Bold Italic
Heavy Italic

HANGULATIN

EINE LATEINISCHE SILBENSCHRIFT NACH DEM VORBILD DES KOREANISCHEN SCHRIFTSYSTEMS

IM VORFELD IHRER KOREAREISE LERNTE ANITA JÜRGENS DAS KOREANISCHE ALPHABET. DAS DORT HERRSCHENDE SCHRIFTSYSTEM, BUCHSTABEN ZU SILBEN ZU GRUPPIEREN, FASZINIERTE SIE SO SEHR, DASS SIE DAS EXPERIMENT WAGTE, EIN SOLCHES SCHRIFTSYSTEM MIT LATEINISCHEN BUCHSTABEN FÜR DIE DEUTSCHE SPRACHE ZU ENTWERFEN. DAS ERGEBNIS IST EIN INTUITIV ERLERNBARES UND ÜBERRASCHEND GUT LESBARES SCHRIFTSYSTEM, WELCHES HEUTE BEREITS RUND 3000 SILBEN ENTHÄLT UND ETWA 95% DES DURCHSCHNITTLICHEN DEUTSCHEN SPRACHGEBRAUCHS ABDECKT.

About

Preparing for a trip to Korea, Anita Jürgeleit studied the Korean alphabet. The prevailing writing system in Korea of grouping characters to syllables fascinated her so much that she dared to experiment with developing such a system of writing with the Latin alphabet for the German language. The result is an intuitively learnable and surprisingly easy to read writing system, which already contains approximately 3,000 syllables.

Awards for Hangulatin, conceived and designed by Anita Jürgeleit: Hangulatin was among the nominated finalists at Hiiibrand Typography Award 2013 & Golden nail in the talent competition of the ADC 2014.

Design
Anita Jürgeleit
2013

Foundry
URW++, Germany
www.urwpp.com

Styles / Weights
Regular

Language support
Latin

OpenType options
Proportional Lining, Standard Ligatures, Superscript, Ordinals, Fractions

Optimized for web
Yes

REGULAR 18PT

abcdefghijklmnopqrstuvwxyzæfjåçéñöûß
ABCDEFGHIJKLMNOPQRSTUVWXYZÆÇØ
0123456789@.,-:;!?')]§*“”«»/–€$&½

REGULAR 30PT

aejgGQR7

REGULAR 12PT

TYPOGRAFEN WOLLEN INTERESSANTE, KLUGE UND GUT AUSGERICHTETE TEXTE IN BÜCHERN

Rhabarber

BLACK

BOLD

hashtag®

nitro glycerin

SEMIBOLD

Yak Milk

REGULAR

Marmelade

LIGHT

1970 GLYPHS IN EACH STYLE
UP TO 14 ALTERNATIVES PER LETTER
DOZENS OF LIGATURES
NIFTY OPENTYPE FEATURES

HapticScript

About

The HapticScript family is a connected brush script with a warm, personal and soft character. The typeface family has five styles from Light through Black. It was designed as a companion and extension to the Haptic sans serif family.

HapticScript has up to 14 variations for each glyph. The almost 2,000 characters per font including 40+ ligatures enable designers to give each word an individual look. Many swash characters for initials and word endings make words looks as if they were hand-lettered.

Design
Henning Skibbe
2015

Foundry
Henning Skibbe – Typefaces, Germany
www.henningskibbe.com

Styles / Weights
Light, Regular, Semibold, Bold, Black

Language support
Latin

OpenType options
Proportional Oldstyle, Standard Ligatures, Discretionary Ligatures, Ordinals, All Alternates, Contextual Ligatures, Fractions, Stylistic Sets

Optimized for web
No

REGULAR 18PT

aaaaa aaaaa abcdefghijklmnopqrstuvwxyzæffjåçéñöûß
ABCDEFGHIJKLMNOPQRSTUVWXYZÆÇØ
0123456789@.,-:;!?')]§*“”«»/–€$&½

BOLD & LIGHT 34PT

BLACK & REGULAR 18PT

Typographers want amazing, exquisite & clever justified text in books

BOLD & LIGHT 11PT

→ **over·view** / noun / a brief summary of something: in the index of the Yearbook of Type the reader can find an overview of all typefaces presented in the book sorted by classification.

SEMIBOLD & LIGHT 18PT

Typographers want amazing, exquisite & clever justified text in books

e possible to them, assuming that
ctions do not infringe on the equal
others. It is also the idea that every
s pleasure should far surpass their
of pain. Ethical hedonism is said to
en started by Aristippus of Cyrene
of Socrates. He held the idea that

FONT FAMILY

Hedon is THICK

modern sans serif

waves OFFIC

playground 329

RAGMENTS mirror

s@lon

SERBIAN jazz

T_D_F_...

raffiné Yetti

Ethical hedonis
that all people h
to do everythin

Hedon

About
Hedon font family is an exotic example of how the geometry of modern grotesques could be blended with thin and thick lines familiar to serif fonts without actually crossing the doorstep of the serif's house. Hedon is a sans serif family benefiting both from legibility and contrast of sans and elegance and beauty of serifs. Staying in the middle between them, Hedon looks neutral yet versatile and easy to read. With its four weights and matching italics, this family is a perfect solution for editorial design, though you could easily use it for wine labels, packaging, corporate ID etc.

Explore the Light weight in extra large sizes for single word headlines or find out how elegant Italics are in a short text paragraph. The Bold style will make everything strong and contrast with enhanced legibility even in small sizes printed on paper or used as web font.

Design
Dušan Jelesijević
2014

Foundry
Tour de Force Font Foundry, Serbia
www.tourdefonts.com

Styles / Weights
Light, Light Italic, Regular, Italic, Semi Bold, Semi Bold Italic, Bold, Bold Italic

Language support
Latin

OpenType options
Fractions

Optimized for web
Yes

REGULAR 18PT

abcdefghijklmnopqrstuvwxyzæfjåçéñöûß
ABCDEFGHIJKLMNOPQRSTUVWXYZÆÇØ
0123456789@.,-:;!?')]§*"" «»/–€$&½

BOLD 36PT

aejgGQR7

BOLD & LIGHT 16PT

Typographers want amazing, exquisite
& clever justified text in books

BOLD & REGULAR 8PT

Year·book of Type/*noun*/book published every second year, giving details on typefaces of the previous two years and also about general current typographic topics–*e.g. OpenType features, font editors like Glyphs etc.*

ALL WEIGHTS 11PT

Light
Regular
Semi Bold
Bold

ITALICS 11PT

Light Italic
Regular Italic
Semi Bold Italic
Bold Italic

Heimat Didone
Heimat Display
Heimat Sans
Heimat Mono
Heimat Stencil

The overall air
define species
season seabird
defined minim
(BDMPS) to e
potential impa
development
season. Speci
are: red-throa
diver, norther
gannet great
Arctic skua &

ATLAS FONT FOUNDRY

About
Heimat Display is the high-contrast sans serif typeface family within the Heimat Collection, also containing Heimat Didone, Heimat Sans, Heimat Mono and Heimat Stencil. Heimat Display is a neo-classical typeface family designed for contemporary typography, especially for use in headlines and on posters, but also for reading purposes. It combines an idiosyncratic appearance with the feeling of a grid-based letter construction of the late 20s.

Since the design might be too extreme for some applications, Heimat Display's character set provides multiple alphabets, the regular one plus alternate designs that come across as less suspenseful.

Design
Christoph Dunst
2015

Foundry
Atlas Font Foundry, Germany
www.atlasfonts.com

Styles / Weights
Family of six optical weights (10, 12, 14, 16, 18, 20), each with six weights (Extralight, Light, Regular, Semi Bold, Bold, Heavy), each with Italics

Language support
Latin

OpenType options
Proportional Oldstyle, Tabular and Proportional Lining, Tabular Oldstyle, Standard Ligatures, Discretionary Ligatures, Historical Ligatures, All Caps, Superscript, Subscript, Ordinals, Swashes, Contextual Swashes, Contextual Alternates, Contextual Ligatures, Fractions, Numerator, Denominator, Ornaments, Arrows, Stylistic Alternates, Stylistic Sets, Historical Forms, Optical size

Optimized for web
Yes

10 REGULAR 18PT

abcdefgghijklmnopqrrstuvwxyyzæfjåçéñöûß
ABCDEFGHIJKLMNOPQRSTUVWXYZÆÇØ
0123456789@.,-:;!?’)]§*“”«»/–€$&⅓

16 EXTRABOLD 30PT

aejgGQR7

14 EXTRABOLD & REGULAR 14PT

Typographers want
amazing, exquisite
& clever justified text
in books

18 LIGHT 30PT

aejgGQR7

16 BOLD & REGULAR 11PT

The Yearbook of Type
compendium works well as
a tool in vexed typography
questions for polarizing jobs

Henriette
Vienna's finest
Available Now
Wiens Typografische Hochkultur
KAFFEEHAUS
Daily Newspaper Cover
Figure 478
The Oldstyle
Reisefieber
Phototype Straße

Henriette

About

The new type family of the Viennese foundry Typejockeys is available in 30 weights and therefore provides a great number of possible applications. Classy, elegant and sophisticated, as well as playful and a little knobbly. Perfect for headlines, logotypes, but also copytexts.

Basis for the alphabet were the letters of Vienna's street signs. Henriette is not a simple digitization, but rather a reinterpretation of 16 different styles you can find on the white-on-blue enamel plates today.

All Roman and all Italic weights offer the same character set and features throughout the width spectrum—normal, condensed, compressed. This offers even more flexibility when it comes to fitting a headline or creating an awesome logotype. The romans come with small caps. The italics with swash caps. All weights provide ligatures, contextual substitutes and several figure styles. A wide range of languages is supported throughout.

Design
Michael Hochleitner
2012

Foundry
Typejockeys, Austria
www.typejockeys.com

Styles / Weights
Family of three widhts (Normal, Condensed, Compressed), each with five weights (Regular, Medium, Bold, Heavy, Black), each with Italics

Language support
Latin

OpenType options
Proportional Oldstyle, Tabular and Proportional Lining, Tabular Oldstyle, Standard Ligatures, All Caps, Small Caps, Capitals to Small Caps, Superscript, Subscript, Ordinals, Titling Alternates, Swashes, Contextual Alternates, Fractions, Alternative Fractions, Numerator, Denominator, Ornaments, Arrows, Stylistic Alternates, Stylistic Sets, Mark Positioning, Circled Figures, new: Frames

Optimized for web
Yes

REGULAR 18PT

abcdefghijklmnopqrsttuvwxyzæfjåçéñöûß
ABCDEFGHIJKLMNOPQRSTUVWXYZÆÇØ
0123456789@.,-:;!?')]§*“”«»/–€$&⅓→

BOLD & REGULAR 9PT

→ **ex·am·ple**/*noun*/an illustration that supports or provides more information: *by showing examples the Yearbook of Type presents each font in different sizes and weights*

CONDENSED BOLD & REGULAR 16PT

Typographers want
amazing, exquisite
& clever justified
text in books

MEDIUM & HEAVY 34PT

aejgGQR7
aejgGQR7

COMPRESSED BOLD & REGULAR 16PT

Typographers want
amazing, exquisite
& clever justified
text in books

KIJK NAAR HET AVONDJOURNAAL

HOLLAND FESTIVAL

THEATER & MUZIEK, KUNSTEN, OPERA & FILM

UITNODIGI NGUITNODI

LARGEST PERFORMING ARTS FESTIVAL @ THE NETHERLANDS

SINDS 1947

LUFTPUTEFARTØYET MITT ER FULLT AV ÅL

83 COMMANDEURS

About
HF Stencil is a typeface specially created for the graphic identity of the Holland Festival in collaboration with Amsterdam design agency Thonik. The design is inspired by all-time classic Glaser Stencil from 1970, and taken to a whole new level by featuring hundreds of ligatures. These unusual fragmented ligatures play with the conventions of readability by simultaneously connecting individual letters and yet also disconnecting them again. Add to that a huge amount of stylistic alternates per glyph, and the result is a sophisticated typographic system that is tailored to look great in large sizes.

Design
Paul van der Laan
2014

Foundry
Bold Monday, The Netherlands
www.boldmonday.com

Styles / Weights
Bold

Language support
Latin

OpenType options
Standard Ligatures, Discretionary Ligatures, Contextual Alternates, Stylistic Alternates, Stylistic Sets

Optimized for web
Yes

BOLD 18PT
ABCDEFGHIJKLMNOPQRSTUVWXYZÆÅÇÉÑÖÛ
0123456789@.,-:;!?')*"" «»/–€$&

BOLD 30PT
AEJGQR7

BOLD 16PT
TYPOGRAPHERS WANT AMAZING, EXQUISITE & CLEVER JUSTIFIED TEXT IN BOOKS

<!DOCTYPE SPECIMEN SYSTEM "-//TDC//NY 2.1//EN">

HELLO WORLD

if (foo != bar * baz) {

Why won't this compile!?

grep "Stardate `date +'%Y%j.%H'`" /var/log/captain

<caption>

define **String cheese;**

```
class cube : public std::basic_os
{
public:
    convertToText() : std::basic_
    void open(std::string host, ur
        buffer * buf = (buffer*)rd
        buf->open(host, port, cate
    }
```

About
Like many programmers, I've always used monospaced fonts for my code. Input questions that convention and proposes a fresh approach for data and programming aesthetics. This flexible type system finds inspiration in early computer consoles but looks towards a richer future, where coding environments allow full control over one's typographic display.

Design
David Jonathan Ross
2014

Foundry
The Font Bureau, USA
www.fontbureau.com

Styles / Weights
168 Styles: Sans, Serif, and Mono Variants with Thin, Extra Light, Light, Regular, Medium, Bold, Black Weights; Normal, Narrow, Condensed, Compressed Widths; each with Italics

Language support
Latin, Cyrillic

OpenType options
Tabular Lining, Superscript, Subscript, Ordinals, All Alternates, Fractions, Numerator, Denominator, Ornaments, Arrows, Stylistic Alternates, Stylistic Sets, Slashed Zero

Optimized for web
Yes

INPUT SANS REGULAR 12PT

abcdefghijklmnopqrstuvwxyzæfjåçéñöûß
ABCDEFGHIJKLMNOPQRSTUVWXYZÆÇØ
01234567890@.,-:;!?')]§*“”«»/–€$&½■→

INPUT SERIF REGULAR 12PT

abcdefghijklmnopqrstuvwxyzæfjåçéñöûß
ABCDEFGHIJKLMNOPQRSTUVWXYZÆÇØ
01234567890@.,-:;!?')]§*“”«»/–€$&½■→

SANS BOLD & REGULAR 8PT

ref·er·ence book / *noun* / a book that contains facts and information that you look at when you need to find out sth. particular—*"I am looking for the right typeface for my project, so I use the Yearbook of Type as a reference book."*

MONO COMPRESSED BOLD & LIGHT 16PT

Typographers want amazing, exquisite
& clever justified text in books ❦

PADRE
RACK
BEAKER
HURL
CLERK
GNOME
STORE

About
The Intro font family consists of 26 unique font weights (+24 Condensed). The family is characterized by excellent legibility both in print and on the web, a well-finished geometric design, optimized kerning, etc.

Intro is most suitable for headlines of all sizes, but it does well in a variety of text lengths as well. The font's various styles give it the versatility necessary to meet any type of graphic design challenge—web, print, motion graphics, etc.—and make it perfect for T-shirts, posters, and logos.

Design
Svetoslav Simov
2012

Foundry
Fontfabric, Bulgaria
www.fontfabric.com

Styles / Weights
Thin, Thin Italic, Thin Alt, Thin Caps, Light, Light Italic, Light Alt, Light Caps, Regular, Italic, Regular Alt, Regular Caps, SemiBold, SemiBold Italic, SemiBold Alt, SemiBold Caps, Bold, Bold Italic, Bold Alt, Bold Caps, Black, Black Italic, Black Alt, Black Caps, Black Inline, Black Inline Caps

OpenType options
Not available

Language support
Latin, Cyrillic

Optimized for web
Yes

REGULAR 18PT

abcdefghijklmnopqrstuvwxyyzæçéñöß
ABCDEFGHIJKLMNOPQRSTUVWXYZÆÇØ
0123456789@.,-:;!?')]§*“”«»/–€$&

BLACK 35PT

aejgGQR7

SEMIBOLD & THIN 14PT

Typographers want
amazing, exquisite
& clever justified text
in books

BLACK INLINE CAPS 36PT

AEJGQR7

BOLD & REGULAR 12PT

The Yearbook of Type
compendium works well as
a tool in vexed typography
questions for polarizing jobs

arrest
SPARK
official
€92.50
умный
Movies!
kicking
93% off
🡅 online
PERFECT
Москва
¿CUÁNDO?
89 Tippett
приоритет

Sparkly light!

LATIN & КИРИЛЛИЦА

современная

Sans serif with a distinct flair

Flemish...!

A spark is an incandescent particle. Such sparks may be produced by pyrotechnics, by metalworking or as a by-product of fires, especially when burning wood. *In pyrotechnics, iron filings and metal alloys such as magnalium may be used to create sparks*. The quanti-

---

Принадлежа по рождению и крещению к православной церкви, Толстой, как и большинство представителей образованного общества своего времени, *в юности и молодости был равнодушен к религиозным вопросам. В середине 1870-х проявлял*

About
A practical sans serif doesn't need to appear dry, constructed, or derivative. It can excel in its sensible role and yet possess a distinct flair. Iskra (spark or flash) is a new sans serif designed by Tom Grace. It was conceived to challenge the limits between utilitarian and decorative. Sporting a low-contrast profile, it is a study of bridled energy in the Cyrillic and Latin scripts. Its eye-catching forms are an oblique tribute to the less-predictable style of brush lettering, and contain daring, elegant curves, economical proportions, and a slight top-heavy asymmetry. Its warmth comes from the subtle emphasis on the structures and details of individual letterforms, whereas its solidity is demonstrated through its balanced rhythm over long spans of text.

Design
Tom Grace
2012

Foundry
TypeTogether, Czech Republic
www.type-together.com

Styles / Weights
Ultra Thin, Ultra Thin Italic, Thin, Thin Italic, Light, Light Italic, Regular, Italic, Medium, Medium Italic, Bold, Bold Italic, Ultra Bold, Ultra Bold Italic

Language support
Latin, Cyrillic

OpenType options
Proportional Oldstyle, Tabular Lining, Proportional Lining, Tabular Oldstyle, Standard Ligatures, All Caps, Superscript, Subscript, Ordinals, Fractions, Numerator, Denominator, Arrows, Stylistic Alternates, Localized Forms

Optimized for web
Yes

REGULAR 18PT

abcdefghijklmnopqrstuvwxyzæfjåçéñöûß
ABCDEFGHIJKLMNOPQRSTUVWXYZÆÇØ
0123456789@.,-:;!?')]§*“”«»/–€$&½↗

BOLD & REGULAR 9PT

→ **ex·am·ple** / *noun* / an illustration that supports or provides more information: *by showing examples the Yearbook of Type presents each font in different sizes and weights*

MEDIUM & THIN 16PT

Typographers want
amazing, exquisite
& clever justified text
in books

BOLD & LIGHT 36PT

aejgGQR7
aejgGQR7

ALL WEIGHTS 12PT

Ultra Thin
Thin
Light
Regular
Medium
Bold
Ultra Bold

ITALICS 12PT

Ultra Thin Italic
Thin Italic
Light Italic
Italic
Medium Italic
Bold Italic
Ultra Bold Italic

A very fast xylophonist

1930–31 | 2013–14

The majestic mountain pass opened slowly.

Eggshell White

Типография каллиграфия и библиотеки

JAPONICA

kinetic typography

Εξαιρετική

◆

Local Time	Direction	**Speed/Gust**	**Temp/Feels Like**	**Humidity**	*Pressure*	Cloud Amount	***Precip Amount***
00:00	ENE	14 / 29 km/h	**21** / 21°C	**84%**	*1012 mb*	3%	***0.2 mm***
03:00	ENE	14 / 30 km/h	**20** / 20°C	**82%**	*1011 mb*	92%	***2.7 mm***
06:00	ENE	15 / 31 km/h	**21** / 20°C	**85%**	*1012 mb*	2%	***5.8 mm***
09:00	NE	17 / 19 km/h	**29** / 33°C	**75%**	*1013 mb*	63%	***0.4 mm***
12:00	NE	18 / 21 km/h	**32** / 39°C	**66%**	*1011 mb*	71%	***0.9 mm***
15:00	NE	17 / 19 km/h	**32** / 39°C	**68%**	*1009 mb*	83%	***1.6 mm***

About
Having been a fan of Eric Gill's work for some time, the slab serif Joanna stood out to Terrance. After initial sketches, Terrance decided to pursue a reimagining of Joanna, in a sans serif form. Ben Jones picked up the update to the serif Joanna, named Joanna Next. After nearly three years of research and development, the pair of families was ready to be released. Joanna Sans borrows heavily from Joanna, but takes a direction of its own. It has influences from other Gill faces, like the low contrast of Gill Sans, and the calligraphic nature of Perpetua. The scale of the body and x-height of Joanna Sans have been increased from the original Joanna, to be better suited for contemporary typographic demands. It has the varying width proportions and open aperture of a Humanists sans serif, but retains an easygoing geometric tone. The fluid details and structure of the italics can be elegant and striking, while remaining very legible.

Design
Terrance Weinzierl
2014

Foundry
Monotype, USA
www.monotype.com

Styles / Weights
Thin, Thin Italic, Light, Light Italic, Regular, Italic, Book, Book Italic, Medium, Medium Italic, Bold, Bold Italic, Extra Bold, Extra Bold Italic, Black, Black Italic

Language support
Latin, Cyrillic, Greek

OpenType options
Proportional Oldstyle, Tabular and Proportional Lining, Tabular Oldstyle, Standard Ligatures, All Caps, Small Caps, Capitals to Small Caps, Superscript, Subscript, Ordinals, All Alternates, Fractions, Numerator, Denominator, Stylistic Alternates, Stylistic Sets, Slashed Zero, Localized Forms, Case Sensitive Forms, Capital Spacing

Optimized for web
Yes

REGULAR 18PT

abcdefghijklmnopqrstuvwxyzæfjåçéñöûß
ABCDEFGHIJKLMNOPQRSTUVWXYZÆÇØ
01234567890@.,-:;!?')]§*“”«»/–€$&⅓

BOLD & REGULAR 36PT

aejgGQR7
aejgGQR7

BLACK & BOOK 13PT

The Yearbook of Type
compendium works well as
a tool in vexed typography
questions for polarizing jobs

MEDIUM & LIGHT 9PT

ar·chive / *noun* / a collection of documents such as letters, photographs or other material: *the Yearbook of Type is an archive of contemporary typefaces from all over the world*

ALL WEIGHTS 10PT

Thin
Light
Regular
Book
Medium
Bold
Extra Bold
Black

ITALICS 10PT

Thin Italic
Light Italic
Italic
Book Italic
Medium Italic
Bold Italic
Extra Bold Italic
Black Italic

خط **كاف**
29LT**Kaff**

رفيع	Thin
خفيف جدًا	Ultra Light
خفيف	Light
عاديّ	Regular
متوسّط	Medium
شبه داكن	Semi Bold
داكن	Bold
أسود	Black

About
29LT Kaff is a contemporary pragmatist typeface drawn with extreme refinement and low pen contrast that unveils an extensive set of fonts suitable for the everyday use and various projects. It is the corporate typeface as well as a sleek fashionable typeface. It can be casual as well as sophisticated depending on its usage.

It is a type family created with maximum legibility and ease of usability mindset. The letterforms were drawn in a certain composition representing neutrality while retaining its connection to calligraphy. It is a humanistic typeface in searching for the essence of the Arabic and Latin typographic structures.

The Arabic ligatures and elongated stylistic sets give the typeface more calligraphic characteristics. These were added to enhance the script's "essentiality," and essential is, after all, what Kaff means.

Design
Ian Party, Pascal Zoghbi, 2015

Foundry
29Letters, Lebanon
www.29lt.com

Styles / Weights
Thin, Ultra Light, Light, Regular, Medium, Semi Bold, Bold, Black

Language support
Latin, Arabic

OpenType options
Standard Ligatures, Discretionary Ligatures, Superscript, Subscript, All Alternates, Contextual Ligatures, Stylistic Alternates, Stylistic Sets, Localized Forms, Required Ligatures, Mark Positioning, Terminal Form, Initial Form, Isolated Form, Medial Form

Optimized for web
Yes

REGULAR 14PT

ا أ ب ببب ت تتت ث ثثث ج ججج ح ححح خ خخخ د د ذ ذ ر ر ز ز س سسس
ش ششش ص صصص ض ضضض ط ططط ظ ظظظ ع ععع غ غغغ
ف ففف ق ققق ك ككك ل للل م ممم ن ننن ه ههه و و ي ييي لا لا

REGULAR 14PT

abcdefghijklmnopqrstuvwxyzæfjåçéñöûß&€$*
ABCDEFGHIJKLMNOPRSTUVWXYZÆÇØ
0123456789·١٢٣۳٤٥٦٧٨٩۴۵۶۲۷@.,-:;!?')]§«»/–

BOLD 32PT

aejgGQR7
ع جم ض س ق

BLACK & ULTRA LIGHT 16PT

Typographers want amazing, exquisite
& clever justified text in books

29LT Kaff

Kailey

A bodacious font with the right amount of whimsy.

Beautiful · Brave · Bold

Kailey

About
Kailey font is a hand lettered, voluptuous typeface that is very special to the Great Lakes Lettering team. This oblique font is inspired by Molly Jacques' "signature" lettering style, using bold brush strokes, fluid flourishes, and distinctive characters. Kailey has a distinct feminine feel that takes on a bold attitude to match her curves.

Design
Great Lakes Lettering, Dathan Boardman & Molly Jacques Erickson
2013

Foundry
Great Lakes Lettering, USA
www.greatlakeslettering.com

Styles / Weights
Regular

Language support
Latin

OpenType options
Standard Ligatures, Swashes, Fractions

Optimized for web
Yes

REGULAR 18PT

abcdefghijklmnopqrstuvwxyzæfjåçéñöû
ABCDEFGHIJKLMNOPQRSTUVWXYZÆÇØ
0123456789@.,–:;!?')]§*""«»/–£$&½

REGULAR 36PT

aejgGQR7

REGULAR 16PT

Typographers want amazing, exquisite & clever justified text in books

Kandel 105

Kandel 205

Ay Ay

Ny Ny

About
Kandel is a geometric, tri-line sans serif in two separate families—Kandel 105 and Kandel 205—each of three weights. Kandel 105 features sharper, more conventional right angles at the junctions of some characters (A, M, N, V, W, Y, v, w, y) while Kandel 205 offers continuous curves at the junctions.

Design
Adrian Talbot
2013

Foundry
Talbot Type, England
www.talbottype.co.uk

Styles / Weights
Family of two styles (105, 205), each in three weights (Light, Medium, Bold), each with Italics

Language support
Latin

OpenType options
Proportional Lining, Standard Ligatures, Fractions, Required Ligatures

Optimized for web
No

105 MEDIUM 18PT

abcdefghijklmnopqrstuvwxyzœfjåçēñöûß
ABCDEFGHIJKLMNOPQRSTUVWXYZÆÇØ
0123456789@.,-:;!?')]*“”«»/–€$&½

205 LIGHT 18PT

abcdefghijklmnopqrstuvwxyzœfjåçēñöûß
ABCDEFGHIJKLMNOPQRSTUVWXYZÆÇØ
0123456789@.,-:;!?')]*“”«»/–€$&½

105 BOLD & BOLD OBLIQUE 36PT

aejgGQR7
aejgGQR7

205 BOLD & MEDIUM 16PT

The Yearbook of Type
compendium works well as
a tool in vexed typography
questions for polarizing jobs

Kelso

Ligh

Med

Bol

Each glyph is represented by a single continuous line

Kelso

About
Kelso is a geometric outline display font available in three weights. Each character is represented by a single continuous stroke, creating a rhythmic, fluid look. Having hit upon the idea for the font, Kelso fell into place quite quickly, although it took a little while to resolve the curved characters with a stroke that connected inner and outer curves in a clean and easy fashion.

Design
Adrian Talbot
2014

Foundry
Talbot Type, England
www.talbottype.co.uk

Styles / Weights
Light, Light Italic, Medium, Medium Italic, Bold, Bold Italic

Language support
Latin

OpenType options
Proportional Lining, Standard Ligatures

Optimized for web
No

MEDIUM 16PT
abcdefghijklmnopqrstuvwxyzœfjàçéñöûß
ABCDEFGHIJKLMNOPQRSTUVWXYZÆÇØ
0123456789@.,-:;!?')]*"«»/–€$&

BOLD & MEDIUM 28PT

BOLD OBLIQUE 15PT
Typographers want amazing, exquisite & clever justified text in books

BOLD & LIGHT 11PT
The Yearbook of Type compendium works well as a tool in vexed typography questions for polarizing jobs

ALL WEIGHTS 9PT
Light
Medium
Bold

ITALICS 9PT
Light Oblique
Medium Oblique
Bold Oblique

As a comet approaches the inner Solar System,
SOLAR RADIATION
causes the volatile materials within the comet
to vaporize and stream out
of the nucleus, carrying dust away with them

Der Halleysche Komet kam zuletzt
1986
IN ERDNÄHE

Orbital Period

ICE, DUST & ROCKY PARTICLES

Galaktische Gezeitenkräfte

Tempel 1 was the target of the
SPACE MISSION
which photographed an impact
upon the comet in 2005

BORRELLYS SURFACE
reflects not more than
3.0%
OF THE SUNLIGHT

Ein Komet oder Schweifstern ist ein kleiner Himmelskörper von meist einigen Kilometern Durchmesser, der in sonnennahen Teilen seiner Bahn eine durch Ausgasen erzeugte Koma und meist auch einen leuchtenden Schweif entwickelt. Kometen sind wie Asteroiden Überreste der Entstehung des Sonnensystems und bestehen aus Eis, Staub und lockerem Gestein.

Texts from wikipedia.org and related pages

About
Komet is a sturdy sans serif typeface with a calm and upright feel. Its low stroke contrast and heavy dots and accents give it an almost monolinear quality. The diagonals are slightly curved and the counters of the round letters such as b, o and q are generously wide. The muted, understated middle weights are built for extended body copy, while Komet's thin and dark weights look brisk and assertive and make for subtly expressive headlines. The Komet family comes in eight weights from Thin to Black, each with a matching Italic. Every font contains around 850 glyphs, including a rich repertoire of OpenType features. Small caps, ligatures, ten different figure sets with matching currency symbols, stylistic alternates and arrows make Komet a comprehensive toolkit for ambitious typography. Komet is an ideal choice for editorial design, branding and corporate design.

Design
Jan Fromm
2015

Foundry
Jan Fromm, Germany
www.janfromm.de

Styles / Weights
Thin, Thin Italic, ExtraLight, ExtraLight Italic, Light, Light Italic, Regular, Italic, Medium, Medium Italic, Bold, Bold Italic, Heavy, Heavy Italic, Black, Black Italic

Language support
Latin

OpenType options
Proportional Oldstyle, Tabular Lining and Prop. Lining, Tab. Oldstyle, Standard Ligatures, Discretionary Lig., All Caps, Small Caps, Capitals to Small Caps, Superscript, Subscript, Ordinals, All Alternates, Fractions, Numerator, Denominator, Arrows, Stylistic Alt., Stylistic Sets, Localized Forms

Optimized for web
Yes

REGULAR 17PT

aabcdefgghijklmnopqrstuvwxyyzæfjåçéñöûß
ABCDEFGHIJKLMNOPQRSTUVWXYZÆÇØ
0123456789@.,-:;!?')]§*“”«»/—€$&⅓↗

BLACK & THIN 30PT

aejgGQR7
aejgGQR7

HEAVY & EXTRALIGHT 16PT

Typographers want
amazing, exquisite
& clever justified text
in books

BOLD & REGULAR 9PT

com·pen·dium / *noun* / (pl. com·pen·dia / or com·pen·diums) a collection of facts, drawings and photographs on a particular subject, especially in a book: *“a compendium of typography.”*

ALL WEIGHTS 10PT

Thin
ExtraLight
Light
Regular
Medium
Bold
Heavy
Black

ITALICS 10PT

Thin Italic
ExtraLight Italic
Light Italic
Regular Italic
Medium Italic
Bold Italic
Heavy Italic
Black Italic

Jan Fromm

Komet

FREE Late Night Jam

FLOWING YET FUNCTIONAL

→*Fabulous Superlatives*←

Ambiance

EDITORIAL AND DISPLAY

Conserve

TEXTURE RICH

Taste makers

Decorum

Nº2467 BARLEY HONEY SPICE

VERSATILE REPERTOIRE

Resorts

CHEERY ENTHUSED

About
The Kopius family is a contemporary serif type that features friendly characteristics with round open counters conveying a relaxed ambiance. The robustness of the characters supports a wide variety of applications including editorial and display use. The allusion to a brush stroke bestows a contemporary texture-rich appearance that is entirely in tune with functionality. The top and bottom slightly curved stems imply flow and reading direction.

Kopius is an exuberant family with a genuinely multifaceted repertoire. This upbeat type comes with a multitude of weights to satisfy any fanciful appetite for a colorful typographic palette. With packaging applications in mind, the family includes sets of expandable and combinable boxes for a boundless range of adjusted composites and labels. Pertinent symbols, weight adjusted arrows, and catchwords complete the Kopius family. OpenType provides advanced layout features including figure sets, small caps, fractions, and more.

Design
Sibylle Hagmann
2015

Foundry
Kontour, USA
www.kontour.com

Styles / Weights
Light, Light Italic, Regular, Italic, Bold, Bold Italic, Black, Black Italic, Condensed Romans, Box Headings, Label Material

Language support
Latin

OpenType options
Proportional Oldstyle, Tabular and Proportional Lining, Tabular Oldstyle, Standard Ligatures, Discretionary Ligatures, All Caps, Small Caps, Superscript, Subscript, Ordinals, Fractions, Numerator, Denominator, Ornaments, Arrows

Optimized for web
Yes

REGULAR 17PT
abcdefghijklmnopqrstuvwxyzæfjåçéñöûß
ABCDEFGHIJKLMNOPQRSTUVWXYZÆÇØ
0123456789@.,-:;!?')]§*“”«»/–€$&½↗

BLACK 30PT
aejgGQR7

BOLD & LIGHT 14PT
Typographers want amazing, exquisite
& clever justified text in books

EXTRAS 30PT

BOLD & REGULAR 9PT
cata·logue/ *noun*/ a complete list of things that people can look at or buy: *a catalogue of typefaces (a book showing the newest fonts, to help people choose the right typeface)*

Modern life is a
continuous
intelligence test.
Korpus A —
150 pt.

About

The term Korpus comes from the Latin and means "body." In the German-speaking printing world, Korpus is used for a medium point size used in metal setting, size ten Didot points. But Korpus (corpus in English) can also refer to a text or extract from a collection of texts or statements that are the subject of a particular presentation or study in various academic disciplines. The development of this typeface took inspiration from intermediary devices, primarily those involved in the technological reproducibility of character drawings.

Inaccuracies, fuzziness, and inconspicuous errors in their transmission from one physical state to the next began to play a part in the development process of the characters. Emerging discretely, they strikingly put into perspective the body of their appearances.

Design

Binnenland, Mischler & Thoenen
2014

Foundry

Binnenland, Switzerland
www.binnenland.ch

Styles / Weights

A, A10, B, B12, C

Language support

Latin

OpenType options

Proportional Oldstyle, Tabular and Proportional Lining, Standard Ligatures, All Caps, Small Caps, Capitals to Small Caps, Superscript, Subscript, Fractions, Numerator, Denominator, Slashed Zero

Optimized for web

Yes

A 18PT

abcdefghijklmnopqrstuvwxyzæfjåçéñöûß
ABCDEFGHIJKLMNOPQRSTUVWXYZÆÇØ
01234567890@.,-:;!?')]§*“”«»/–€$&½

C 36PT

aejgGQR7

B & A 16PT

Typographers want
amazing, exquisite
& clever justified text
in books

B 36PT

aejgGQR7

C & A 9PT

ar·chive / *noun* / a collection of documents such as letters, photographs or other material: *the Yearbook of Type is an archive of contemporary typefaces from all over the world*

Ce soir j'écrirai un
poème pour la postérité –
pour présenter les
caractères typographiques
Korpus Grotesk.

Korpus Grotesk – B
ABCDEFGHIJKLMNOP
QRSTUVWXYZ
0123456789

Korpus Grotesk

About
Korpus Grotesk is a continuation and translation of the typographic vocabulary of the serif typeface Korpus into a sans serif font family. It is both an interpretation and a development of its shape, while retaining the proportions and the rhythm of the underlying typeface. Where the Korpus refers to features of hot metal typesetting, Korpus Grotesk imitates the technical characteristics of phototypesetting. Inaccuracies and fuzziness in the transmission through exposure onto the carrier medium of film and printing plate—as for example light bleeding—are rendered discretely visible, relativizing the character of the font. The two font families Korpus and Korpus Grotesk have been harmonized to allow alternating use in body text.

Design
Binnenland, Mischler & Thoenen
2014

Foundry
Binnenland, Switzerland
www.binnenland.ch

Styles / Weights
A, A8, B, B8, C, C8, D

Language support
Latin

OpenType options
Proportional Oldstyle, Tabular and Proportional Lining, Standard Ligatures, All Caps, Small Caps, Capitals to Small Caps, Superscript, Subscript, Fractions, Numerator, Denominator, Arrows, Stylistic Alternates, Slashed Zero

Optimized for web
Yes

A 18PT
abcdefghijklmnopqrstuvwxyzæfjåçéñöûß
ABCDEFGHIJKLMNOPQRSTUVWXYZÆÇØ
0123456789Ø@.,-:;!?')]§*""«»/–€$&½→

D 36PT
aejgGQR7

C & A 14PT
The Yearbook of Type
compendium works well as
a tool in vexed typography
questions for polarizing jobs

B 36PT
aejgGQR7

C & A 9PT
Year·book of Type / *noun* / book published every second year, giving details of typefaces of the previous two years and about general current typographic topics—*e.g. OpenType features, font editors like Glyphs etc.*

Blick von der Londoner Tate Modern Galerie über die Themse zur Kirche St. Paul's, Oktober 2013.

Lammerhuber

Schriftfamilie für einen Photographie Verlag

DIE *LAMMERHUBER* IST DIE ERSTE maßgeschneiderte Hausschrift für einen österreichischen Verlag und somit ein historisch wichtiger Schritt.

Der Kunde, Edition Lammerhuber, ist ein mehrfach preisgekrönter Photographie Verlag aus Baden, Niederösterreich. Die Produktionsstandards des Hauses sind kompromisslos, Materialien und Verarbeitung sowie Fertigungstechniken sind von höchster Qualität. Um diesen Ansprüchen typographisch Genüge zu leisten wurde 2013 eine Hausschrift in Auftrag gegeben.

Eines der wichtigsten Genres des Verlages ist Dokumentar Photographie und die Schrift *Lammerhuber* ist davon inspiriert. Sie entspricht dem sachlichen Beobachter, der kommentiert und festhält, sich jedoch nicht in den Vordergrund drängt. Sie spricht ihre eigene Sprache, die in Details zur Geltung kommt, ist aber unsichtbar, wenn es darum geht, Inhalte zu vermitteln. Ausgehend von Proportionen der amerikanischen Grotesken des frühen 20. Jahrhunderts hat sich die *Lammerhuber* in eine eigenständige, zeitgenössische Serifenlose mit europäischem Charakter entwickelt.

Wie für einen zentraleuropäischen Verleger passend kann man 98 Sprachen aus ihr setzen, zudem erleichtern und verbessern zahlreiche typographische Funktionen die Gestaltung von Text. Eine ungewöhnliche Besonderheit der Schrift sind schmale Formen der häufigsten Buchstaben durch deren Einsatz man Blocksatz verbessern und ein regelmäßiges Satzbild erzeugen kann, ohne den Leser zu irritieren.

Die hier präsentierte Familie wird in Zukunft weiter ausgebaut und nach Ablauf der Exklusivität zur allgemeinen Lizensierung angeboten werden.

About
Lammerhuber was conceived as a bespoke typeface for the homonymous Austrian publisher. As the first typeface ever commissioned by an Austrian publishing house, Lammerhuber is of historic significance. Edition Lammerhuber is an award-winning photography publisher with exacting production standards. The principal genre of the publisher is documentary photography and Lammerhuber derives its inspiration from the subject. The type resembles the factual observer who comments and captures images, yet does not push to the fore. It has its own voice which emerges in the details, yet it is invisible where content needs to be conveyed. Initially inspired by the proportions of the American Grotesque types, Lammerhuber developed into a fully independent, contemporary sans with a distinct European character. As fitting for a central-European publisher, one can set 98 languages with the type, and its many typographic features facilitate and improve the design of text.

Design
Titus Nemeth
2014

Foundry
tntypography, Austria
www.tntypography.eu

Styles / Weights
Thin, Light, Regular, Italic, Medium, Semibold, Bold, Semilight, Negative, Positive, Extrabold

Language support
Latin

OpenType options
Proportional Oldstyle, Tabular and Proportional Lining, Tabular Oldstyle, Standard Ligatures, Discretionary Ligatures, All Caps, Small Caps, Capitals to Small Caps, Superscript, Subscript, Ordinals, Contextual Alternates, Fractions, Numerator, Denominator, Stylistic Alternates, Stylistic Sets, Localized Forms

Optimized for web
No

REGULAR 18PT
abcdefghijklmnopqrstuvwxyzæfjåçéñöûß
ABCDEFGHIJKLMNOPQRSTUVWXYZÆÇØ
0123456789@.,-:;!?')]§*“”«»/—€$&½

EXTRABOLD 36PT
aejgGQR7

NEGATIVE & THIN 16PT
Typographers want
amazing, exquisite
& clever justified text
in books

BOLD & REGULAR 8PT
ref·er·ence book / *noun* / a book that contains facts and information that you look at when you need to find out sth. particular—*"I am looking for the right typeface for my project, so I use the Yearbook of Type as a reference book."*

SEMIBOLD & SEMILIGHT 16PT
Typographers want
amazing, exquisite
& clever justified text
in books

ECLIPSE
Solaire

LE BATEAU IVRE
Drunken boat

MÉCANIQUE CÉLESTE
Physiques Quantique

ELEKTROLOKOMOTIVE
Electricity rules

I SET TEXT, THEREFORE I AM
But does it mean anything?

About
A monospace typeface inspired by the Age of Reason and fine steel.

What if an 18th century mathematician would have possessed an Amiga computer? Such a gadget would have required a very specific typeface. Let's imagine how its letter shapes would look like: They would surely follow classical forms, probably with dominating vertical emphasis. Capitals would strive towards a divine width-to-height ratio rectangle. It would incorporate evenly spaced numerals. Due to the simplicity of the machine, it could only be a monospaced font. Thanks to refined metal techniques, thin strokes would be very fine. Italics would be created with the aid of the most recent mathematical innovations, such as Pierre-Simon Laplace's Z-transform. Spacing and typesetting would be close to celestial mechanics. The curves would be Fibonacci spirals. Kerning values would be = 0.

Holy moly, such a machine would inspire unlike any other! With Laplace and an Amiga at hand, publishing a thesis would be a breeze.

Design
Anton Koovit
2014

Foundry
Fatype, Germany / Switzerland
www.fatype.com

Styles / Weights
Light, Regular, Bold

Language support
Latin, Cyrillic

OpenType options
Standard Ligatures

Optimized for web
Yes

REGULAR 15PT

abcdefghijklmnopqrstuvwxyzæfjåçéñöûß
ABCDEFGHIJKLMNOPQRSTUVWXYZÆÇØ
0123456789@.,-:;!?')]§*“”«»/–€$&

BOLD 36PT

aejgGQR7

BOLD & LIGHT 14PT

TYPOGRAPHERS WANT
AMAZING, EXQUISITE
& clever justified
text in books

LIGHT 36PT

aejgGQR7

BLACK & LIGHT 9PT

YEAR·BOOK OF TYPE / noun / book published every second year, giving details on typefaces of the previous two years and also about general current typographic topics–e.g. OpenType features, font editors like Glyphs etc.

LASKI SLAB STENCIL

$159.55 at online retailers

HUMAN

Kartki świąteczne

Number

Süddeutsche Zeitung

Reflexão

Sales of new cars drop

REPRESENTATIVE

Laski Slab

About
Laski Slab is a comprehensive suite of 20 fonts conceived for editorial purposes.

Belying the intrinsic robustness of the slab serif genre, Laski's humanistic construction and subtle calligraphic details lend it a friendly appearance. Round, open letter forms and generous horizontal proportions make it easy to read. The regular weights perform impeccably in text sizes, while the bolder versions produce expressive and very effective subheadings and headlines. Two idiosyncratic stencil variants considerably expand Laski's creative potential.

Laski Slab is a suite of feature-rich OpenType fonts fully equipped to tackle complex, professional typography. The character set includes five sets of numerals, Small Caps, Fractions, alternate characters and case-sensitive forms. Besides standard Latin, its extensive character set supports Central European, Baltic and Turkish languages.

Design
Ramiro Espinoza, Paula Mastrangelo
2014

Foundry
Retype, Netherlands
www.re-type.com

Styles / Weights
Thin, Thin Italic, Extralight, Extralight Italic, Light, Light Italic, Regular, Italic, Book, Book Italic, Semi Bold, Semi Bold Italic, Bold, Bold Italic, Heavy, Heavy Italic, Black, Black Italic, Stencil Black, Stencil Black Italic

Language support
Latin, Central European, Baltic, Turkish

OpenType options
Proportional Oldstyle, Tabular Lining, All Caps, Capitals to Small Caps, Fractions, Numerator, Denominator, Stylistic Sets

Optimized for web
Yes

REGULAR 18PT

aabcdefgghijklmnopqrstuvwxyzæfjåçéñöûß
ABCDEFGHIJKLMNOPQRSTUVWXYZÆÇØ
0123456789@.,-:;!?')]§*“”«»/–€$&⅓

BOLD 30PT

aejgGQR7

BOLD & REGULAR 14PT

Typographers want amazing, exquisite
& clever justified text in books

STENCIL BLACK 30PT

aejgGQR7

BOLD & REGULAR 9PT

cata·logue / *noun* / a complete list of things that people can look at or buy: *a catalogue of typefaces (a book showing the newest fonts, to help people choose the right typeface)*

magazine

on paper or distributed online

tidskriften

περιοδικό

εβδομαδιαία, μηνιαία κλπ.

журнал

дневник, подённая записка

zeitschrift

14-tägig oder monatlich

Lava was originally designed for *Works That Work* magazine, but far transcends its original application. It's a no-nonsense workhorse typeface that can handle large quantities of text with ease. It's legible and harmonious at small sizes, sophisticated and elegant at large sizes, designed to perform optimally in both high- and low-resolution environments. Supports Latin, Cyrillic, Greek, and Arabic.

About
Lava was originally designed for Works That Work magazine, but far transcends its original application. It's a no-nonsense workhorse typeface that can handle large quantities of text with ease. It's legible and harmonious at small sizes, sophisticated and elegant at large sizes.

Since the magazine exists both in print and on screen, Lava was designed to perform optimally in both high and low resolution environments.

Design
Peter Biľak
2013

Foundry
Typotheque, The Netherlands
www.typotheque.com

Styles / Weights
Regular, Italic, Medium, Medium Italic, Bold, Bold Italic, Heavy, Heavy Italic

Language support
Latin, Cyrillic, Greek, Arabic

OpenType options
Proportional Oldstyle, Tabular and Proportional Lining, Tabular Oldstyle, Standard Ligatures, Discretionary Ligatures, All Caps, Small Caps, Capitals to Small Caps, Superscript, Subscript, Ordinals, All Alternates, Contextual Alternates, Fractions, Numerator, Denominator, Ornaments, Arrows, Stylistic Alternates, Stylistic Sets, Slashed Zero

Optimized for web
Yes

REGULAR 18PT

abcdefghijklmnopqrstuvwxyzæfjåçéñöûß
ABCDEFGHIJKLMNOPQRSTUVWXYZÆÇØ
01234567890@.,-:;!?')]§*""«»/–€$&⅓☝↗

BLOLD & MEDIUM 30PT

aejgGQR7
aejgGQR7

HEAVY & REGULAR 16PT

Typographers want amazing, exquisite
& clever justified text in books

BOLD & REGULAR 8PT

☞ **ex·am·ple** / *noun* / an illustration that supports or provides more information: *by showing examples the Yearbook of Type presents each font in different sizes and weights*

ALL WEIGHTS 11PT

Regular
Medium
Bold
Heavy

ITALICS 11PT

Regular Italic
Medium Italic
Bold Italic
Heavy Italic

or el azul, símbolo
del medio es blanca, símbolo de la
Y la inferior es de color rojo, símbo
angre derramada por la libertad y
endencia. En la franja del medio l
nda **«libertad o muerte».** La ba
riginal fue robada por la organiza
rrillera OPR-33 y no ha aparecido
cha. En el cuadro del pintor urugu
n Manuel Blanes se puede ver la ba
on la leyenda. Finalmente, el 19 de
desembarcaron en Soriano, más
te en la Playa de la Agraciada y a
sar tierra firme todos clamaron e
o en Montevideo antes de partir. C
do listo para retornar a la patria,
barcaron en el puerto bonaerens
nbarcaron lanchones. Eligieron p

Libertad

About
Design can do without images, but not without typefaces.

Libertad is a sans serif typeface that mixes humanist and grotesk models. Its most interesting feature is the combination of balanced regulars with dynamic Italics, which makes it a very versatile font for different uses.

This typeface follows the Luc(as) de Groot's Interpolation Theory, that's why it has seven specially calculated weights plus their matching italics, from Thin to Extra Bold. This allows it to be useful in big headlines and also small texts. It has more than 800 characters per weight and support for more than 70 languages.

Design
Fernando Díaz, Vincente Lamónaca, Martin Sommaruga
2014

Foundry
TipoType, Uruguay
www.tipotype.com

Styles / Weights
Thin, Thin Italic, Light, Light Italic, Book, Book Italic, Regular, Italic, Medium, Medium Italic, Bold, Bold Italic, ExtraBold, ExtraBold Italic

Language support
Latin

OpenType options
Proportional Oldstyle, Tabular Lining, Proportional Lining, Tabular Oldstyle, Standard Ligatures, Discretionary Ligatures, Historical Ligatures, Small Caps, Titling Alternates, Contextual Ligatures, Fractions, Ornaments, Arrows, Slashed Zero, Localized Forms, Required Ligatures

Optimized for web
Yes

REGULAR 18PT

abcdefghijklmnopqrstuvwxyzæfjåçéñöûß
ABCDEFGHIJKLMNOPQRSTUVWXYZÆÇØ
0123456789ø@.,-:;!?')]§*"" «»/–€$&½✪↗

BOLD & REGULAR 9PT

→ **over·view** / noun / a brief summary of something: *in the index of the Yearbook of Type the reader can find an overview of all typefaces presented in the book sorted by classification*

BOOK & THIN 16PT

Typographers want
amazing, exquisite
& clever justified text
in books

EXTRABOLD & MEDIUM 36PT

aejgGQR7
aejgGQR7

ALL WEIGHTS 8PT

Thin
Light
Book
Regular
Medium
Bold
ExtraBold

ROUNDED, ALL WEIGHTS 8PT

Thin Italic
Light Italic
Book Italic
Italic
Medium Italic
Bold Italic
ExtraBold Italic

NOW PLAYING
"HOUSE BY THE RIVER"
A FILM NOIR

GET YOUR TICKET FOR THE
BLUE GARDENIA

TODAY AT 8 PM

TUESDAY AND WEDNESDAY
FOR SPECIAL PRICES

POPKORN & KOLA!

PARKETT LOGE KOLA bitte

OHNE ABRISS UNGÜLTIG & AUFBEWAHREN

AUF VERLANGEN VORZEIGEN.

About

Cinemas from the early 20th century are called "Lichtspiele" in Germany. Lichtspiele transports you back to a time where neon lights and marquee letters decorated cinema facades.

Of the five styles, three have two versions of italics—one for each perspective. Display is your basic style. Neon is inspired by the old neon letters found outside cinemas.

Add Neon Outline to Display or Neon to add another layer to your artwork. Neon 3D is a extruded version of Neon. Screen Credits is based on the liner notes of movie posters.

Get more out of life, go to a movie.

Design
Stefan Hübsch
2014

Foundry
Typocalypse, Germany
www.typocalypse.com

Styles / Weights
Display, Display Italic, Display Contra Italic, Neon, Neon Italic, Neon Contra Italic, Neon 3D, Neon Outline, Neon Outline Italic, Neon Outline Contra Italic, Screen Credits, Trailer (free)

Language support
Latin

OpenType options
Standard Ligatures, Discretionary Ligatures, Small Caps, Contextual Alternates, Contextual Ligatures, Fractions, Stylistic Alternates, Stylistic Sets

Optimized for web
No

DISPLAY 26PT

abcdefghijklmnopqrstuvwxyzæfjåçéñöüß
ABCDEFGHIJKLMNOPQRSTUVWXYZÆÇØ
0123456789@.,-:;!?')]s*"" «»/-€$& ½

NEON & SCREEN CREDITS 43PT

aejgGQR7
AEJGGQR7

NEON OUTLINE CONTRA ITALIC 24PT

Typographers want amazing, exquisite & clever justified text in books

NEON OUTLINE & NEON 3D 43PT

aejgGQR7
aejgGQR7

DISPLAY ITALIC 24PT

Typographers want amazing, exquisite & clever justified text in books

TypeTogether presents **LIPA AGATE** By Ermin Međedović

TILO · TILLEUL · LÍPA · HÁRSFA · TÍLIA · BLI · TIĿLER · LÕHMUS · LEHMUS · TIGLIO · LIEPA · TEI

Honest workhorse

Global equity-research budgets have dropped from $8.2 billion in 2007 to $4.8 billion last year; this will now drop down to

AGATE: a standard unit of measurement 5 ½ points or 1⁄14 of an inch or 1.814 mm

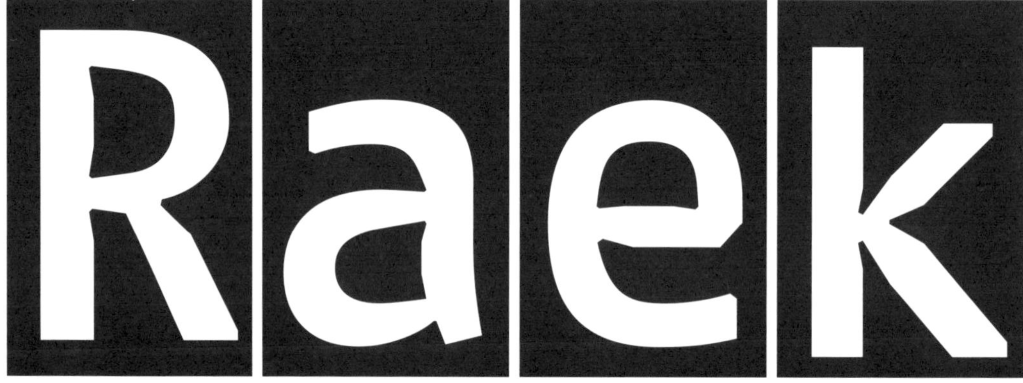

SARCASM AND INDIFFERENCE HAVE driven me from you. I sail for Europe with the next steamer. Shall I purchase

THAT PERFORMS WELL IN SMALL SIZES

HIGH & LOW: 2 X-HEIGHTS, ONE LETTER-WIDTH, FOR ANY EDITORIAL NEED

€ ⅜ + 6 £ ÷ ▼ × ¬ ↕ € ⑧ ? ⅓ ¢ % ⅖ × ® $ ¢ = = ÷

~ 1 € ← ▲ 7 € ¥ ¢ 5 ↘ 8 ▲ ↗ + 6 ❽ € + % ❹ ↖ ¬ ¢

¥ ½ > 5 0 ¥ 3 ↘ 4 × 3 ⅕ ¡ º ½ € ¶ 1 € 6 ¦ ÷ ¢ #

2 ↕ + ≠ ❶ ÷ → ↙ ❾ 6 ⓿ § = $ 5 ¥ ¢ 0 ¥ ⑥ % ▼ €

1 ⑦ $ ¢ = ¬ > ↙ 9 8 ^ % ÷ 1 ↙ + # 2 ¶ 5 0 7 * ¥

× ® % ⅔ ❺ ¢ $ < 3 ② ¥ # 3 ▲ ¾ ¢ 1 ⑦ ↕ + ≠ ⑨ 4 8

24 styles: High & Low / Roman, Narrow & Condensed / Light, Regular, **Medium & Bold** ←

Fine print, SMALL PRINT, or **'mouseprint'** is less noticeable print smaller than the more obvious larger print it accompanies that advertises or otherwise describes or partially describes a commercial product or service.[1] The larger print that is used in conjunction with fine print by the merchant often has the effect of deceiving the consumer into believing the offer is more advantageous than it really is, via a legal **technicality** which requires full disclosure of all (even unfavourable) terms or conditions, but does not specify the

About
Lipa Agate is part of a bigger type collection, comprising various type groups into one coherent system which Ermin developed over the past ten years. Lipa Agate is the first to be released; a sans serif designed and engineered to be used in the smallest text sizes, best under 10pt, and in very bad printing conditions. It is perfect for phone books, classified ads, directories or any other job requiring economy without jeopardizing legibility. To achieve this, Lipa Agate employs a range of tools, such as deep ink-traps, narrow proportions and a tall x-height.

Lipa Agate—with its three levels of condensation, four weights and two sets of different x-heights, "High" and "Low," which share the same width—fulfils these requirements wonderfully. That's a total of 24 fonts!

Design
Ermin Međedović
2014

Foundry
TypeTogether, Czech Republic
www.type-together.com

Styles / Weights
Three levels of condensation (Regular, Narrow, Condensed) in four weights (Light, Regular, Medium, Bold) with two sets of different x-heights (High, Low)

Language support
Latin

OpenType options
Tabular and Proportional Lining, Standard Ligatures, Discretionary Ligatures, All Caps, Small Caps, Capitals to Small Caps, Superscript, Subscript, Ordinals, Fractions, Alternative Fractions, Numerator, Denominator, Arrows, Stylistic Alternates, Stylistic Sets, Slashed Zero, Superior, Inferior

Optimized for web
Yes

HIGH REGULAR 18PT

abcdefghijklmnopqrstuvwxyzæfjåçéñöûß
ABCDEFGHIJKLMNOPQRSTUVWXYZÆÇØ
01234567890@.,-:;!?')]§*"" «» / –€$&⅓↗

HIGH BOLD & BOLD CONDENSED 30PT

aejgGQR7
aejgGQR7

HIGH BOLD & REGULAR 16PT

Typographers want amazing, exquisite
& clever justified text in books

LOW BOLD & LIGHT 9PT

→ **com·pen·dium** / noun / (pl. com·pen·dia / or com·pen·diums) a collection of facts, drawings and photographs on a particular subject, especially in a book: "a compendium of typography."

HIGH NARROW ALL WEIGHTS 14PT

Light
Regular
Medium
Bold

HIGH CONDENSED ALL WEIGHTS 14PT

Light
Regular
Medium
Bold

LUNCHBOX

A QUIRKY HAND DRAWN TYPE FAMILY

YOU SEE... THE THING ABOUT LUNCHBOX IS IT BRINGS A LOT TO THE TABLE

IT COMES IN SANS AND SLAB

LIGHT · REGULAR · BOLD

ALL CAPS · SMALL CAPS · lowercase

BUT WHAT'S COOLER... THERE ARE OVER 1,500 TOTAL CHARACTERS

THAT'S A LOT

HOW YOU SAY? HERE... LET'S BREAK IT DOWN

CONTEXTUAL ALTERNATIVES

BASICALLY GIVE EACH LETTER 4 DIFFERENT VERSIONS

HERE, LET'S TAKE A LOOK

AAAA BBBB CCCC

THIS TRICK IS SUPER DUPER HELPFUL WHEN A CHARCTER APPEARS MULTIPLE TIMES IN THE SAME WORD OR SENTENCE.

[which is pretty much always]

ADD SOME PIZZAZZ USING Stylistic Alternatives

HAVE SOME FUN WITH THESE Pretty Sweet Swashes

DISCRETIONARY LIGATURES!

FOR MOST COMMON LETTER COMBINATIONS, THESE SPECIALIZED LIGATURES GIVE USERS HEAPS OF CUSTOMIZABLE OPTIONS

SAY WHAT!?

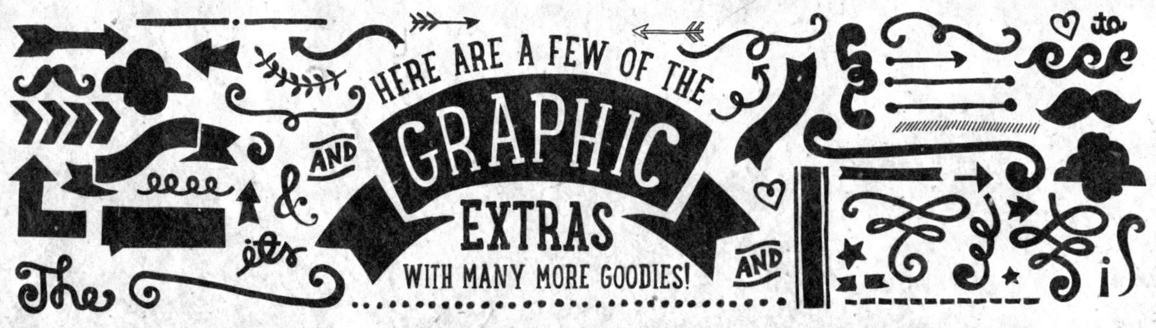

HERE ARE A FEW OF THE
GRAPHIC
EXTRAS
WITH MANY MORE GOODIES!
AND
&
AND
The
its
to

Lunchbox Family

About
LunchBox is a uniquely hand-drawn typeface that gives infinite customizable options and a fully authentic look. Using Lunchbox's Open-Type features gives access to over 1,500 different characters. Contextual alternatives give each letter four different character styles, all cycling through each other to ensure that no two letters ever show up together. There is also a custom set of small caps, each with four style variations as well. Stylistic alternates give an extra hand-drawn flourish, loop and slight variation, also with four different styles per letter. Discretionary ligatures pertain to both regular all caps Lunchbox as well as stylistic alternatives. It takes special letters and gives a unique interaction with the characters around them, giving your design a unique and personalized look. Swashes also have four style variations to both the regular and stylistic alternatives, as well as lowercase letters with ascenders and descenders.

Design
Kimmy Kirkwood
2013

Foundry
Kimmy Design, United States
www.kimmydesign.com

Styles / Weights
Light, Regular, Bold, Ornaments

Language support
Latin, Cyrillic, Greek, Armenian

OpenType options
Standard Ligatures, Discretionary Ligatures, All Caps, Small Caps, Capitals to Small Caps, Swashes, Contextual Swashes, Contextual Alternates, Contextual Ligatures, Fractions, Ornaments, Stylistic Alternates, Stylistic Sets, Slashed Zero

Optimized for web
Yes

SANS REGULAR 22PT

aabcdefghijklmnopqrstuvwxyzæfjåçéñöûß
AABCDEFGHIJKLMNOPQRSTUVWXYZÆÇØ
01234567890@.,-:;!?')]§*""«»/-€$&½

SLAB REGULAR 22PT

aabcdefghijklmnopqrstuvwxyzæfjåçéñöûß
AABCDEFGHIJKLMNOPQRSTUVWXYZÆÇØ
01234567890@.,-:;!?')]§*""«»/-€$&½

ORNAMENTS 30PT

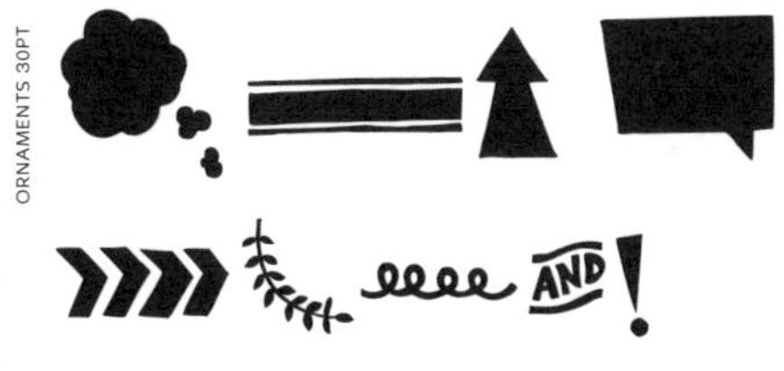

SANS BOLD & REGULAR 19PT

THE YEARBOOK OF TYPE
COMPENDIUM WORKS WELL AS
A TOOL IN VEXED TYPOGRAPHY
QUESTIONS FOR POLARIZING JOBS

Una donna nella luna è un melodramma fanta-scientifico e un film muto

---

du directeur Fritz Lang, adapté du roman de sa femme Thea von Harbou.

It is often considered to be one of the first serious science fiction films.

Filmen *Frau im Mond* hade världspremiär den 5 oktober 1929 i Berlin.

♡

Lunica

Lunica

About
Lunica is a single line weight serif font available in four styles: Thin, Light, Regular and Medium. Inspired by the basic letterforms of the cinema subtitles he grew familiar with during his years in Stockholm, the designer was compelled to add serifs to reflect the charm of the Swedish language. The serifs are abstracted with a geometric quarter circle leading to a highly individual typeface with poetic character. Nonetheless, Lunica offers great readability at small sizes.

Design
Thomas Hirter
2014

Foundry
Gestalten, Germany
www.gestaltenfonts.com

Styles / Weights
Thin, Light, Regular, Medium

Language support
Latin

OpenType options
Proportional Oldstyle, Tabular and Proportional Lining, Tabular Oldstyle, Superscript, Ordinals, Fractions

Optimized for web
No

REGULAR 18PT

abcdefghijklmnopqrstuvwxyzæfjåçéñöûß
ABCDEFGHIJKLMNOPQRSTUVWXYZÆÇØ
0123456789@.,-:;!?')]§*""«»/–€$&½♡

MEDIUM 36PT

aejgGQR7

MEDIUM & LIGHT 13PT

The Yearbook of Type compendium works well as
a tool in vexed typography questions for polarizing jobs

LIGHT 36PT

aejgGQR7

MEDIUM & LIGHT 9PT

ar·chive / noun / a collection of documents such as letters, photographs or other material: the Yearbook of Type is an archive of contemporary typefaces from all over the world

Luxus Brut
Sparkling

Drinks

Hors d'œuvre

Anzüge nach Maß
Modefrisuren für Sie und Ihn
Künstlerbedarf

Luxus Brut Sparkling

phospho

Script, Display

About
The story behind this font began back in 2001, when Roland Hörmann moved into the neighborhood of an abandoned book binding workshop in Vienna. His fascination for their ancienthand-painted shop sign lead to the release of a formal script font named Luxus Brut in 2009, drawing its wide spaced letterforms with low x-height and distinctive capital letters from the original signage. Five years later, sketches for a bolder version ended in a complete rework of the typeface. Slightly tightened spacing, emphasized stroke contrast and lowered cap height allow the new release for a broader range of use. Luxus Brut Sparkling now also offers an extended array of glyph shape variants, accessible via two Stylistic Sets as well as automated contextual substitution.

Design
Roland Hörmann
2014

Foundry
phospho, Austria
www.phospho.at

Styles / Weights
Regular

Language support
Latin

OpenType options
Standard Ligatures, Discretionary Ligatures, Superscript, Subscript, Contextual Swashes, Fractions, Numerator, Denominator, Stylistic Alternates, Stylistic Sets, Localized Forms, Terminal Form, Initial Form

Optimized for web
No

REGULAR 18PT

abcdefghijklmnopqrstuvwxyzæfjàçéñöüß

ABCDEFGHIJKLMNOPQRSTUVWXYZÆÇØ

0123456789@.,-:;!?)]§*"" «»/–€$&

REGULAR 36 PT

aejgGQR

REGULAR 30 PT

Typographers want amazing, exquisite & clever justified text in books

CAFÉ-AU-LAITMACULA

YELLOW

BEDEUTET FLECK

MANCHA

SITUÉE AU FOND DE L'ŒIL

THE HUMAN EYE

RETINA

XANTHOPHYLL CAROTENOIDS

PHOTORECEPTORS

FOVEOLA

BLINDE VLEKJE

About
Macula can be described as the "impossible typeface," since its design is based on the concept of impossible objects. This optical illusion was explored in great detail in the 1930s by the Swedish artist Oscar Reutersvärd, and simultaneously made very famous by Dutch artist M.C. Escher. Every character in Macula has been designed in two versions, and to enhance typographic liveliness, these two versions are alternated automatically by OpenType features. Macula comes in five styles—some are great to use just by themselves and some are specifically meant for use in layers. By stacking different styles of Macula on top of each other, multicolored (impossible) typography becomes possible.

Design
Jacques Le Bailly
2013

Foundry
Bold Monday, The Netherlands
www.boldmonday.com

Styles / Weights
Line, Solid, Shaded, Background, Shading

Language support
Latin

OpenType options
Superscript, Ordinals, Contextual Alternates, Fractions, Stylistic Sets

Optimized for web
Yes

SOLID 16PT

ABCDEFGHIJKLMNOPQRSTUVWXYZ
ÆÅÇÉÑÖÛ
0123456789@.,-:;!?')*“”«»/—€$&½

LINE 28PT

BACKGROUND & SHADING 13PT

TYPOGRAPHERS WANT
AMAZING, EXQUISITE
& CLEVER JUSTIFIED
TEXT IN BOOKS

SHADED 28PT

LINE 13PT

TYPOGRAPHERS WANT
AMAZING, EXQUISITE
& CLEVER JUSTIFIED
TEXT IN BOOKS

Azienda Vinicola

Prädikatswein

Fill your life with friends and your glass with wine

Petit Château

CASA LUIGI

Wine is poetry in a bottle

Baguette

TAFELWEIN

I cook with wine, sometimes I even add it to the food.

Tartufo Bianco

ZOPF

Magnum Sans Pro

About
Magnum Sans Pro is a strong neutral sans serif consisting of eleven weights with true Italic, Oblique and an alt upright set called Alfa. The definition of Magnum is a large wine bottle that's twice the capacity of one 750 ml bottle. Today, the name is used in any product offering double the capacity, and Magnum Sans achieves this by offering two slanted and two upright versions plus a standard and pro set.

Designed to be highly readable, Magnum Sans Pro is ideal for text, signage, headlines and media broadcasting or anywhere else that requires quick readable lettering. With the stylistic alternates and swash caps, you can expand your creativity in logo designing. Sprinkle in an alternate letter or two to create a dynamic appeal that's sure to get attention in advertising.

This Pro set includes additional language support for Vietnamese, Pin Yin and Greek.

Design
Michael Hagemann
2014

Foundry
FontMesa LLC, USA
www.fontmesa.com

Styles / Weights
Family of two slanted and two upright versions and a standard and pro set in eleven weights (Thin, Extralight, Light, Regular, Medium, Semi Bold, Bold, Heavy, Black, Extra Black, Extra Bold), each with Italics, Oblique and Alfa versions

Language support
Latin, Greek, Vietnamese, Pin Yin

OpenType options
Proportional Oldstyle, Tabular Lining, Prop. Lining, Tabular Oldstyle, Standard Ligatures, Discretionary Lig., Superscript, Subscript, Ordinals, Swashes, All Alternates, Fractions, Alternative Fractions, Numerator, Denominator, Arrows, Stylistic Alt., Stylistic Sets, Slashed Zero, Scientific Inferiors, Case Sensitive Forms

Optimized for web
Yes

REGULAR 16PT

aabcdefgghijklmnopqrstuvwxyyzæfjåçéñöûß
ABCDEFGHIJKLMNOPQRSTUVWXYZÆÇØ
01234567890@.,-:;!?')]§*“”«»/–€$&⅓↗

ALFA HEAVY 32PT

aejgGQR7

ALFA BOLD & LIGHT 12PT

The Yearbook of Type compendium works well as a tool in vexed typography questions for polarizing jobs

THIN 32PT

aejgGQR7

BOLD & REGULAR 9PT

→ **cata·logue** / noun / a complete list of things that people can look at or buy: *a catalogue of typefaces (a book showing the newest fonts, to help people choose the right typeface)*

Overbearing advertising,
god of consumerism,
and all your crooked pictures,
looking good, mirrorism,
filtering information,
for the public eye,
designed for profiteering ...

System of a Down

Randglovies
Randglovies
Randglovies
Randglovies
Randglovies
Randglovies
Randglovies
Randglovies
Randglovies
Randglovies
Randglovies

PTL Magsans by Ole Schaefer 2015 for primetype.com

About
PTL Magsans is a text typeface family, originally designed for a magazine. The latest version is redesigned and extended for all purposes of reading.

Design
Ole Schäfer
2015

Foundry
primetype GmbH, Germany
www.primetype.de

Styles / Weights
Thin, Thin Italic, Extralight, Extralight Italic, Light, Light Italic, Regular, Italic, Book, Book Italic, Medium, Medium Italic, Semi Bold, Semi Bold Italic, Bold, Bold Italic, Heavy, Heavy Italic, Black, Black Italic, Ultra, Ultra Italic

Language support
Latin, Latin Extended

OpenType options
Proportional Oldstyle, Tabular and Proportional Lining, Tabular Oldstyle, Small Caps

Optimized for web
Yes

BOOK 18PT

abcdefghijklmnopqrstuvwxyzæfjß
ABCDEFGHIJKLMNOPQRSTUVWXYZÆØ
0123456789@.,-:;!?')]§*“”«»/–€$&½

BOLD & BOOK 36PT

aejgGQR7
aejgGQR7

BOLD & THIN 16PT

Typographers want amazing, exquisite
& clever justified text in books

BLACK & LIGHT 9PT

Year·book of Type / noun / book published every second year, giving details on typefaces of the previous two years and also about general current typographic topics–*e.g. OpenType features, font editors like Glyphs etc.*

ULTRA & BOOK 16PT

Typographers want amazing, exquisite
& clever justified text in books

Maja*

(pronounced My-ya)

A bright, bubbly display and text type. Young, fresh and informal!

Distinctively warm, soft and rounded shapes with assured and fluent lines. A typeface full of punchy personality.

---

*Maja is popular name in: Sweden, Slovenia, Serbia, Macedonia, Poland, Croatia and Albania.

FS Maja

About
Fontsmith received the brief to develop a font that would form part of the broadcast identity for the UK's first digital Freeview channel—E4. It needed to work seamlessly in text and display, both in print and on-screen, and please the eye of the target audience, 18–34-year-olds. So, young, fresh and informal.

FS Maja's soft, rounded shapes and assured, fluent lines encompass lots of notable features that contribute to its warm, fun-loving personality, including: a very large x-height; a short, rounded serif to allow for close spacing and give texture to body text; a slight convexity, or bulge, in the stroke terminals; a calligraphic fluidity in the entry to the down-stroke of most lowercase letters; open, generous curves, especially in the "B," "P" and "R"; and a "w" made of two "u"s.

Design
Jason Smith
2013

Foundry
Fontsmith, Great Britain
www.fontsmith.com

Styles / Weights
Regular, Italic, Bold, Bold Italic

Language support
Latin

OpenType options
Tabular Lining, Discretionary Ligatures, Fractions

Optimized for web
Yes

REGULAR 18PT
abcdefghijklmnopqrstuvwxyzæfjåçéñöûß
ABCDEFGHIJKLMNOPQRSTUVWXYZÆÇØ
0123456789@.,-:;!?')]§*“”«»/–€$&½

BOLD 30PT
aejgGQR7

BOLD REGULAR 14PT
Typographers want
amazing, exquisite
& clever justified text
in books

REGULAR 30PT
aejgGQR7

BOLD & REGULAR 8PT
ex·am·ple / *noun* / an illustration that supports or provides more information: *by showing examples the Yearbook of Type presents each font in different sizes and weights*

hello ⟨world⟩

→ subscribe online ←

gadget guide

⑥Export ❼Office ⑤Import

$C_4H_6O_5$ & H_2O

formular$^{(4+5=9)}$

mail@somepeople

new ***keywords***

About
Mantika Book was designed as a companion serif typeface to Mantika Sans that can be set for lengthy like those in books. It shares the same x-height with Mantika Sans but has longer ascenders and descenders, making for better word shapes in long, continuous reading. The approach of an "old-style" looking typeface with large minuscules makes Mantika Book also a choice for magazine text settings where one often needs smaller point sizes to fit in a multiple columns layout. The unique details of Mantika Book are the assymmetric bracketed serifs and its higher stroke contrast which is not likely to be found in a Renaissance style. The stems are slightly curved inwards. The Italic has a low degree of inclination, which makes longer passages of text set in Italic rather pleasing to read. The regular weight has small caps. There is a kind of an old-style feeling to Mantika Book, yet these citations from the past were turned into a contemporary serif typeface with a soft but sturdy character.

Design
Jürgen Weltin
2014

Foundry
Monotype, USA
www.monotype.com

Styles / Weights
Regular, Italic, Bold, Bold Italic

Language support
Latin

OpenType options
Proportional Oldstyle, Tabular and Proportional Lining, Tabular Oldstyle, Standard Ligatures, Discretionary Ligatures, Superscript, Subscript, Ordinals, Fractions, Numerator, Denominator, Arrows, Stylistic Alternates, Stylistic Sets, Localized Forms

Optimized for web
Yes

REGULAR 16PT

abcdefghijklmnopqrstuvwxyzæfjåçéñöûß
ABCDEFGHIJKLMNOPQRSTUVWXYZÆÇØ
0123456789@.,-:;!?')]§*"" «»/–€$&⅓ ↗

BOLD 35PT

aejGQR7

BOLD & REGULAR 16PT

Typographers want
amazing, exquisite
& clever justified text
in books

BOLD & REGULAR 12PT

The Yearbook of Type
compendium works well as
a tool in vexed typography
questions for polarizing jobs

BOLD & REGULAR 8PT

→ **ref·er·ence book** / *noun* / a book that contains facts and information that you look at when you need to find out sth. particular—*"I am looking for the right typeface for my project, so I use the Yearbook of Type as a reference book."*

P22
Marcel
Mes chères petites
Kontroleret
CENSOR
CONTROLE
3
LUFTPOST
PAR AVION
VERIFICATO PER CENSURA
OPENED BY EXAMINER
PASSED BY
CENSURA DE GUERRA

P22 Marcel Pro

About

The multi-award winning font Marcel is named in honor of Marcel Heuzé, a Frenchman who was conscripted into labor during World War II. During the months Marcel was in Germany, he wrote letters to his beloved wife and daughters back home in rural France. Marcel's letters contain rare first-person testimony of day-to-day survival in a labor camp, along with the most beautiful expressions of love imaginable. The letters—stained and scarred with censor marks—were the original source documents used to create this script font.

As a result of years of research and design work, Marcel Script features more than 1,300 glyphs. The font is a highly readable running script that includes textural details that capture the look of ink on paper. The font Marcel Caps is a hand-lettered titling face intended as a companion to the Script. Marcel EuroPost features more than 200 postmarks, cancellation and censor marks, and other embellishments found on historical letters and documents.

Design
Carolyn Porter
2014

Foundry
P22 Type Foundry, USA
www.p22.com

Styles / Weights
Script, Euro Post One, Euro Post Two, Caps, Ornament

Language support
Latin

OpenType options
Standard Ligatures, Discretionary Ligatures, All Caps, Swashes, Contextual Swashes, Contextual Alternates, Contextual Ligatures, Stylistic Alternates

Optimized for web
Yes

SCRIPT 20PT

abcdefghijklmnopqrstuvwxyzæffjàçéñöüß
ABCDEFGHIJKLMNOPQRSTUVWXYZÆÇØ
0123456789@.,-:;!?')]$*“”«»/–€$%½

EURO POST ONE & TWO 40PT

CAPS 19PT

TYPOGRAPHERS WANT AMAZING, EXQUISITE & CLEVER JUSTIFIED TEXT IN BOOKS

ORNAMENTS 9PT

SCRIPT 16PT

The Yearbook of Type compendium works well as a tool in vexed typography questions for polarizing jobs

99 Luftballons

Infrastruktur

Autobahn

Begrüßungsgeld

Federweißer

Pünktlichkeit

Dieter Rams

FF Mark

About
New meets old meets technic: FF Mark is not an average geometric sans. Born from the idea of creating an up-to-date typeface rooted in 1920s German geometry, FF Mark is a special project, as it is a self-initiated collaboration between Hannes von Döhren, FontFont's very own Christoph Koeberlin, and the entire FontFont Type Department.

This distinctive typeface was designed with the creative support no less than Erik Spiekermann, they designed a distinctive typeface: FF Mark is strong, simple and bold in form and at a glance may appear to be typical of its predecessors. On closer inspection, letter shapes are wider, letter proportions are better balanced and the x-height is uncharacteristically "normal" or higher, which increases its versatility tremendously.

With carefully crafted diacritics, extensive kerning, consistent stroke endings and a sizeable contemporary character set, FF Mark has been developed with the intention to be expressed across a wide range of applications.

See also: *www.ffmark.com*

Design
Christoph Koeberlin, Hannes von Döhren
2013

Foundry
FontFont, Germany
www.fontfont.com

Styles / Weights
Hairline, Thin, Extra Light, Light, Regular, Book, Medium, Bold, Heavy, Black, each with Italics

Language support
Latin

OpenType options
Proportional Oldstyle, Tabular and Prop. Lining, Tabular Oldstyle, Standard Ligatures, Discretionary Lig., Historical Ligatures, Small Caps, Capitals to Small Caps, Superscript, Subscript, Ordinals, Fractions, Numerator, Denominator, Ornaments, Arrows, Stylistic Alternates, Stylistic Sets, Historical Forms, Slashed Zero, Case Sensitive Forms, Capital Spacing, Scientific Inferiors, Alt. Annotation Forms

Optimized for web
Yes

REGULAR 16PT

aabcdefghijklmnopqrstuvwxyzæfjåçéñöûß
ABCDEFGHIJKLMNOPQRSTUVWXYZÆÇØ
01234567890@.,-:;!?')]§*""«»/–€$&⅓♥↗

BOLD 32PT

aejgGQR7

BOLD & BOOK 16PT

Typographers want
amazing, exquisite
& clever justified text
in books

BLACK & LIGHT 8PT

→ **Year·book of Type** / *noun* / book published every second year, giving details on typefaces of the previous two years and also about general current typographic topics—*e.g. OpenType features, font editors like Glyphs etc.*

ALL WEIGHTS 8PT

Thin
Extra Light
Light
Regular
Book
Medium
Bold
Heavy
Black

ITALICS 8PT

Thin Italic
Extra Light Italic
Light Italic
Italic
Book Italic
Medium Italic
Bold Italic
Heavy Italic
Black Italic

Egg in — a box*

Royal Festival Hall Southbank, SE1 8XX

Inaugurated: 3 May 1951

London's Southbank is full of interest. The Royal Festival hall is exceptional and a great example of compelling architecture. Built by Sir Robert Hogg Matthew as part of the post-war reconstruction of Greater London on the Festival of Britain's South Bank site, the hall has foyers beneath and to either side that are all connected by stairwells. *Subsequently it became known as the 'egg in a box'.*

FS Matthew

About

Not for the first time, Fontsmith was commissioned to develop a font for one of the UK's terrestrial TV channels. The product was a clearly-defined three-weight family. When italics were added, it became FS Matthew, a clean, stylish, structured sans serif with swooping, open curves and a bright, lively personality.

Inspiration for many of the forms of FS Matthew came from details found within the modernist buildings and architecture of London's Southbank, such as the Royal Festival Hall. During the font's gestation, Jason had found himself at London Studios, a TV studio on Southbank, and a wander around the neighboring arts buildings proved thought-provoking. The result was a font with a very British character: solid forms that provide the platform for innovation and distinctiveness. FS Matthew's trademark is efficiency with a feel good factor: disciplined enough for corporate identities, websites and signing systems, and colorful enough for logotypes and advertising.

Design
Jason Smith
2013

Foundry
Fontsmith, Great Britain
www.fontsmith.com

Styles / Weights
Light, Light Italic, Regular, Italic, Medium, Medium Italic, Bold, Bold Italic

Language support
Latin

OpenType options
Tabular Lining, Standard Ligatures, Fractions

Optimized for web
Yes

REGULAR 18PT

abcdefghijklmnopqrstuvwxyzæfjåçéñöûß
ABCDEFGHIJKLMNOPQRSTUVWXYZÆÇØ
0123456789@.,-:;!?')]§*“”«»/–€$&½

REGULAR 36PT

aejgGQR7

BOLD & REGULAR 16PT

Typographers want
amazing, exquisite
& clever justified text
in books

BOLD & REGULAR 9PT

cata·logue / *noun* / a complete list of things that people can look at or buy: *a catalogue of typefaces (a book showing the newest fonts, to help people choose the right typeface)*

MEDIUM & LIGHT 14PT

The Yearbook of Type
compendium works well as
a tool in vexed typography
questions for polarizing jobs

FS Millbank

Crafted for clarity
brimming with personality

Accessible

Versatile

Rhythmic

Economical

Informative

Distinctive

Approachable

Legible

About

When designer Stuart de Rozario surveyed the fonts used in signage on London's public trans-port systems, he reached a dead end. They seemed staid, sterile, lacking in personality, and ill-suited to be used by modern brands.

Stuart decided to create FS Millbank: "The driving force behind my thoughts was to design something more current and fresh without compromising legibility and clarity. A font with both personality and function, that's versatile at large and small sizes and effortless to read."

Reading signs is different to reading a book or a newspaper. Text on signs needs to be deciphered quickly and effortlessly. Legibility criteria for signage letterforms are also different to those for normal reading. Characters have been given features for extra definition.

FS Millbank provides the solution whenever optimum clarity is absolutely essential. The overall result is a font with a distinct beauty. It flows exquisitely, is defiantly human and brimming with personality.

Design
Stuart de Rozario
2014

Foundry
Fontsmith, Great Britain
www.fontsmith.com

Styles / Weights
Light, Light Italic, Regular, Italic, Bold, Bold Italic, Heavy, Heavy Italic

Language support
Latin

OpenType options
Proportional Oldstyle, Tabular and Proportional Lining, Tabular Oldstyle, Standard Ligatures, Discretionary Ligatures, All Caps, Fractions, Arrows

Optimized for web
Yes

REGULAR 18PT

abcdefghijklmnopqrstuvwxyzæfjåçéñöûß
ABCDEFGHIJKLMNOPQRSTUVWXYZÆÇØ
0123456789@.,-:;!?')]§*"”«»/–€$&½↗

BOLD 36PT

aejgGQR7

HEAVY & LIGHT 14PT

Typographers want
amazing, exquisite
& clever justified text
in books

LIGHT 36PT

aejgGQR7

ALL WEIGHTS 12PT

Light
Regular
Bold
Heavy

ITALICS 12PT

Light Italic
Italic
Bold Italic
Heavy Italic

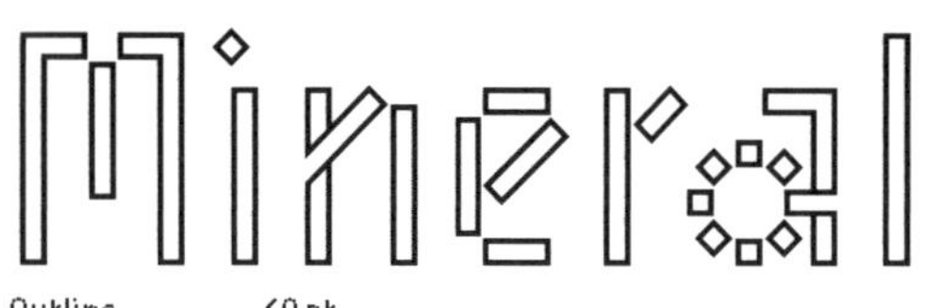 is a naturally occurring

Outline 60 pt Solid 21 pt

substance that is solid and stable

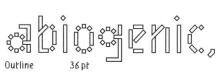

36 pt 21 pt Border 36 pt

at room temperature, representable

Blunt 24 pt

by a chemical formula, usually abiogenic,

14 pt 36 pt 14 pt Outline 36 pt

and has an ordered atomic structure.

Border 21 pt Solid

It is different from a rock, which can

Blunt 36 pt 21 pt Outline 36 pt Blunt 21 pt

be an aggregate of minerals or non-minerals and does not have a

Smooth 14 pt

specific chemical composition.

32 pt

The exact definition of a mineral is under debate,

14 pt Border 24 pt Smooth 14 pt Blunt 24 pt

especially with respect to the requirement a valid species be abiogenic,

11 pt Outline 24 pt Blunt 11 pt

and to a lesser extent with regards to it having

18 pt 32 pt 18 pt

an ordered atomic structure.

Solid Border 36 pt

document line spacing: 44 pt

source: en.wikipedia.org/wiki/Mineral

www.bb-bureau.fr www.volcano-type.de

Outline 48 pt

Tetragonal type and derivative

Solid 14 pt

Solid, Border, Outline, Blunt & Smooth 7 pt

About
Mineral is a glittering font, fractured into multiple tetragonal splinters, rectangular modules slightly spaced, like quartz and pixels. A Kapla style construction, with stencil properties—Solid version—however offers a great readability to the font. Mineral Solid has four stylistic titling alternatives: Border, Outline, Smooth and Blunt.

Design
Benoît Bodhuin
2013

Foundry
VolcanoType, Germany
www.volcano-type.de

Styles / Weights
Solid, Outline, Border, Blunt, Smooth

Language support
Latin

OpenType options
Standard Ligatures

Optimized for web
No

BLUNT 18PT

abcdefghijklmnopqrstuvwxyzæfjäçéñöûß
ABCDEFGHIJKLMNOPQRSTUVWXYZÆÇØ
0123456789@.,-:;!?')]§*"""«»/–€$&

BORDER 18PT

abcdefghijklmnopqrstuvwxyzæfjäçéñöûß
ABCDEFGHIJKLMNOPQRSTUVWXYZÆÇØ
0123456789@.,-:;!?')]§*"""«»/–€$&

OUTLINE & SMOOTH 36PT

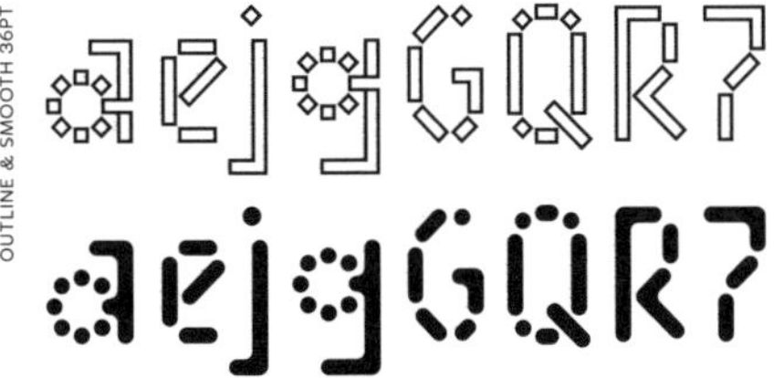

SOLID & OUTLINE 16PT

Typographers want
amazing, exquisite
& clever justified
text in books *

Geomythology Bile
Katawa-Guruma
Chibaiskweda Kirin
Theriocephalus
Corycian nymphs
Warg Yatagarasu
Chinese Dragon
Horned Serpent
Greek Mythology
Hind Ceryneian
Pendragon Eetion
Ponaturi Undead
Three-Legged Bird

About
How does one reference Cubism in a typeface? The most obvious tack would be to disassemble each letter and render it broken. That might produce something interesting to look at, but not something that can be used. Minotaur Serif and Sans is a practical family of straight lines inspired by the Cubist movement. Its roots are Venus, a landmark Grotesque from the era that gave rise to Cubism, and two serif models: Bruce's Scotch Roman and A. V. Hershey's series for early vector-based computing. Not only are the letters' outlines atypical, but their set number of widths, derived from historical technical limitations, play with expectations. Despite their seemingly primitive restraints, these fonts are legible at any size and have their own beauty: Minotaur Serif, in particular, balances its harsh contours with the elegant skeleton of its early 20th century model. Minotaur offers a richness not found in most type; one that rewards viewers in new ways as they step closer to the canvas.

Design
Jean-Baptiste Levée
2014

Foundry
Production Type, France
www.productiontype.com

Styles / Weights
Family of three styles (Sans, Serif, Beef), Sans and Serif each in three weights (Light, Regular, Bold), each with Italics

Language support
Latin

OpenType options
Proportional Oldstyle, Tabular and Proportional Lining, Tabular Oldstyle, Standard Ligatures, Discretionary Ligatures, Historical Ligatures, All Caps, Superscript, Subscript, Ordinals, Swashes, All Alternates, Contextual Alternates, Contextual Ligatures, Fractions, Numerator, Denominator, Ornaments, Arrows, Stylistic Alternates, Stylistic Sets, Historical Forms, Slashed Zero

Optimized for web
Yes

SANS REGULAR 15PT

abcdefghiijklmnopqrstuvwxyzæfjåçéñöûß
AABCDEFGHIJKLMNOPQRSTUVWXYZÆÇØ
0123456789ø@.,-:;!?')]§*“”«»/–€$&½♡↗

BEEF BOLD 30PT

aejgGQR7

SERIF BOLD & LIGHT 14PT

Typographers want
amazing, exquisite
and clever justified text
in books ♡

SANS LIGHT 30PT

aejgGQR7

SANS BOLD & LIGHT 9PT

▸ **ar·chive** / *noun* / a collection of documents such as letters, photographs or other material: *the Yearbook of Type is an archive of contemporary typefaces from all over the world*

Møñitêurs
Møñitêurs
Møñitêurs
Møñitêurs
Møñitêurs

Museen sind ein guter Ort, wenn die Besichtigung der Gegenwart ans Unerträgliche grenzt.

Development

Identity
Information
Digital

Gateways
Shengen
1234567890

↓ News

About
We developed the first version of Monico in 1994 for the design company Moniteurs, which was launched at the same time as xplicit. As a customized modification of the Mac monospaced font Monaco, we equipped them with a proportional character set, minuscule digits and a distinctive bold weight. In the course of technical development, the font experienced many an update. For their (and our) 20th anniversary, the Berlin office for CI and Information Design presented them with a completely newly designed Monico with five weights, from Thin to Bold, which was first used as the web font for the new Moniteurs website. xplicit partner Alexander Branczyk drew the curves, while the finish was developed in collaboration with Georg Seifert, of course using his font editor Glyphs.

Design
Alexander Branczyk
2014

Foundry
czyk, Germany
www.xplicit.de

Styles / Weights
Thin, Light, Regular, Medium, Bold

Language support
Latin, Greek

OpenType options
Proportional Oldstyle, Standard Ligatures, Historical Ligatures, Arrows, Stylistic Alternates

Optimized for web
Yes

czyk

REGULAR 18PT

abcdefghijklmnopqrstuvwxyʒæfjåçéñöûß
ABCDEFGHIJKLMNOPQRSTUVWXYZÆÇØ
0123456789@.,-:;!?')]§*“”«»/–€$&→

BOLD & MEDIUM 30PT

aejgGQR7
aejgGQR7

BOLD & THIN 16PT

Typographers want amaʒing, exquisite & clever justified text in books

REGULAR & LIGHT 30PT

aejgGQR7
aejgGQR7

MEDIUM & LIGHT 14PT

The Yearbook of Type compendium works well as a tool in vexed typography questions for polariʒing jobs

Monico

PAULY
RAIN
BEAUTY
HUGE
CLEAN
GOLD
JINNY
GULF
SUNDAE
NOURISH

FONTFABRIC

About
The very first Muller sketches were made about four years ago. During this process they changed so much that they no longer resembled the original idea. As it is with most work we do, when we seek perfection, changes are inevitable.

It was specifically designed with a wider structure for better appearance in small sizes and the extra attention to detail was needed for the big sizes. We managed to find the right balance for the perfect universal font family.

The family consists of 20 weights, ranging from Thin to Heavy with matching Italics. This font family is suited for everything, ranging from advertising, packaging, editorial and branding, to web and screen projects.

Muller comes with a complete range of figure options, including proportional and old style figures, each in its tabular version. It also includes advanced typographic features such as ligatures, fractions, alternate characters, case-sensitive forms, superscripts and subscripts.

Design
Radomir Tinkov
2015

Foundry
Fontfabric, Bulgaria
www.fontfabric.com

Styles / Weights
Hairline, Thin, UltraLight, Light, Regular, Medium, Bold, ExtraBold, Black, Heavy, each with Italics

Language support
Latin, Cyrillic

OpenType options
Proportional Oldstyle, Tabular and Proportional Lining, Tabular Oldstyle, Standard Ligatures, Discretionary Ligatures, Superscript, Subscript, Titling Alternates, Fractions, Numerator, Denominator, Stylistic Alternates, Stylistic Sets, Localized Forms

Optimized for web
Yes

REGULAR 17PT

aabcdefghijklmnopqrstuvwxyyzæfjåçéñöûß
ABCDEFGHIJKLMNOPQRSTUVWXYZÆÇØ
0123456789@.,-:;!?')]§*""«»/–€$&½

BLACK 32PT

aejgGQR7

MEDIUM & LIGHT 16PT

Typographers want
amazing, exquisite
& clever justified text
in books

BLACK & LIGHT 8PT

Year·book of Type / *noun* / book published every second year, giving details on typefaces of the previous two years and also about general current typographic topics—*e.g. OpenType features, font editors like Glyphs etc.*

ALL WEIGHTS 8PT

Hairline
Thin
UltraLight
Light
Regular
Medium
Bold
ExtraBold
Black
Heavy

ITALICS 8PT

Hairline Italic
Thin Italic
UltraLight Italic
Light Italic
Italic
Medium Italic
Bold Italic
ExtraBold Italic
Black Italic
Heavy Italic

About
Multi is a sans serif typeface family designed for editorial design on paper and screen, available in two series: Multi Display and Multi Text. Multi Display consists of seven roman weights with their italics: Thin, Light, Regular, Medium, Bold, ExtraBold, and Poster. Multi Text consists of three Roman weights with their Italics: Regular, SemiBold and Bold. All were manually hinted and optimized as webfonts. All the fonts comprise special characters designed for specific languages requirements. Their design intends to match specific emotional attributes: warmth, dynamism, optimism, contemporary, human ... Its main purpose is to bring a fresh and strong personality to printed and online publications.

Design
Laura Meseguer
2015

Foundry
Type-Ø-Tones, Spain
www.type-o-tones.com

Styles / Weights
Family of two styles, Multi Display with seven weights (Thin, Light, Regular, Medium, Bold, ExtraBold, Poster), each with Italics and Multi Text with three weights (Regular, SemiBold, Bold), each with Italics

Language support
Latin

OpenType options
Tabular and Proportional Lining, Standard Ligatures, Superscript, Ordinals, Fractions, Stylistic Alternates, Stylistic Sets, Localized Forms, Optical size

Optimized for web
Yes

MULTI TEXT REGULAR 16PT

abcdefghijklmnopqrstuvwxyzæfjåçéñöûß
ABCDEFGHIJKLMNOPQRSTUVWXYZÆÇØ
0123456789@.,-:;!?')]§*“”«»/–€$&½

MULT IDISPLAY BOLD 30PT

aejgGQR7

MULTI DISPLAY POSTER & MEDIUM 12PT

The Yearbook of Type
compendium works well as
a tool in vexed typography
questions for polarizing jobs

MULTI TEXT BOLD & REGULAR 9PT

cata·logue / *noun* / a complete list of things that people can look at or buy: *a catalogue of typefaces (a book showing the newest fonts, to help people choose the right typeface)*

MULTI DISPLAY ALL WEIGHTS 7PT

Thin
Thin Italic
Light
Light Italic
Regular
Regular Italic
Medium
Medium Italic
Bold
Bold Italic
ExtraBold
ExtraBold Italic
Poster
PosterItalic

MULTI TEXT ALL WEIGHTS 7PT

Regular
Regular Italic
SemiBold
SemiBold Italic
Bold
Bold Italic

VON BAD RADKERSBURG BIS BAD AUSSEE

Steirische Weinstraße

47° 36′ **N**, 15° 40′ **O**

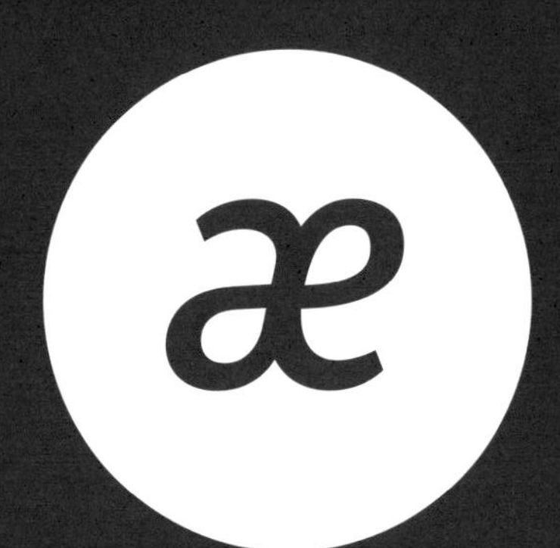

Schoeller Bleckmann Stahlwerke AG ↳ 1924

Metaalbewerking

Gipfeltreffen

agy ⤜ agy
agy* ⤜ *agy

effective office

Kurfürstendamm

Joseph mag's!

Apfelspatzn & Kürbiskernöl

About
Styrian rooted and with a name dedicated to a region with soft rocks, forested mountains, narrow valleys and clear air, Muriza is a modest slab serif with tempting curves: Its clear and economic typography linked to peculiarly shapes—like curved spurs instead of serifs—combines well working normalcy with refreshing uniqueness.

With a range of nine well graduated weights—from delicate Hairline to sturdy Black—and a conventional but distinctive italic, Muriza can fulfill almost every typographic wish until it is related to a sober design. Furthermore, OpenType layout features like Oldstyle figures, Small Caps and Stylistic Alternates or dingbats and arrows are included as well as an extended language support with most Latin-based scripts supported.

Design
Jakob Runge, Jürgen Schwarz
2014

Foundry
type me! fonts, Germany
www.typemefonts.com

Styles / Weights
Hairline, Hairline Italic, Thin, Thin Italic, Light, Light Italic, Regular, Italic, Medium, Medium Italic, SemiBold, SemiBold Italic, Bold, Bold Italic, ExtraBold, ExtraBold Italic, Black, Black Italic

Language support
Latin

OpenType options
Proportional Oldstyle, Tabular and Proportional Lining, Tabular Oldstyle, All Caps, Small Caps, Capitals to Small Caps, Superscript, Subscript, Ordinals, Fractions, Numerator, Denominator, Ornaments, Arrows, Stylistic Alternates, Stylistic Sets, Slashed Zero, Localized Forms

Optimized for web
No

REGULAR 18PT

aɑbcdefgghijklmnopqrstuvwxyyzæfjåçéñöûß
ABCDEFGHIJKLMNOPQRSTUVWXYZÆÇØ
0123456789ø@.,-:;!?’)]§*“”«»/–€$&⅓☞⇒→

REGULAR 36PT

aejgGQR7

SEMIBOLD & REGULAR 16PT

Typographers want
amazing, exquisite
& clever justified text
in books ☆

MEDIUM & LIGHT 9PT

ref·er·ence book / *noun* / a book that contains facts and information that you look at when you need to find out sth. particular—*“I am looking for the right typeface for my project, so I use the Yearbook of Type as a reference book.”*

ALL WEIGHTS 9PT

Hairline
Thin
Light
Regular
Medium
SemiBold
Bold
Extrabold
Black

ITALICS, ALL WEIGHTS 9PT

Hairline Italic
Thin Italic
Light Italic
Regular Italic
Medium Italic
SemiBold Italic
Bold Italic
ExtraBold Italic
Black Italic

If I had

I'd try to make **more mistakes** next time.

I would **relaxe.**

I would **be sillier** than I have been this trip.

I know of **very few things** I would **take seriously.**

I would take **more chances.**

my life

I would take **more trips.**

I would climb **more mountains, swim more rivers** and **watch more sunsets.**

I would eat **more ice cream** and less beans.

I would have **more actual troubles** and fewer imaginary ones.

to live

You see I am one of those people who live prophylactically

and sanely and sensibly, hour after hour and day after day.

Oh, I have had my moments and if I had to do it over again, I'd have more of them.

In fact, I'd try to have nothing else. Just moments, one after another.

– If I had my life to live over –

over

I would start **barefoot earlier in the spring** and **and stay that way until late in the fall.**

I would play **hooky more.** *I would* ride on **more merry-go-rounds.**

I'd pick **more daisies.**

Nadine Star

NarzissGrotesk

About
Many of you know Hubert Jocham's neoclassic typeface Narziss. It can be found in headlines all over the world. Creating a sans serif version did not mean to just take away all the serifs and thicken the hairlines. Back in 1998, Arena magazine used Venus in text, one of the few interesting digital versions of a classic grotesque. It worked perfect in a lifestyle magazine. After some experiments, Hubert decided to create a grotesque as a companion for the neoclassic Narziss. Inspired by 19th century specimens and of course by the Narziss family.

Design
Hubert Jocham
2015

Foundry
Hubert Jocham, Germany
www.hubertjocham.de

Styles / Weights
Light, Light Italic, Book, Book Italic, Regular, Regular Italic, Medium, Medium Italic, Semibold, Semibold Italic, Bold, Bold Italic, Heavy, Heavy Italic, Extrabold, Extrabold Italic, Ultrabold, Ultrabold Italic

Language support
Latin, Latin Extended

OpenType options
Ligatures, Oldstyle Figures

Optimized for web
Yes

REGULAR 18PT

abcdefghijklmnopqrstuvwxyzæfjåçéñöûß
ABCDEFGHIJKLMNOPQRSTUVWXYZÆÇØ
0123456789@.,-:;!?')]§*“”«»/–€$&

HEAVY 36PT

aejgGQR7

BOLD & BOOK 16PT

Typographers want
amazing, exquisite
& clever justified text
in books

SEMIBOLD & LIGHT 9PT

cata·logue / *noun* / a complete list of things that people can look at or buy: *a catalogue of typefaces (a book showing the newest fonts, to help people choose the right typeface)*

ALL WEIGHTS 10PT

Light
Book
Regular
Medium
Semibold
Bold
Heavy
Extrabold
Ultrabold

ITALICS, ALL WEIGHTS 10PT

Light Italic
Book Italic
Regular Italic
Medium Italic
Semibold Italic
Bold Italic
Heavy Italic
Extrabold Italic
Ultrabold Italic

Mediterraneo

Venti caldi del Sud

47/15 Knots

Ponente & Tramontana

Mar Jónico

The successor state of the Ottoman Empire

Nautica

About

Nautica is an elegant script typeface based on classic Copperplate's ductus. It was designed using high contrast strokes to give this typeface a strong character. A beautiful collection of alternates, ligatures, swashes and extensive language support complete the over 900 glyphs included, offering fully professional typographic features. It has been designed as three weights, including an additional font with decorative nautical elements such as ropes, knots, wind roses and many others which significantly enhance the visual impact and complement the style of this family beautifully.

Design
Paco González, Giuseppe Salerno
2014

Foundry
Resistenza, Spain
www.resistenza.es

Styles / Weights
Regular, Medium, Bold, Icons and Knots

Language support
Latin

OpenType options
Standard Ligatures, Discretionary Ligatures, Historical Ligatures, All Caps, Small Caps, Capitals to Small Caps, Swashes, Contextual Swashes, All Alternates, Contextual Alternates, Contextual Ligatures, Ornaments, Arrows, Stylistic Alternates, Stylistic Sets, Terminal Form, Initial Form, Medial Form

Optimized for web
No

REGULAR 12PT

abcdefghijklmnopqrstuvwxyzæfjaçéñöüß
ABCDEFGHIJKLMNOPQRSTUVWXYZÆÇØ
0123456789@.,-:;!?()/§/-€$&*

REGULAR 28PT

aejgGQR7

REGULAR 19PT

Typographers want amazing, exquisite & clever justified text in books

ICONS AND KNOTS 28PT

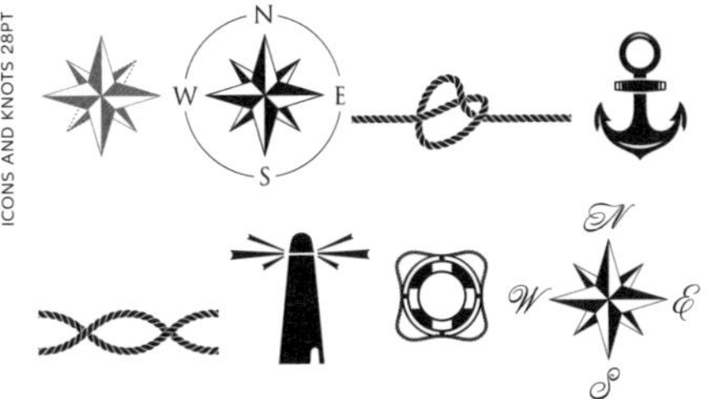

BOLD 19PT

The Yearbook of Type compendium works well as a tool in vexed typography questions from polarizing jobs

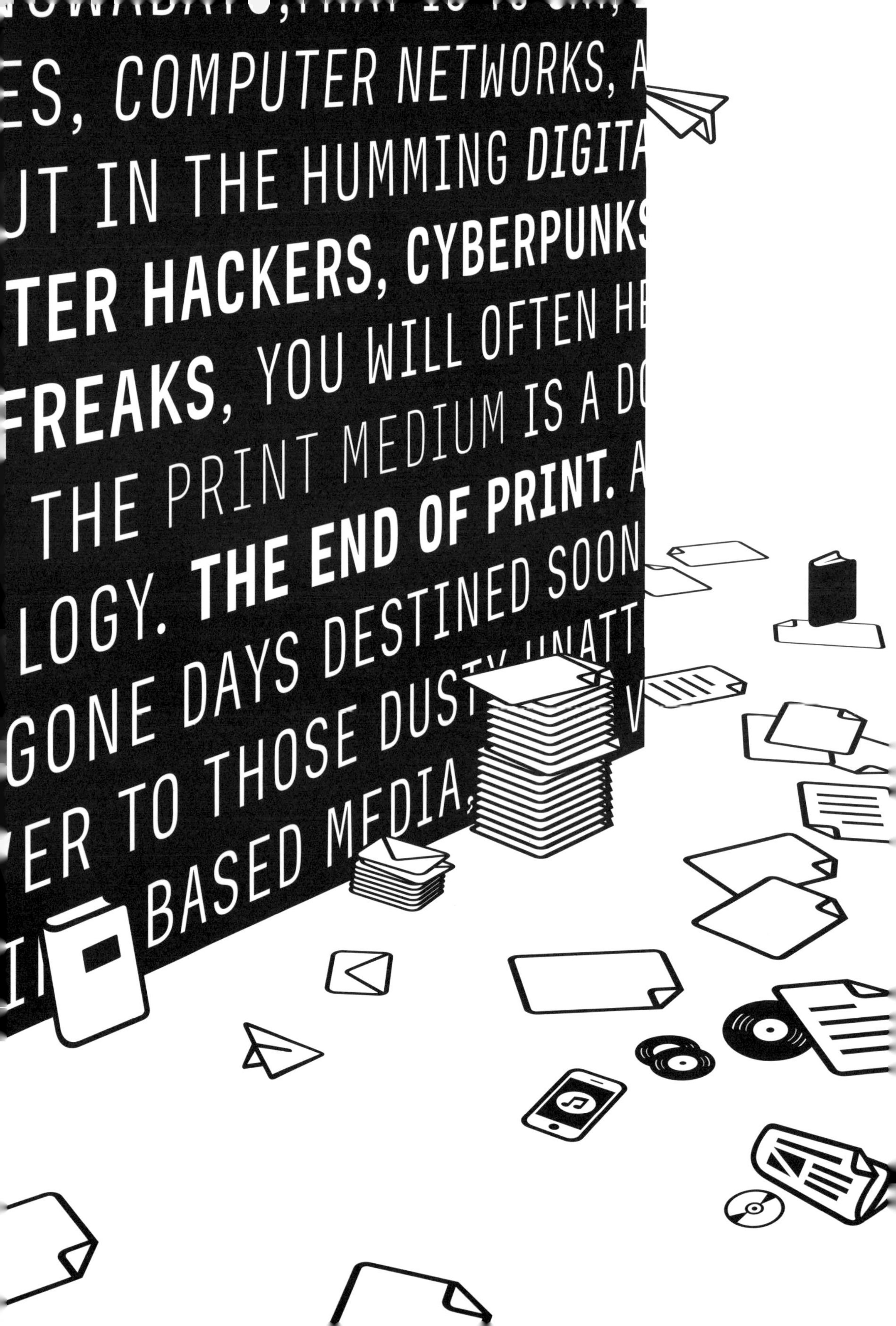

ES, *COMPUTER NETWORKS*, A
UT IN THE HUMMING *DIGITA*
TER HACKERS, CYBERPUNKS
FREAKS, YOU WILL OFTEN HE
THE PRINT MEDIUM IS A DO
LOGY. **THE END OF PRINT.** A
GONE DAYS DESTINED SOON
ER TO THOSE DUSTY UNATT V
BASED MEDIA,
I

Newsletter Pro

About
Monospaced but no mono space.

Created from 2013 to 2015, this font family is an extensive update of the font Newsletter. It is influenced by fonts like OCR-B, DIN and the work of Erik Spiekermann. Newsletter Pro is not a real monospaced font but has the ease of recognition these fonts have—even though these fonts are often criticized for their aesthetic qualities. Newsletter Pro has a computer-related impression but is more legible and aesthetic than real monospaced fonts are.

Design
Ingo Krepinsky, Gunnar Link
2015

Foundry
Die Typonauten, Germany
www.typonauten.de

Styles / Weights
Thin, Thin Italic, Light, Light Italic, Normal, Normal Italic, Medium, Medium Italic, Bold, Bold Italic, Black, Black Italic, Icons

Language support
Latin, Greek

OpenType options
All Caps, Small Caps, All Alternates, Fractions, Alternative Fractions, Numerator, Denominator, Arrows, Slashed Zero

Optimized for web
Yes

NORMAL 18PT

abcdefghijklmnopqrstuvwxyzæfjåçéñöûß
ABCDEFGHIJKLMNOPQRSTUVWXYZÆÇØ
01234567890@.,-:;!?’)]§*“”«»/–€$&½

BOLD 30PT

aejgGQR7

BLACK & LIGHT 14PT

The Yearbook of Type compendium works well as
a tool in vexed typography questions for polarizing jobs

ICONS 9PT

ALL WEIGHTS 12PT

Thin
Light
Normal
Medium
Bold
Black

ITALICS 12PT

Thin Italic
Light Italic
Normal Italic
Medium Italic
Bold Italic
Black Italic

The East End Underworld

Criminale con possibilità economiche molto elevate

Bankovní lupič

GENERAL THIEF AND BAD CHARACTER

Hodder & Stoughton

§ 129 Bildung krimineller Vereinigungen

Ruby Sparks

Howard Journal of Criminal Justice

Hensynsløs framferd

Sa façon d'agir est particulièrement odieuse

BRIGHTON

The nightclub scene in London's West End 1930

sources of money

About
Nitti Grotesk is the proportional companion to the monospaced Nitti. Both typefaces have gained worldwide recognition through their prominent role in iA Writer Pro—a professional writing suite. Nitti Grotesk is inspired by the quirky and often idiosyncratic shapes of the early English sans serifs of the 19th century. These so-called "grotesques" contain a humanity and warmth which is still appreciated among many graphic designers today. Pieter van Rosmalen incorporated the peculiarities into a versatile, contemporary family of seven weights plus Italics and extended Latin character set.

Design
Pieter van Rosmalen
2014

Foundry
Bold Monday, The Netherlands
www.boldmonday.com

Styles / Weights
Light, Light Italic, SemiLight, SemiLight Italic, Normal, Italic, Medium, Medium Italic, Bold, Bold Italic, ExtraBold, ExtraBold Italic, Black, Black Italic

Language support
Latin

OpenType options
Tabular and Proportional Lining, Standard Ligatures, Superscript, Subscript, Ordinals, Contextual Alternates, Fractions, Numerator, Denominator, Arrows, Stylistic Alternates, Stylistic Sets, Slashed Zero

Optimized for web
Yes

NORMAL 18PT
aabcdefgghijklmnopqrstuvwxyzæfjåçéñöûß
ABCDEFGHIJKLMNOPQRSTUVWXYZÆÇØ
01234567890@.,-:;!?')]§*“”«»/–€$&⅓↗

BOLD 36PT
aejgGQR7

BLACK & MEDIUM 15PT
Typographers want
amazing, exquisite
& clever justified text
in books

BLACK & NORMAL 9PT
ex·am·ple / *noun* / an illustration that supports or provides more information: *by showing examples the Yearbook of Type presents each font in different sizes and weights*

ALL WEIGHTS 11PT
Light
SemiLight
Normal
Medium
Bold
ExtraBold
Black

ITALICS 11PT
Light
SemiLight Italic
Normal Italic
Medium Italic
Bold Italic
ExtraBold Italic
Black Italic

Niveau

Grotesk

& Serif

Arte Nova

GRANDE ROYALE

Princess Cheesecake

Niveau Grotesk & Niveau Serif is a type system of 36 fonts in total: 12 weights *plus matching italics* and SMALL CAPS. It was designed by Hannes von Döhren. Influenced by classical nineteenth-century faces, the fonts are based on geometric forms. Because of its straight architecture, Niveau has a "PUNCH" in big sizes but is very legible in smaller sizes and longer texts – in print or on screen.

Niveau Grotesk & Serif

About
Niveau Grotesk and Niveau Serif is a type system of 36 fonts in total: twelve weights plus matching italics and small caps.

It was designed by Hannes von Döhren. Influenced by classical 19th century faces, the fonts are based on geometric forms. Because of its straight architecture, Niveau has a "punch" in big sizes but is very legible in smaller sizes and longer texts—in print or on screen.

Design
Hannes von Döhren
2013

Foundry
HVD Fonts, Germany
www.hvdfonts.com

Styles / Weights
Family of two styles (Grotesk, Serif), each in six weights (ExtraLight, Light, Regular, Medium, Bold, Black), each with Italics

Language support
Latin

OpenType options
Proportional Oldstyle, Tabular and Proportional Lining, Tabular Oldstyle, Standard Ligatures, All Caps, Small Caps, Superscript, Subscript, Ordinals, Fractions, Numerator, Denominator, Arrows, Stylistic Alternates, Stylistic Sets, Localized Forms

Optimized for web
Yes

GROTESK REGULAR 18PT

aabcdefghijklmnopqrstuvwxyzæfjåçéñöûß
ABCDEFGHIJKLMNOPQRSTUVWXYZÆÇØ
0123456789@.,-:;!?')]§*""«»/–€$&⅓↗

SERIF REGULAR 18PT

aabcdefghijklmnopqrstuvwxyzæfjåçéñöûß
ABCDEFGHIJKLMNOPQRSTUVWXYZÆÇØ
0123456789@.,-:;!?')]§*""«»/–€$&⅓↗

GROTESK BLACK & SERIF MEDIUM 36PT

aejgGQR7
aejgGQR7

GROTESK BOLD & SERIF LIGHT 16PT

Typographers want
amazing, exquisite
& clever justified text
in books

MIX THE 4 STYLES

NORD

OR USE IT SEPARATLY

KOPENHAGEN

TROMSØ

HELSINKI OSLO STOCKHOLM

VANCOUVER

www.Letterwerk.ch

About
Nord is a capital letter font made for display use. The four styles can either stand alone or be used for effects by adding different colors to each stackable style. The Nord Inline style and the Nord Form style are predestinated for really big size usage because of the very thin line inside.

Design
Fabian Widmer
2014

Foundry
Letterwerk, Switzerland
www.letterwerk.ch

Styles / Weights
Black, Sun, Inline, Form

Language support
Latin

OpenType options
Not available

Optimized for web
No

BLACK 16PT

ABCDEFGHIJKLMNOPQRSTUVWXYZÅÇÉÑÖÛ
0123456789@.,-:;!?')*“”«»/–€$&

INLINE 16PT

ABCDEFGHIJKLMNOPQRSTUVWXYZÅÇÉÑÖÛ
0123456789@.,-:;!?')*“”«»/–€$&

SUN 35PT

AEJGQR7

BLACK 8PT

HAND•BOOK / NOUN / A BOOK GIVING INSTRUCTIONS ON HOW TO USE STH. OR INFORMATION ABOUT A PARTICULAR SUBJECT LIKE TYPEFACES~COMPARE MANUAL OR YEARBOOK OF TYPE

**My daddy was an astronaut.
That is what I was often taught.
My daddy went away too soon.
Now he is living on the moon.**

Nick Cave

Randgloyes
Randgloyes
Randgloyes
Randgloyes
Randgloyes
Randgloyes
Randgloyes
Randgloyes
Randgloyes
Randgloyes
Randgloyes

PTL Notes Nova by Ole Schaefer 2015 for primetype.com

PTL Notes Nova

About
PTL Notes Nova is a newly redesigned and extended version of the well-known original PTL Notes.

Design
Ole Schäfer
2015

Foundry
primetype GmbH, Germany
www.primetype.de

Styles / Weights
Thin, Thin Italic, Extralight, Extralight Italic, Light, Light Italic, Regular, Italic, Book, Book Italic, Medium, Medium Italic, Semi Bold, Semi Bold Italic, Bold, Bold Italic, Heavy, Heavy Italic, Black, Black Italic, Ultra, Ultra Italic

Language support
Latin, Latin Extended

OpenType options
Proportional Oldstyle, Tabular Lining, Proportional Lining, Tabular Oldstyle, Standard Ligatures, Small Caps, Arrows

Optimized for web
Yes

REGULAR 18PT
abcdefghijklmnopqrstuvwxyzæfjß
ABCDEFGHIJKLMNOPQRSTUVWXYZÆØ
0123456789@.,-:;!?')]§*“”«»/–€$&½

BOLD 36PT
aejgGQR7

ULTRA & REGULAR 16PT
Typographers want amazing, exquisite
& clever justified text in books

THIN 10PT
aejgGQR7

BOLD & THIN 16PT
Typographers want amazing, exquisite
& clever justified text in books

Novel
Novel Sans Hair
Novel Sans
Novel Sans Office
Novel Sans Condensed
Novel Mono
Novel Sans Rounded

In general atmospheric circu
exist equatorial regions and a
a difference in temperature.
air at the poles to flow along
pattern of air circulation is co
several forces, the most imp
force created by the rotatio
not perceptible to humans a
and travel relatively short di
Earth. However, the Corioli
great distances, such as an a
right in the Northern Hemis
straight line. The amount of
greatest at the poles, and d
Coriolis force also differs w
speed, the greater the devi
Earth deflects moving air to
the air. The speed of the Ea
three distinct cells in each
the equator rises upward f
eastward by the rotation o
distance from the equator
eastward. This air cools ar
area of high pressure as it

Atlas Font Foundry

About
Novel Sans Hair is the new package of 24 ultra light weights of Novel Sans Pro, the humanist grotesque typeface family within the largely extended award winning Novel Collection, also containing Novel Pro, Novel Sans Condensed Pro, Novel Mono Pro, Novel Sans Rounded Pro and Novel Sans Office Pro.

Novel Sans Hair has a carefully attuned character design and a well-balanced weight contrast. Classic proportions and the almost upright italic makes Novel Sans Pro a modern humanist with the calligraphic warmth of a real Italic. Many similarities with the other typeface families within the Novel Collection enable designers to combine the families and reach highest quality in typography.

Design
Christoph Dunst
2014

Foundry
Atlas Font Foundry, Germany
www.atlasfonts.com

Styles / Weights
Hairline in twelve optical weights (6, 8, 10, 12, 14, 18, 24, 30, 36, 42, 48, 54), each with Italics

Language support
Latin

OpenType options
Proportional Oldstyle, Tabular and Proportional Lining, Tabular Oldstyle, Standard Ligatures, Discretionary Ligatures, Historical Ligatures, All Caps, Small Caps, Capitals to Small Caps, Superscript, Subscript, Ordinals, Titling Alternates, Contextual Alternates, Fractions, Alternative Fractions, Numerator, Denominator, Arrows, Stylistic Alternates, Stylistic Sets, Historical Forms

Optimized for web
Yes

42 16PT

abcdefghijklmnopqrstuvwxyzæfjåçéñöûß
ABCDEFGHIJKLMNOPQQRSTUVWXYZÆÇØ
0123456789@.,-:;!?')]§*"‚'«»/–€$&⅓↗

10 ITALIC 30PT

aejgGQR7

54 & 6 14PT

Typographers want
amazing, exquisite
& clever justified text
in books

36 30PT

aejgGQR7

48 & 12 11PT

→ cata·logue / *noun* / a complete list of things that people can look at or buy: *a catalogue of typefaces (a book showing the newest fonts, to help people choose the right typeface)*

Today is the greatest
Day I have ever known
Cannot live for tomorrow
Tomorrow is much too
long ...

The Smashing Pumpkins

Onlinetypefacedesign
Onlinetypefacedesign
Onlinetypefacedesign

ONLINETYPEFACEDESIGN
ONLINETYPEFACEDESIGN
ONLINETYPEFACEDESIGN

Onlinetypefacedesign
Onlinetypefacedesign

Onlinetypefacedesign
Onlinetypefacedesign

ORF On by Ole Schaefer 2014 - for
ORF Online & Teletext GmbH & Co KG
Artdirection: Claudia Bogun · news.orf.at

About
ORF On—“On” means online—is the new typeface for *news.orf.at*. It is the news portal of ORF Fernsehen in Austria. The implementation is still in progress, so far the typeface is used for news, sport and the sport app and other solutions.

This original typeface is specially designed for screen display. The typeface design is optimized for a good legibility on screen for web and smartphones applications. The art direction for the application for web and apps is from Claudia Bogun and the typeface design from Ole Schäfer for primetype GmbH.

Design
Ole Schäfer
2014

Foundry
primetype GmbH, Germany
www.primetype.de

Styles / Weights
Family of two styles (Normal, Condensed), each in three weights (Regular, Medium, Bold), Normal with Italics and Caps

Language support
Latin, Latin Extended

OpenType options
Tabular and Proportional Lining, Small Caps, Fractions

Optimized for web
Yes

REGULAR 18PT

abcdefghijklmnopqrstuvwxyzæfjåçéñöûß
ABCDEFGHIJKLMNOPQRSTUVWXYZÆÇØ
0123456789@.,-:;!?’)]§*“”«»/–€$&⅓

BOLD 35PT

aejgGQR7

CONDENSED BOLD & BOOK 16PT

Typographers want amazing, exquisite
& clever justified text in books

BOLD & REGULAR 8PT

Year•book of Type / *noun* / book published every second year, giving details on typefaces of the previous two years and also about general current typographic topics–e.g. *OpenType features, font editors like Glyphs etc.*

BOLD & REGULAR 12PT

The Yearbook of Type
compendium works well as
a tool in vexed typography
questions for polarizing jobs

ORF On

primetype GmbH

An informal type family for display & text

VELLUM

inspired by twisted strips of paper, almost calligraphic

Make truffles 1627

Inspiratǎ dupǎ mōdelul fâșiilor de hârtie îndoite, nĕbunātiça vorbește mạị mûlte łimbi

define organic sausages

in the office, at work, or in the magazines

Kvindekjøn

240 hungry sailors experienced @typemuseum

Qarboncharity

Quasimodo (1745–1836) practiced yoga and {quantum mechanics}

£78.93 always look good on Paiper

About
Paiper is a type family for display and text use. The roman weights have slightly flared serifs and low contrast, while the italics feature higher contrast and more pronounced serif shapes. Each family member delivers a unique personality to the mix, from elegant and skinny to poetic and chubby. Its intended use is for designing movie posters, book covers and logos, as well as flyers, magazines, and funky packages.

Design
Diana Ovezea
2014

Foundry
Gestalten, Germany
www.gestaltenfonts.com

Styles / Weights
Thin, Thin Italic, Regular, Italic, Black, Black Italic

Language support
Latin

OpenType options
Proportional Oldstyle, Tabular and Proportional Lining, Tabular Oldstyle, Standard Ligatures, Discretionary Ligatures, Ordinals

Optimized for web
No

REGULAR 18PT
abcdefghijklmnopqrstuvwxyzæfjåçéñöûß
ABCDEFGHIJKLMNOPQRSTUVWXYZÆÇØ
0123456789@.,-:;!?')]§*“”«»/–€$&

BLACK & REGULAR 9PT
cata·logue / noun / a complete list of things that people can look at or buy: *a catalogue of typefaces (a book showing the newest fonts to help people choose the right typeface)*

BLACK & REGULAR 16PT
Typographers want
amazing, exquisite
& clever justified text
in books

BLACK 36PT
aejgGQR7

ALL WEIGHTS 12PT
Thin
Regular
Black

ITALICS 12PT
Thin Italic
Regular Italic
Black Italic

LOVE
is
in
the
Air

PARIS PRO | THE ULTIMATE TYPEFACE FOR FASHION & LUXURY
MOSHIK NADAV TYPOGRAPHY

Paris Pro

About
The ultimate typeface for fashion and luxury

This fashion-forward type family has two center weights, Regular and Bold, each consisting of four enticing styles. An extra light style and five different sans serif weights are also available. With more than 1,200 glyphs, Paris Pro takes any lettering to a whole new level of refined luxury. These multiple glyphs and ligatures empower the user to customize each individual messaging, so no word is destined to look the same twice—sometimes it may have to burst with boldness, other times whisper quietly with impact. This innovative type system puts users in control, which is rare for typefaces.

The stylish swashes and amazing OpenType features are distinct qualities of Paris Pro's opulent typefaces. Readymade words for modular, eye-catching headlines in fashion magazines and mouthwatering logotypes for luxury brands have already proven to work.

This unique typeface has been utilized around the world, making Paris Pro live up to its name of a global city's style. The regular and bold weights include 1,200 glyphs per style.

Design
Moshik Nadav
2014

Foundry
Moshik Nadav Typography, USA
www.moshik.net

Styles / Weights
Hairline, Thin, Extralight, Light, Regular, Book, Medium, Bold

Language support
Latin

OpenType options
Swashes, Ligatures, Alternate Glyphs, Ready-Made Words

Optimized for web
Yest

REGULAR 17PT

abcdefghijklmnopqrstuvwxyzaefjåçéñöû
ABCDEFGHIJKLMNOPQRSTUVWXYZÆÇØ
0123456789@.,-:;!?)]*»/$&

BOLD & REGULAR STRIP 36PT

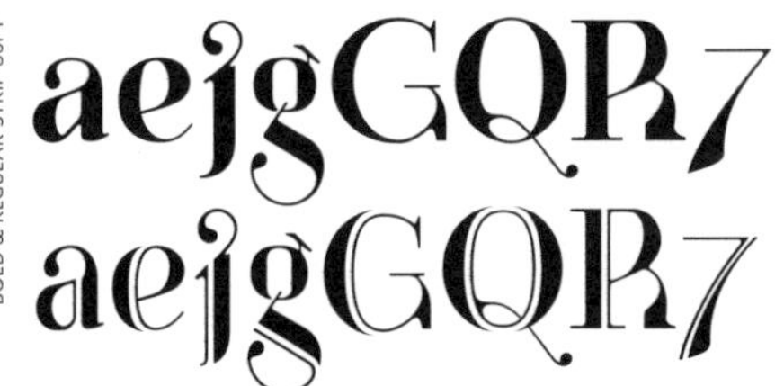

BOLD STRIP & BOLD EXIT 16PT

Typographers want amazing, exquisite & clever justified text in books

REGULAR STRIP READY-MADE WORD 36PT

LIGHT BOOK & HAIRLINE 12PT

The Yearbook of Type compendium works well as a tool in vexed typography questions for polarizing jobs

from paradise to the park
is just a very small step

DF-Park

About
DF-Park originates from an opportunistic attempt to develop a visual language for a huge theme pavilion for a country hosting a universal exhibition about food. The subject of the strip of greenhouses dealt with the history of biodiversity and the scope of food production. The font set (six styles) is designed not only to transfer the content of the exhibition but also to dress up the greenhouses facades with its lines and patterns. All the characters are composed of hand-painted lines and, when superimposed, form an endless variety of (letter) forms. Executed in transparent colorful layers, you will find yourself entering a cathedral on a sunny day.

Design
Ko Sliggers
2014

Foundry
dutchfonts, France
www.dutchfonts.com

Styles / Weights
DF-parkone, DF-parktwo, DF-parkthree, DF-parkfour, DF-parkfive, DF-parksix

Language support
Latin

OpenType options
Not available

Optimized for web
Yes

DF-PARKONE 18PT

abcdefghijklmnopqrstuvwxyzáçêñöü

DF-PARKTWO 36PT

DF-PARKFIVE 16PT

typographers want amazing, exquisite and clever justified text in books

DF-PARKSIX 36PT

DF-PARKTHREE 24PT

Parmigiano

Aa Aa Aa Aa Aa Aa

PICCOLO

Aa Aa Aa Aa Aa Aa

PICCOLO ITALICS

Aa Aa Aa Aa Aa Aa

CAPTION

Aa Aa Aa Aa Aa Aa

CAPTION ITALICS

Aa Aa Aa Aa Aa Aa

TEXT

Aa Aa Aa Aa Aa Aa

TEXT ITALICS

Aa Aa Aa Aa Aa Aa

HEADLINE

Aa Aa Aa Aa Aa Aa

HEADLINE ITALICS

The Parmigiano Typographic System (named after Parma, the city where Bodoni established his printing house) is the most extensive family of fonts ever to have been inspired by this great designer. The project started with a thorough analysis of the *Manuale Tipografico*, yet Parmigiano goes beyond it to imagine what would Bodoni have done if he had worked with digital media. The authors consider Parmigiano an 'irreverent descendant' of Bodoni's work rather than a revival, as it includes styles that Bodoni never created or even considered creating.

About
The Parmigiano Typographic System (named after Parma, the city where Bodoni established his printing house) is the most extensive family of fonts ever to have been inspired by this great designer. Their biggest challenge was to create coherent relationships between various optical sizes (Piccolo, Caption, Text, Headline) and weights, something that Bodoni himself didn't concern himself with much. The project started with a thorough analysis of the Manuale, yet Parmigiano goes beyond it to imagine what would Bodoni have done if he had worked with digital media. The authors consider Parmigiano an "irreverent descendant" of Bodoni's work rather than a revival, as it includes styles (e.g. Sans) that Bodoni never created or even considered creating.

Design
Riccardo Olocco, Jonathan Pierini
2014

Foundry
Typotheque, The Netherlands
www.typotheque.com

Styles / Weights
Family of four styles (Piccolo, Caption, Text, Headline), each with six weights (Thin, Light, Regular, Medium, Bold, Black), each with Italics

Language support
Latin, Cyrillic, Greek

OpenType options
Proportional Oldstyle, Tabular and Proportional Lining, Tabular Oldstyle, Standard Ligatures, Discretionary Ligatures, All Caps, Small Caps, Capitals to Small Caps, Superscript, Subscript, Ordinals, All Alternates, Contextual Alternates, Contextual Ligatures, Fractions, Numerator, Denominator, Ornaments, Arrows, Stylistic Alternates, Stylistic Sets, Slashed Zero

Optimized for web
Yes

PICCOLO REGULAR 17PT

abcdefghijklmnopqrstuvwxyzæfjåçéñöûß
ABCDEFGHIJKLMNOPQRSTUVWXYZÆÇØ
0123456789o@.,-:;!?')]§*“”«»/–€$&⅓ ☛↗

PICCOLO BOLD & REGULAR 8PT

☞ **Year·book of Type** / noun / book
published every second year, giving details of typefaces of the previous two years and about general current typo-graphic topics—*e.g. OpenType features, font editors like Glyphs etc.*

CAPTION MEDIUM & THIN 13PT

The Yearbook of Type
compendium works well as
a tool in vexed typography
questions for polarizing jobs

CAPTION BLACK & HEADLINE THIN 32PT

aejgGQR7
aejgGQR7

HEADLINE BOLD & LIGHT 13PT

The Yearbook of Type
compendium works well as
a tool in vexed typography
questions for polarizing jobs

Calligraphy

SLABSERIF

Humanist

crossover

Pepone

Maximilien & Longueval

stencil

ZE STROPNICE DO VEVEŘÍ

Spitzweg

CHALOUPKY

1957 är tillbaka på Kungliga Operan

This typeface is primarily designated for the setting belles-lettres. The regular styles are balanced to suit nall text sizes and enable reading of long portions text. The development of e typeface was guided by the goal of creating a conporary, discreet book ser-, with modern expression numerous functions. Letfeature reduced contrast, lighter styles may evoke d letters, while the heavies bear distinct slab serif ences. The extremes thus rk in harmony and fulfill demanding requirements advertising and magazine yout. The typeface is suitle for bottle labels, invitans, exhibition catalogues d posters, for printed and nline presentations alike. name Pepone was chosen s an homage to Josef Kroor. His novels and poems d meticulous typography, nely they ask for a careful oice of a typeface. Up unl now, his books were set randomly selected fonts, some better, some worse. n now on, the situation is t to change. The new, cusm-made typeface was creed specifically for the pur-

Today, every other restauran or steel factory boast their o typeface; why not every indi ual writer and author? Just each of us has unique hand ing as well as individual wr and spoken expression, each every writer should have the ilege of having a unique ima a page in a book. The classic Style or transitional serif ty faces are too decorative and ile to suit Josef's texts, Didc modern typefaces are too str and uptight, and the other r ern serif typefaces lack expre sion and character. The solu cannot be found "in betwee On the contrary, we must tr to express Josef's literary wc through type. The alphabet to deal with a number of inf ences, such as the landscape Italy and South Bohemia, w European history, with curre and long forgotten painters, ets, photographers, graphic ists, ceramicists, and plenty other inspiration sources. Th letters are constructed with writer letterforms in mind, w may remind of Josef K.'s beg nings in the samizdat era. T italics, on the other hand, v ly remind of the scripts of th Italian Renaissance, narrov fulfill the need for economy per-saving in mind) in the c

About
This typeface is primarily designated for the setting of belles-lettres. The regular styles are balanced to suit small text sizes and enable the reading of long portions of text. The development of the typeface was guided by the goal of creating a contemporary, discreet book serif, with modern expression and numerous functions. Letters feature reduced contrast, the lighter styles may evoke wired letters, while the heavier ones bear distinct slab serif references. The extremes thus work in harmony and fulfill the demanding requirements of advertising and magazine layout. The typeface is suitable for bottle labels, invitations, exhibition catalogues and posters, for printed and online presentations alike. The name Pepone was chosen as an homage to Josef Kroutvor. His novels and poems need meticulous typography, namely they ask for a careful choice of a typeface.

Design
František Štorm
2014

Foundry
Storm Type Foundry, Czech Republic
www.stormtype.com

Styles / Weights
Family of two styles (Regular, Stencil), each with five weights (Light, Book, Regular, Bold, Black), each with Italics

Language support
Latin

OpenType options
Proportional Oldstyle, Tabular and Proportional Lining, Tabular Oldstyle, Standard Ligatures, Discretionary Ligatures, Historical Ligatures, All Caps, Small Caps, Capitals to Small Caps, Swashes, Fractions, Numerator, Denominator, Ornaments, Arrows, Stylistic Sets, Slashed Zero

Optimized for web
Yes

REGULAR 17PT

abcdefghijklmnopqrstuvwxyzæfjåçéñöûß
ABCDEFGHIJKLMNOPQRSTUVWXYZÆÇØ
01234567890@.,-:;!?')]§*“”«»/–€$&❦↗

STENCIL BOLD 30PT

aejgGQR7

BLACK & REGULAR 14PT

Typographers want
amazing, exquisite
& clever justified text
in books

BOLD & REGULAR 8PT

☛ **cata·logue** / *noun* / a complete list of things that people can look at or buy: *a catalogue of typefaces (a book showing the newest fonts, to help people choose the right typeface)*

ALL WEIGHTS 10PT

Light
Light Italic
Book
Book Italic
Regular
Italic
Bold
Bold Italic
Black
Black Italic

STENCILS 10PT

Light
Light Italic
Book
Book Italic
Regular
Italic
Bold
Bold Italic
Black
Black Italic

LP Philharmonia

Peter Schmidt, a well-known designer from Hamburg, browsed in a fashion magazine on a return flight from the United States. At the time he was thinking about a logo for a philharmonic orchestra. In the magazine, he noticed some interesting typography. He removed the page from the magazine and later sent it to Peter Langpeter. That inspired the creation of the logo. Since Peter Langpeter really liked the classic aesthetics of the resulting letters, he developed a whole new alphabet from it. Initially, only capital letters. Now he has completed this exceptionally beautiful font.

2014

Peter

LANGPETER

AN ORCHESTRA is a large instrumental ensemble that contains sections of string, brass, woodwind, and percussion instruments. Other instruments such as the piano and celesta may sometimes be grouped into a fifth section such as a keyboard section or may stand alone, as may the concert harp and electric and electronic instruments. The term orchestra derives from the Greek.

DIE LIEBE ZUR HARMONIE

classic aesthetics

Boethius weist der musica mundana die dominierende Rolle zu. Der Mensch hat die Pflicht, diese zu erkennen und selbst ein geregeltes Leben zu führen.

ELBPHILHARMONIE

CORNET

The cornet was initially derived from the post horn around 1820 in France. Among the first manufacturers of modern cornets was Parisian Jean Asté in 1828. Cornets first appeared as separate instrumental parts in 19th century French compositions.

symphony orchestra

An orchestra is a large instrumental ensemble that contains sections of string, brass, woodwind, and percussion instruments.

About
Peter Schmidt, a well-known designer from Hamburg, browsed in a fashion magazine on a return flight from the United States. At the time he was thinking about a logo for a philharmonic orchestra. In the magazine, he noticed some interesting typography. He removed the page from the magazine and later sent it to Peter Langpeter. That inspired the creation of the logo. Since Peter Langpeter really liked the classic aesthetics of the resulting letters, he developed a whole new alphabet from it. Initially, only capital letters. Now he has completed this exceptionally beautiful font.

Design
Peter Langpeter
2013

Foundry
URW++, Germany
www.urwpp.com

Styles / Weights
Regular

Language support
Latin

OpenType options
Proportional Lining, Standard Ligatures, Superscript, Ordinals, Fractions

Optimized for web
Yes

REGULAR 18PT

abcdefghijklmnopqrstuvwxyzæfjåçéñöûß
ABCDEFGHIJKLMNOPQRSTUVWXYZÆÇØ
0123456789@.,-:;!?')]§*“”«»/–€$&½

REGULAR 30PT

aejgGQR7

REGULAR 16PT

Typographers want amazing, exquisite & clever justified text in books

A famished fox crept into a vineyard where ripe, luscious grapes were draped high upon arbors in a most tempting display. In his effort to win a juicy prize, the fox jumped and sprang many times but failed in all his attempts. When he finally had to admit defeat, he retreated and muttered to himself, "Well, what does it matter anyway? The grapes are sour!"

Seven Sublime Interchangeable Scripts

by João Henrique Lopes

About
Seven superb scripts that can be freely mixed with one another. Alone, each of them flows nicely, but combined they reach ultimate vitality and grace. The Pleiades are one of the most beautiful constellations in the sky, and in Greek mythology they were seven divine sisters. Luxurious freedom of choice and excellent readability make Pleiad the perfect face for a variety of projects, from stylish invitations to magazine ads, from poetry books to restaurant logos. Sometimes calm, sometimes flittering—but always fair and graceful—this sublime calligraphic type family will hold an everlasting fascination.

Design
João Henrique Lopes
2014

Foundry
URW++, Germany
www.urwpp.com

Styles / Weights
Alcyone, Celeno, Electra, Maia, Merope, Sterope, Taygete

Language support
Latin

OpenType options
Proportional Oldstyle, Standard Ligatures, Ordinals

Optimized for web
Yes

STEROPE 23PT

abcdefghijklmnopqrstuvwxyzæfjåçéñöûß
ABCDEFGHIJKLMNOPQRSTUVWXYZÆÇØ
0123456789@.,'-:;!?()[]§*"" « » /–€$&

ELECTRA 54PT

aejgGQR7

TAYGETE 25PT

Typographers want amazing, exquisite & clever justified text in books

CELENO 54PT

aejgGQR7

MAIA 23PT

Typographers want amazing, exquisite & clever justified text in books

›Now, Mr. Anderson, I put it to you: if you had had only one orgasm in your **WHOLE** life, would you be sure that you had had one? It seems to me that a continuum is REQUIRED; that if an experience of this sort is unique, it is impossible to know if it has really been experienced at all.‹

A Letter from Wanda Tinasky, April 27, 1988

About
The concave logo design for the label Holger Records in 2013 was the basis for the expansion to Polja-Sans. Polja then arose as a counterpoint and was awarded with the first prize of the People's Choice in the Morisawa Type Design Competition 2014.

Design
Reymund Schroeder
2014

Foundry
Zeugler, Germany
www.zeugler.de

Styles / Weights
Bold

Language support
Latin

OpenType options
Standard Ligatures

Optimized for web
No

REGULAR 18PT

abcdefghijklmnopqrstuvwxyzæfjöß
ABCDEFGHIJKLMNOPQRSTUVWXYZÆ
0123456789@.,-:;!?')*“”«»/–&

REGULAR 30PT

aejgGQR7

REGULAR 14PT

Typographers want amazing, exquisite & clever justified text in books

HUNGRY YOUNG MAN

BREAKFAST

KOBRA

---

infinite

space

---

321 | IT'S TIME TO BE ON TOP

METAL

monster

Quantum

About
A very friendly-looking sans, Quantum is Hitesh Malaviya's first published typeface for Latin script. Its five styles are very, very wide, but the letterforms do not look too technical. Stroke endings are vertical, like in a humanist sans. Don't overlook the tails on "K," "Q," "R," and "k!"

Design
Hitesh Malaviya
2015

Foundry
Indian Type Foundry, India
www.indiantypefoundry.com

Styles / Weights
Light, Regular, Medium, Semibold, Bold

Language support
Latin

OpenType options
Proportional Lining, Standard Ligatures, Superscript, Fractions

Optimized for web
Yes

REGULAR 11PT

abcdefghijklmnopqrstuvwxyzæfjåçéñöûß
ABCDEFGHIJKLMNOPQRSTUVWXYZÆÇØ
0123456789@.,-:;!?')]§*""«»/-€$&½

BOLD 22PT

BOLD & REGULAR 10PT

The Yearbook of Type compendium works
well as a tool in vexed typography questions for polarizing jobs

MEDIUM 22PT

SEMIBOLD & LIGHT 10PT

The Yearbook of Type compendium works
well as a tool in vexed typography questions for polarizing jobs

Quendel

Happy Family

Quendel Regular
Quendel Bold

Quendel Fingertip
Quendel Wood

Quendel Marking Pen
Quendel Crayon

Dès Noël où un zéphyr haï me vêt de glaçons würmiens, je dîne d'exquis rôtis de bœuf au kir à l'aÿ d'âge mûr & cætera
Blåbærgrød
A quick movement of the enemy will jeopardize six gunboats.
@
Marmelade
Schweißgequält zündet Typograf Jakob verflixt öde Pangramme an.
Call me!
The quick brown fox jumps over the lazy dog.

About
The basic form of Quendel was written with a Japanese bamboo tip and therefore embodies a form letter of natural flow. The variants show other features that provide the feel of written scripts. The wood relief of Quendel Wood was created by a freehand wood relief drawn with oiled chalk. Quendel Marking Pen seems to be written with a felt-tip pen soon depleted. At the same time it is also reminiscent of the blooming effect, which we know from photography. The name of Quendel Fingertip suggests what can be seen—someone seems to have written with the finger in a grainy material. One would like to try it himself. The effect of broken lines which can be gained by writing with chalk as reflected in Quendel Crayon. Almost like parched sandy soil, the writing material seems to crumble.

Design
Anita Jürgeleit
2013

Foundry
URW++, Germany
www.urwpp.com

Styles / Weights
Regular, Bold, Crayon, Fingertip, Marking Pen, Wood

Language support
Latin

OpenType options
Proportional Lining, Standard Ligatures, Superscript, Ordinals, Fractions

Optimized for web
Yes

REGULAR 18PT

abcdefghijklmnopqrstuvwxyzæfjåçéñöüß
ABCDEFGHIJKLMNOPQRSTUVWXYZÆÇØ
0123456789@.,-:;!?')]§*""«»/-€$&%

MARKING PEN D 36PT

CRAYON D 16PT

Typographers want amazing, exquisite & clever justified text in books

FINGERTIP 36PT

WOOD D 16PT

The Yearbook of Type compendium works well as a tool in vexed typography questions for polarizing jobs

Quercus
user's special offline codex
navigation
Braganza Institute Library
REGIONAL
Putzentfernungsmittel
Настоящий
Tons of indistinguishable typefaces in the world
Thirsty & Holy Motors
Язык машин
Чемодан индустрияльной свёклы

Hairline *Silent*, Rational skele
Thin *yet little-spicy*, transpare
Light *fresh*, legible & toner sa
Book *informal*, decent conce
Regular *legible* workhorse fo
Medium *very visible*, protruc
Bold *for branding &* headlin
Black *loud* for street and bil

Quercus Sans

About
Quercus is characterized by open, yet a little bit condensed drawing with sufficient spacing so that the neighboring letters never touch. It has eight interpolated weights with respective italics. Their fine gradation allows finding an exact valeur for any kind of design, especially on the web. Quercus serif styles took inspiration from neo-classical typefaces with vertical shadows, ball terminals and thin serifs. The italics have the same width proportion as upright styles. This "modern" attitude is applied to both families and calls for use on the same page, e. g. in dictionaries and cultural programs. Serif styles marked by "10" are dedicated to textual point sizes and long reading. The sans serif principle is rather minimalistic, with subtle shadows and thinned joints between curved shapes and stems.

It excels in informational and magazine design, corporate identity and branding, but it is suited for book covers, catalogues and posters as well.

Design
František Štorm
2015

Foundry
Storm Type Foundry, Czech Republic
www.stormtype.com

Styles / Weights
Hairline, Hairline Italic, Thin, Thin Italic, Light, Light Italic, Book, Book Italic, Regular, Italic, Medium, Medium Italic, Bold, Bold Italic, Black, Black Italic

Language support
Latin, Cyrillic

OpenType options
Proportional Oldstyle, Tabular and Proportional Lining, Tabular Oldstyle, Standard Ligatures, Discretionary Ligatures, Historical Ligatures, All Caps, Small Caps, Capitals to Small Caps, Swashes, Fractions, Numerator, Denominator, Ornaments, Arrows, Stylistic Alternates, Historical Forms, Slashed Zero

Optimized for web
Yes

REGULAR 18PT

abcdefgghijklmnopqrstuvwxyzæfjåçéñöûß
ABCDEFGHIJKLMNOPQRSTUVWXYZÆÇØ
01234567890@.,-:;!?')]§*""«»/–€$&⅓↗

BOLD 36PT

aejgGQR7

BLACK & MEDIUM 14PT

Typographers want
amazing, exquisite
& clever justified text
in books

LIGHT 36PT

aejgGQR7

ALL WEIGHTS 12PT

Hairline
Thin
Light
Book
Regular
Medium
Bold
Black

ITALICS 12PT

Hairline Italic
Thin Italic
Light Italic
Book Italic
Italic
Medium Italic
Bold Italic
Black Italic

Playing on both sides of the field

Slender but sturdy

CLASSIC FORM, MODERN STYLING

Pilcrows & fleurons

VENETIAN TO MODERN

A new voice in the chorus

&&*¶❦

Sjung när du kernar

Aangename letterspasiëring

Syng mens du spatierer

Le crénage en chantant

Nuo venetų iki modernių šriftų

Quire Sans

About
A classical term for a "signature" of printed leaves, folded and ready for binding with other signatures into a book or manuscript. With one foot in the world of pilcrows, fleurons and traditional book typography, and another in modern electronic media, the Quire Sans design plays both sides of the field. It's a typeface for all media, and a mirror for whatever's going on around it. Smiling but sometimes assertive. Slender but sturdy, when the need arises. And always eminently legible, large or small, on the page or on-screen.

Design
Jim Ford
2014

Foundry
Monotype, USA
www.monotype.com

Styles / Weights
Thin, Thin Italic, Extralight, Extralight Italic, Light, Light Italic, Regular, Italic, Medium, Medium Italic, Semi Bold, Semi Bold Italic, Bold, Heavy, Heavy Italic, Black, Black Italic, Fat, Fat Italic

Language support
Latin

OpenType options
Proportional Oldstyle, Tabular and Proportional Lining, Tabular Oldstyle, Standard Ligatures, All Caps, Small Caps, Capitals to Small Caps, Superscript, Subscript, Fractions, Numerator, Denominator, Stylistic Alternates, Stylistic Sets

Optimized for web
Yes

REGULAR 18PT

abcdefgghijklmnopqrstuvwxyzæfjåçéñöûß
ABCDEFGHIJKLMNOPQRSTUVWXYZÆÇØ
0123456789@.,-:;!?')]§*"" «»/–€$&½

THIN & BLACK 30PT

aejgGQR7
aejgGQR7

HEAVY & LIGHT 16PT

Typographers want
amazing, exquisite
& clever justified text
in books ❦

FAT & REGULAR 9PT

ref·er·ence book / *noun* / a book that contains facts and information that you look at when you need to find out sth. particular—*"I am looking for the right typeface for my project, so I use the Yearbook of Type as a reference book."*

ALL WEIGHTS 9PT

Thin
Extralight
Light
Regular
Medium
Semi Bold
Bold
Heavy
Black
Fat

ITALICS 9PT

Thin Italic
Extralight Italic
Light Italic
Italic
Medium Italic
Semi Bold Italic
Bold Italic
Heavy Italic
Black Italic
Fat Italic

A designed visual to show the potential of each typeface.

Quist
X
SMALL
CAPS
viẻẽţṇâṁệsẻ
@Ắю
Открытие небес
Ελληνικά
space
gothic
Greyscale
Colour mode:
2130870918
This is an opportunity to present the font design's specific qualities in the best way.
contemporary
SAMPLE
&

About
The wonderful fictional character Onno Quist gave this typeface its name. Quist is a contemporary space-efficient gothic typeface and comes with a huge scope of language support and OpenType features.

"If written in the three-letter words of the four-letter alphabet, a human being is determined by a genetic narrative long enough to fill the equivalent of 500 Bibles. In the meantime human beings have discovered this for themselves. That's right. They have uncovered our profoundest concept—namely, that life is ultimately reading. They themselves are the Book of Books." Quote from Harry Mulish: *The Discovery of Heaven*

Design
Ralph du Carrois
2014

Foundry
Carrois Type Design, Germany
www.carrois.com

Styles / Weights
Regular, Medium, Bold, Head

Language support
Latin, Cyrillic, Greek, Vietnamese

OpenType options
Proportional Oldstyle, Tabular and Proportional Lining, Tabular Oldstyle, Standard Ligatures, All Caps, Capitals to Small Caps, Superscript, Subscript, Fractions, Numerator, Denominator, Arrows, Historical Forms, Slashed Zero

Optimized for web
Yes

REGULAR 18PT

abcdefghijklmnopqrstuvwxyzæfjåçéñöûß
ABCDEFGHIJKLMNOPQRSTUVWXYZÆÇØ
01234567890@.,-:;!?')]§*""«»/–€$&⅓↗

HEAD 48 PT

aejgGQR7

BOLD & REGULAR 16PT

Typographers want amazing, exquisite
& clever justified text in books

MEDIUM 39PT

aejgGQR7

HEAD 16PT

The Yearbook of Type compendium works well as a tool in vexed typography questions for polarizing jobs

NEWS FROM GIZEH

fluid excerpt

LIONS TIGERS AND BEARS

nova

MORE LIQUID TEQUILA

Black Pearl

young minds to write,
sing, draw & play daily

9 flying monkeys

perception

circle yellow brick roads in

The 23 carnival lights

About
A modern slab serif that mirrors the zeitgeist. It is no accident that the letter "Q" is the first letter in the name of the font. Freytag designed the "Q" as the first letter of the new font and derived the other characters from it. It was designed as a monolinear font, so that only a few letters have careful variations in the weights. Along with the upright styles, Quitador has a true Italic. The lightly tilted letters have round, extended line ends, which lends them a soft and dynamic character while allowing them to maintain their shape extensively. With seven weights, Quitador covers an enormous bandwidth, and as a result is suited to the most diverse applications. In headlines, the font can set the tone; in the smaller sizes, it is also easily legible.

Design
Arne Freytag
2014

Foundry
Monotype, USA
www.monotype.com

Styles / Weights
UltraLight, Light, Regular, Medium, Bold, ExtraBold, UltraBold, each with Italics

Language support
Latin, Afrikaans, Basque, Breton, Catalan, Croatian, Czech, Danish, Dutch, English, Estonian, Finnish, French, Gaelic (Irish, Scots), German, Hungarian, Icelandic, Indonesian, Irish, Italian, Latvian, Lithuanian, Norwegian, Polish, Portuguese, Romanian, Saami (Southern), Serbian, Slovak, Slovenian, Spanish, Swahili, Swedish, Turkish.

OpenType options
Tabular and Proportional Lining, Standard Ligatures, Superscript, Subscript, Fractions, Numerator, Denominator

Optimized for web
Yes

REGULAR 17PT

abcdefghijklmnopqrstuvwxyzæfjåçéñöûß
ABCDEFGHIJKLMNOPQRSTUVWXYZÆÇØ
0123456789@.,-:;!?')]§*""«»/–€$&½

BOLD & MEDIUM 30PT

aejgGQR7
aejgGQR7

EXTRABOLD & ULTRALIGHT 16PT

Typographers want
amazing, exquisite
& clever justified
text in books

BOLD & REGULAR 8PT

com·pen·dium / *noun* / (pl. com·pen·dia / or com·pen·diums) a collection of facts, drawings and photographs on a particular subject, especially in a book: *"a compendium of typography."*

ALL WEIGHTS 9PT

UltraLight
Light
Regular
Medium
Bold
ExtraBold
UltraBold

ITALICS 9PT

UltraLight Italic
Light Italic
Italic
Medium Italic
Bold Italic
ExtraBold Italic
UltraBold Italic

The Rebellion of the Lambs

Cape Arcona Type Foundry

CA Recape

About
CA Recape is a weird and beautiful vintage script family with two styles. It's an excellent choice for creating logotypes, headlines, signs, posters and any design that requires a custom-made feeling. The basic inspiration for CA Recape comes from American '50s lettering. But instead of reviving one special style, it is a kind of "Best of" remix. It takes the weirdest and most beautiful letterforms of a weird and beautiful time and merges them into one font. The outcome is a charming bastard. Guess what it looks like: weird and beautiful.

CA Recape is packed with a lot of OpenType features like underlining swashes, Stylistic, Discretionary, Titling and Contextual Alternates and Ligatures for use in OpenType-savvy programs. It also comes with some nice Ornaments.

Derived from the original typeface, Cape Arcona Type Foundry also offers a Raw style that has the distressed look of a poorly printed raw font.

Design
Thomas Schostok
2014

Foundry
Cape Arcona Type Foundry, Germany
www.cape-arcona.com

Styles / Weights
Regular, Raw

Language support
Latin

OpenType options
Standard Ligatures, Discretionary Ligatures, Titling Alternates, Swashes, Contextual Alternates, Ornaments, Stylistic Alternates

Optimized for web
No

REGULAR 15PT

aa, bcdefghhijklmnopqrstuvwxyzæfjåçéñöûß
AAABCDEFGHIJKLMNOPQRSTUVWXYZÆŒÇØ
0123456789@.,-:;!?')]§*"" «»/-€$&♥

REGULAR 30PT

aejgGQR7

REGULAR 19PT

Typographers want amazing, exquisite, & clever justified text, in books ★

RAW 30PT

aejgGQR7

RAW 19PT

Typographers want amazing, exquisite & clever justified text in books

Museum

Rektorat Black

Fassade

Rektorat Bold

Korridor

Rektorat Medium

Rektorat

Rektorat Regular

Baustelle

Rektorat Light

Sekretär

Rektorat Thin

Eingang B

Rektorat Hairline

NN Rektorat

About
The building where the Zurich University of the Arts (formerly called the School of Applied Arts) was housed from the 1930s to 2014 was built during the Bauhaus period. During its renovation in 2001 Rudolf Barmettler was asked to derive a new signage typeface from existing lettering. Together with students he traced parts of characters that were discovered during the renewal of the building's wallpapers. These letters were completely redrawn in ink and then refined. The aim was to create a typeface that could be used in-house for writing phrases like "WC Damen" (ladies' room), "Kein Durchgang" (no passage), "Galerie" (gallery) etc.

In 2002 while teaching at the F+F Design School, Barmettler created additional weights together with the students. Reinhard Haus helped to digitize the drawings and to create and extend the fonts using Fontographer software. The plan was to create a family of 18 typestyles but, unfortunately, these were never realized. Since 2014 Rudolf Barmettler and Anton Studer have reworked the entire typeface. The current seven weights form the first part of an ever-growing superfamily.

Design
Rudolf Barmettler
2015

Foundry
Nouvelle Noire, Switzerland
www.nouvellenoire.ch

Styles / Weights
Hairline, Thin, Light, Regular, Medium, Bold, Black

Language support
Latin

OpenType options
Tabular and Proportional Lining, Ligatures, Superscript, Subscript, Fractions, Numerator, Denominator, Arrows, Stylistic Sets, Slashed Zero

Optimized for web
Yes

REGULAR 18PT

abcdefghijklmnopqrstuvwxyzfjåcéñöû
ABCDEFGHIJKLMNOPQRSTUVWXYZ
0123456789.,-:;!?')]"«»/–€$

BOLD 35PT

aejGQR7

HEAVY & THIN 16PT

Typographers want amazing, exquisite
and clever justified text in books

HAIRLINE 35PT

aejGQR7

MEDIUM & LIGHT 16PT

Typographers want amazing, exquisite
and clever justified text in books

Mi Investigación
CORAZÓN
IMPRESOS
Guadalajara
MALLORCA
Spanish
San Salvador de Leyre
Tipografico
Estilo
TOLEDO
ESCRITURA
Retiro
ALICANTE
humanista
Sabadell
CAPITAL CATALANA
Historia
MUNDO
Miranda del Castañar
GOLDEN AGE
Oranges
ALMODOVAR
Oficio
Castrojeriz
Experiencia
Montserrat
Costa de la Luz
Flamenco
Mediterranean
humanista
Guadalquivir
TORREMOLINOS
Carrer de Montcada

Retiro

About
Retiro is a daring interpretation of Spanish typography. Severe, austere and yet full of life, Retiro is a vernacular version of Castilian and Andalusian in a typical Didot. Named after a lovely park in Madrid, Retiro started life as a bespoke typeface designed to give a unique voice to the magazine *Madriz*. In 2006, the founder of *Madriz* was looking for a Didot for his new magazine. The Didot is the archetypal typeface used in high-end magazines. In 2014, in order to keep its originality, the unique weight was retained, but complemented with optical size variants to set highly contrasted headlines into various sizes, visually balanced. The Retiro Pro glyph set is available in five optical sizes and offers 1,100 signs and variations we have refined to the extreme for several months. Via multiple OpenType features combined to infinity, the Retiro offers your graphic projects a unique but never austere typographic identity as it is “multiple” and full of life.

Design
Jean François Porchez
2014

Foundry
Typofonderie, France
www.typofonderie.com

Styles / Weights
Regular

Language support
Latin

OpenType options
Proportional Oldstyle, Tabular and Proportional Lining, Tabular Oldstyle, Standard Ligatures, Discretionary Ligatures, Historical Ligatures, All Caps, Small Caps, Capitals to Small Caps, Superscript, Subscript, Ordinals, Titling Alternates, Swashes, All Alternates, Contextual Alternates, Fractions, Numerator, Denominator, Ornaments, Arrows, Stylistic Alternates, Stylistic Sets, Historical Forms, Slashed Zero, Optical size

Optimized for web
No

REGULAR 17PT

aabcdefgghijklmnopqrstuvwxyyzzæfjåçéñöûß
AAAABCDEFGHIJKLMNOPQRSTUVWXYZÆÇØ
0123456789ø@.,-:;!?')]§*“”«»/–€$&

REGULAR 36PT

aejgGQR7

REGULAR 16PT

Typographers want amazing, exquisite & clever justified text in books

REGULAR STYLISTIC SET 36PT

ORNAMENTS REGULAR 24PT

It was a pleasure to burn

Igor Stravinsky

sometimes I left messages

Las Vegas

MY KEEPER IS WATCHING ME

Nottinghamshire

gently smiling jaws

Dostoyevsky

All this happened, more or less.

PUFFING DEVIL

About
Riga is a space-saving and highly legible typeface designed to work equally well on paper and on screen. Its personality is clear and practical, yet warm and polite. Economical proportions, high x-height and open letter forms result in a very useable typeface, particularly for delicate tasks such as narrow columns or tight headlines. Riga is exceptionally readable at small point sizes and elegant at larger ones.

Riga Screen has been designed to work particularly well on screen. Responsive websites and office applications will appreciate its economic proportions. Riga has been specially engineered and optimized for exceptional readability in small sizes on all current computer monitors, including tablets and smartphones. This small family of four weights can be perfectly combined with the Riga type family.

Design
Ludwig Übele
2014

Foundry
LudwigType, Germany
www.ludwigtype.de

Styles / Weights
Extralight, Extralight Italic, Light, Light Italic, Regular, Italic, Medium, Medium Italic, Bold, Bold Italic, Black, Black Italic

Language support
Latin

OpenType options
Proportional Oldstyle, Tabular Lining, Proportional Lining, Tabular Oldstyle, Standard Ligatures, Discretionary Ligatures, All Caps, Small Caps, Capitals to Small Caps, Superscript, Subscript, Ordinals, Contextual Alternates, Fractions, Numerator, Denominator, Arrows, Stylistic Alternates, Stylistic Sets, Slashed Zero

Optimized for web
Yes

REGULAR 18PT

abcdefgghijklmnopqrstuvwxyzæfjåçéñöûß
ABCDEFGHIJKLMNOPQRSTUVWXYZÆÇØ
01234567890@.,-:;!?')]§*""«»/–€$&½↗

BOLD 35PT

aejGQR7

BLACK & REGULAR 16PT

Typographers want
amazing, exquisite
and clever justified
text in books

BOLD & REGULAR 10PT

ex·am·ple / *noun* / an illustration that supports or provides more information: by showing examples the Yearbook of Type presents each font in different sizes and weights

ALL WEIGHTS 10PT

Extralight
Light
Regular
Medium
Bold
Black

ITALICS 10PT

Extralight Italic
Light Italic
Italic
Medium Italic
Bold Italic
Black

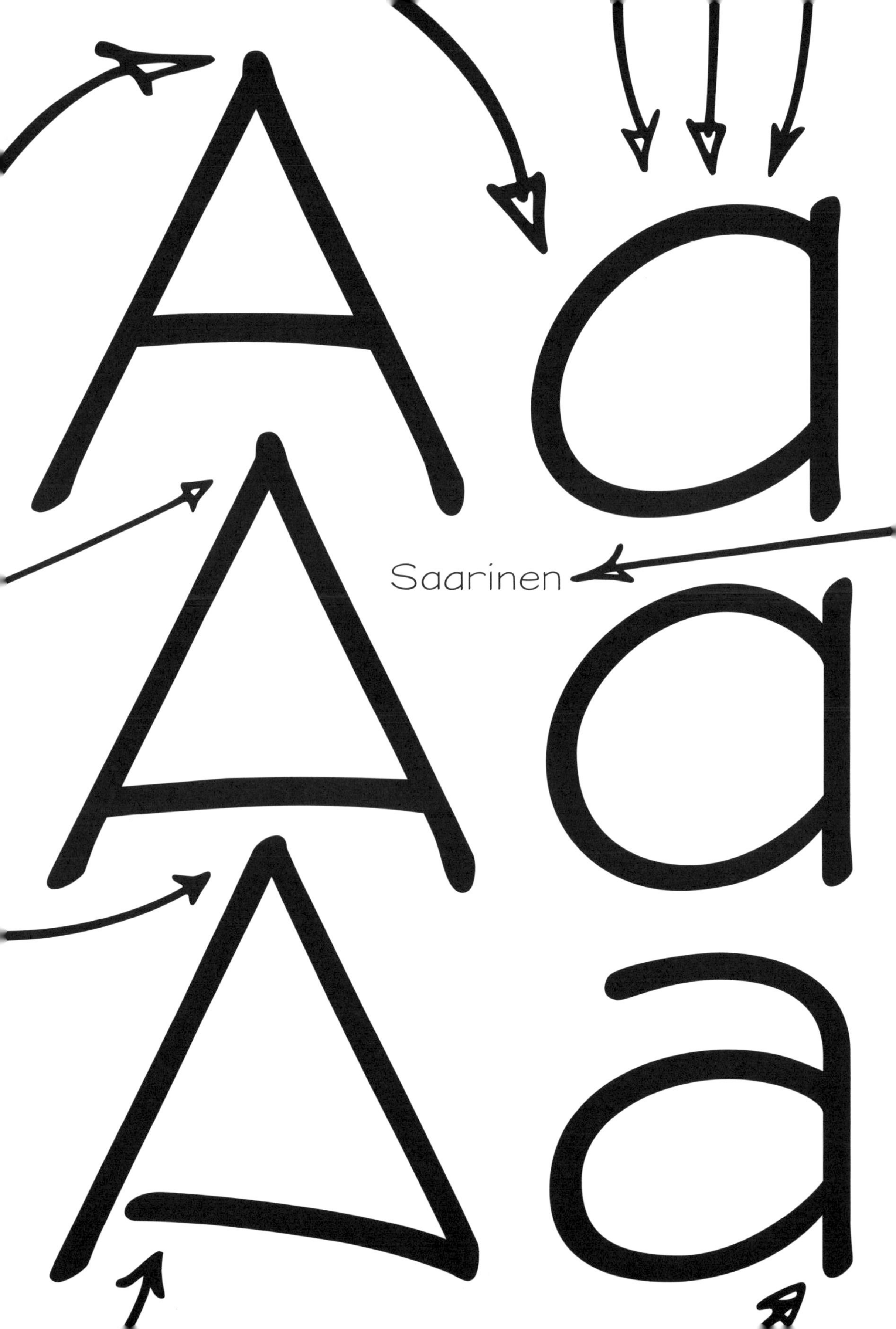
Saarinen

P22 Saarinen

About
P22 Saarinen is a typeface based on the architectural lettering of Finnish American architect Eero Saarinen. The Saarinen fonts were created to help commemorate the 75th anniversary of Kleinhans Music Hall in Buffalo, NY, which was designed by Saarinen in collaboration with his father Eliel Saarinen and is recognized as one of the greatest concert halls ever built in the United States.

Saarinen's own lettering styles were combined with various lettering manual suggestion for proper lettering to create a flexible casual lettering style in regular and bold weights.

The Pro fonts include multiple variations of each letter for a more natural lettering style as well as stylistic variants to achieve various highs for crossbars and other customizable variants. The Pro fonts also include Central European character set, fractions, small caps and an array of hand-drawn directional arrows.

Design
Miranda Roth
2014

Foundry
International House of Fonts
(P22 Type Foundry), USA
www.p22.com

Styles / Weights
Family of four styles (Regular, Pro, Alternate 1, Alternate 2), each in two weights (Regular, Bold), plus Arrows

Language support
Latin

OpenType options
Standard Ligatures, Contextual Alternates, Arrows, Stylistic Alternates

Optimized for web
Yes

REGULAR 13PT

abcdefghijklmnopqrstuvwxyzæfjåçéñöûß
ABCDEFGHIJKLMNOPQRSTUVWXYZÆÇØ
0123456789@.,-:;!?')]§*"" «»/—€$& ½

BOLD 28PT

aejgGQR7

BOLD & REGULAR 13PT

Typographers want amazing, exquisite
& clever justified text in books

ARROWS 24PT

ALTERNATE 2 BOLD & REGULAR 10PT

The Yearbook of Type compendium works well as
a tool in vexed typography questions for polarizing jobs

Crowds were a huge thing.

SIGNO

Still are!

THIN & ITALIC

Sed ut perspiciatis unde omnis iste natus error sit voluptatem *accusantium dolorem que laudantium, totam rem aperiam*

LIGHT & ITALIC

Sed ut perspiciatis unde omnis iste natus error sit voluptatem *accusantium dolorem que laudantium, totam rem aperiam*

BOOK & ITALIC

Sed ut perspiciatis unde omnis iste natus error sit voluptatem *accusantium dolorem que laudantium,*

REGULAR & ITALIC

Sed ut perspiciatis unde omnis iste natus error sit voluptatem *accusantium dolorem que laudantium,*

MEDIUM & ITALIC

Sed ut perspiciatis unde omnis iste natus error sit voluptatem *accusantium dolorem que laudantium, totam*

BOLD & ITALIC

Sed ut perspiciatis unde omnis iste natus error sit voluptatem ***accusantium dolorem que laudantium, totam***

About
Signo is a dynamic sans serif with reverse contrast, designed for editorial and branding. Signo is a charismatic typeface for headlines, but its tall x-height and open counters also make it perform well in small sizes, resulting in a versatile typeface across weights. The cursive italics are a good complement to the roman fonts and will add variety and warmth to the page. The Signo family comes in six weights, from Thin to Bold, and includes two weights for text: the Book and the Regular.

Design
Rui Abreu
2014

Foundry
Rui Abreu / R-typography, Portugal
www.r-typography.com

Styles / Weights
Thin, Thin Italic, Light, Light Italic, Book, Book Italic, Regular, Italic, Medium, Medium Italic, Bold, Bold Italic

Language support
Latin

OpenType options
Standard Ligatures, All Caps, Fractions, Numerator, Denominator, Historical Forms, Slashed Zero

Optimized for web
Yes

REGULAR 16PT

abcdefghijklmnopqrstuvwxyzæfjåçéñöûß
ABCDEFGHIJKLMNOPQRSTUVWXYZÆÇØ
01234567890@.,-:;!?')]§*""«»/–€$&½

BOLD 30PT

aejgGQR7

BOLD REGULAR 16PT

Typographers want amazing, exquisite
& clever justified text in books

BOLD & REGULAR 9PT

over·view / *noun* / a brief summary of something: *in the index of the Yearbook of Type the reader can find an overview of all typefaces presented in the book sorted by classification*

ALL WEIGHTS 10PT

Thin
Light
Book
Regular
Medium
Bold

ITALICS 10PT

Thin Italic
Light Italic
Book Italic
Italic
Medium Italic
Bold Italic

Sindelar

Sindelar Bold, set in 60 pt ►

▼ Sindelar Regular A, set in 112 pt

a

3 Regulars
A, B, and C
3 Regular Italics
A, B, and C
Medium
Medium Italic
Semibold
Semibold Italic
Bold
Bold Italic
Extrabold
Extrabold Italic
Black
Black Italic
Extrablack
Extrablack Italic

Willerstorfer
FONT FOUNDRY

▼ various weights of Sindelar

Foco, determinação e motivação

Wunderteam

Happels Trainerkarriere begann in den Niederlanden bei ADO Den Haag

første landslagsmål

c'est ce qu'a déclaré le Premier Ministre

raccogliere

Polacy rozpoczynają walkę o potrójną koronę

technically outstanding

la superluna ha iniziato a farsi vedere nel Pacifico, in Nuova Zelanda e Australia

Maradona

WIEN – Ogris ist kein Mann großer Worte. Erst recht nicht, wenn es um die eigene Vergangenheit geht. Will man heute mit ihm über seinen fulminanten WM-Treffer gegen die USA sprechen, ist er perplex: »Nicht Ihr Ernst, oder?« Doch, doch. Wie könnte man nur vergessen. Energieanfall, dein Name am 19. Juni 1990 war Andi Ogris. In der 49. Minute trat Tab Ramos einen Corner für die USA, der Ball wird am kurzen Eck aus der Gefahrenzone geköpfelt und von Gerhard Rodax präzise in den Lauf der mit hellseherischen Fähigkeiten ausgestatteten roten Rakete verlängert.

Der Rest spielt sich im sommerlichen Florenz in Zeitraffer ab, die Gegner in Zeitlupe. Drei US-Spieler werden gnadenlos überlaufen, zu Hydranten degradiert. Und so brutal er diesen Konter lief, so gefühlvoll schloss er ihn ab, mit einem Lupfer ins lange Eck. Ogris hat für das Solo eine simple Erklärung. [...]

8.4/10.5 Reg. A | Der Standard, Vienna, 7 Oct. 2014

Sindelar

About
Sindelar is a capable, contemporary text face addressing today's news design requirements. Its large x-height, low contrast and robust serifs grant a high legibility in small sizes. The balanced, well-chosen proportions make the typeface economic without giving it a too narrow appearance. These characteristics make it the ideal choice for extensive text setting in newspapers and magazines. Named after Austrian soccer player Matthias Sindelar (1903–1939), one of the best players of his time, the typeface shares two major qualities with its namesake: their technical brilliance and their way of performing aesthetically to the last detail. The football player's nickname "Der Papierene" (the Paper Man) elegantly refers to the media, too. Although optimized for small sizes, Sindelar's low contrast and robust serifs give the typeface a strong impact in larger sizes. Sindelar comes in 18 styles. Each font is equipped with a character set of about 980 glyphs and various OpenType features.

Design
Stefan Willerstorfer
2014

Foundry
Willerstorfer Font Foundry, Austria
www.willerstorfer.com

Styles / Weights
Regular (A, B, C), Medium, Semibold, Bold, Extrabold, Black, Extrablack, each with Italics

Language support
Latin

OpenType options
Small Caps, Case Sensitive Forms, Capital Spacing, Ligatures, Discretionary Ligatures, Proportional Oldstyle Figures, Proportional and Tabular Lining Figures, Tabular Oldstyle Figures, Small Cap Figures, Numerators, Denominators, Prebuilt Fractions, Superiors, Inferiors, Superscript, Subscript, Ordinals, Titling Alternates, Localized Forms, Historical Forms, Stylistic Sets, Circled Figures, Geometric Shapes, Arrows, Circled Arrows, Mark Positioning

Optimized for web
Yes

REGULAR A 16PT

abcdefghijklmnopqrstuvwxyzæfjåçéñöûß
ABCDEFGHIJKLMNOPQRSTUVWXYZÆÇØ
0123456789@.,-:;!?')]§*""«»/–€$&⅓↗

BLACK 30PT

aejgGQR7

EXTRABOLD & REGULAR C 15PT

Typographers want
amazing, exquisite
& clever justified text
in books

BOLD & REGULAR A 8PT

↗ **Year·book of Type** / *noun* / book published every second year, giving details on typefaces of the previous two years and also about general current typographic topics—*e.g. OpenType features, font editors like Glyphs etc.*

ALL WEIGHTS 8PT

Regular A
Regular B
Regular C
Medium
Semibold
Bold
Extrabold
Black
Extrablack

ITALICS 8PT

Regular A Italic
Regular B Italic
Regular C Italic
Medium Italic
Semibold Italic
Bold Italic
Extrabold Italic
Black Italic
Extrablack Italic

STENCIL ALLROUND

→ CAPITAL LETTER FONT FOR DISPLAY USE

BLUEBERRIES

LUCKY BUDDAH

FRISBEE

www.Letterwerk.ch

About
Stencil Allround is a rounded stencil capital letter font made for display use.

Design
Dominique Boessner
2011

Foundry
Letterwerk, Switzerland
www.letterwerk.ch

Styles / Weights
Regular

Language support
Latin

OpenType options
All Caps, Fractions, Arrows

Optimized for web
Yes

REGULAR 18PT
ABCDEFGHIJKLMNOPQRSTUVWXYZÆÀÇÉÑÖÛ
0123456789@.,-:;!?')*"“«»/–€$&½→

REGULAR 36PT
AEJGQR7

REGULAR 16PT
TYPOGRAPHERS WANT
AMAZING, EXQUISITE
& CLEVER JUSTIFIED TEXT
IN BOOKS

Stencil Allround

TAZ WIDE & EXTENDED

▪ ▪ ▪ ▪ ▪ ▪ ▪

Inimitablemente!

Wide – UltraBlack

czasami biorą najbliższą książkę

Wide – SemiLight

*24. August 1899 in Buenos Aires

Wide – Black Italic [Discretionary Ligatures]

ONBEGRENSD

Wide – UltraLight Italic

zusammenhängende Wortfügungen

Wide – Black

natuurlĳkerwĳs

Wide – Regular [Stylistic Set 16 + Discretionary Ligatures]

▪ ▪ ▪ ▪ ▪ ▪ ▪

grande

Extended – UltraBlack

Mar del Plata, 1941

Extended – UltraLight [Stylistic Set 1]

¿Cómo localizar el venerado hexágono secreto?

Extended – Italic

tiefschwarz

Extended – UltraBlack

EXTRAVAGANT HAPPINESS

Extended – SemiLight

eşit öğelerden oluşuyordu

Extended – ExtraBold Italic

Taz Wide & Extended

About
Taz Wide and Taz Extended complement the Taz family. Ten weights, each with 812 glyphs including Vietnamese (!), stylistic alternates, and eight figure sets. Like all Taz fonts, they have square dots and punctuation marks, which can be switched to rounded versions for a softer look. Taz Wide has a generous width and saves vertical space. Taz Extended, as one of the widest fonts on the market, makes a vigorous impression and is ideally suited for contemporary editorial design, striking art and advertising.

Design
Luc(as) de Groot
2014

Foundry
LucasFonts, Germany
www.lucasfonts.com

Styles / Weights
UltraLight, ExtraLight, Light, SemiLight, Regular, SemiBold, Bold, ExtraBold, Black, UltraBlack, each with Italics

Language support
Latin

OpenType options
Proportional Oldstyle, Tabular and Proportional Lining, Tabular Oldstyle, Standard Ligatures, Discretionary Ligatures, Superscript, Subscript, Ordinals, All Alternates, Contextual Alternates, Fractions, Numerator, Denominator, Stylistic Alternates, Stylistic Sets, Historical Forms

Optimized for web
Yes

TAZ EXTENDED REGULAR 13PT

aabcdefgghiijjklmnopqrstuvwxyyzæfjåçéñöûß
ABCDEFGHIJKLMNOPQRSTUVWXYZÆÇØ
0123456789@.,-:;!?')]§*""«»/—€$&⅓

TAZ WIDE REGULAR 13PT

aabcdefgghiijjklmnopqrstuvwxyyzæfjåçéñöûß
ABCDEFGHIJKLMNOPQRSTUVWXYZÆÇØ
0123456789@.,-:;!?')]§*""«»/—€$&⅓

TAZ EXT BOLD & REGULAR 9PT

com·pen·dium / *noun* / (pl.com·pen·dia / or com·pen·diums) a collection of facts, drawings and photographs on a particular subject, especially in a book: *"a compendium of typography."*

TAZ WIDE ALL WEIGHTS 8PT

UltraLight
ExtraLight
Light
SemiLight
Regular
SemiBold
Bold
ExtraBold
Black
UltraBlack

TAZ WIDE ITALICS 12PT

UltraLight Italic
ExtraLight Italic
Light Italic
SemiLight Italic
Italic
SemiBold Italic
Bold Italic
ExtraBold Italic
Black Italic
UltraBlack Italic

Aa Bb Cc Dd Ee Ff Gg Hh Ii Jj Kk Ll Mm Nn Ññ Oo
Pp Qq Rr Ss Tt Uu Vv Ww Xx Yy Zz 1 2 3 4 5 6 7 8 9 0

GLYPHS · MEDIUM, 21 PTS

The three dimensional shape or configuration of a molecule is an important characteristic. This shape is dependent on the preferred spatial orientation of covalent bonds to atoms having two or more bonding partners. Three dimensional configurations are best viewed with the aid of models. In order to represent such configurations on a two-dimensional surface (paper, blackboard or

PARAGRAPH · BOOK, 14 PTS

Torres del Paine

BLACK · 70 PTS

Counterbalancing

HEAVY · 63 PTS

Ciudad de Barcelona

BOLD · 55 PTS

Meat is Animal Murder

MEDIUM · 50 PTS

I Worked Hard for 38 Years

REGULAR · 45 PTS

IMPRESIONISTAS
AU REVOIR LEA
BRANDS
JEAN

THIN

DESARROLLADO
REPUBLICANO
HORSES
CERA

BOLD

CIGARRETES
AUTOMOBILE
FRANCE
KIDS

BLACK

Ra REGULAR
Ra BOOK
Ra LIGHT
Ra THIN

Ra REGULAR ITALIC
Ra BOOK ITALIC
Ra LIGHT ITALIC
Ra THIN ITALIC

Ra BLACK
Ra HEAVY
Ra BOLD
Ra MEDIUM

Ra BLACK ITALIC
Ra HEAVY ITALIC
Ra BOLD ITALIC
Ra MEDIUM ITALIC

a a

THIN & THIN ALT · 165 PTS

$79.28
€46.30
£32.95

NUMBERS · 58 PTS

fsß

ESZETT COMPARISION · 72 PTS

g g

BOLD · 156 PTS

A B C
D E F
G H I

GLYPHS · BLACK, 72 PTS

Citroën

BRAND · BOLD, 58 PTS

About
Texta. A Sans for All.

Through studying humanists' models from Edward Johnston to Adrian Frutiger and the Gothic Alphabet made by sign painters comes Texta, a contemporary, rational, transparent and useful Sans to compose all kind of texts. We incorporated an Alt version that replaces lower cases like a-g-y with geometric constructions to get more versatility in neutral compositions.

Design
Daniel Hernández, Miguel Hernández
2014

Foundry
Latinotype, Chile
www.latinotype.com

Styles / Weights
Family of two styles (Regular, Alt), each in eight weights (Thin, Light, Regular, Book, Medium, Bold, Heavy, Black), each with Italics

Language support
Latin

OpenType options
Fractions

Optimized for web
No

REGULAR 18PT

abcdefghijklmnopqrstuvwxyzæfjåçéñöûß
ABCDEFGHIJKLMNOPQRSTUVWXYZÆÇØ
0123456789@.,-:;!?')]§*“”«»/-€$&½

BLACK & ALT BLACK 36PT

aejgGQR7
aejgGQR7

BOLD & THIN 16PT

Typographers want
amazing, exquisite
& clever justified text
in books

ALT BOLD & ALT BOOK 8PT

com·pen·dium / noun / (pl. com·pen·dia / or com·pen·diums) a collection of facts, drawings and photographs on a particular subject, especially in a book: *"a compendium of typography."*

REGULAR 10PT

Thin
Light
Book
Regular
Medium
Bold
Heavy
Black

REGULAR ITALICS 12PT

Thin Italic
Light Italic
Book Italic
Italic
Medium Italic
Bold Italic
Heavy Italic
Black Italic

STOLTENBERG

12,400 CHARACTERS

Each ThreeDee character is partly covered by its predecessor and is creating a three-dimensional effect.

ThreeDee

URW++

About

Axel Stoltenberg, longtime IKARUS program developer at URW++, had the idea for this completely new font design with overlapping characters. Each character is partly covered by its predecessor and thereby creates a three-dimensional effect. This technique was not available before digital fonts. The implementation of this unusual notation for digital setting required a lot of programming until all necessary character variants were produced and set properly, always using the correct form. In order to achieve this, the OpenType Pro font ThreeDee contains about 12,400 characters and all the necessary OpenType features for the automatic setting in OTF savvy application programs.

The slightly playful basic design was created by Anna Stoltenberg, the daughter of Axel, specially devised for the innovative representation and support of its special nature. ThreeDee is a headline font that will unveil all its charisma and exceptional quality at appropriate, larger sizes.

Design

Anna Stoltenberg, Axel Stoltenberg
2014

Foundry

URW++, Germany
www.urwpp.com

Styles / Weights

Regular

Language support

Latin

OpenType options

Proportional Lining, Standard Ligatures, Superscript, Ordinals, Fractions, Custom OpenType Feature Programming for Automatic Setting

Optimized for web

Yes

REGULAR 16PT

abcdefghijklmnopqrstuvwxyzæfjåçéñöüß
ABCDEFGHIJKLMNOPQRSTUVWXYZÆÇØ
0123456789@.,-:;!?')]§*"" «»/–€$&

REGULAR 30PT

REGULAR 16PT

Typographers want amazing, exquisite & clever justified text in books

Tilda Grande

& Tilda Petite

About
Jessica Hische's typeface for Moonrise Kingdom set the tone for a sweet movie about youthful innocence. Inspired by director Wes Anderson's quaint aesthetic and the titles from La Femme Infidéle (1969), Tilda is formally dressed, without hiding its raw, intentional naïveté. Unusual for a script typeface, it comes in two size-specific styles to preserve its delicate qualities for uses big and small, on page or screen.

Design
Jessica Hische
2014

Foundry
The Font Bureau, USA
www.fontbureau.com

Styles / Weights
Grande, Petite

Language support
Latin

OpenType options
Proportional Oldstyle, Proportional Lining, Standard Ligatures, All Caps, Superscript, Subscript, Ordinals, Fractions, Ornaments, Arrows, Stylistic Alternates

Optimized for web
Yes

GRANDE 18PT

abcdefghhijklmnopqrstuvwxyyzœfiffbåçéñöûß

AABCDEFGHIJKLMNOPQRSTUVWXYZÆÇØ

0123456789@.,-:;!?)]§*""«»/-€$&½

GRANDE 48PT

aejgGQRT

PETITE 18PT

The Yearbook of Type compendium works well as a tool in vexed typography questions for polarizing jobs

PETITE 40PT

aejgGQRT

GRANDE 15PT

cata·logue / noun / a complete list of things that people can look at or buy:a catalogue of typefaces (a book showing the newest fonts, to help people choose the right typeface)

From THIN —To
BLACK

Thin Light Regular **Bold & Black**

About
Designed in 2009 for the corporate visual identity of a digital television channel, Tomica was completely redesigned in 2011 and published by AinsiFont in 2012.

Tomica is a sans serif geometric character. Even though it is of original design, Tomica is a descendant of Paul Renner's Futura (1927).

Design
Sébastien Delobel
2012

Foundry
AinsiFont, France
www.ainsifont.com

Styles / Weights
Thin, Light, Regular, Bold, Black

Language support
Latin

OpenType options
Proportional Oldstyle, Tabular and Proportional Lining, Standard Ligatures, Discretionary Ligatures, Small Caps, Capitals to Small Caps, Superscript, Subscript, Ordinals, Titling Alternates, Fractions, Numerator, Denominator, Stylistic Alternates, Stylistic Sets, Petite Caps, Capitals to Petite Caps

Optimized for web
No

REGULAR 18PT

abcdefghijklmnopqrstuvwxyzæfjåçéñöûß
ABCDEFGHIJKLMNOPQRSTUVWXYZÆÇØ
0123456789@.,-:;!?')]§*""«»/–€$&⅓

BOLD 30PT

aejgGQR7

BOLD & THIN 14PT

Typographers want amazing, exquisite
& clever justified text in books

LIGHT 30PT

aejgGQR7

BLACK & REGULAR 10PT

The Yearbook of Type compendium works well as
a tool in vexed typography questions for polarizing jobs

SOY MUY POPULAR EN TWITTER Y ME GUSTA

TRENDING

I'M SEXIST AND I KNOW IT

FACUNDO HERNÁNDEZ NAZAL

HIPSTER

BUENOS AIRES, CONCEPCIÓN, SANTIAGO

About
Trend, Trend Hand Made and Trend Rough are fonts made of layers, taking as a basis a sans and a slab font. It is the result of observation, search and study of the latest global trends. Trend tries to capture the aesthetics of fashion or even fashion itself, integrating elements of a very popular and current trend.

It is a typeface designed to be used without need to add anything external to it, because it has all components required for this.

Trend is trending.

Design
Daniel Hernández, Paula Nazal Selaive
2013

Foundry
Latinotype, Chile
www.latinotype.com

Styles / Weights
Family of two styles (Sans, Slab), each with five weights (One, Two, Three, Four, Five), each with Italics, Ornaments

Language support
Latin

OpenType options
Fractions

Optimized for web
No

SANS ONE 16PT

ABCDEFGHIJKLMNOPQRSTUVWXYZ
ÆÅÇÉÑÖÛ
0123456789@.,-:;!?')*“”«»/–€$&½

SLAB FOUR 16PT

ABCDEFGHIJKLMNOPQRSTUVWXYZ
ÆÅÇÉÑÖÛ
0123456789@.,-:;!?')*“”«»/–€$&½

ORNAMENTS 27PT

SANS, ALL WEIGHTS 9PT

ONE
ONE ITALIC
TWO
TWO ITALIC
THREE
THREE ITALIC
FOUR
FOUR ITALIC
FIVE
FIVE ITALIC

SLAB, ALL WEIGHTS 9PT

ONE
ONE ITALIC
TWO
TWO ITALIC
THREE
THREE ITALIC
FOUR
FOUR ITALIC
FIVE
FIVE ITALIC

Trola Text Family
Prolonged Readings

COMPARISON OF TROLA (LOW CONTRAST) AND TROLA TEXT (HIGH CONTRAST)

EOHàndgêks

EOHàndgêks

Wider proportions — *Straight serifs* — *Pure rounded forms* — *More aperture* — *Larger ascenders & descenders* — *Slightly inclination*

HO

Wider

Wide increase Trola Text characters, particularly the upper case, are noticeably wider than in Trola, so they are perfectly adjusted to be used in text sizes. The wider proportions and a looser spacing help to avoid a condensed texture.

Crisp

Harmonic texture Some changes in the letterforms resulted in a more harmonic and balanced texture with more white space: circular forms are more rounded and have a different tension, diagonal strokes have been adjusted and flare towards the serifs.

cknow shpgie

Robust

Serifs totally straight In Trola Text the serifs have been simplified and strengthen so it is more robust when used in smaller sizes. A slight adjust in the contrast helps to resist better in reduced sizes.

Warm

Dynamic reading The characters in Trola Text have a slight inclination to the right which increases the reading speed, becoming more dynamic and lighter. The aperture in the letterforms have also been increased.

Trola Text

About

Trola Text keeps the original spirit of Trola, but some of the letterform features have been modified so it can perfectly adapt to the needs of typefaces used in text of continued reading.

Trola Text characteristics result in a somewhat crisp texture, with an increased contrast, and a high level of legibility. Proportions in Trola Text are noticeably wide, particularly in the upper case, but also the serifs are simpler, their construction is more robust, and the shapes are totally straight. White space becomes more prominent through a generous spacing and letterforms with larger aperture. A little increase in the curves' tension in every character and a slight flare in the strokes, particularly evident in the diagonal shapes, add a pinch of warmth. Additionally, the lowercase had some inclination to the right, increasing the speed of reading in prolonged readings.

Design
Jordi Embodas
2014

Foundry
Tipografies, Spain
www.tipografies.com

Styles / Weights
Light, Light Italic, Regular, Italic, Bold, Bold Italic, Heavy, Heavy Italic

Language support
Latin

OpenType options
Proportional Oldstyle, Tabular Lining, Proportional Lining, Standard Ligatures, Discretionary Ligatures, All Caps, Small Caps, Superscript, Subscript, Ordinals, Fractions, Numerator, Denominator, Optical size

Optimized for web
Yes

REGULAR 18PT

abcdefghijklmnopqrstuvwxyzæfjåçéñöûß
ABCDEFGHIJKLMNOPQRSTUVWXYZÆÇØ
0123456789@.,-:;!?')]§*""«»/–€$&½

BOLD & REGULAR 10PT

cata·logue / *noun* / a complete list of things that people can look at or buy: *a catalogue of typefaces (a book showing the newest fonts, to help people choose the right typeface)*

HEAVY & LIGHT 16PT

Typographers want
amazing, exquisite
& clever justified text
in books

BOLD & REGULAR 36PT

aejgGQR7
aejgGQR7

ALL WEIGHTS 10PT

Light
Regular
Bold
Heavy

ITALICS 12PT

Light Italic
Regular Italic
Bold Italic
Heavy Italic

REGULAR · 70 PTS

AA

LIGHT CONDENSED & WIDE ALT · 92 PTS

VALPARAÍSO

REGULAR · 70 PTS

NEW × YORK

BLACK · 70 PTS

ANGOULÊME

BLACK · 70 PTS

TECNO CITY BOYS

BLACK · 70 PTS

TACOS

BLACK · 70 PTS

CARNAVAL DO *RIO DE JANEIRO*

BLACK · 70 PTS

FRUSTRA LABORANT QUOTQUOT SE CALCULATIONIBUS FATIGANT PRO INVENTIONE QUADRATURAE CIRCUL · EXPRESSIO UNIUS EST EXCLUSIO ALTERIUS · AB HONESTO VIRUM BONUM NIHIL DETERRET · RADIX OMNIUM MALORUM EST CUPIDITAS · MATER ARTIUM NECESSITAS

PARAGRAPH · BOOK, 14 PTS

$39.28
¥2.690,50
£634.95
€46.30

BRAND · BOLD, 58 PTS

FSB

BRAND · BOLD, 58 PTS

MOTEL MOTEL MOTEL MOTEL

BRAND · BOLD, 58 PTS

RAD	RAD	RAD	CONDENSED	*RAD*	*RAD*	*RAD*
RA	RA	RA	ROMAN	*RA*	*RA*	*RA*
R	R	R	EXPANDED	*R*	*R*	*R*
R	R	R	WIDE	*R*	*R*	*R*
LIGHT	REGULAR	BOLD			*MATCHING ITALICS*	

EXTRAS  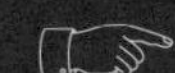    9

PICCOLO *THE FAMILY INCLUDES A VERSATILE "PICCOLO" SMALL CAPS WEIGHT WITH ITALICS*

PARIS
GOLDEN
LA FEMME
VÊTEMENTS
PIERROT LE FOU

BRAND · BOLD, 58 PTS

About
Uomo is a contemporary typographic system that explores sans geometric style and Italian Art Deco that allows to combine four widths and three weights. Includes small caps and extras with illustrations, ornaments and words to design with no necessity of external elements. From the refined and classic to the postmodern and vernacular in only one family.

Design
Tania Chacana, Miguel Hernández
2014

Foundry
Latinotype, Chile
www.latinotype.com

Styles / Weights
Family of four widths (Regular, Condensed, Expanded, Wide), each in three wights (Regular, Light, Bold), each with Italics, Regular width with Piccolo weight, Extras

Language support
Latin

OpenType options
Fractions

Optimized for web
No

REGULAR 18PT

ABCDEFGHIJKLMNOPQRSTUVWXYZ
ÆÅÇÉÑÖÛ
0123456789@.,-:;!?')*“”«»/-€$&½

BOLD 36PT

CONDENSED BOLD & LIGHT 16PT

THE YEARBOOK OF TYPE
COMPENDIUM WORKS WELL A
A TOOL IN VEXED TYPOGRAPHY
QUESTIONS FOR POLARIZING JOBS

EXTRAS 22PT

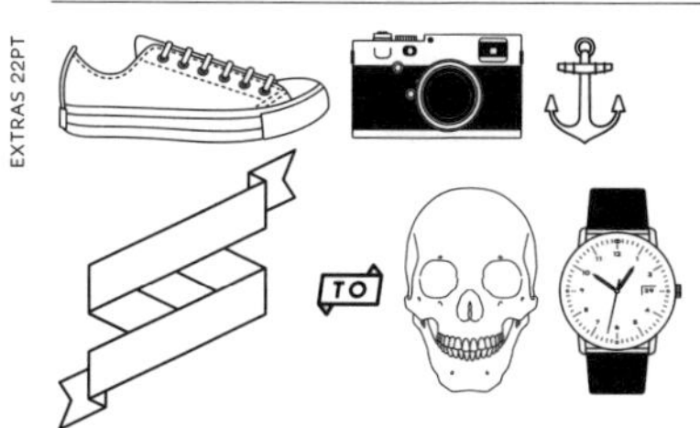

EXPANDED BOLD & REGULAR 8PT

THE YEARBOOK OF TYPE
COMPENDIUM WORKS WELL AS
A TOOL IN VEXED TYPOGRAPHY
QUESTIONS FOR POLARIZING JOBS

Urban Grotesk™

A B C D E
F G H I J
K L M N O
P Q R S T
U V W X Y

Light *Italic* SMAL
Regular *Italic* SM
Medium *Italic* SM
Semibold *Italic*
Bold *Italic* SMAL
Black *Italic* SMA

Urbanism as a Way of Life

Louis Wirth

A
Albania, Tirana
Andorra, Andorra la Vella
Armenia, Yerevan
Austria, Vienna
Azerbaijan, Baku

B
Belarus, Minsk
Belgium, Brussels
Bosnia and Herzegovina, Sarajevo
Bulgaria, Sofia

C
Croatia, Zagreb
Cyprus, Nicosia
Czech Republic, Prague

D
Denmark, Copenhagen

E

G
Georgia, Tbilisi
Germany, Berlin
Greece, Athens

H
Hungary, Budapest

I
Iceland, Reykjavík
Ireland, Dublin
Italy, Rome

K
Kazakhstan, Astana
Kosovo, Pristina

L
Latvia, Riga
Liechtenstein, Vaduz
Lithuania, Vilnius

About
Urban Grotesk attempts to follow the best of traditions of Grotesk typefaces: rounded arches, slightly thinner connecting strokes and a vertical shadowing axis, where outstrokes are terminated strictly perpendicular to the stroke direction. The primary characteristics are the connection of the rounded stroke to the stem, a round dot, lower and more thrifty uppercase, and generous numerals. The width proportions of characters is almost unified, the text color creates a unified grey area on a page. An airy metric aids good legibility in shorter texts.

Design
Tomas Brousil
2014

Foundry
Suitcase Type Foundry, Czech Republic
www.suitcasetype.com

Styles / Weights
Light, Light Italic, Regular, Italic, Medium, Medium Italic, Semibold, Semibold Italic, Bold, Bold Italic, Black, Black Italic

Language support
Latin

OpenType options
Proportional Oldstyle, Tabular and Proportional Lining, Tabular Oldstyle, Standard Ligatures, Discretionary Ligatures, All Caps, Small Caps, Capitals to Small Caps, Superscript, Subscript, Ordinals, Fractions, Numerator, Denominator, Arrows, Stylistic Sets, Slashed Zero, Localized Forms

Optimized for web
Yes

REGULAR 18PT

aabcdefgghijklmnopqrstuvwxyzæfjåçéñöûß
ABCDEFGHIJKLMNOPQRSTUVWXYZÆÇØ
01234567890@.,-:;!?')]§*“”«»/–€$&⅓↗

BOLD 36PT

aejgGQR7

BLACK & MEDIUM 14PT

Typographers want
amazing, exquisite
& clever justified text
in books

REGULAR 36PT

aejgGQR7

ALL WEIGHTS 12PT

Light
Regular
Medium
Semibold
Bold
Black

ITALICS 12PT

Light Italic
Italic
Medium Italic
Semibold Italic
Bold Italic
Black Italic

70% 245° 65′ 40″

MIX THE CITY

TOP 5 SOURCES OF GLOBAL C02 BY INDUSTRY

4 Sports & Symbols

get ready

25 Years Of Discovery

what's next?

Sensible Software 1986–1999

Chamberlain Collection

About
The idea of Urby is to combine striking character with technical functionality. The vibrant tension of active and dynamic shapes fused with geometric construction makes Urby a distinctive typeface for branding related to sports, outdoor activities, energy or technology.

Having the different weights and styles with identical character widths, the type family allows you to change weight or style without reformatting the text—ideal for interface design.

Extremely wide opened apertures like in "a," "e," "c" or "s" plus organic stroke endings like in "v" or "x" bring some playfulness into the overall geometric, mono-lined construction. Reduced shapes as in "t," "f" or "4" and quirky details of "g," "y" or "G" are underlining Urby's distinctiveness.

Beside its catchy qualities for headline sizes, Urby works surprisingly well for short text.

The rich character set supports most Latin languages and is providing helpful dingbats and geometric shapes—Urby is ready to rumble. Are you?

Design
Jakob Runge
2015

Foundry
type me! fonts, Germany
www.typemefonts.com

Styles / Weights
Thin, Light, Regular, Book, Bold, Black

Language support
Latin

OpenType options
Tabular and Proportional Lining, Superscript, Subscript, Ordinals, All Alternates, Fractions, Alternative Fractions, Numerator, Denominator, Arrows, Stylistic Alternates, Stylistic Sets, Slashed Zero, Localized Forms, Mark Positioning

Optimized for web
No, but available as webfont, with auto-hinting

REGULAR 16PT

abcdefghijklmnopqrstuvwxyzæfjåçéñöûß
ABCDEFGHIJKLMNOPQRSTUVWXYZÆÇØ
0123456789@.,-:;!?')]§*“”«»/-€$&½↗

BLACK 30PT

aejgGQR7

BOLD & LIGHT 14PT

Typographers want amazing, exquisite
& clever justified text in books

THIN 30PT

aejgGQR7

BOLD & REGULAR 9PT

☞ **cata·logue** / noun / a complete list of things that people can look at or buy: a catalogue of typefaces (a book showing the newest fonts, to help people choose the right typeface)

When in doubt, use the usual.

Usual is a utilitarian typeface.

About
Usual is a utilitarian typeface, suitable for whenever typographic sobriety and neutrality is needed. With a clear modernist inspiration, Usual was born of the attempt at using a scale of proportions in type design.

Similarly to Le Corbusier's Modulor, the scale of proportions used in Usual works as a tool or program for the typeface's metrics, and consequently, the rhythm of the stems.

Usual comprises five weights from Light to Extra Bold, with matching italics. It was designed to work well in a broad range of body sizes, from text settings to headlines. In addition to Stylistic Alternates and Arrows, Usual's OpenType features include letters with shorter descenders, useful for setting headlines with tight line-spacing.

Design
Rui Abreu
2014

Foundry
Rui Abreu / R-typography, Portugal
www.r-typography.com

Styles / Weights
Light, Light Italic, Regular, Italic, Medium, Medium Italic, Bold, Bold Italic, ExtraBold, ExtraBold Italic

Language support
Latin

OpenType options
Standard Ligatures, All Caps, Titling Alternates, Fractions, Arrows, Stylistic Alternates, Historical Forms, Slashed Zero

Optimized for web
Yes

REGULAR 16PT

aabcdefgghijklmnopqrstuvwxyzæfjåçéñöûß
ABCDEFGHIJKLMNOPQRSTUVWXYZÆÇØ
01234567890@.,-:;!?')]§*""«»/–€$&½↗

LIGHT 34PT

aejgGQR7

EXTRABOLD & LIGHT 11PT

The Yearbook of Type
compendium works well as
a tool in vexed typography
questions for polarizing jobs

BOLD & REGULAR 8PT

Year·book of Type / *noun* / book published every second year, giving details on typefaces of the previous two years and also about general current typographic topics—*e.g. OpenType features, font editors like Glyphs etc.*

ALL WEIGHTS 10PT

Light
Regular
Medium
Bold
ExtraBold

ITALICS 10PT

Light Italic
Italic
Medium Italic
Bold Italic
ExtraBold Italic

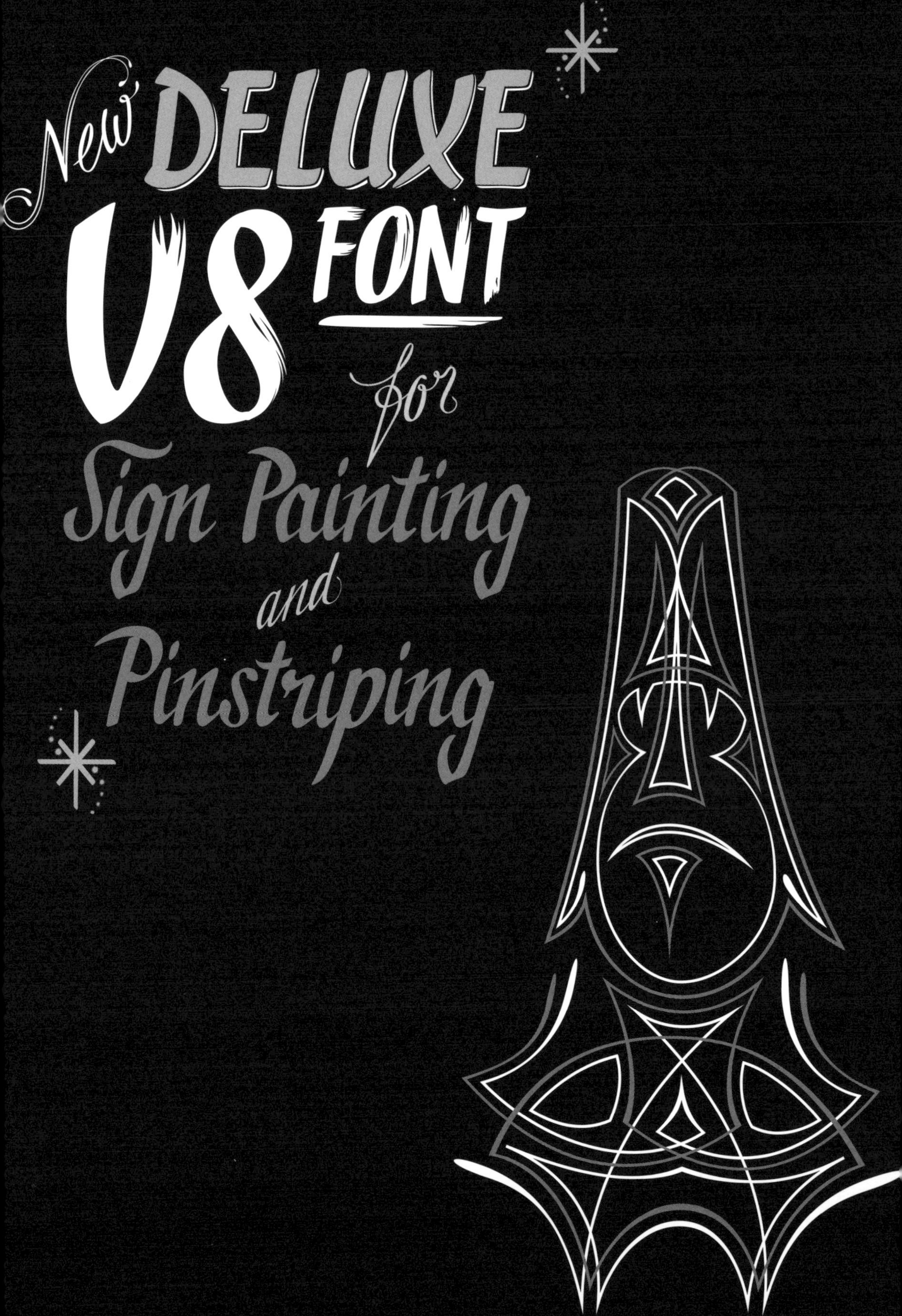
New DELUXE
V8 FONT
for
Sign Painting
and
Pinstriping

About
V8 is the high-octane typeface for lovers of sign painting and pinstriping. Beside the mixed regular and caps figures, the font contains a bunch of extra styles, such as "dry brush" and "shadows." All weights roll with alternative swash letters and a jumping baseline for a more crafted impression. Pinstripes, catchwords and icons perfect this red-hot old school font in one shot.

Design
Stefan Krömer, Gunnar Link
2015

Foundry
Die Typonauten, Germany
www.typonauten.de

Styles / Weights
Regular, DryBrush, Outline, Catchwords, Icons, Pinstripes, Caps

Language support
Latin

OpenType options
All Caps, Small Caps, Swashes, Contextual Swashes, All Alternates, Contextual Alternates, Stylistic Alternates, Unicase, Jumping Baseline

Optimized for web
Yes

REGULAR 18PT
abcdefghijklmnopqrstuvwxyzfjåéñöûß
ABCDEFGHIJKLMNOPQRSTUVWXYZ
0123456789@.,-:;!?'"" –€$

CAPS 36PT
AEJGQR7

OUTLINE 14PT
TYPOGRAPHERS WANT AMAZING, EXQUISITE & CLEVER JUSTIFIED TEXT IN BOOKS

REGULAR 36PT
aejgGQR7

REGULAR 17PT
Typographers want amazing, exquisite and clever justified text in books

THE SPECTACULAR STORY OF

100 HUNDREDS

Because Records Don't Lie

51 Test Centuries

49 Odi Centuries

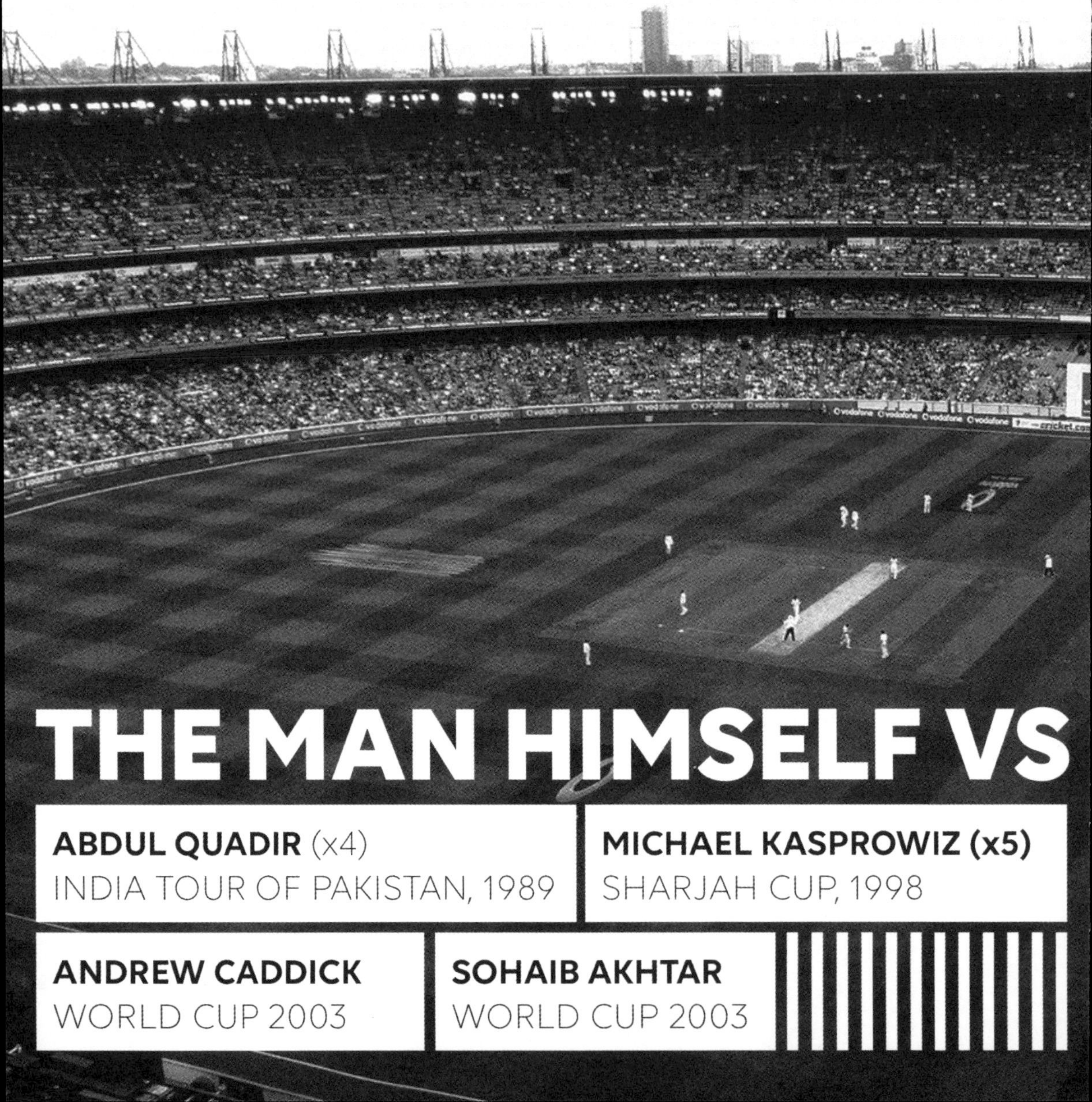

THE MAN HIMSELF VS

ABDUL QUADIR (x4)
INDIA TOUR OF PAKISTAN, 1989

MICHAEL KASPROWIZ (x5)
SHARJAH CUP, 1998

ANDREW CADDICK
WORLD CUP 2003

SOHAIB AKHTAR
WORLD CUP 2003

Volte

About
Graphic designers always search for new geometric sans faces appropriate for our times. ITF is pleased to present them with Volte. Including the five most essential font weights (Light–Bold), Volte Latin differentiates itself from the geometric sans pack through its simplification and reduction. For a geometric sans, Volte's letters are very open. Some letters appear constructed, but they all retain the necessary geometric and mono-linear spirt. Volte's openness increases its legibility, too. Coupled with its clear style, this helps make Volte Latin an effective workhorse typeface.

Design
Namrata Goyal
2015

Foundry
Indian Type Foundry, India
www.indiantypefoundry.com

Styles / Weights
Light, Regular, Medium, Semibold, Bold

Language support
Latin, Indic

OpenType options
Proportional Lining, Standard Ligatures, Superscript, Fractions

Optimized for web
Yes

REGULAR 18PT

abcdefghijklmnopqrstuvwxyzæfjåçéñöûß
ABCDEFGHIJKLMNOPQRSTUVWXYZÆÇØ
0123456789@.,-:;!?')]§*""«»/–€$&½

MEDIUM & LIGHT 9PT

cata·logue / noun / a complete list of things that people can look at or buy: a catalogue of typefaces (a book showing the newest fonts, to help people choose the right typeface)

BOLD & REGULAR 16PT

Typographers want amazing, exquisite
& clever justified text in books

BOLD & MEDIUM 36PT

aejgGQR7
aejgGQR7

SEMIBOLD & LIGHT 13PT

The Yearbook of Type compendium works well as
a tool in vexed typography questions for polarizing jobs

Wishes Script
Best Wishes
LA MEJOR FORMA DE EXPRESAR TUS SENTIMIENTOS Y DESEOS
Save the Date
15•04
Romeo and Juliet
1562 • VERONA
WEDDING INVITATION
We ♥ Letters
Amor
Lovely
BE•MY Valentine
MERRY Christmas
Angel
With all my Love
Sabrina M. Lopez

Wishes Script

About
Wishes Script is the best way to express your greetings! All you want to say is more gorgeous when using this pretty font, since it beautifies every message. Programed with OpenType, Wishes offers the designer a complete range of possibilities: frames, ribbons, hearts, flowers, ornaments, swashes, endings, ligatures and all the alternates you need to make a wonderful work. With delicate and flowing curves which blend English style with lettering, Wishes Script works perfectly in greeting cards, invitations, weddings, posters, magazines, fashion world, logos, packagings, etc. Additionally, it can be used in small and big formats, due to its Display and Text styles. It works perfectly in both small and large sizes, preserving the delicacy of its thin strokes and ensuring them to be printed accurately in smaller sizes. You can get both styles in the Light, Regular and Bold weights.

Design
Sabrina Lopez
2013

Foundry
Typesenses, Argentina
www.typesenses.tumblr.com

Styles / Weights
Family of three styles (Pro, Ornament, Caps), each with Text and Display versions in three weights (Light, Regular, Bold)

Language support
Latin

OpenType options
Standard Ligatures, Discretionary Ligatures, Small Caps, Titling Alternates, Swashes, All Alternates, Contextual Alternates, Fractions, Ornaments, Stylistic Alternates, Stylistic Sets, Slashed Zero, Terminal Form, Initial Form

Optimized for web
Yes

TEXT REGULAR 17PT

abcdefghijklmnopqrstuvwxyzæfjàçéñöü ß
ABCDEFGHIJKLMNOPQRSTUVWXYZÆÇØ
0123456789ø@.,-:;!?')]§*"" « »/-€$&½

TEXT BOLD & DISPLAY LIGHT 30PT

CAPS DISPLAY BOLD 18PT

TYPOGRAPHERS WANT AMAZING, EXQUISITE & CLEVER JUSTIFIED TEXT IN BOOKS

ORNM DISPLAY BOLD 30PT

TEXT BOLD & REGULAR 22PT

Typographers want amazing, exquisite & clever justified text in books

CHERRY
OAK TEAK
BEECH
CHESTNUT
LIME ASH
DOUGLAS
BAMBOO
FIR PINE
SPRUCE

About

Woodkit is a type system inspired by wood type and letterpress consisting of three families—Solid, Print and Reprint, each with six distinct styles covering various alphabet designs, components and miscellaneous ornaments. Woodkit supports Latin, Cyrillic and Greek scripts.

From both aesthetic and functional reasons, the most important feature of Woodkit is that every single glyph fills a square, not just horizontally, but also vertically. This is a reference and homage to the physicality of the real life wooden blocks. It didn't only induce some new and unexpected constructional solutions, it also gave the final font broad versatility, mutual interchangeability, many visual treats unavailable in proportional typefaces and most importantly—playfulness. Some of the fonts and shapes are outright inspired by wooden blocks and alphabets for kids. Therefore with Woodkit, typing also means building.

Design
Ondrej Jób
2014

Foundry
Typotheque, The Netherlands
www.typotheque.com

Styles / Weights
Family of three styles (Solid, Print, Reprint), each with six weights (Letterpress, Alphabet A, Alphabet B, Blocks, Figures, Ornaments)

Language support
Latin, Cyrillic, Greek

OpenType options
Standard Ligatures, Discretionary Ligatures, Contextual Alternates, Randomize

Optimized for web
Yes

BLOCKS 12PT

SOLID LETTERPRESS 26PT

PRINT ALPHABET B 8PT

TYPOGRAPHERS WANT
AMAZING, EXQUISITE
AND CLEVER JUSTIFIED
TEXT IN BOOKS

PRINT ALPHABET A & REPRINT ALPHABET A 24PT

PRINT ORNAMENTS 30PT

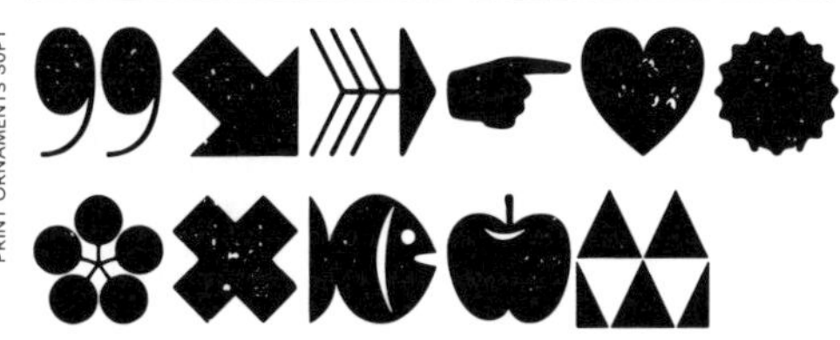

Xylophone Jams

♥

Crazy Rock Stars

it happened

← *in 1369* →

cutting edge band

A GREAT CONNECTION

George & Zelda

Yalta Sans

About
Yalta Sans combines the warmth of a humanist typeface with the clarity of a grotesque and the linearity of a square sans. The main aspects in the design were to combine readability, kindness and technicality. The emphasized horizontal curves hit the stem nearly orthogonally, but due to their conic form they need nearly no incision. This has a comforting effect on the whole appearance of the type. Moreover the openness of the forms leads to a good connection between the glyphs. Although the typeface has emancipated from its calligraphic ancestors, one may find many details that quote the vividness and the contrast of a humanist antiqua. Thanks to the tapering of the horizontals, the font looks more dynamic and vivid than a linear grotesque while angled endings refer to an imaginary calligraphic pen. The real cursive is narrower than the upright and with its upstrokes and alternative upper cases it transfers the humanist touch onto the italic weight.

Design
Stefan Claudius
2013

Foundry
Monotype, USA
www.monotype.com

Styles / Weights
Thin, Light, Book, Regular, Medium, Bold, Extra Bold, Black, each with Italics

Language support
Latin

OpenType options
Proportional Oldstyle, Tabular and Proportional Lining, Tabular Oldstyle, Standard Ligatures, Small Caps, Capitals to Small Caps, Superscript, Subscript, Fractions, Numerator, Denominator, Stylistic Alternates, Stylistic Sets, Slashed Zero, Localized Forms

Optimized for web
Yes

REGULAR 18PT

abcdefggghijklmnopqrstuvwxyzæfjåçéñöûß
ABCDEFGHIJKLMNOPQRSTUVWXYZÆÇØ
01234567890@.,-:;!?')]§*""«»/–€$&½

BLACK 30PT

aejgGQR7

BOLD & LIGHT 14PT

Typographers want
amazing, exquisite
& clever justified text
in books

BOLD & REGULAR 8PT

ref·er·ence book / *noun* / a book that contains facts and information that you look at when you need to find out sth. particular—*"I am looking for the right typeface for my project, so I use the Yearbook of Type as a reference book."*

ALL WEIGHTS 10PT

Thin
Light
Book
Regular
Medium
Bold
Extra Bold
Black

ALL ITALICS 10PT

Thin Italic
Light Italic
Book Italic
Italic
Medium Italic
Bold Italic
Extra Bold Italic
Black Italic

مثل الطبيب والجاهل

زعموا أنّه كان في بعض المدن طبيب له رفق وعلم وكان ذا فطنة فيما يجري على يده من المعالجات. فكبر ذلك الطبيب وضعف بصره. وكان لملك تلك المدينة ابن وحيد. فاصابه المرض، فجيء بهذا الطبيب. فلما سأل الفتى عن وجعه، فأخبره، فعرف داءه ودواءه وقال: لو كنت أبصر لجمعت الأخلاط على معرفتي بأجناسها ولا أثق في ذلك بأحد غيري. وكان في المدينة رجل جاهل فبلغه الخبر فأتاهم وادّعى علم الطب وأعلمهم أنّه خبير بمعرفة أخلاط الأدوية والعقاقير. فأمره الملك أن يدخل خزانة الأدوية فيأخذ من أخلاط الدواء حاجته. فلما دخل الجاهل الخزانة وعرضت عليه الأدوية ولا يدري ما هي أخذ في جملة ما أخذ منها صرّة فيها سمّ قاتل وخلطه بالأدوية ولا علم له به ولا معرفة عنده بجنسه. فلما تمّت أخلاط الأدوية سقى الفتى منه فمات. فلما عرف الملك ذلك دعا بالجاهل

About
Zapfino Arabic is designed by Nadine Chahine as the Arabic companion to Hermann Zapf's iconic Zapfino typeface, with the approval of Prof. Zapf. The design is an evolution of Arabic calligraphic traditions that combines Naskh and Nastaaliq to form a backward slanted calligraphic style. The character proportions refer to Naskh traditions but the isolated and final forms bring with them an exaggerated swash-like movement that references the extravagant ascenders and descenders of Zapfino. The font contains a large number of contextual variants that work to create a smooth flow of pen movement, as well as ten stylistic sets. The character set supports the Arabic language as well as basic Latin. It's meant to be used as a display typeface, for logos, greeting cards and short headlines. It could also work for short pieces of text, for poetry or chapter introduc-tions, when used in a generous type size and with ample space around it. Its design leaves a lot of room for typographic playfulness.

Design
Nadine Chahine
2014

Foundry
Monotype, USA
www.monotype.com

Styles / Weights
Regular

Language support
Arabic

OpenType options
Standard Ligatures, Superscript, Subscript, Contextual Alternates, Fractions, Numerator, Denominator, Stylistic Sets, Localized Forms, Mark Positioning, Terminal Form, Initial Form, Medial Form, Cursive Positioning, Glyph Composition / Decomposition

Optimized for web
Yes

REGULAR 22PT

abcdefghijklmnopqrstuvwxyyzæçéñöß
ABCDEFGHIJKLMNOPQRSTUVWXYZÆÇØ
0123456789@.,-:;!?’)]§*“”«»/–€$@

REGULAR 36PT

ا ك ب ت ث ف
ج ح خ ع غ م
ل ن س ش ص ض
ق ي د ذ ر ز و ط ظ ه
١٢٣٤٥٦٧٨٩٠

REGULAR 18PT

الى صديقة جديدة ...
ودعتك الأمس وعدت وحدي
مفكرًا ببوحك الأخير
كتبت عن عينيك ألف شيءٍ
كتبت بالضوء وبالعبير عباس

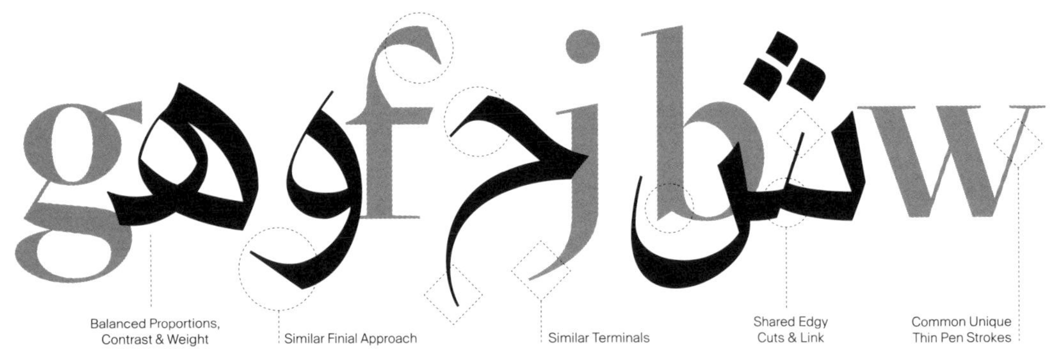

29LT Zeyn

عبد الوهاب البياتي Abdel Wahab Al Bayati

وطني

Bold

المنفى

Medium

منفاي

Regular

الكلمات

Light

My nation is the exile.

My exile is my words.

فكلكُمْ

في بَني البَشَر شَرٌّ ضَروريّ يَمرحُ ويَمْزح

Extensive set of **ligatures** and **stylistic sets**

About
29LT Zeyn is an elegant, contemporary Arabic and Latin typeface. It covers all western European languages as well as Arabic, Persian and Urdu. The Arabic is inspired from both the Naskh and Thuluth calligraphic styles, while the Latin is drawn based on the Modern Serif Roman style. The letterforms are drawn with extreme refinement and extreme contrast between the thick and thin pen strokes that unveil modernity in a stylish approach. Both scripts were created simultaneously and without any sacrifice from one script on behalf of the other. The elements that bring both scripts together are the design approach, the proportions, the weight, and the contrast. It encloses an extended set of Arabic ligatures and stylistic sets offering the typeface a unique contemporary characteristic with a calligraphic posture. The Arabic is drawn with a free spirit and challenges the Arabic calligraphic standards in a unique manner. “Zeyn” is an Arabic word meaning beautiful, graceful, and elegant.

Design
Ian Party, Pascal Zoghbi
2014

Foundry
29Letters, Lebanon
www.29lt.com

Styles / Weights
Light, Regular, Medium, Bold

Language support
Latin, Arabic

OpenType options
Standard Ligatures, Discretionary Ligatures, Superscript, Subscript, All Alternates, Contextual Ligatures, Stylistic Alternates, Stylistic Sets, Localized Forms, Required Ligatures, Mark Positioning, Terminal Form, Initial Form, Isolated Form, Medial Form

Optimized for web
Yes

MEDIUM 18PT

لالا أأ ب ببب ت تتت ث ثثث ج ججج حححح خ خخخ دد ذذ رر زز
س سسس ش ششش ص صصص ض ضضض ط ططط ظ ظظظ ع ععع
غ غغغ ف ففف ق ققق ك ككك ل للل م ممم ن ننن ه ههه و و ي ييي

MEDIUM 18PT

abcdefghijklmnopqrstuvwxyzæfjåçéñöûß&€$*
ABCDEFGHIJKLMNOPRSTUVWXYZÆÇØ
0123456789٠١٢٣٣٤٥٦٧٨٩۴۵۶۷@.,-:;!?')]§«»/–

BOLD 36PT

BOLD & REGULAR 18PT

Typographers want amazing, exquisite
& clever justified
text in books

Index B

ABeZeh, 8 / 9

agGR

aefgjkmstzß
AEFGKMQRSZ
13570?&$@»

FS Albert Arabic, 12 / 13

agGR

aefgjkmstzß
AEFGKMQRSZ
13570?&$@»

AM Sans One, 18 / 19

agGR

aefgjkmstzß
AEFGKMQRSZ
13570?&$@»

Anisette, 22 / 23

AGGR

AEFGJKMST
AEFGKM
13570?&$@»

Areal BL, 28 / 29

agGR

aefgjkmstzß
AEFGKMQRSZ
13570?&$@»

Arquitecta, 32 / 33

agGR

aefgjkmstzß
AEFGKMQRSZ
13570?&$@»

Bague Sans, 36 / 37

agGR

aefgjkmstzß
AEFGKMQRSZ
13570?&$@»

Basetica, 40 / 41

agGR

aefgjkmstzß
AEFGKMQRSZ
13570?&$@»

FF Bauer Grotesk, 42 / 43

agGR

aefgjkmstzß
AEFGKMQRSZ
13570?&$@»

Beausite, 44 / 45

agGR

aefgjkmstzß
AEFGKMQRSZ
13570?&$@»

Berlingske Sans, 50 / 51

agGR

aefgjkmstzß
AEFGKMQRSZ
13570?&$@»

AB BLine, 54 / 55

agGR

aefgjkmstzß
AEFGKMQRSZ
13570?&$@»

Brezel Grotesk, 64 / 65

agGR

aefgjkmstzß
AEFGKMQRSZ
13570?&$@»

Brix Sans, 66 / 67

agGR

aefgjkmstzß
AEFGKMQRSZ
13570?&$@»

BTP, 70 / 71

agGR

aefgjkmstzß
AEFGKMQRSZ
13570?&$@»

Burg Grotesk, 74 / 75

agGR

aefgjkmstzß
AEFGKMQRSZ
13570?&$@»

Burlingame, 76 / 77

agGR

aefgjkmstzß
AEFGKMQRSZ
13570?&$@»

Campton, 80 / 81

agGR

aefgjkmstzß
AEFGKMQRSZ
13570?&$@»

Caput (SF), 82 / 83

agGR

aefgjkmstzß
AEFGKMQRSZ
13570?&$@»

Caravel, 84 / 85

agGR

aefgjkmstzß
AEFGKMQRSZ
13570?&$@»

Cera, 90 / 91

agGR

aefgjkmstzß
AEFGKMQRSZ
13570?&$@»

Darwin, 100 / 101

agGR

aefgjkmstz
AEFGKMQRSZ
13570&$@›

David, 102 / 103

agGR

aefgjkmstzß
AEFGKMQRSZ
13570?&$@»

Decima, 104 / 105

agGR

aefgjkmstzß
AEFGKMQRSZ
13570?&$@»

Duru, 110 / 111

agGR

aefgjkmstzß
AEFGKMQRSZ
13570?&$@»

Echo, 114 / 115

agGR

aefgjkmstzß
AEFGKMQRSZ
13570?&$@»

AB Eiffel, 116 / 117

agGR

aefgjkmstzß
AEFGKMQRSZ
13570?&$@»

FS Elliot Pro, 118 / 119

agGR

aefgjkmstzß
AEFGKMQRSZ
13570?&$@»

FS Emeric, 120 / 121

agGR

aefgjkmstzß
AEFGKMQRSZ
13570?&$@»

Flanders Art Sans, 128 / 129

agGR

aefgjkmstzß
AEFGKMQRSZ
13570?&$@»

Sans Serif

Formular, 132 / 133

agGR

aefgjkmstzß
AEFGKMQRSZ
13570?&$@»

Galano Classic, 136 / 137

agGR

aefgjkmstzß
AEFGKMQRSZ
13570?&$@»

GarySans, 140 / 141

agGR

aefgjkmstzß
AEFGKMQRSZ
13570?&$@»

GE Inspira Sans, 142 / 143

agGR

aefgjkmstzß
AEFGKMQRSZ
13570?&$@»

Gedau Gothic, 144 / 145

agGR

aefgjkmstzß
AEFGKMQRSZ
13570?&$@»

Gerbera, 146 / 147

agGR

aefgjkmstzß
AEFGKMQRSZ
13570?&$@»

Gibbs, 148 / 149

agGR

aefgjkmstzß
AEFGKMQRSZ
13570?&$@»

Glober, 150 / 151

agGR

aefgjkmstzß
AEFGKMQRSZ
13570?&$@»

FS Hackney, 156 / 157

agGR

aefgjkmstzß
AEFGKMQRSZ
13570?&$@»

Hangulatin, 158 / 159

agGR

aefgjkmstzß
AEFGKMQRSZ
13570?&$@»

Hedon, 162 / 163

agGR

aefjkmstz
AEFGKMQRSZ
13570?&$@»

Heimat Display, 164 / 165

agGR

aefgjkmstzß
AEFGKMQRSZ
13570?&$@»

Intro, 172 / 173

agGR

aefgjkmstzß
AEFGKMQRSZ
13570?&$@»

Iskra, 174 / 175

agGR

aefgjkmstzß
AEFGKMQRSZ
13570?&$@»

Joanna Sans, 176 / 177

agGR

aefgjkmstzß
AEFGKMQRSZ
13570?&$@»

29LT Kaff, 178 / 179

agGR

aefgjkmstzß
AEFGKMQRSZ
13570?&$@»

Komet, 186 / 187

agGR

aefgjkmstzß
AEFGKMQRSZ
13570?&$@»

Korpus Grotesk, 192 / 193

agGR

aefgjkmstzß
AEFGKMQRSZ
13570?&$@»

Lammerhuber, 194 / 195

agGR

aefgjkmstzß
AEFGKMQRSZ
13570?&$@»

Libertad, 202 / 203

agGR

aefgjkmstzß
AEFGKMQRSZ
13570?&$@»

Lipa Agate, 206 / 207

agGR

aefgjkmstzß
AEFGKMQRSZ
13570?&$@»

Magnum Sans Pro, 216 / 217

agGR

aefgjkmstzß
AEFGKMQRSZ
13570?&$@»

PTL Magsans, 218 / 219

agGR

aefgjkmstzß
AEFGKMQRSZ
13570?&$@»

FF Mark, 226 / 227

agGR

aefgjkmstzß
AEFGKMQRSZ
13570?&$@»

FS Matthew, 228 / 229

agGR

aefgjkmstzß
AEFGKMQRSZ
13570?&$@»

FS Millbank, 230 / 231

agGR

aefgjkmstzß
AEFGKMQRSZ
13570?&$@»

Monico, 236 / 237

agGR

aefgjkmstʒß
AEFGKMQRSZ
13570?&$@»

Muller, 238 / 239

agGR

aefgjkmstzß
AEFGKMQRSZ
13570?&$@»

Multi Text, 240 / 241

agGR

aefgjkmstzß
AEFGKMQRSZ
13570?&$@»

NarzissGrotesk, 244 / 245

agGR

aefgjkmstzß
AEFGKMQRSZ
13570?&$@»

Nitti Grotesk, 250 / 251

agGR

aefgjkmstzß
AEFGKMQRSZ
13570?&$@»

Niveau Grotesk, 252 / 253

agGR

aefgjkmstzß
AEFGKMQRSZ
13570?&$@»

PTL Notes Nova, 256 / 257

agGR

aefgjkmstzß
AEFGKMQRSZ
13570?&$@»

Novel Sans Hair, 258 / 259

agGR

aefgjkmstzß
AEFGKMQRSZ
13570?&$@»

ORF On, 260 / 261

agGR

aefgjkmstzß
AEFGKMQRSZ
13570?&$@»

Paiper, 262 / 263

agGR

aefgjkmstzß
AEFGKMQRSZ
13570?&$@»

Paris Pro, 264 / 265

agGR

aefgjkmstz
AEFGKMQRSZ
13570?&$@

Quantum, 278 / 279

agGR

aefgjkmstzß
AEFGKMQRSZ
13570?&$@»

Quercus Sans, 282 / 283

agGR

aefgjkmstzß
AEFGKMQRSZ
13570?&$@»

Quire Sans, 284 / 285

agGR

aefgjkmstzß
AEFGKMQRSZ
13570?&$@»

Quist, 286 / 287

agGR

aefgjkmstzß
AEFGKMQRSZ
13570?&$@»

NN Rektorat, 292 / 293

agGR

aefgjkmstz
AEFGKMQRSZ
13570?$»

Riga, 296 / 297

agGR

aefgjkmstzß
AEFGKMQRSZ
13570?&$@»

P22 Saarinen, 298 / 299

agGR

aefgjkmstzß
AEFGKMQRSZ
13570?&$@»

Signo, 300 / 301

agGR

aefjkmstz
AEFGKMQRSZ
13570?&$@»

Taz Extended, 306 / 307

agGR

aefgjkmstzß
AEFGKMQRSZ
13570?&$@»

Taz Wide, 306 / 307

agGR

aefgjkmstzß
AEFGKMQRSZ
13570?&$@»

Texta, 308 / 309

agGR

aefgjkmstzß
AEFGKMQRSZ
13570?&$@»

A.F. Tomica, 314 / 315

agGR

aefgjkmstzß
AEFGKMQRSZ
13570?&$@»

Trend, 316 / 317

AGR

AEFGJKMQRSTZ
13570?&$@»

Uomo, 320 / 321

AGR

AEFGJKMQRSTZ
13570?&$@»

Urban Grotesk, 322 / 323

agGR

aefgjkmstzß
AEFGKMQRSZ
13570?&$@»

Urby, 324 / 325

agGR

aefgjkmstzß
AEFGKMQRSZ
13570?&$@»

Usual, 326 / 327

agGR

aefgjkmstzß
AEFGKMQRSZ
13570?&$@»

Volte, 330 / 331

agGR

aefgjkmstzß
AEFGKMQRSZ
13570?&$@»

Yalta Sans, 336 / 337

agGR

aefgjkmstzß
AEFGKMQRSZ
13570?&$@»

Serif / Antiqua

Alverata, 16 / 17

agGR

aefgjkmstzß
AEFGKMQRSZ
13570?&$@»

Amster Pro, 20 / 21

agGR

aefgjkmstzß
AEFGKMQRSZ
13570?&$@»

Aria Text, 30 / 31

agGR

aefgjkmstzß
AEFGKMQRSZ
13570?&$@»

Begum, 46 / 47

agGR

aefgjkmstzß
AEFGKMQRSZ
13570?&$@»

Berenjena Pro, 48 / 49

agGR

aefgjkmstzß
AEFGKMQRSZ
13570?&$@»

Berlingske Serif, 50 / 51

agGR

aefgjkmstzß
AEFGKMQRSZ
13570?&$@»

Diogenes, 108 / 109

agGR

aefgjkmstzß
AEFGKMQRSZ
13570?&$@»

Duwal Pro, 112 / 113

agGR

aefgjkmstzß
AEFGKMQRSZ
13570?&$@»

Essay Text, 122 / 123

agGR

aefgjkmstzß
AEFGKMQRSZ
13570?&$@»

Fantasy, 124 / 125

agGR

aefgjkmstzß
AEFGKMQRSZ
13570?&$@»

Fazeta, 126 / 127

agGR

aefgjkmstzß
AEFGKMQRSZ
13570?&$@»

Flanders Art Serif, 128 / 129

agGR

aefgjkmstzß
AEFGKMQRSZ
13570?&$@»

FF Franziska, 134 / 135

agGR

aefgjkmstzß
AEFGKMQRSZ
13570?&$@»

Garden, 138 / 139

agGR

aefgjkmstzß
AEFGKMQRSZ
13570?&$@»

GE Inspira Serif, 142 / 143

agGR

aefgjkmstzß
AEFGKMQRSZ
13570?&$@»

Kopius, 188 / 189

agGR

aefgjkmstzß
AEFGKMQRSZ
13570?&$@»

Korpus, 190 / 191

agGR

aefgjkmstzß
AEFGKMQRSZ
13570?&$@»

Lava, 200 / 201

agGR

aefgjkmstzß
AEFGKMQRSZ
13570?&$@»

Mantika Book, 222 / 223

agGR

aefgjkmstzß
AEFGKMQRSZ
13570?&$@»

Minotaur, 234 / 235

agGR

aefgjkmstzß
AEFGKMQRSZ
13570?&$@»

Niveau Serif, 252 / 253

agGR

aefgjkmstzß
AEFGKMQRSZ
13570?&$@»

Parmigiano, 268 / 269

agGR

aefgjkmstzß
AEFGKMQRSZ
13570?&$@»

Pepone, 270 / 271

agGR

aefjkmstz
AEFGKMQRSZ
13570?&$@»

LP Philharmonia, 272 / 273

agGR

aefgjkmstzß
AEFGKMQRSZ
13570?&$@»

Retiro, 294 / 295

agGR

aefgjkmstzß
AEFGKMQRSZ
13570?&$@»

Sindelar, 302 / 303

agGR

aefgjkmstzß
AEFGKMQRSZ
13570?&$@»

Trola Text, 318 / 319

agGR

aefgjkmstzß
AEFGKMQRSZ
13570?&$@»

29LT Zeyn, 340 / 341

agGR

aefgjkmstzß
AEFGKMQRSZ
13570?&$@»

Slab Serif

ABeZeh Slab, 8 / 9

agGR
aefgjkmstzß
AEFGKMQRSZ
13570?&$@»

Adria Slab, 10 / 11

agGR
aefgjkmstzß
AEFGKMQRSZ
13570?&$@»

Berlingske Slab, 50 / 51

agGR
aefgjkmstzß
AEFGKMQRSZ
13570?&$@»

Brando, 58 / 59

agGR
aefgjkmstzß
AEFGKMQRSZ
13570?&$@»

Bree Serif, 62 / 63

agGR
aefgjkmstzß
AEFGKMQRSZ
13570?&$@»

Brix Slab, 66 / 67

agGR
aefgjkmstz
AEFGKMQRSZ
13570?&$@»

Caput (SF), 82 / 83

agGR
aefgjkmstzß
AEFGKMQRSZ
13570?&$@»

Colón, 92 / 93

agGR
aefgjkmstzß
AEFGKMQRSZ
13570?&$@»

NN Colroy, 94 / 95

agGR
aefgjkmstzß
AEFGKMQRSZ
13570?&$@»

Columbia Titling, 96 / 97

AGR
AEFGJKM
QRSTZ
13570?&$@»

DIN Next Slab, 106 / 107

agGR
aefgjkmstzß
AEFGKMQRSZ
13570?&$@»

Garden, 138 / 139

AGR
AEFGJKM
QRSTZ
13570?&$@»

Henriette, 166 / 167

agGR
aefgjkmstzß
AEFGKMQRSZ
13570?&$@»

Laski Slab, 198 / 199

agGR
aefgjkmstzß
AEFGKMQRSZ
13570?&$@»

Muriza, 242 / 243

agGR
aefgjkmstzß
AEFGKMQRSZ
13570?&$@»

Quitador, 288 / 289

agGR

aefgjkmstzß
AEFGKMQRSZ
13570?&$@»

Trend, 316 / 317

AGR

AEFGJKM
QRSTZ
13570?&$@»

Stencil

Berlingske Slab Stencil, 50 / 51

agGR

aefgjkmstzß
AEFGKMQRSZ
13570?&$@»

NT Bixa, 52 / 53

AGR

AEFGJKMQRSTZ
13570

Cera, 90 / 91

agGR

aefgjkmstzß
AEFGKMQRSZ
13570?&$@»

HF Stencil, 168 / 169

AGR

AEFGJKMQRSTZ
13570?&$@»

Laski Slab Stencil, 198 / 199

agGR

aefgjkmstzß
AEFGKMQRSZ
13570?&$@»

Mineral, 232 / 233

agGR

aefgjkmstzß
AEFGJKMQRSTZ
13570?&$@»

Pepone Stencil, 270 / 271

agGR

aefgjkmstzß
AEFGKMQRSZ
13570?&$@»

Stencil Allround, 304 / 305

AGR

AEFGJKMQRSTZ
13570?&$@»

Monospace / Typewriter

Berlingske Typewriter 50 / 51

agGR

aefgjkmstzß
AEFGKMQRSZ
13570?&$@»

Burg Grotesk, 74 / 75

agGR

aefgjkmstzß
AEFGKMQRSZ
13570?&$@»

Catalina Typewriter, 88 / 89

agGR

aefgjkmstz
AEFGJKMQRSTZ
13570?&$@»

Colón Mono, 92 / 93

agGR

aefgjkmstzß
AEFGKMQRSZ
3570?&$@»

Decima Mono, 104 / 105

agGR

aefgjkmstzß
AEFGKMQRSZ
13570?&$@»

Formular Mono, 132 / 133

agGR

aefgjkmstzß
AEFGKMQRSZ
13570?&$@»

Input, 170 / 171

agGR

aefgjkmstzß
AEFGKMQRSZ
13570?&$@»

Laplace, 196 / 197

agGR

aefgjkmstzß
AEFGKMQRSZ
13570?&$@»

Newsletter Pro, 248 / 249

agGR

aefgjkmstzß
AEFGKMQRSZ
13570?&$@»

Script

Asterism, 34 / 35

agGR
aefgjkmstz
AEFGKMQRSZ
13570?&$@»

Brush Up, 68 / 69

AGR
AEFGJKMQRSTZ
13570?&$@»

Caligo, 78 / 79

agGR
aefgjkmstzß
AEFGKMQRSZ
13570?&$@»

Catalina Script, 88 / 89

agGR
aefgjkmstzß
AEFGJKMQRSTZ
13570?&$@»

Daft Brush, 98 / 99

AGGR
AEFGJKMQRSTZ
13570?&$@»

Garden, 138 / 139

agGR
aefgjkmstzß
AEFGKMQRSZ
13570?&$@»

HapticScript, 160 / 161

agGR
aefgjkmstzß
AEFGKMQRSZ
13570?&$@»

Kailey, 180 / 181

agGR
aefgjkmstz
AEFGKMQRSZ
13570?&$@»

Luxus Brut Sparkling, 212 / 213

agGR
aefgjkmstzß
AEFGKMQRSZ
13570?&$@»

P22 Marcel Pro, 224 / 225

agGR
aefgjkmstzß
AEFGKMQRSZ
13570?%$@»

Nautica, 246 / 247

agGR
aefgjkmstzß
AEFGKMQRSZ
13570?&$@

Pleiad, 274 / 275

agGR
aefgjkmstzß
AEFGKMQRSZ
13570?&$@»

CA Recape, 290 / 291

agGR
aefgjkmstzß
AEFGKMQRSZ
13570?&$@»

P22 Saarinen, 298 / 299

agGR
aefgjkmstzß
AEFGKMQRSZ
13570?&$@»

Tilda, 312 / 313

agGR
aefgjkmstzß
AEFGKMQRSZ
13570?&$@»

Script

V8, 328 / 329

agGR
aefgjkmstzß
AEFGKMQRSZ
13570?$@

Wishes Script, 332 / 333

agGR
aefgjkmstzß
AEFGKMQRSZ
13570? &$@ »

Zapfino Arabic, 338 / 339

agGR
aefgjkmstzß
AEFGKMQRSZ
13570?&$@»

Display

Algo FY, 14 / 15

agGR
aefgjkmstzß
AEFGKMQRSZ
13570?&$@»

Anisette, 22 / 23

AGGR
AEFGJKMST
AEFGKM
13570?&$@»

Aniuk, 24 / 25

agGR
aefgjkmstzß
AEFGKMQRSZ
13570?&$@»

Apeloig Type Library, 26 / 27

AGGR
AEFGJKMSTZß
GKMQRSZ
13570?&$@»

Baker Street, 38 / 39

agGR
aefgjkmstzß
AEFGKMQRSZ
13570?&$@»

Beausite, 44 / 45

agGR
aefgjkmstzß
AEFGKMQRSZ
13570?&$@»

Berlingske Display, 50 / 51

agGR
aefgjkmstzß
AEFGKMQRSZ
13570?&$@»

NT Bixa, 52 / 53

AGR

AEFGJKMQRSTZ
13570?&$@»

Brahmos, 56 / 57

agGR

aefgjkmstzß
AEFGKMQRSZ
13570?&$@»

Brandon Printed, 60 / 61

AGR

AEFGJKMQRSTZ
13570?&$@»

Brush Up, 68 / 69

AGR

AEFGJKMQRSTZ
13570?&$@»

BTP, 70 / 71

agGR

aefgjkmstzß
AEFGKMQRSZ
13570?&$@»

Burford, 72 / 73

AGR

AEFGJKMQRSTZ
13570?&$@»

Caligo, 78 / 79

agGR

aefjkmstz
AEFGKMQRSZ
13570?&$@»

Carrosserie, 86 / 87

AGR

AEFGJKMQRSTZ
13570?&$@»

Catalina Family, 88 / 89

AGR

AEFGJKMQRSTZ
13570?&$@»

Columbia Titling, 96 / 97

AGR

AEFGJKM
QRSTZ
13570?&$@»

Daft Brush, 98 / 99

AGgR

AEFGJKMQRSTZ
13570?&$@»

AB Eiffel, 116 / 117

agGR

aefgjkmstzß
AEFGKMQRSZ
13570?&$@»

Fantasy, 124 / 125

agGR

aefgjkmstzß
AEFGKMQRSZ
13570?&$@»

Fazeta, 126 / 127

agAR

aefgjkmstzß
AEFGKMQRSZ
13570?&$@»

Flynt, 130 / 131

agGR

aefgjkmstzß
AEFGKMQRSZ
13570?&@

Display

Garden, 138 / 139

agGR
aefgjkmstzß
AEFGKMQRSZ
13570?&$@»

LTC Goudy Initials, 152 / 153

AGR
AEFGJKMQRSTZ

Graphique Pro Next, 154 / 155

AGR
AEFGJKMQRSTZ
13570?&$@»

Hangulatin, 158 / 159

agGR
aefgjkmstzß
AEFGKMQRSZ
13570?&$@»

HapticScript, 160 / 161

agGR
aefgjkmstzß
AEFGKMQRSZ
13570?&$@»

Heimat Display, 164 / 165

agGR
aefgjkmstzß
AEFGKMQRSZ
13570?&$@»

Intro, 172 / 173

agGR
aefgjkmstzß
AEFGKMQRSZ
13570?&$@»

Kandel 105 & 205, 182 / 183

agGR
aefgjkmstzß
AEFGKMQRSZ
13570?&$@»

Kelso, 184 / 185

agGR
aefgjkmstzß
AEFGKMQRSZ
13570?&$@»

Libertad, 202 / 203

agGR
aefgjkmstzß
AEFGKMQRSZ
13570?&$@»

Lichtspiele, 204 / 205

agGR
aefgjkmstzß
AEFGKMQRSZ
13570?&$@»

Lunchbox Family, 208 / 209

agGR
aefgjkmstzß
AEFGKMQRSZ
13570?&$@»

Lunica, 210 / 211

agGR
aefgjkmstzß
AEFGKMQRSZ
13570?&$@»

Luxus Brut Sparkling, 212 / 213

agGR
aefgjkmstzß
AEFGKQRSZ
13570?&$@»

Macula, 214 / 215

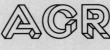

AGR
AEFGJKM
QRSTZ
13570?&$@»

FS Maja, 220 / 221

agGR

aefgjkmstzß
AEFGKMQRSZ
13570?&$@»

Mineral, 232 / 233

agGR

aefgjkmstzß
AEFGKMQRSZ
13570?&$@»

Multi Display, 240 / 241

agGR

aefgjkmstzß
AEFGKMQRSZ
13570?&$@»

Nord, 254 / 255

AGR

AEFGJKM
QRSTZ
13570?&$@»

Novel Sans Hair, 258 / 259

agGR

aefgjkmstzß
AEFGKMQRSZ
13570?&$@»

Paris Pro, 264 / 265

agGR

aefgjkmstz
AEFGKMQRSZ
13570?&$@

DF-Park, 266 / 267

agr

aefgjkmqrstz
13570?&$@

Polja, 276 / 277

agGR

aefgjkmstzß
AEFGKMQRSZ
13570?&@»

Quendel Happy F., 280 / 281

agGR

aefgjkmstzß
AEFGKMQRSZ
13570?&$@»

Retiro, 294 / 295

agGR

aefgjkmstzß
AEFGKMQRSZ
13570?&$@»

ThreeDee, 310 / 311

agGR

aefgjkmstz
AEFGKMQRSZ
13570?&$@»

Trend, 316 / 317

AGR

AEFGJKMQRSTZ
13570?&$@»

V8, 328 / 329

agGR

aefgjkmstz
AEFGKMQRSZ
13570?$@

Wishes Script, 332 / 333

agGR

aefgjkmstz
AEFGKMQRSZ
13570?$@»

Woodkit, 334 / 335

AGR

AEFGJKM
QRSTZ
13570?&$@»

Abbink, Mike
USA
www.mikeabbink.com

Mike Abbink earned two BFAs: one in Fine Arts, and one in Graphic Design and Packaging from Art Center in Pasadena. He has been designing letter forms since 1992, and his first completed typeface, FF Kievit, is used around the world and has won awards from the ISTD and ATypI. Mike Abbink is a multidisciplinary creative director, typeface designer and educator. MetaDesign San Francisco served as a launch pad for Abbink and after three years, he went on and to co-found Method Inc. He has since also worked as Design Director at Apple, Design Director at Wolff Olins, Creative Director for Saffron and Creative Director at Wolff Olins. His most recent post is now Sr. Creative Director of The Museum of Modern Art (MoMa) in New York.

→ Brando 58 / 59
→ GE Inspira Sans 142 / 143
→ GE Inspira Serif 142 / 143

Abreu, Rui
Portugal
www.r-typography.com

Rui Abreu is a Portuguese type designer living in Lisbon. He studied Graphic Design at the University of Porto—School of Fine Arts, where he graduated in 2003. Rui started experimenting with typography during his student years and in 2006 released his first attempts with fonts. In 2008, he launched *r-typography.com*, a showcase with a selection of his work. From 2009, Rui Abreu has published fonts with the Swedish type foundry Fountain, while releasing typefaces under his own label.

→ Aria Text 30 / 31
→ Signo 300 / 301
→ Usual 326 / 327

Ackermann, Thomas
Germany
www.pblcdsgn.de

Thomas Ackermann studied Communication Design at Hamburg University of Applied Arts (HAW Hamburg) and Shenkar School of Engineering and Design in Tel Aviv. He worked as freelance designer for blottodesign in Berlin and teaches typography at the design department of HAW Hamburg. He specializes in corporate design, typography and type design favoring big letters in architectural spaces. In 2010, he founded PBLC—Büro für Visuelle Kommunikation with three other partners in Hamburg.

→ FF Bauer Grotesk 42 / 43

Apeloig, Philippe
France
www.apeloig.com

Philippe Apeloig was born in Paris in 1962. In 1985, he was hired as a graphic designer at the Musée d'Orsay in Paris. Apeloig was art director of the Musée du Louvre from 2003 to 2008. Among others, he designed posters for the exhibition *Yves Saint Laurent* at the Petit Palais and the *Saut Hermès au Grand Palais* in 2013. Apeloig has also created numerous logos, from the Châtelet Musical Theater to the Instituto Universitario di Architettura di Venezia or the silversmith Puiforcat. Apeloig is currently working on the visual identity of the Louvre in Abu Dhabi. Apeloig's design compositions have won numerous prizes, including the Premier Awards at the 2014 International Society of Typographic Designers Award in London.

→ Apeloig Type Library 26 / 27

Bagdasaryan, Gayaneh
Russia
www.brownfox.org

A graduate of Moscow State University of Printing Arts, Gayaneh has designed Cyrillic localizations for most major type libraries, including Linotype, Bitstream, The Font Bureau, ITC, Berthold, Typotheque, Emigre, and ParaType. She began her type design career at ParaType in 1996 and started her independent business with Brownfox in 2012. Her work has won awards from a number of international type design competitions, including Kyrillitsa '99, TDC^2 2000, and Granshan 2013. Gayaneh is the mastermind behind Serebro Nabora, a prominent annual international type conference held in Russia.

→ Formular 132 / 133
→ Formular Mono 132 / 133
→ Gerbera 146 / 147

De Baerdemaeker, Jo
Belgium
www.typojo.com

Jo De Baerdemaeker is an independent Belgian typeface designer and researcher, and founder of Studio Type. He holds a PhD in Typography and Graphic Communication and an MA in Typeface Design from the University of Reading. His interests are designing, researching and writing about world script typefaces (particularily on Tibetan

and Mongolian typefaces) and multilingual typography. He is elected ATypI board member and ATypI Country Delegate for Belgium, and currently teaches at LUCA School of Arts (campus Sint-Lukas Brussels), at the Plantin Institute for Typography (Antwerp), and at the European Lettering Institute (Bruges). He was the external examiner for the department of TypeMedia 2014 at KABK in The Hague.
→ Flanders Art 128 / 129

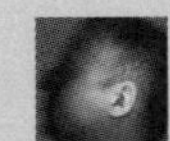

Baggar, Yassin
Switzerland
www.fatype.com

Yassin Baggar is a Swiss graphic and type designer. After studying Graphic Design in La Chaux-de-Fonds in Switzerland, he worked for various studios and clients, designing visual identities, books, magazines, posters, or websites. After receiving his Master's in Type Design from the Type and Media program at the Royal Academy of Art (KABK), The Hague, Yassin Baggar formed Fatype with Anton Koovit to distribute high quality typefaces and create custom typefaces for clients. He now lives between Berlin and Switzerland.
→ Beausite 44 / 45

Le Bailly, Jacques
The Netherlands
www.baronvonfonthausen.com

Jacques Le Bailly worked in Berlin for a number of years after graduating as a graphic designer. Upon returning to The Netherlands, he started working for The Enschedé Type Foundry. Since then, he also worked as a tutor at the WdKA art academy in Rotterdam, and Sint Joost art academy in Den Bosch. After working for three years as a senior designer at Studio Bauwinkel, he started his own company Baron von Fonthausen in 2009 and is focusing now on type design. He is currently working on personal type projects and for type foundries like Lineto, Monotype, House Industries, Bold Monday and custom projects for several branding design agencies.
→ Macula 214 / 215

Baldinger, André
Switzerland
www.abtypefoundry.com

André Baldinger studied in Zurich under Hans Rudolf Bosshard, then at the ANRT in Paris. In 1995, he founded his own workshop. He has been awarded grants from the French Ministry of Culture, the Swiss Federal Office of Culture and the Cnap. His creations can be found in the collections of the French National Library, the Zurich Museum of Design, and the Toyama Museum of Modern Art. In 2005, he was invited by the Swiss National Bank to participate in the competition for the new Swiss bank notes. In 2008, he founded Baldinger•Vu-Huu, along with Toan Vu-Huu. He teaches at Ensad in Paris, co-directs the EnsadLab Type research program, and lectures at the ANRT in Nancy and at the Zurich University of the Arts. He is a member of AGI.
→ AB Bline 54 / 55
→ AB Eiffel 116 / 117

Barmettler, Rudolf
Switzerland
www.typetypo.ch

Studied graphic design at the Lucerne University of Art and Design and at Pentagram Design, Zurich. Research project in visual communication with Hans-Rudolf Lutz, Zurich. Graphic designer at Jean Widmer, Paris. Freelancer for different design studios and publishers in Zurich and Munich. Freelancer for the Department of Artistic Design at the ETH Zurich. Studied film and graduated from the University of Television and Film, Munich. Since 1989, lecturer in Type and Typography in the Department of Visual Communication. 1999–2008 head of the Department of Visual Communication. Founder and head of the post-diploma courses CAS Schriftgestaltung, CAS Typography and Print, CAS Digital Typography and MAS Type Design / Typography.
→ NN Rektorat 292 / 293

Bieder, René
Germany
www.renebieder.com

René Bieder is a Berlin-based designer and art director. Before becoming a self-taught type designer, he worked in various advertising agencies. Since 2012, he has been developing font families like Galano Classic, Galano Grotesque, Campton, Choplin, Canaro and Quadon,

ranging from display to text usage. Four of his font families became Myfonts' most successful releases of the year 2012, 2013 and 2014.
→ Campton 80 / 81
→ Galano Classic 136 / 137

Bil'ak, Peter
The Netherlands
www.typotheque.com

Peter Bil'ak was born in Czechoslovakia and lives in the Netherlands. He works in the field of editorial, graphic, and type design, as well as teaching at the Royal Academy of Art in The Hague. He started Typotheque in 1999, Dot Dot Dot in 2000, Indian Type Foundry in 2009, and *Works That Work* magazine in 2012.
→ Lava 200 / 201

Binnenland
Mischler & Thoenen
Austria, Switzerland
www.binnenland.ch

Binnenland was founded in 2007 by Michael Mischler and Niklaus Thoenen to publish their font developments and to distribute their own typefaces via the Internet. Nik Thoenen lives and works as independent designer in Vienna, Austria. Michael Mischler lives and works as independent designer in Bern, Switzerland.
→ Korpus 190 / 191
→ Korpus Grotesk 192 / 193

Bodhuin, Benoît
France
www.bb-bureau.fr

Mathematical then graphics studies and a short stint in an agency persuaded him to work as freelancer. For the last ten years he has divided his time between completing orders for customers and personal projects often focused on typography. Since 2010, he also teaches Type Design and regularly leads workshops.
→ Mineral 232 / 233

Boessner, Dominique
Germany
www.letterwerk.ch

Dominique Boessner lives and works in Berlin as a designer of typography, type and objects. She studied design at the Free University of Bolzano—Faculty of Design and Art, Italy, and typography and type design at the Basel School of Design, Switzerland. In 2008, Dominique Boessner founded, together with Fabian Widmer Letterwerk, a design studio based in Berlin and Zurich.
→ Stencil Allround 304 / 305

Bonge, Felix
Germany
www.allerzeiten.com

Felix Bonge was born in 1982 in Hamburg, Germany. He first began experimenting with type design in 2005, studying Communication Design at the Hamburg University for Applied Arts (HAW Hamburg). From the second semester on he was hooked on type, thanks to Jovica Veljović and his type design class. Having had some experience with calligraphy before, this was a totally new and exciting insight in the world of letter shapes. From then on he further specialized in typography and type design, leading up to his first commercial release, Levato. Since 2012, he teaches Type Design at the HAW Hamburg and is part of the design studio allerzeiten, where he works on everything type-related and draws new typefaces in the meantime.
→ FF Bauer Grotesk 42 / 43

Branczyk, Alexander
Germany
www.czyk.de

Alexander Branczyk (*1959) studied Visual Communication at the HfG Offenbach academy under professor Friedrich Friedl. 1988–1994 he was project manager at Erik Spiekmann's MetaDesign. Since 1994, Alexander is partner of xplicit Gesellschaft für visuelle Kommunikation mbH based in Frankfurt / Main and Berlin. In addition, he is a self-clicking graphic designer, typeface designer, art director emeritus of the 1990s cult magazine *Frontpage* and founding member of the collaborative type'n'typo project Face2Face. 2003–2005 Alex was professor for typography at the Bauhaus University Weimar. Since 2012 at FH Dortmund, University of Applied Sciences and Arts. As a typeface designer, Branczyk designs corporate fonts like BER Airport Berlin-Brandenburg.
→ Monico 236 / 237

Brousil, Tomas
Czech Republic
www.suitcasetype.com

Tomas Brousil devotes himself primarily to fonts and typography. He graduated from the Prague Academy of Arts, Architecture and Design in 2009 with the project of 96 typefaces of the Tabac font. He founded his own Suitcase Type Foundry in 2003, serving as an outlet for his creative work; he currently holds several awards. He currently resides in Prague, also serving as a pedagogue at the Type Design and Typography department of the Prague Academy of Arts, Architecture and Design.
→ Urban Grotesk 322 / 323

Burian, Veronika
Czech Republic, Germany
www.type-together.com

Veronika Burian originally studied Industrial Design before graduating with distinction from the MA in Typeface Design in Reading, UK, in 2003. After working as full-time type designer at DaltonMaag in London, she co-founded with José Scaglione the independent type label TypeTogether. She also continues to give lectures and workshops at international conferences and universities. Several of her typefaces have been recognized by international competitions, including ED-Awards and TDC.
→ Bree Serif 62 / 63

du Carrois, Ralph
Germany
www.carrois.com

Ralph du Carrois was born 1975 in Füssen im Allgäu. He graduated as diploma designer with a degree in Product Design from the Karlsruhe University of Art and Design in 2004. He later founded the Berlin-based studio Carrois Type Design. In cooperation with Erik Spiekermann, FontShop and Monotype he and his team also work on multiple corporate type projects for clients such as Mozilla, ZDF, Cisco, Deutsche Bahn and many more.
→ Quist 286 / 287

Chacana, Tania
Chile
www.latinotype.com

Tania Chacana was born in Santiago de Chile in 1985, studied Graphic Design in Chile and at the University of Buenos Aires (AR) and completed the Type Design Specialization Career after two years. After graduating in 2012, she made type design the permanent focus of her work and now concentrates on the research of modern aesthetics for useful fonts.
→ Uomo 320 / 321

Chahine, Nadine
Germany
www.arabictype.com

Dr. Nadine Chahine is an award-winning Lebanese type designer working as the Arabic specialist at Monotype. She studied Graphic Design at the American University of Beirut, has an MA in Typeface Design from the University of Reading, UK, and a PhD from Leiden University, The Netherlands. In 2005, she joined Linotype as Arabic specialist and has been living in Germany ever since. Nadine's research focus is on legibility studies for the Arabic script. She has won an Award for Excellence in Type Design from the Type Directors Club in 2008 and 2011. Her work has been featured in the 5th edition of Megg's History of Graphic Design and in 2012 she was selected by Fast Company as one of its 100 Most Creative People in Business.
→ Zapfino Arabic 338 / 339

Claudius, Stefan
Germany
www.cape-arcona.com

Stefan Claudius (born 1971) is a German-Swiss typographer, typeface designer and graphic designer. After studying Industrial Design in Essen and Wuppertal, he started as a freelance designer in 2000. In 2002, he founded the Cape Arcona Type Foundry together with Thomas Schostok. Since 2007, he has taught at the Folkwang University of the Arts, the FH Dortmund, University of Applied Sciences and Arts and the HFBK Hamburg Typography, Type Design and Conceptual Design. His handwriting typeface Texteron has been awarded the European Design Award and was nominated for the Design Award of the Federal Republic of Germany.
→ Yalta Sans 336 / 337

Conidi, Emanuela
Great Britain
www.fontsmith.com

Emanuela Conidi joined Fontsmith in 2008 after studying Typeface Design at Reading University. With a background in graphic design, experience in hot-metal type hand composition and letterpress printing, she is passionate about typographic history, 19th century typefaces and Arabic typography.
→ FS Albert Arabic 12 / 13

Cortat, Matthieu
France
www.nonpareille.net

Born in 1982 in Delémont (Switzerland), Matthieu Cortat is a type and graphic designer. He graduated from the École d'Art de Lausanne (ECAL) and the Atelier National de Recherche Typographique (ANRT) in Nancy, France. Now living in Lyon, he creates new typefaces, but also works with several publishers as a typographer, and regularly offers guided tours of the Lyon Printing Museum. Within the framework of the latter institution, he has set up the Corpus typographique français (which collects all typefaces designed in France between 1850 and today). He also contributes articles to the website dedicated to the 450th anniversary of Claude Garamond's death.
→ Basetica 40 / 41

Crossgrove, Carl
USA
www.monotype.com

If there's such a thing as a born type designer and typographer, it is Carl Crossgrove. Since learning to read at the age of two, he has been obsessed with how letters look, and has been drawing them all his life, beginning with the chalk alphabets he drew on the driveway of his Connecticut home. Growing up, he soaked up influences. His interests shifted from fantastical display lettering inspired by comics, album covers and the 1970s art nouveau revival to classical type and lettering, calligraphy and botanical illustration. After earning a degree in Printing with a focus on Typography from Rochester Institute of Technology in 1994, he started his association with Monotype.
→ Burlingame 76 / 77

Dell, Natascha
Germany
www.fontfarm.de

Natascha Dell was born 1981 in Saarlouis. From 2000 to 2004 she studied Visual Communication at the University of Applied Sciences, Aachen. She graduated in 2004 with a diploma, supervised by Prof. Klaus Endrikat and Prof. Doris Casse-Schlüter. Since 2003, she gained practical experiences in type design and founded Fontfarm.de, an independent type foundry, in cooperation with Kai Oetzbach in 2006. Since 2012, she is a lecturer at the Folkwang University of the Arts where she teaches Communication Design and Type Design.
→ Caput (SF) 82 / 83
→ Gedau Gothic 144 / 145

Delobel, Sébastien
France
www.ainsifont.com

Sébastien Delobel was born in Lille, France, in 1972, and studied Graphic Design at l'École Supérieure des Arts Décoratifs de Strasbourg, France. He designs custom fonts for a large variety of projects: brand identities, press, signage systems. Since 1998, he has been co-founder and associated graphic designer at Atelier Télescopique studio, Lille. Atelier Télescopique works in multiple media—print, design, web and art exhibitions. He is co-founder of the digital foundry AinsiFont which has distributed original typefaces since 2007. It was formerly called La Fonderie Nordik (1999–2007).
→ A.F. Tomica 314 / 315

Derre, Michel
France
www.fontyou.com

Michel Derre was born in 1955. Typesetter at first, he oriented himself to graphic design through various experiences in editorial and advertising agencies. In the eighties, he got credibility with letterings, logotypes and his first passion, calligraphy. In 1991, he created an advanced degree class in Type Design at École Estienne in Paris with Franck Jalleau. He also teaches Calligraphy and Letter Drawing at the famous ESAG Penninghen in Paris. Michel Derre has been the calligraphy teacher of many type lovers. Good friend of the foundry since its creation, Michel choose to develop his first font Algo FY with the Fontyou team.
→ Algo FY 14 / 15

Design Partnership Areal BL
Switzerland
www.bivgrafik.ch
www.hi-web.ch
www.binnenland.ch

Design Partnership: Bringolf Irion Vögeli, Visuelle Gestaltung, Zurich and Hi—Visuelle Gestaltung, Lucerne, Claudio Barandun in collaboration with Binnenland.

→ Areal BL 28 / 29

Díaz, Fernando
Uruguay
www.ferfolio.com

Fernando Díaz Morales is a Lic. graphic designer born in Montevideo, Uruguay, in 1988. Co-founder and partner at *TipoType.com*. Founding member of Sociedad Tipográfica de Montevideo (Montevideo's Tipographic Society). Country delegate for AtypI (Association Typographique International). Selected in TiposLatinos 2008 and BID 2010. Instructor at TypeCamp Brazil 2012. Jury of TiposLatinos 2014. Speaker at PechaKucha 2014. Speaker at DiaTipo 2014. Participated in the book *Tipografía Latinoamericana {Un panorama actual y futuro}* compiled by Vicente Lamónaca.

→ Libertad 202 / 203

Dieneš, Andrej
Slowakei
www.adtypo.com

Andjrey Dieneš was born 11.5.1985 in Myjava, Slovakia. Fine art attracted him from an early age. He always preferred drawing (shapes), rather than painting (colors), which led him to study at the School of Applied Art in Bratislava, department of Promotional Graphics (2000–2004). Then he continued to study at the Academy of Fine Arts and Design in Bratislava in the department of Visual Communication (2005–2011). In the 3rd year, he became interested in type design. He did not know anything about it, but it fascinated him, so he endured difficult beginnings and began to improve. He got an internship at the Academy of Arts, Architecture and Design in Prague, Department of Type Design and Typography (2010), where he gained valuable experience. After studying, he worked as graphic designer in a small advertising agency, then as graphic designer for the town Senica (SK). Today, he teaches the course of Typography at the Technical College in Hodonín (CZ).

→ Fazeta 126 / 127

Dietzel, Livius
Germany
www.liviusdietzel.de

Livius Dietzel studied Visual Communication at the University of the Arts in Berlin as well as in London and Barcelona. In 2008, he graduated from Fons Hickmann's Design Class. Beside his work at MetaDesign, he works as an art director and type designer. Livius has received honors like the reddot, the iF Award and the Certificate of Typographic Excellence from the Type Directors Club New York. Together with Hannes von Döhren, he designed the typefaces ITC Chino, Livory and FF Basic Gothic.

→ Brix Sans & Slab 66 / 67

von Döhren, Hannes
Germany
www.hvdfonts.com

Hannes von Döhren was born in Berlin, Germany. After completing his studies in Graphic Design, he worked in an advertising agency in Hamburg. Since 2008, he runs his own type foundry HVD Fonts. Within the last years he has released several type families like Brevia, Livory, ITC Chino, FF Basic Gothic, Reklame Script, Pluto, Pluto Sans and Brandon Grotesque which was the most successful release at MyFonts in 2010. In 2011, he received the Certificate of Excellence in Type Design from the Type Directors Club NY.

→ Brandon Printed 60 / 61
→ Brix Sans & Slab 66 / 67
→ FF Mark 226 / 227
→ Niveau Grotesk 252 / 253
→ Niveau Serif 252 / 253

Droz, Marc
Switzerland
www.dreh-gmbh.ch

Marc Droz lives and works in Zurich. In 1989, he completed his apprenticeship as a graphic designer in the Studio U. Hiestand. From 1990–2011, he ran his own studio and worked in the field of print and motion design as well as architectural visualization. In 2011, he graduated in CAS Type Design at the Zurich University of the Arts. In 2011, he founded with Regula Ehrliholzer the graphic design studio dreh gmbh—bureau for professional deformation.

→ NN Colroy 94 / 95

Dünnwald, Dennis
Germany
www.volcano-type.de

Dennis Dünnwald is a German designer based in Berlin. Currently he is working as senior art director and is mainly at home in the digital world. Nevertheless, he finds himself getting pulled back into working with print media or in front of a simple blank sheet of paper to draw letters.

→ Duwal Pro 112 / 113

Dunst, Christoph
Germany
www.atlasfonts.com

Christoph Dunst studied at the Royal Academy of Art in The Hague, The Netherlands, where he graduated with a degree in Graphic and Typographic Design and a master in Type Design. Bureau Christoph Dunst was founded in 2006. Since 2011, he teaches typographic design, typeface design, brand communication and corporate identity at universities and art academies, nationally and internationally. The Atlas Font Foundry, founded in 2012, publishes new original typefaces for professional use such as editorial and corporate typography. The growing collection of high quality font families is finely crafted and provides many features for fine typography and innovative design solutions.

→ Heimat Display 164 / 165
→ Novel Sans Hair 258 / 259

Embodas, Jordi
Spain
www.tipografies.com

Jordi Embodas (Barcelona, 1977) is a Barcelona-based graphic designer passionate about letterforms. He studied Graphic Design in Elisava 1995–1999 and he studied one term at Universität GH Essen (Germany). Since 2001, he works at Estudi Juste Calduch and he has been designing text typefaces since 2005. He teaches Typography at various design schools in Barcelona and sometimes he offers educational talks within the Spanish typographic scene. Noe Blanco has collaborated in the development of Bulo Rounded and Trola Text.

→ Trola Text 318 / 319

Espinoza, Ramiro
The Netherlands
www.re-type.com

Ramiro Espinoza became interested in type design when he was a student at the Universidad Nacional del Litoral in Santa Fe, Argentina. After graduation, he taught Typography at the Universidad de Buenos Aires—under the direction of Silvia Gonzalez. In 2003, he moved to The Netherlands and studied at the KABK in The Hague. Since then, he has been a contributor to *Tipográfica* and *Tipo* design magazines, researched vernacular Dutch lettering and worked in numerous freelance assignments for FontShop International. In 2007, he founded ReType type foundry to market his typefaces.

→ Laski Slab 198 / 199

Ford, Jim
USA
www.monotype.com

A graduate in Graphic Design from Columbia College Chicago in 2005, Jim has notched up custom typefaces from agencies and publishers to software manufacturers and game developers. Jim has also created his own designs from traditional text faces to innovative display lettering, and includes art and illustration in his portfolio. He counts the books of Frederic Goudy and a Hyphen Press text by Fred Smeijers, Counterpunch, as serious influences on his development as a designer. "It's often an aim of mine to make my typefaces shine at display sizes and perform gracefully in text sizes as well. It's a balancing act." Other fonts from Jim include the Ayita Pro™, Ford's Folly™ and Pokerface™ designs.

→ Quire Sans 284 / 285

Freytag, Arne
Germany
www.fontador.de

Arne Freytag was born in Hamburg in 1967. In 1995, he won a scholarship to study Graphic Design at the Kunstschule Alsterdamm art school in Hamburg. As a postgraduate in 1998, he attended the Atelier National de Recherche Typographique in Paris. He has published various articles in Tipografica, *étapes* and the *Typografische Monatsblätter.* He has been working as a freelance typographic and graphic designer since 2000.

→ Quitador 288 / 289

Fromm, Jan
Germany
www.janfromm.de

Jan Fromm studied Communication design at Potsdam University of Applied Sciences. An initial curiosity about typography quickly became a passion when he began to attend Luc(as) de Groot's Type Design classes. In that time he gained a deep understanding of typography as a fundamental visual component of graphic design. Jan has worked as a freelance type designer since 2003, and besides drawing letters and logos, he works with web and screen-based design projects.
→ Komet 186 / 187

Gabriel, Thomas
Austria
www.typejockeys.at

Thomas Gabriel was born and lives in Vienna, Austria. He studied Graphic and Communication design at Die Graphische in Vienna. After that he completed the one year master class with diploma in 2004. That was followed by one year civil service for the Red Cross. In 2006 he went abroad to study typeface design at the Royal Academy of Art, The Hague (NL). Graduated in 2007 at the type]media Master Course. Since then, he has been working in different graphic design fields, always pushing quality typeface design. In 2008, he founded Typejockeys together with Anna Fahrmaier and Michael Hochleitner.
→ Aniuk 24 / 25

Gálvez Pizarro, Francisco
Chile
www.pampatype.com

Francisco Gálvez Pizarro is a Chilean graphic designer and a self-taught type designer. He teaches at the Universidad Católica and he wrote the book *Educación tipográfica* that is popular in Spanish-speaking countries. His type Australis gained the Gold Prize at Morisawa Japan, 2002. His type Elemental won the Chilean prize Altazor, 2002. Together with Rodrigo Ramírez, he created the types for the newspapers *La Discusión* (Chillán) and *La Cuarta* (Santiago), the type for the transport system Transantiago, and also the type for the highways signs in Chile.
→ Amster Pro 20 / 21

Garnham, Phil
Great Britain
www.fontsmith.com

Phil Garnham's journey through art school began at the Colchester Institute, Essex and then through Middlesex University, London, where he studied Visual Communication—Graphic Design. A new-found fascination for type, its tone, texture and placement, later propelled Phil on a journey of typographic investigation. Phil joined Fontsmith in 2003 and has since created letterforms and alphabets for a diverse global client list. He is typeface design director of Fontsmith, co-leads the Fontsmith team creatively and helps to manage the company.
→ FS Emeric 120 / 121

González, Paco
Spain
www.resistenza.es

Paco González is a Spanish designer from Valencia. His background varies from the tourism industry to marketing and graphic design. He develops corporate identity and typographic projects. His typographic work is focused on handwritten typefaces, scripts and illustrative icons, dingbats and little sketches later transformed into type sets. He co-founded Resistenza.es with Giuseppe Salerno. Being a part of a type foundry gives him all the creative freedom.
→ Nautica 246 / 247

Goyal, Namrata
India
www.indiantypefoundry.com

Born in Rajasthan, India, Namrata is a good mix of traditional and contemporary. She is a Visual Communication Design graduate from the Srishti School of Art, Design and Technology, Bangalore. Her interest in typography in her design explorations eventually led her to do a Gurmukhi type design project as her final (diploma) project. After working for six months as a graphic designer at FITCH—Mumbai, Namrata joined the Indian Type Foundry based in Ahmedabad, India, in 2014. Growing up all over the country, she loves to travel, read and is annoyingly curious about everything.
→ Volte 330 / 331

Grace, Tom
USA
www.virgotype.com

Tom Grace is an independent typeface designer and font developer whose skill and experience span both the aesthetic and technical aspects of digital typography. He creates custom and retail typeface designs as well as adapting existing designs for specialized roles (eg. reading on-screen). His collaborative style has allowed him to work closely with many of the world's most prominent typeface designers and foundries, and their work has received awards for excellence. He has lectured on typeface design and has participated in type design workshops. He has gained a formal education in type from the Rhode Island School of Design (RI, USA) and the University of Reading (UK), where he received his MA in typeface design.
→ DIN Next Slab 106 / 107
→ Iskra 174 / 175

Grall, Guillaume
France
www.buildingparis.fr

Guillaume Grall is a graphic designer and started his own studio Building Paris in 2012 with Benoît Santiard. He works in the fields of editorial project and visual identity, always paying great attention to typography.
→ BTP 70 / 71

Great Lakes Lettering
USA
www.greatlakeslettering.com

Dathan Boardman and Molly Jacques Erickson founded Great Lakes Lettering with a mutual appreciation for artful calligraphy. "In 2012 I had been working on lots of calligraphic fonts and came across Molly's work and was immediately struck by how visceral it was and how it didn't really look like any other kind of calligraphy that I've come across," Dathan says. "I reached out to her wondering if she had any interest in turning her lettering into fonts." The duo's first typeface, Frosted, was released later that year. Dathan and Molly's bestselling typefaces include Asterism, a calligraphy style font with a moving baseline and lots of shining personality, and Kailey, a hand lettered typeface that was inspired by Molly's signature style.
→ Asterism 34 / 35
→ Kailey 180 / 181

de Groot, Luc(as)
Germany
www.lucasfonts.com

Dutch type designer Luc(as) de Groot is best-known for his superfamily Thesis: TheSans, TheSerif, TheMix, TheSansMono, TheAntiqua etc. He designed custom fonts for periodicals like *taz*, *Der Spiegel*, *Folha de S.Paulo*, *Le Monde*; and corporate type for clients like *Sun Microsystems*, *Volkswagen*, *Miele*, *Bell South*, *Heineken*. For *Microsoft* he designed Consolas and Calibri. Luc(as) developed an interpolation theory, teaches and gives lectures Waround the world. He runs his foundry LucasFonts in Berlin.
→ Taz Wide 306 / 307
→ Taz Extended 306 / 307

Guseynov, Ramiz
USA
www.tipografiaramis.com

Ramiz Guseynov is an American designer, born and educated in Russia. In 1991, he moved from Moscow to Chicago as an already accomplished and highly regarded graphic designer. In the US, he has spent over 20 years working for various design studios and Fortune 500 corporations. After a long career in print design, he was able to realize his dream of dedicating himself completely to his longtime passion of typeface design. In 2004, he established the TipografiaRamis font foundry to create and market his digital fonts.
→ Colón 92 / 93
→ Decima 104 / 105

Hagemann, Michael
USA
www.fontmesa.com

Michael Hagemann's career as an artist started out in product advertising photography where he achieved a great level of success as photographer for Automobili Lamborghini in 1993. While studying Digital Photography in 1995, he bought a font design application and became interested in type design, and after practicing for five years, he released his first type designs in 2000. Since then he has continued work on improving his skill as a type designer with a growing collection of font revivals and original designs.
→ Magnum Sans Pro 216 / 217

Hagmann, Sibylle
USA
www.kontour.com

Sibylle Hagmann began her career in Switzerland after earning a BFA from the Basel School of Design in 1989. She explored her passion for type design and typography while completing her MFA at the California Institute of the Arts. Over the years, she developed award winning typeface families, such as Cholla and Odile. Cholla was originally commissioned by Art Center College of Design in 1999 and released by the type foundry Emigre in the same year. Cholla was among the winning entries of bukva:raz! The typeface family Odile, published in 2006, was awarded the Swiss Federal Design Award. Her work has been featured in numerous publications and she presented her work nationally and internationally at typography conferences and other venues.

→ Kopius 188 / 189

Hecksher, Jonas
Denmark
www.playtype.com

Jonas Hecksher holds a degree from The Royal Danish Academy of Fine Arts—The School of Design, and École Supérieure d'Arts Graphiques et d'Architecture, Paris, where he specialized in graphic design and typography design. Heckscher is partner and creative director at the design agency e-Types which he co-founded in 1997. He is also co-founder of type foundry and type design brand Playtype.

→ Berlingske Family 50 / 51

Hernández, Daniel
Chile
www.latinotype.com

Daniel Hernández is a graphic designer who received his BA in Design from the Universidad Mayor in 2006 and and was awarded a diploma in diploma in Typography from the Pontificia Universidad Católica de Chile in 2007. In 2006, he received from *tipoGráfica*—an Argentinean typography magazine—the tpG award for his display font Stgotic. Daniel is a specialist in display fonts design and has taught at several Chilean universities and colleges. In 2010, he began selling his fonts through the Sudtipos font foundry. Daniel is one of the partners of Latinotype and he currently lives in Santiago de Chile. On Typographica, MyFonts, FontShop and I Love Typography, his fonts have consistently remained best-sellers throughout this year.

→ Arquitecta 32 / 33
→ Texta 308 / 309
→ Trend 316 / 317

Hernández, Miguel
Chile
www.latinotype.com

Miguel Hernández, born in Chile in 1977, is a graphic designer and self-taught type designer, founder of Latinotype and author of diverse font families like Mija, Tikal, Arquitecta, Texta and Uomo. He's interested in mixing all timeless classics and post-modernist typographic aesthetics into versatile graphic design tools.

→ Arquitecta 32 / 33
→ Texta 308 / 309
→ Uomo 320 / 321

Hirter, Thomas
Switzerland
www.thomashirter.ch

Thomas Hirter has been working as an independent graphic designer for nearly 10 years. He graduated from the school of design in the Swiss city of Biel and now works from a small former packaging factory in Bern, a space he shares with two dozen other freelancers. "I consider myself more of a craftsman than an artist. Type design has always fascinated me, but in recent years I have become more serious and passionate, so it was only a question of time until my first typeface was released."

→ Lunica 210 / 211

Hische, Jessica
USA
www.jessicahische.is

Jessica Hische is a letterer and illustrator working in San Francisco and Brooklyn. She has worked for clients from Wes Anderson to Tiffany & Co. and the *New York Times*. Jessica has been featured in design and illustration annuals around the globe and was named a Print Magazine New Visual Artist (20 under 30), one of Forbes 30 under 30 in Art and Design two years in a row, an ADC Young Gun, a "Person to Watch" by GD USA, and one of 25 Emerging Artists by *STEP Magazine*. She serves on the Type Directors Club Board of Directors. Aside from her illustrious client work, she has created side projects including *Daily Drop Cap*, *Should I Work for Free?*, *Mom This is How Twitter Works*, and *Don't Fear the Internet* (created along with Russ Maschmeyer).

→ Tilda 312 / 313

Hochleitner, Michael
Austria
www.typejockeys.at

Michael Hochleitner was born and lives in Vienna, Austria. He studied Graphic and Communication Design in Vienna, completing his diploma in 2003. After one year of civil service, he studied media science in Vienna, while driving a cab for money. Michael worked as a freelance graphic designer from 2004 to 2007. In 2007, he completed his MA in Typeface Design at the University of Reading (UK), where he laid the foundation for his successful typeface Ingeborg. In 2008, he founded the design studio and foundry Typejockeys together with Anna Fahrmaier and Thomas Gabriel. Michael gives lectures and workshops about type design, lettering and typography. He is the proud father of two girls.
→ Henriette 166 / 167

Hörmann, Roland
Austria
www.phospho.at

Austrian graphic designer, born 1976 in Krems. His father's Letraset catalogues early aroused his fascination for type, which led to first experimental pixel font creations on the Commodore64 in the early nineties. After studying Graphic Design in Vienna and graduating in Communication Design in 1999 he worked as freelance graphic designer in Vienna. In 2007 he became a freelance art director for Perndl+Co and shortly thereafter started releasing fonts on his label phospho type foundry, which soon specialized in display typefaces inspired by the typographical heritage of the city of Vienna. In 2012, he co-founded Stadtschrift, an association for the collection, preservation and documentation of historic façade signs.
→ Luxus Brut Sparkling 212 / 213

Hornus, Jérémie
France
www.fontyou.com

Jérémie Hornus studied graphic design at Le Scriptorium de Toulouse, France, (2000–2004) and then completed a Master of Arts in Typeface Design at the University of Reading, UK, in 2006. He worked in London for DaltonMaag before joining Fontyou in 2013.
→ Algo FY 14 / 15

Hübsch, Stefan
Germany
www.typocalypse.com

Stefan Hübsch, son of a sign painter, studied communication design and is currently working as a freelance graphic designer, typographer and independent photographer. Typocalypse is a typographic collective and type foundry based in southwest Germany—founded in 2008. Kai Merker, Stefan Hübsch and Sven Fuchs are the three horsemen of the typocalypse.
→ Lichtspiele 204 / 205

Jancsó, Áron
Hungary
www.aronjancso.com

Gestalten scouted out the amazingly fresh Hungarian talent Áron Jancsó and released his first commercial fonts Ogaki and Sensaway, which became quickly two of the top selling fonts of the foundry. Jancso, who has liked to build, carve wood, and draw since childhood, has grown up to be a real type addict, and he now devotes his time to meticulously drawing and designing letters. "I like to play and experiment, a bit like an explorer or scientist in the visual world. I'm fascinated by visual languages of the cultures of the world and their writing systems and how these can be mixed with modern and clean styles."
→ Caligo 78 / 79

Jelesijević, Dušan
Serbia
www.dusanjelesijevic.com

Dušan Jelesijević was born in Gornji Milanovac, Serbia, in 1983. He graduated from the Graphic Design department at the Faculty FILUM in Kragujevac.
→ Hedon 162 / 163

Job, Nick
Great Britain
www.fontsmith.com

Nick Job joined the exclusive list of Fontsmith designers in 2012, releasing the hugely successful FS Elliot geometric sans serif family. A lover of design grids and maps, Nick has a straightforward approach to executing clean, fresh, no-nonsense fonts that read beautifully.
→ FS Elliot Pro 118 / 119
→ FS Hackney 156 / 157

Jób, Ondrej
Slovakia
www.urtd.net

Ondrej Jób is a Graphic and Type designer currently living in Bratislava. He holds MA degrees in graphic design from the Academy of Fine Art and Design in Bratislava, Slovakia (2008), and in type design from the Type-Media master's program at The Royal Academy of Art (KABK) in The Hague, The Netherlands (2009).
→ Woodkit 334 / 335

Jocham, Hubert
Germany
www.hubertjocham.de

After his education in lead setting, Hubert Jocham studied Graphic Design in Germany and England. His degree project dealt with the history of italic old style printing type. He worked for Henrion in London in corporate branding, designing logotypes and design manuals. During that time, he also designed typefaces for British magazines like *FRANK* and *ARENA*. Today, Hubert Jocham designs brand marks for most of the leading branding Networks like Interbrand, The Brand Union, Landor or Futurebrand. He develops text and headline systems for international magazines like *GQ London*, Russian, Turkish and French *Vogue*, *L'Officiell Paris*, *Details* and *W magazine* in New York. He created corporate typefaces for Bally, Agfa Photo and Vattenfall Sweden.
→ GarySans 140 / 141
→ NarzissGrotesk 244 / 245

Jung, Erica
Brazil
www.pintassilgoprints.com

Erica Jung is a type designer from Brazil. She graduated from Federal University of Rio de Janeiro in 1998, with a monograph on typography. Along with Ricardo Marcin, she runs their independent foundry, PintassilgoPrints, based in Florianópolis, Brazil. With a solid background in hand printing techniques besides a long time love for typography and lettering, they have been developing a consistent font library of original typefaces which reflects a vigorous handcrafted feel. Often packed with dynamic OpenType features, their fonts encourage users to craft unique typographic pieces. PintassilgoPrints works have been featured in specialized publications such as *8 Faces*, *Creative Characters*, *Slanted*, *Computer Arts*, *Page Magazine* and *Typolyrics*.
→ Brush Up 68 / 69
→ Daft Brush 98 / 99

Jürgeleit, Anita
Germany
www.anitajuergeleit.de

For Anita Jürgeleit, typefaces are more than just a shape: "A typeface is the most important tool for a designer. It's a requirement for creating good and targeted design." Amazed by the important matter of type design of our everyday life, Anita Jürgeleit published her first typeface at URW++ in 2013. After she had finished her education in logistics business, she found her way into the creative field through an apprenticeship as a media designer and by graduating in Communication Design. Her work focuses on type and the clarity of its shape. "I just never knew how type is created and where it comes from. Otherwise I would have been engaged with it much earlier."
→ Hangulatin 158 / 159
→ Quendel Happy Family 280 / 281

Kirilenko, Vyacheslav
Russia
www.brownfox.org

A graduate of Kazakh National Pedagogical University Abai, Vyacheslav currently works as a freelance graphic designer and as a type designer for Brownfox. His work has been widely acclaimed, included in numerous international books and periodicals, and won an award from Granshan international type design competition, 2013.
→ Formular 132 / 133
→ Formular Mono 132 / 133
→ Gerbera 146 / 147

Kirkwood, Kimmy
USA
www.kimmydesign.com

Kimmy Kirkwood is a type designer currently based out of Santa Monica, CA. She specializes in complex typefaces utilizing the full range of OpenType features. Most recognized are her organic fonts, each one made to look completely hand crafted. She loves traveling and everything typography, finding inspiration all over the world.

→ Baker Street 38 / 39
→ Burford 72 / 73
→ Catalina Family 88 / 89
→ Lunchbox Family 208 / 209

Kobayashi, Akira
Japan
www.linotype.com

The DIN Next Slab family is the result of a collaboration between Monotype's Akira Kobayashi, as the design director, and freelance designers Sandra Winter and Tom Grace, who did much of the heavy lifting. Winter and Grace have worked previously with Kobayashi, who comments, "Part of Sandra and Tom's competence is that, with very little direction, they produce excellent results."

→ DIN Next Slab 106 / 107

Koeberlin, Christoph
Germany
www.typefacts.com

Christoph Koeberlin worked from 2006 to 2015 as a type designer and font developer at FontShop International and runs the independent typography website *typefacts.com.* He likes vinyl records, gingham-checkered shirts and a bit of chocolate after every meal. He is a big fan of 1. FC Kaiserslautern and had recently the chance to design the jersey figures of The Club.

→ FF Mark 226 / 227

Koovit, Anton
Germany
www.korkork.com

Anton Koovit was born in Tallinn, Estonia, in 1981. He studied Graphic Design at Estonian Academy of Arts, ESAG Paris and at Gerrit Rietveldt Academy in Amsterdam, the Netherlands. After finishing his Graphic Design studies in 2005, he continued to specialize in type design in the postgraduate course Type and Media (KABK) in The Hague, the Netherlands. In 2007, he moved to Berlin, Germany. In collaboration with Yassin Baggar he set up Fatype, a digital type foundry, to distribute his fonts and work on custom type projects.

→ Laplace 196 / 197

Krepinsky, Ingo
Germany
www.typonauten.de

Ingo Krepinsky is founder and manager of the Bremen-based (German) design agency Die Typonauten. He studied Communication Design at the University of the Arts Bremen and the University of Applied Sciences and Arts Hannover. He has won several design contests such as iF communication design award, The German Design Award (nominated) or Stiftung Buchkunst (best designed books). The design performance and font work of Die Typonauten are consistently presented in international journals. The foundry was selected as German independent type foundry for *Typography, Referenced—A Comprehensive Visual Guide to the Language, History, and Practice of Typography*, a publication of Rockport Publishers.

→ Newsletter Pro 248 / 249

Krömer, Stefan
Germany
www.typonauten.de

Stefan Krömer is founder and manager of the Bremen-based (German) design agency Die Typonauten. He studied Communication Design at the University of the Arts Bremen and the University of Applied Sciences and Arts Hannover. He has won several design contests such as iF communication design award, The German Design Award (nominated) or Stiftung Buchkunst (best designed books). The design performance and font work of Die Typonauten are consistently presented in international journals. The foundry was selected as German independent type

foundry for *Typography, Referenced—A Comprehensive Visual Guide to the Language, History, and Practice of Typography*, a publication of Rockport Publishers.
→ V8 328 / 329

van der Laan, Paul
The Netherlands
www.boldmonday.com

Paul van der Laan is founding partner of Bold Monday type foundry, and lives near the seaside in The Hague working as a designer of type and typography. Since 2003, Van der Laan has been staff member and tutor in Type Design at the Type & Media Master's course at the Royal Academy of Art (KABK) in The Hague. He travels regularly to give workshops and lectures at schools and international conferences. Paul van der Laan is also the designer of acclaimed typefaces including Oskar, Flex, Feisar, and has worked on custom type for worldwide clients including *Audi AG, USA Today, General Electric, NBCUniversal, WDR,* and *Rijksmuseum Amsterdam*.
→ GE Inspira Sans 142 / 143
→ GE Inspira Serif 142 / 143
→ HF Stencil 168 / 169

Lamónaca, Vicente
Uruguay
www.tipotype.com

Vincente Lamónaca is a Lic. graphic designer living in Montevideo, Uruguay, since 1985. Teacher in the area of typography and editorial design at ORT University since 2000. He has served since 1993 as a senior graphic designer, where he has been involved in organizing conferences and exhibitions related to design and typography. He has published articles related to type design. Jury for the typography biennial Letras Latinas 2006 and Tipos Latinos 2008, and organizer of Tipos Latinos 2010. Finally, he was the compiler of the book *Tipografía Latinoamericana {Un panorama actual y futuro}*.
→ Libertad 202 / 203

Langpeter, Peter
Germany
www.lp-design.de

Peter Langpeter first trained as a cartographer, with the focus on drawing fonts of all kinds. This was followed by years of practice draughtsmanship activities on city and street maps as well as nautical charts. Later he also drew illustrations for the graphical content. As digital interfaces became increasingly popular for developing maps, he switched to graphic design. The designer Peter Schmidt became aware of him and asked Peter Langpeter to come to Hamburg, where he then spent five years. During this time he designed many well-known letterings and logos. Since then Peter Langpeter works as freelance font and logo designer, calligrapher and illustrator. Lately he has begun developing his own fonts, inspired from the daily needs in graphic design and designed to be especially user-friendly.
→ LP Philharmonia 272 / 273

Levée, Jean-Baptiste
France
www.productiontype.com

Jean-Baptiste Levée works methodically in a process that combines history and technology with the nuances of artistry. He manufactures functional, yet versatile digital platforms for designers to build upon. He has designed over a hundred typefaces for industry, moving pictures, fashion and publishing. He leads the digital typeface foundry Production Type. he has exhibited his work internationally, and is featured in the permanent collections of the French national library (BnF) and the National Center of Arts (Cnap); of the Newberry Library in Chicago, and several printing museums in Europe. He is also the country delegate for France at ATypI. He teaches Typeface Design at the Amiens School of Arts & Design, among others.
→ Minotaur 234 / 235

Link, Gunnar
Germany
www.gunnarlink.net

Gunnar Link is a German graphic and type designer living in a small town in the black forest. After his apprenticeship as a digital media designer, he studied Communication Design at the University of Applied Scienes Mainz. Since 2011, he has been working as a freelance graphic designer, mainly focusing on type design projects.
→ Newsletter Pro 248 / 249
→ V8 328 / 329

Lopes, João Henrique
Brazil
www.urwpp.com

Born in Brazil in 1986, Joao Henrique Lopes has always been interested in professional drawing. He has been selected for several cartoon exhibitions around the world, did some comic books, and wrote a book about the art of drawing (Elements of Manga Style). He graduated in Visual Arts in 2011, worked as an art teacher in various schools, and in 2012 he started converting the typefaces he had sketched over the years in Bezier curves. He doesn't create fonts just because he likes it. Each of his projects originates from a need. He feels that "it would be good if a font existed that could be used for diverse occasions," then he searches for it. And if he sees that such a font doesn't exist yet, he takes it as his mission to create it.
→ Pleiad 274 / 275

Lopez, Sabrina
Argentina
www.typesenses.tumblr.com

Sabrina Lopez was born in Buenos Aires, Argentina, in 1987. She is a graphic designer and graduated from Buenos Aires University. She has also studied calligraphy with the best teachers: Eugenia Roballos and Betina Naab in Buenos Aires, and she took classes with Julian Waters, Georgia Deaver and Carl Rohrs in Boston. Since 2009, she has been designing fonts in Typesenses, her own foundry. Every font she publishes is a great success. She is a demanding type designer, focused on studying calligraphy to learn more about the letter forms. As she enjoys the contact with paper and ink so much, she decided to make this the focus of her work.
→ Fantasy 124 / 125
→ Wishes Script 332 / 333

Malaviya, Hitesh
India
www.indiantypefoundry.com

After finishing art school in Baroda in 2007, Hitesh Malaviya joined Ogilvy, Delhi, and later moved to Wieden+Kennedy, Delhi in 2008. After working in advertising for five years, he quit both W+K and advertising. He currently works for the Indian Type Foundry in Ahmedabad.
→ Quantum 278 / 279

Marcin, Ricardo
Brazil
www.pintassilgoprints.com

Ricardo Marcin is a type designer and graphic artist born in Rio de Janeiro in 1973. Together with Erica Jung, he runs their independent foundry, PintassilgoPrints, based in Florianópolis, Brazil. With a solid background in hand printing techniques besides a lasting love for typography and lettering, they have been developing a consistent font library of original typefaces that reflects a vigorous handcrafted feel. Often packed with dynamic OpenType features, their fonts encourage users to craft unique typographic pieces. Pintassilgo-Prints works have been featured in specialized publications such as *8 Faces*, *Creative Characters*, *Slanted*, *Computer Arts*, *Page Magazine* and *Typolyrics*.
→ Brush Up 68 / 69
→ Daft Brush 98 / 99

Mastrangelo, Paula
Spain
www.paulamastra.com

Paula Mastrangelo is an Argentinian designer living in Barcelona. After graduating from Escola d'art i Disseny (EINA), she worked at La Vanguardia. Since then she has focused on corporate magazines and became an editorial art director. The past 15 years, Paula has designed or managed the media of many of the most important local and international firms operating in Spain. In 2012, Paula decided to further specialize in typography and completed a post-graduate Master course in Type Design at EINA. Upon graduation, she started to collaborate with Retype, participating in the production process of the calligraphic script Medusa. The Laski Slab type family—her graduation project—has now been released commercially by Retype.
→ Laski Slab 198 / 199

Međedović, Ermin
Slovenia
www.lettermin.com

Ermin Međedović, a native Croat living in Slovenia for the past 20 years, is an accomplished graphic and type designer. In the past, he has worked for big advertising agencies, run his own design studio and created several custom typefaces. He taught Type Design at the Design Academy in Ljubljana and works as design director at the Delo Publishing house. The Lipa type collection originated as custom project for his employer Delo.
→ Lipa Agate 206 / 207

Meiners, Anja
Germany
www.carrois.com

Anja Meiners was born in 1988 in Staaken (Berlin). After graduating with a degree in Communication Design from the Design Akademie in Berlin in 2010, she did an internship at Carrois Type Design. She decided to stay and is now working as a freelancer focusing on typeface design and kid's stuff. In 2015, she had her first child who will hopefully learn to read and write soon.
→ ABeZeh 8 / 9

Menacher, Alois
Germany
www.urwpp.de

Alois Menacher trained as a lead typesetter. Since his apprenticeship, he has worked intensively with typography and type design. His artistic focus was always on logo and corporate design. His knowledge in the field of graphic design and Mac computers is all self-taught.
→ AM Sans One 18 / 19

Mendoza, Guisela
Chile
www.mendozavergara.com

Guisela A.K.A. Coto Mendoza is a graphic designer who received her BA in Design and Innovation from Universidad Mayor, and a diploma in Visual Communication from the Pontificia Universidad Católica de Chile. Coto is a typographer, calligrapher and co-founder of Mendoza & Vergara, specializing in calligraphy, hand lettering and typography. She designs fonts and sells them through Latinotype font foundry. Mendoza specializes in handmade typefaces designing, based on calligraphy and the use of different materials and tools. Coto is co-creator of the blog TypeMenu: a place where you can find trendy typefaces and interviews with prominent people from the field of typography. Also, she has taught design at different universities for over ten years.
→ Garden 138 / 139

Meseguer, Laura
Spain
www.type-o-tones.com

Laura Meseguer is a freelance graphic designer, specialized in typography. Her activities involve the fields of commercial work and personal projects. As a typographer, she specializes in editorial design, as a type designer in the design of any kind of bespoke lettering and typefaces for identity and publications. She also teaches Typography and Type Design in Barcelona. She is the author of the book *TypoMag.Typography in Magazines* (Index Book) and co-author of the book *Cómo crear tipografías. Del boceto a la pantalla* (Tipo e). Through her own digital foundry, Type-Ø-Tones, she releases and promotes her typefaces. Her typefaces are: Cortada, Frankie, Girard Sansusie (for House Industries), Guapa, Magasin, Lalola and Multi.
→ Multi Display 240 / 241
→ Multi Text 240 / 241

Milne, Ross
Canada
www.workingformat.com

Ross Milne lives in Vancouver, Canada, and works under the name Working Format, a design practice that spans type and lettering, identities, public art and new product development. In 2009, Ross completed the acclaimed Type and Media Master's course in The Hague, The Netherlands. His typefaces are available through Typotheque and Commercial Type. Alongside his practice, Ross teaches regularly at the Emily Carr University in Vancouver.
→ Echo 114 / 115

Nadav, Moshik
USA
www.moshik.net

Born and raised in Israel, Moshik Nadav lives and breathes for typography and seeing design through the sophisticated form of type. This passion for type design has always run deep. At a young age, Moshik has always been surrounded by design and typography. His father, Jacob Nadav, is an inspiration not only as a person, but also as a graphic designer and skilled calligrapher. Moshik's view of beauty is and always has been truly shaped by typography. Moshik established his type design firm Moshik Nadav Typography LLC in 2009, serving international clients, and in 2013, relocated to New York City; to not only expand his business, but once again, to draw further inspiration.
→ Paris Pro 264 / 265

Nazal Selaive, Paula
Chile
www.latinotype.com

Paula Nazal Selaive is a graphic designer focused on typeface design. She was born on April 16 1987 in Los Angeles, a small town in southern Chile. She studied design at Universidad mayor, Santiago de Chile, Universidad de Palermo, Buenos Aires, and Universidad de Buenos Aires, Buenos Aires, Argentina. Most of her knowledge in typography is self-taught, with mentoring partner Daniel Hernandez and some calligraphy workshops and drawing letters.
→ Trend 316 / 317

Nemeth, Titus
Austria
www.tntypography.eu

Titus Nemeth is an independent type designer and typographer with specialist expertise in Arabic script culture. His internationally recognized practice spans commercial and cultural work, and his interests and activities extend to academic research and teaching in higher education. His original type designs have won multiple renowned awards and are widely used for complex cross-cultural visual communications. Titus holds a PhD in Typography and Graphic Communication from the University of Reading, UK, an MA in Typeface Design from the same institution, and a diploma in Graphic Design from Die Graphische in Vienna, Austria. He has taught Type Design and Typography at schools in Austria, France, Morocco, Qatar and the United Kingdom.
→ Lammerhuber 194 / 195

Nowak, Alisa
France
www.alisa-nowak.de

Alisa Nowak studied Graphic Design at the University of Applied Sciences in Düsseldorf. After her diploma (2009), she specialized in designing typefaces in the context of formation "Post-diplôme Typographie & Langage" at École supérieure d'art et de design d'Amiens, where she's now teaching type design in addition to type design missions for Fontyou.
→ Algo FY 14 / 15

Oelsner, Jörn
Sweden
www.oedesign.info

Jörn Oelsner is a graphic designer, specialized in typography and type design. He has worked in several graphic and corporate design studios in Europe. Besides his logo and graphic artworks for several international companies, he also develops custom fonts. Since 2010, he has also published several retail fonts. Currently he leads his own studio in Gothenburg, Sweden.
→ Graphique Pro Next 154 / 155

Oetzbach, K.-F. (Kai)
Germany
www.fontfarm.de

Kai Oetzbach was born in 1965 in Velbert (Germany). Since 1989, he studied Communication Design at BUGH Wuppertal, supervised by design experts like Günther Kieser, Uwe Loesch, Klaus Winterhager, Hans Günter Schmitz and Bazon Brock. He studied for his diploma from 1997–1998, supervised by Prof. Dr. Siegfried Maser and Prof. Hans Günter Schmitz. Since 2000, he has worked as a lecturer for Visual Communication, Typography and Typedesign at University of Applied Sciences, Aachen. Since 2002 he has been gaining practical experience in type design and founded Fontfarm.de, an independent type foundry, in cooperation with Natascha Dell in 2006.
→ Caput (SF) 82 / 83
→ Gedau Gothic 144 / 145

Olocco, Riccardo
Italy
www.c-a-s-t.com

Riccardo Olocco is a type designer. Prior to a four-year stint as a lecturer in Typography at the Faculty of Design and Art of the Free University of Bolzano, he freelanced as a graphic designer in Milan and elsewhere in northern Italy. He is currently studying for his Master's in Typeface Design at the University of Reading. Riccardo also writes on type design and type history. In addition to his ongoing investigation into Francesco Griffo's roman types, the research he is now doing with James Clough on Bodoni's types should be published by Codex in 2016. Along with other Italian type designers, Riccardo has recently launched the foundry CAST (Cooperativa Anonima Servizi Tipografici).
→ Parmigiano 268 / 269

Ovezea, Diana
The Netherlands
www.ovezea.com

Diana Ovezea was born in a small Romanian town called Medgidia, close to the Black Sea coast. When she was twelve, her family moved to Vienna (Austria), where she attended the American International School. She now lives in Amsterdam (The Netherlands) and is very thankful for being so international and culturally flexible. Diana has been working independently as a graphic designer since 2010, mainly on book and corporate design projects. She graduated from the TypeMedia Master's course in Type Design in 2013. In addition to designing typefaces, she has recently taught a Typography class at the Royal Academy of Art in The Hague.
→ Paiper 262 / 263

Parikh, Manushi
India
www.indiantypefoundry.com

Manushi Parikh is a Graphic Design graduate from the National Institute of Design, Ahmedabad. She has been associated with ITF since her college time and has been helping ITF with many retail and custom fonts. In 2014, she joined ITF as a permanent typeface designer.
→ Begum 46 / 47

Party, Ian
Switzerland
www.swisstypefaces.com

Ian Party, born in Lausanne in 1977, lives and works in Lausanne, Switzerland, as type designer. After studying at ECAL, Ecole Cantonale d'Art de Lausanne, Ian completed a master in type design at KABK, The Royal Academy of Art, in The Hague, the Netherlands. He is the co-founder of B&P Type Foundry and teaches type design at ECAL.
→ 29LT Kaff 178 / 179
→ 29LT Zeyn 340 / 341

Perrodeau, Jeremy
France
www.jeremyperrodeau.com

Jeremy Perrodeau is both a graphic designer and a typeface designer.
→ BTP 70 / 71

Petrov, Ivan
Russia
www.cargocollective.com/ malamaka

Ivan Petrov was born 1982 in Volkhov, Russia. In 2007, he graduated from baron Stieglitz Art and Industry Academy of St. Petersburg, department of Communication Design. He moved to the capital, Moscow, to study designing type in British School of Art and Design, from where he graduated in 2011 and then continued his professional activity in the design of typefaces. Within three years after the end of the course, he created the corporate font for the touristic brand of Bulgaria, some corporate typefaces for leading Russian companies as well as two fonts (Glober and Panton) in collaboration with Fontfabric. Glober received the diploma for excellence in typeface design at the international competition Modern Cyrillic in 2014. Currently co-founder and designer in KL N.
→ Glober 150 / 151

Pierini, Jonathan
Italy
www.jonathanpierini.com

Jonathan Pierini is a graphic and type designer. He studied Graphic Design and visual communication at ISIA (Istituto Superiore per le Industrie Artistiche) in Urbino and later earned an MA in Type Design and Media Studies at the Royal Academy of Art (KABK) in The Hague. He is currently working at the Free University of Bolzano (Faculty of Design and Art) as a researcher and lecturer in Graphic Design. His research projects focus on the relationship between written communication and inhabited spaces.
→ Parmigiano 268 / 269

Pinhorn, Jonny
India
www.indiantypefoundry.com

Jonny Pinhorn graduated from Birmingham Institute of Art and Design in 2008 with a 1st Class BA (Hons) degree in Visual communication. That same year, he was accepted onto the highly regarded post-graduate MA in Type Design at the University of Reading where he graduated in 2009. Throughout this time, and continuing on into his professional life, Jonny has developed

and indulged his broad interests in type design and particularly that of non-Latin types. He now designs Indian typefaces full-time here at ITF, and so far has worked on Tamil, Gujarati and Malayalam scripts. In his spare time, Jonny enjoys the often weird and exotic lifestyle that comes with being a foreigner living in India.
→ Caravel 84 / 85

Porchez, Jean François
France
www.typofonderie.com

Founder of Typofonderie, type director of ZeCraft, Jean François Porchez's (*1964) expertise covers both the design of bespoke typefaces, logotypes and typographic consultancy. Since 2012, he is the program director for the typographic design master at ECV (France). He is honorary president of the Association Typographique Internationale (was ATypI president in 2004–2007). Introduced to French Who's Who in 2009. He was awarded the Prix Charles Peignot in 1998 and numerous prizes for his typefaces. In 2014, Perrousseaux published his monograph.
→ Anisette 22 / 23
→ Retiro 294 / 295

Porter, Carolyn
USA
www.porterfolioinc.com

Carolyn Porter is an award-winning freelance graphic designer based in St. Paul, Minnesota (USA). Carolyn provides print design and communication solutions for clients in the financial, medical, environmental and business service industries through her business, Porterfolio Inc. She has only recently added type designer to her resume, though she's been a student of typography for more than 20 years.
→ P22 Marcel Pro 224 / 225

Preis, Stefanie
Switzerland
www.burri-preis.ch

Zurich-based graphic designer Stefanie Preis studied at the University of Design Schwäbisch Gmünd and Type Design at the Zurich University of the Arts. In 2009, she co-founded Burri-Preis, a graphic design studio focused on typography and printed matter. Since 2012, she is a vocational teacher for Graphic Design at the Berufsschule für Gestaltung Zurich and guest lecturer at the Lucerne University of Applied Sciences and Arts.
→ Brezel Grotesk 64 / 65

Priez, Julien
France
www.julienpriez.com

After graduating with an advanced degree in Type Design from the Ecole Estienne in Paris in 2010, Julien Priez worked as a freelance graphic designer in collaboration with different design studios, and as a graphic design and calligraphy teacher for various Parisian art schools before he started the Fontyou adventure in 2013.
→ Algo FY 14 / 15

Quintana Godoy, Javier
Chile
www.pampatype.com

Javier Quintana Godoy is an editorial and type designer and a teacher born in Punta Arenas, Chile. He currently devotes himself to type design, book design and consultancy in type matters. He co-founded the agency cooperative design agency Toro. His typefaces have been recognized at different Tipos Latinos biennale editions. He holds a Visual Communication Design diploma from the Universidad Tecnológica Metropolitana and a diploma in Typography from the Universidad Católica. His typefaces are distributed internationally via PampaType and Latinotype.
→ Berenjena Pro 48 / 49

Rajpurohit, Satya
India
www.indiantypefoundry.com

Satya Rajpurohit is the co-founder of Indian Type Foundry (ITF) in Ahmedabad, India. He studied Graphic Design at the National Institute of Design (NID) in India and interned with Linotype in Germany. He has also worked at Dalton Maag in London and L2M3 in Stuttgart. He now works full time at ITF, creating original fonts in all major Indian scripts along with Latin. His fonts are being used by some of the world's most iconic brands including Apple, Sony, Panasonic, Starbucks, News Corporation, Viacom, Unicef and Discovery Channel to name a few. In 2010, he received the prestigious SoTA Catalyst Award presented by the Society of Typographic Aficionados.
→ Brahmos 56 / 57

Rigaud, Émilie
France
www.aisforapple.fr

After completing her Master's in Graphic Design at the ENSAD, Émilie Rigaud entered Reading University to follow the Master's course in Typeface Design, where she developed the Coline typeface family, awarded with the Type Design Prize 2011 of the Tokyo Type Director's Club. She now works as a freelancer, both in book design and typeface design. She recently designed the typeface for the Gardens by the Bay in Singapore. In November 2010, she launched her own type foundry: A is for (www.aisforapple.fr). Since 2013 she she has worked as a teacher at ANRT (Atelier National de Recherche Typographique) and does research about Japanese typography.

→ BTP 70 / 71
→ David 102 / 103

van Rosmalen, Pieter
The Netherlands
www.boldmonday.com

Pieter van Rosmalen studied advertising and graphic design at Sint Lucas in Boxtel and graduated again in 2002 from the postgraduate course Type and Media at the Royal Academy of Art (KABK) in The Hague. He runs the Eindhoven office and is typically working on ten different typefaces at the same time. He has worked on custom typefaces for worldwide clients such as NBCUniversal, Audi AG, General Electric and KPN. In South Korea, a design of Pieter is used for street signs.

→ GE Inspira Sans 142 / 143
→ GE Inspira Serif 142 / 143
→ Nitti Grotesk 250 / 251

Ross, David Jonathan
USA
www.djr.com

Hailing from Southern California, David Jonathan Ross started drawing type during his time at Hampshire College in western Massachusetts. He joined The Font Bureau in 2007, where he draws letters of all shapes and sizes for custom and retail typeface designs. From reversed stress slab serifs of the nineteenth century to Art Deco sans serifs of the twentieth, he ransacks forgotten and pigeon-holed lettering styles and searches for new approaches to the same old alphabet. David's work has been recognized by the Type Directors Club and featured in *the pages of Print* and *HOW* magazines. Until 2013, David taught typeface design at The Art Institute of Boston and could often be found in the woods of New Hampshire. He now lives in Los Angeles.

→ Input 170 / 171

Roth, Miranda
USA
www.p22.com

Miranda Roth graduated from Daemen College (Buffalo, NY) with a BFA in Graphic Design. Her background in letterpress printing, passion for typography and determination for precision have served her well. Working as a freelance designer, Miranda's journey into typography began in 2012 at P22 type foundry where she is currently an in-house type designer and graphic designer.

→ LTC Goudy Initials 152 / 153
→ P22 Saarinen 298 / 299

de Rozario, Stuart
Great Britain
www.fontsmith.com

Stuart de Rozario joined Fontsmith in the summer of 2012. He draws inspiration from ancient manuscripts to abstract modernism, primitive marks to urban calligraphy. Stuart is driven by his passion for beautiful typographical forms and a modernist approach to design and theory.

→ FS Millbank 230 / 231

Runge, Jakob
Germany
www.jakob-runge.de

Jakob Runge is specialized in developing typefaces and custom letterings. After studying Communication Design in Würzburg (BA) and Kiel (MA), he currently is working as an independent type designer in Munich.

→ Cera 90 / 91
→ FF Franziska 134 / 135
→ Muriza 242 / 243
→ Urby 324 / 325

Salerno, Giuseppe
Italy
www.resistenza.es

Giuseppe Salerno mixes his calligraphic skills with his type knowledge and has been in the creative field for 14 years passing through Berlin, Madrid, Valencia, and Seattle to work for clients all over the globe. Together with Paco González he founded the Resistenza.es studio. Their most recognizable style characteristics are brushy types, calligraphic strokes, and originality in the typefaces. They create typefaces to improve their graphic design projects and they practice calligraphy as a basic method for the script typefaces. Salerno shares his skills organizing calligraphy workshops all over Europe.

→ Nautica 246 / 247

Scaglione, José
Argentina
www.type-together.com

José Scaglione is an Argentinian graphic and multimedia designer, and a graduate from the MA in Typeface Design at the University of Reading, UK. He has been working in branding, editorial design and multimedia projects since 1995. José is co-founder of the independent type foundry TypeTogether, and additionally leads his own design studio, consults and lectures on typography and graphic communication matters. He also teaches Typography at post-graduate level at the National University of Rosario.

→ Bree Serif 62 / 63

Schäfer, Ole
Germany
www.primetype.com

Ole Schäfer is a type designer specializing in corporate design, logo design and typeface systems as well as typography and type design consultancy. The primetype GmbH is an independent font label, dedicated to create and produce original contemporary fonts for retail and custom use.

→ PTL Magsans 218 / 219
→ PTL Notes Nova 256 / 257
→ ORF On 260 / 261

Schostok, Thomas
Germany
www.cape-arcona.com

{ths} aka Thomas Schostok is a German graphic designer, typographer and artist and known for his uncompromising graphics works, full of powerful, brutal and dirty aesthetic. {ths} works at the crossroads of art and graphic design. His studio is based in Essen, Germany. In 2002, Schostok co-founded, together with Stefan Claudius, the Cape Arcona Type Foundry, a type foundry that produces and distributes digital typefaces.

→ CA Recape 290 / 291

Schroeder, Reymund
Germany
www.zeugler.de

Reymund Schroeder was born in 1979 in Wismar and studied Typedesign at the Academy of Visual Arts in Leipzig. For his diploma project, Reymund constructed a poster-press and corresponding oligospaced typefaces. After graduation, he worked on various projects for the Swiss type foundry Lineto and developed a custom font for the newspaper *Die Zeit.* He also has a substantial interest in hybrid and timeless shapes. This led to an interaction of historical influences and his own ideas. With a taste for odd shapes, he designs typefaces primarily for larger applications. Apart from his own projects, he sets a distinct focus on the design of custom fonts and logo development. He lives and works in Leipzig.

→ Flynt 130 / 131
→ Polja 276 / 277

Schwarz, Jürgen
Germany
www.schwarzsehen.com

Jürgen Schwarz is an Austrian designer based in Berlin. For his studies in Communication Design he moved to Würzburg (BA). In autumn 2014, he finished his Master's thesis at University of Applied Science in Potsdam. Jürgen is freelancer for corporate and editorial design.

→ Muriza 242 / 243

Shutters, Gregory
USA
www.typetanicfonts.com

Gregory Shutters is an American type designer and lettering artist. Shutters began designing type in 2009 and graduated from the Type@Cooper type design program in New York in 2014. He founded Typetanic Fonts in 2013.

→ Columbia Titling 96 / 97
→ Gibbs 148 / 149

Simov, Svetoslav
Bulgaria
www.fontfabric.com

Svetoslav Simov (Svet to his friends and colleagues) was born 1984 in Novi Pazar, Bulgaria. By the end of 2008 he founded the Fontfabric Type Foundry, working on his first fonts which are mostly free for download, allowing both personal and commercial use. The first bestseller created by Svet is named Uni Sans and is implemented in seven weights and their corresponding Italics. Some of his most popular fonts by date are Intro, Nexa and Nexa Slab and Code Pro. The

Fontfabric portfolio currently presents as many as 40+ fonts, including bestsellers and designers favorites. Svet's work has been featured in online and printed design editions and respected exhibitions for creatives.
→ **Intro 172 / 173**

Skibbe, Henning
Germany
www.henningskibbe.com

Henning Skibbe is a managing partner and art director at the brand and design agency Erler-SkibbeTönsmann in Hamburg, Germany. He works for brands such as *Rosenthal*, *Küchenwerk Hummel*, *Theater Bremen*, *Staatstheater Stuttgart*, *Architektur & Wohnen* and *747 Studios*. The redesign and relaunch of Norway's oldest weekly newspaper *Morgenbladet* was headed by him. As an expert on typography, editorial design and typeface design, Henning Skibbe is a regular speaker at conferences such as TYPO Berlin and TYPO Day. He has taught Editorial Design and Typography at HAW university in Hamburg. Henning Skibbe (*1979) studied Communication Design and Typeface Design at the University of Applied Science Potsdam and RMIT Melbourne.
→ **HapticScript 160 / 161**

Sliggers, Ko
France
www.dutchfonts.com

Ko Sliggers is a writing chef and a nomad type foundry combining his curiosity for culinary history and culture with traveling, researching, cooking, writing, graphic design, illustration and photography. His typefaces are a by-product of graphic design commissions or the outcome of personal projects which have the aim of keeping his mental health in shape.
→ **DF-Park 266 / 267**

Smith, Jason
Great Britain
www.fontsmith.com

Jason Smith is the founder and creative director of Fontsmith. Jason studied Calligraphy, Lettering and Signwriting at Art College before he went on to produce lettering styles for consumer brands. Jason quickly established a reputation in typeface design and collaborated with a host of other font designers and graphic designers. Jason set up Fontsmith in London in 1999 and became involved with corporate identities. His true passion was graphic design and branding and Fontsmith gave him an opportunity to follow this passion. In 2001, Fontsmith released its own font library. Fontsmith now employs six staff and has a retail library of 30 typefaces, as well as a long list of bespoke typefaces for international brands.
→ **FS Maja 220 / 221**
→ **FS Matthew 228 / 229**

Sommaruga, Martin
Uruguay
www.tipotype.com

Martin Sommaruga was born in Montevideo, Uruguay. He has a degree in Graphic Design from the ORT University in Uruguay. Since 2001, he has also been teaching Communication and Design at the sames university. Since 2010, he has been part of the collective Sociedad Tipografica de Montevideo. Co-founder partner at *TipoType.com*.
→ **Libertad 202 / 203**

Stefan, Ellmer
Austria
www.ellmerstefan.net

Ellmer Stefan (*1982) grew up in the Austrian Alps and later trained in analogue and digital prepress techniques. He studied Graphic Design, with growing tendencies towards type, in Vienna, Arnhem and Leipzig. Today based in Vienna and Oslo, he is working as an independent type designer and lecturer, trying to balance profound historical awareness with a ludic attitude and idiosyncratic necessity. At the moment deeply fascinated by the typographic lunacies of the 19th century.
→ **Essay Text 122 / 123**

Sterz, Marcus
Austria
www.facetype.org

Marcus Sterz, born 1971 in Vienna, Austria, runs the small independent foundry FaceType. Coming from a background as graphic designer, he enjoys creating typefaces for talented creatives. And this might be the shortest bio in the book.
→ Adria Slab 10 / 11

Stoltenberg, Anna
Stoltenberg, Axel
Germany
www.urwpp.com

Axel Stoltenberg has been working as a software developer at URW++ since 1984. He was involved in the development of the IKARUS Framework, the font production software of the URW++ type foundry. Furthermore his his work focuses on digital image processing, graphical editors, the support for Kanji productions and the support for TrueType and OpenType productions. As a SysAdmin at URW++, he is also responsible for networking and hardware integration. Anna Stoltenberg, his 17-year-old daughter, is very artistic. She not only draws and paints is also playing various instruments. While Axel is responsible for programming the technical background of their outstanding type projects, Anna is the one responsible for the visual design.
→ ThreeDee 310 / 311

Štorm, František
Czech Republic
www.stormtype.com

František Štorm was born in 1966. He studied at AAAD in Prague under Prof. Jan Solpera. From 2003 to 2008 he worked at the same school as head of the Type & Typography studio. In 1993, he founded Storm Type Foundry. The catalogue currently contains over one thousand original fonts, including numerous classical revivals. Apart from font making and graphic design, he does woodcuts, illustrations, hard music and watercolor paintings. He lives and works in Prague and South Bohemia.
→ Pepone 270 / 271
→ Quercus Sans 282 / 283

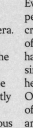

Talbot, Adrian
Great Britain
www.intro-uk.com

Adrian Talbot is a design director and partner at London creative agency Intro, where he's worked since 1990, mainly on identity design. In 2012, he launched his digital online foundry Talbot Type, selling his typeface designs. Influenced by the classic movements of the twentieth century—Modernism, Constructivism, the Bauhaus and Art Deco—, he aspires to create timeless, practical, hard-working text and display fonts.
→ Kandel 105 182 / 183
→ Kandel 205 182 / 183
→ Kelso 184 / 185

Tinkov, Radomir
Bulgaria
www.fontfabric.com

Even though his name is Radomir, people call him Rado. He loves creating fonts and been doing it officially since 2009. Although it has been officially his occupation since the middle of last year when he started working at Fontfabric. Occasionally, he is a designer of Brand and Web projects. Those are also part of his everyday work, a multi-disciplinary designer of some sort. In his spare time, if he has any, he enjoys reading manga, watching movies / anime / TV shows and designing random stuff in general. And last but not least he loves his woman and quality beer!
→ Muller 238 / 239

Tinnes, Andrea
Germany
www.typecuts.com

Andrea Tinnes is a type designer and typographer living and working in Berlin. In 2004, she founded her own font label typecuts. After several years of teaching at Norway's Bergen National Academy of the Arts, she took on a professorship of Type and Typography at Burg Giebichenstein University of Art and Design Halle in 2008. From 2010 till 2014 she was prorector of the school and was responsible for the school's new visual identity. Andrea has a degree in communication design from the University of Applied Sciences Mainz and an MFA in Graphic Design from CalArts. Her work has been featured in many national and international publications and exhibitions. She received a red dot in

2001/2002 and a Certificate of Typographic Excellence (TDC53) in 2007.
→ Burg Grotesk 74/75

Übele, Ludwig
Germany
www.ludwigtype.de

Ludwig Übele studied graphic design in Germany and Finland. He has worked for various design agencies across Europe. In 2007, he graduated from the postgraduate Type and Media course at the Royal Academy of Art (KABK) in The Hague, the Netherlands. In the same year, he also started his own Ludwig-Type Foundry. Today Ludwig lives in Berlin and works in the fields of type design and brand development. He has received several awards for his type design work: TDC² 2008, TDC² 2010, MyFonts Top 10 Fonts 2008, Granshan 2009, ATypI Letter.2 2011. Besides his own type design work, Ludwig collaborates with the great type designer Georg Salden and digitally reproduces and distributes his fonts exclusively on TypeManufactur.
→ Diogenes 108/109
→ Riga 296/297

Unger, Gerard
The Netherlands
www.gerardunger.com

Born in Arnhem, the Netherlands in 1942, he studied graphic design, typography and type design from 1963–67 at the Gerrit Rietveld Academy. He teaches as visiting Professor at the University of Reading, UK, department of Typography and Graphic Communication, and he is professor of Typography at Leiden University, the Netherlands. He has designed stamps, coins, magazines, newspapers, books, logos, corporate identities, annual reports and many other objects, and typefaces. He has been awarded several Dutch and international prizes and honors, such as two honorary doctorates by the universities of Hasselt, Belgium, and Tallinn, Estonia. He has written articles for the trade press, and several larger publications, such as Landscape with Letters (1989).
→ Alverata 16/17

Vassiliou, Panos
Greece
www.parachute.gr

Panos Vassiliou studied Applied Science and Engineering at the University of Toronto. In his transition years from engineering to typography, he got involved with a theater company, founded a design studio and pursued a college teaching career. A few years later, he established a publishing company. He designs typefaces since 1993, including including commercial fonts as well as custom solutions for national and international companies. He is the founder of the independent type foundry Parachute, which specializes in multilingual contemporary typefaces. Panos has received more than fifteen international awards and distinctions for his typefaces.
→ Bague Sans 36/37

Vergara, Luciano
Chile
www.mendozavergara.com

Luciano Vergara is a graphic designer who received his B.A. in Design from Universidad Mayor, and got a diploma in Typography from the Pontificia Universidad Católica de Chile in 2003. Luciano works as a designer at Mendoza & Vergara Design Studio, which he co-founded with Guisela Mendoza. He has been selling his fonts through T26 Digital Type Foundry since 2005. Luciano is founding partner of Latinotype and has been selling his fonts through this foundry since 2008. His work was featured in the 2004 and 2006 Latin American typography biennials. He took part as a jury member in the 2008 Tipos Latinos Biennial. His work has appeared in several publications including *Carácter Latino* and *Yearbook of Type I*.
→ Darwin 100/101
→ Garden 138/139

van Wageningen, Mark
The Netherlands
www.novotypo.nl

Novo Typo is an independent (typo)graphic design studio and foundry, based in Amsterdam, the Netherlands. With Novo Typo typefaces we try to make the world a little bit more beautiful, happier and less boring. We consider a typeface as a set of beautifully shaped abstract signs. Novo Typo was founded by Mark van Wageningen on January 1, 2012.
→ NT Bixa 52/53

Weinzierl, Terrance
USA
www.typeterrance.com

Terrance Weinzierl is a type designer working with Monotype, and he's been exclusively designing typefaces and lettering since 2008. Along with the font development team at Monotype, he's worked on fonts for Microsoft, Google, Barnes & Noble, and Domino's, as well as various design firms, ad agencies, and publishers. When not working on custom fonts, Terrance fills out his professional practice by doing calligraphy, lettering, and letterpress. He recently attended the Type Design short course at the University of Reading, where he focused on Greek and Cyrillic scripts.

→ Joanna Sans 176 / 177

Weltin, Jürgen
Germany
www.typematters.de

Jürgen Weltin runs the independent type design studio Type Matters, located south of Munich. He received awards for his first typeface family Linotype Finnegan, a D&AD award for the exclusive telephone book typeface Yellow and an award at Granshan International Eastern Type Design Competition for Mantika Sans. He began creating typefaces during his studies in the mid-nineties, worked as a type designer at The Foundry in London and is now designing type independently, doing custom type work for various clients and lecturing typography at design schools. His own designs also include the display typeface Balega, the 33 styles of the Agilita sans serif typeface family and Mantika Informal, an easy to read typeface with reading beginners in mind.

→ Mantika Book 222 / 223

Widmer, Fabian
Switzerland
www.letterwerk.ch

Fabian Widmer lives and works as a graphic and type designer in Zurich, Switzerland. He studied Type Design / Typography at The Basel School of Design. After working for two years as a typographer, he launched his own type design studio in 2008 together with Dominique Boessner. The studio is called Letterwerk.

→ Carrosserie 86 / 87
→ Nord 254 / 255

Willerstorfer, Stefan
Austria
www.willerstorfer.com

Stefan Willerstorfer was born in Vienna in 1979 and studied design in Austria, in the Netherlands and in England. In The Hague (NL), at the Royal Academy of Art, he completed the Type Design course Type and Media with a Master of Design degree. At the University of Reading (UK), he completed the course in Information Design with a Master of Arts degree. In 2010, he started the Willerstorfer Font Foundry and released the type family Acorde. He then received the Joseph Binder Award and the Communication Arts Award of Excellence. In 2011, the Japan Typography Association awarded him the Grand Prize of Applied Typography. Willerstorfer lives and works in Vienna as an independent designer and has been teaching at Die Graphische since 2009.

→ Sindelar 302 / 303

Winter, Sandra
Germany
www.w4gestaltung.de

The DIN Next Slab family is the result of a collaboration between Monotype's Akira Kobayashi, as the design director, and freelance designers Sandra Winter and Tom Grace, who did much of the heavy lifting. Winter and Grace have worked previously with Kobayashi, who comments, "Part of Sandra and Tom's competence is that, with very little direction, they produce excellent results."

→ DIN Next Slab 106 / 107

Yazıcıgil, Onur
Turkey
www.onuryazicigil.com

Onur Yazıcıgil is a typographer and educator who currently lives and works in Istanbul, Turkey. He received his MFA from Purdue University in the USA. In 2007, he won first prize in typographic excellence from the Society of Typographic Arts in Chicago. He has spoken at TypeCon, ATypI, TYPO Berlin, and lectured on various topics in the field of typography. He is currently a faculty member at Sabancı University. He has recently developed a humanist sans serif typeface, Duru, with partial availability on Google Web Fonts. In addition to his research in Latin typefaces, he has been most focused on the Ottoman metal typeface production of the 19th century, in particular Ottoman naskh typefaces. He designs Arabic books for the Dutch publisher Brill, and since 2011 has been the creator and organizer of the ISType conferences held in the heart of Istanbul.

→ Duru 110 / 111

Zoghbi, Pascal
Lebanon
www.29lt.com

Type designer and typographer Pascal Zoghbi founded 29Letters in 2006. After he graduated from The Royal Academy of Art in the Netherlands with a Master of Design in Type and Media, Pascal created a notable collection of contemporary corporate Arabic and multilingual typefaces alongside corporate identities. Since 2006, he has been teaching typography courses at design schools in Beirut. He frequently gives lectures and workshops independently. He co-authored and edited the *Arabic Graffiti* book published in 2010. He was one of the 10 finalists for the Jameel Prize 3 in 2013 / 2014. He founded Horouf: Type Design Competition in 2014 in partnership with Nuqat. He was awarded the Red Ribbon of TDC Typeface Design Competition in 2014.

→ 29LT Kaff 178 / 179
→ 29LT Zeyn 340 / 341

D

Essays & Tutorials

Typography and Typedesign on Screen …

OLE SCHÄFER

While communication continues to evolve, our requirements to read remain the same. Therefore we must adapt typography and typefaces to the media web and apps (smartphones). Despite all the technological differences between web and app, there is a lot of common ground: we read illuminated screens and the resolution of the typefaces is not nearly as good as on paper, even when compared to high-quality smartphone screens. This requires another typography than in printed media.

I consciously do not discuss technical but rather formative aspects here, as the text would otherwise become too complex.

Screen Typography

Let us look at the details: Due to the backlighting of the screens, typography will appear considerably lighter and contrast-poorer than on paper. Simultaneously, most of the used typeface spacings are significantly too narrow. If the space is too low, the characters touch each other and degrade readability. A slight spacing of the letters helps a little bit. However, one must make sure that the character spacing does not appear too wide. That would be the case if you do not read the words, but must spell them. We now need to increase the word spacing, due to the larger character spacing, so that the eye is better able to read the row, even compared to the print.

Apart from that, the classical typographic parameters are valid. The row should not be too short or too long, taking into consideration that today's smartphone screens make too long rows (significantly more than 85 characters) rather unlikely anyway. I am always referring to a dark font and bright background. Light text on dark background should not be used for long texts. In any case, the used typeface should be stable enough for such an application in small to medium sizes. In particular, you should make sure that the font size is not too small. Letting users choose between two font sizes in apps is ideal. The font size is extremely important. We live in a society in which people are growing older and small font sizes are a problem, especially in mobile applications. People aged 50 and over will not read articles that cannot be read easily. The company behind an application wants to make money and does this through the number of users. If you lose the older target groups because of bad typography, you lose the richest part of society.

The quality of an app is not defined by the quantity of text but by its readability. Another important aspect is that you can find the text. This depends on a logical structure, good database connectivity, timeliness and a good programming. Good programming offers a fast screen display because it does not contain data garbage, fonts with large storage requirements or images adapted to the screen size. If you are then able to add an attractive, friendly design, you have the ideal app. All this may sound simple, but it is obviously difficult to implement if you look at today's applications.

Find the Right Type

In order to establish a good on-screen typography, you need the right font. If you do not use custom fonts, ensure that the fonts are bold enough. Light and Regular fonts are only suitable to a limited extent, it is better to use Medium or Book fonts. Unfortunately, Bold is then often too light and Italic is rarely used in apps or on the web.

You will also need the fonts to be suitable for different linguistic areas. You should think carefully about what is needed before you recommend a typeface. Usually, a customer would like to cover several linguistic areas. Standard is western, it is practically the old Europe; Latin extended includes the states of Eastern Europe without Cyrillic and Greek. Fonts in the European Union contain Cyrillic due to Bulgaria, which is often forgotten. Asian fonts are very complex due to the wide variety of languages, so consider this if necessary.

Apart from all the conflicting doctrines about whether fonts with or without serifs are more readable, we are used to reading serif typefaces in books and newspapers and often find sans serif fonts on the screen. This development is due to the web. Many people still use very old systems and not high-resolution displays, so serif typefaces are harder to read on the web. They are simply too rough and the serifs are usually too light, as well as many forms within the characters. You could also say web applications have led to simplification of fonts or better, to the use of simpler drawn fonts. But simpler does not mean worse or even easier to draw.

Nothing comes for Free

Once again: nothing comes for free. Very many designers believe that they were well cared for with system fonts or free fonts. This is wrong. All fonts are subject to terms and conditions of use (EULA). People usually ignore the End User License Agreements and this is a mistake. Fonts without Terms of Use are often stolen. If you follow the principle "where no plaintiff, there is no error," your customer consulting is wrong.

And while we are at it, cheaply online manufactured web fonts are almost always illegal, and often of poor technical quality. In principle, there are rights for print, web, and app. This also applies to special applications such as programs, equipment etc. If the designer is not able to find the right solution or specialists that can do it, he or she does not deserve to get the job.

Corporate Type

There are reasons why font foundries offer web fonts. A company that has chosen a corporate typeface would like to use the same fonts in all media. Apart from the licensing rights and applications, this is understandable and makes sense. Unfortunately, few check the requirements a typeface must fulfill in various media.

This then often leads to bad text typography. Or, to give an example, the corporate font is only in use for large sizes or in the headlines on screen. A different font for text needs to be selected; the usual solution is a system font. This is not a good solution.

From my perspective, offers that don't allow the font to be installed in the applications are of doubtful nature. In some linguistic areas it is necessary, due to the large character set, that third-party servers are involved (at least 65,000 characters fit in a font). For most users, a server solution for fonts is not ideal. Large companies usually do not want a third party informed about their data, which is necessarily the case, if the typeface is not on their server.

It is also often difficult to customize existing font foundry typefaces. This is due to the time and costs involved including the licensing costs and the limited uses due to terms and conditions of use. A reasonable and good solution for medium-sized and large companies is always to draw custom-designed corporate typefaces. With good planning, this is faster than you might think.

The Design of Screen Typefaces

It is much easier to build in the solutions that are needed in the typeface itself, than it is to attempt to make adaptations to an existing font in programs. Letter spacing, word spacing and weights should be optimized for the use so that designers and programmers can focus on their job and not have to deal with micro typography, which is the job of a type designer. The designer uses the optimized fonts and they work.

Backlight Backlight

Backlight Backlight

Backlight Backlight

Backlight Backlight

Backlight Backlight

Find the right typeface: Have a look at the weights and the character spacing

Before you start, you should define the main tasks of the corporate font with the customer. Many still believe that print is the larger part of use. Many are surprised that often screen applications represent more than half of the applications, especially if the accounting is included. If you design a good readable font for screen, this always works better than the previous fonts that were used in accounting and mail.

In Detail

In principle, there are many possibilities if your type and media design harmonize with each other. Thin and Light fonts work the same way as Black and Ultra in large font sizes for headlines, products and brands. It's the same with condensed fonts. Special attention must be paid to the text design for various text sizes. You should refrain from tricks such as scaling the outlines inside the fonts. For example, this can lead to 10pt actually representing 12 pt, increasing the weight and the space inside the letters. This is not a good solution and the automatic settings of the systems and programs will not work optimally. You must define the design parameters on the basis of the sizes that are used mainly.

The Typeface Form

Screen displays demand a large x-height of the characters. The minimum requirements for the design of a text typeface are the following: one quarter descender, one quarter ascender, two quarters x-height. You may still add, at the expense of descender and ascender length, something to the x-height.

It is ideal if you get a lot of space inside the letters with a large x-height. You can also do this through wider letters, but then the typeface is also often too wide. The effect of a large x-height is that the typeface seems larger. Therefore, a wide character spacing is also necessary.

The character spacing with variations for curves and straights is chosen the following way: You divide the space inside of an "n," subtract 20 percent and put this new space on both sides of the "n;" if two "n" are set after each other the space between the characters is a bit narrower than the space inside of one character. For rounded characters, you subtract a bit more.

Decisions must be based on individual situations, but you can use this as a basic guideline. This calculation extends the character spacing, but not too far. Hence the larger y-height compared to the character width, as the font should not be too wide if you also want to use it in the print sector. This is still based on a sans serif typeface.

A nice side-effect of such a draft is that even a Bold font has still enough space inside the characters. This brings us to the topic of typeface weight. Concerning continuous text, we look at Regular and Bold. In principle, it is good not to draw Regular and Bold too light.

Due to our lager x-height and open character spacing, we need a stronger weight than normal for the Regular weight. The classic weights of Regular and Bold are mostly too light regarding the backlit screen on which we read. Our eyes love to read typefaces with a stronger weight for longer text and a Regular font often looks like a Light one on screen.

When you design your typeface, you have to find a weight between Book and Medium that will work for most applications. Your Bold weight needs to be heavier than a normal Bold font as you need a higher contrast than on paper.

The new Bold needs to be in between Bold and Extrabold to have the right contrast inside a text. In many applications, this is not the case. The designer noticed the problem and uses the Bold only in headlines or changes the point size a bit to a bigger size. If you want to use both weights, in sport charts for example, different sizes will not work. You can design condensed typefaces with the same principles; they work well in short texts and even better in sub-headlines.

A lot can be said about the design of a typeface. It seems important to me that it helps to work with uniform heights. The capital letters have the same height as the ascender of lower-case

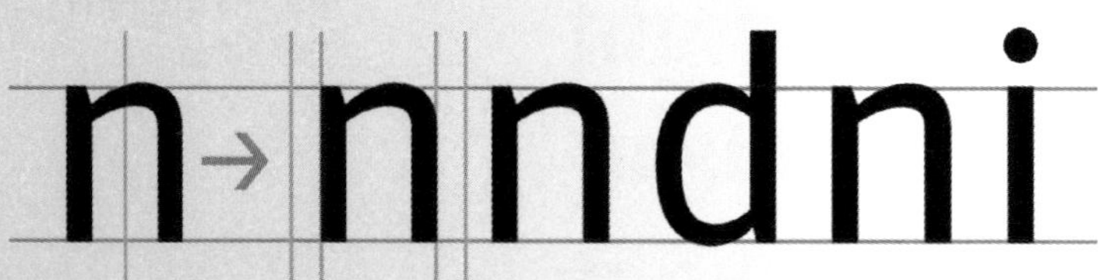

How to find the right spacing: An example for an open character spacing

characters. All heights do not differ between Regular and Bold. Using the same x-height of the weights is also very important if you want to create a continuous line. It greatly benefits the reading. For optical reasons, the round parts in the Bold character should go up and down a little further to prevent floating letters.

No matter which form you choose, the weight of the characters within a font should be created exactly the same. The curves are usually a bit thicker. So an "i" corresponds to an "l," an "n" corresponds to a "d" (straight part) etc. The weight of the uppercase letters can be somewhat stronger, but not much. On the screen, it is important that small form changes are hardly noticed. However, major form changes between the characters create enormous disturbances in the text; but used in headline types, they can be important to create a unique design.

You should work with uniform and clean outlines. The memory requirements are important and increase with the number of points used for a character. The smaller the font, the faster the image buildup; and users do not want to wait for their apps.

To everyone complaining and asking why they cannot take any web fonts and why everything has to be so complicated, it must be said: there are experts who can help. Of course, you can find and use good existing web fonts. But you can also search for the best possible solution. I have only roughly outlined the topic here, but I hope I could give some helpful suggestions. I am always happy to see attractive design and easy-to-read text. Today we can draw better fonts, with better technology, cover greater linguistic areas and create better detailed typography than ever before ... we should do it.

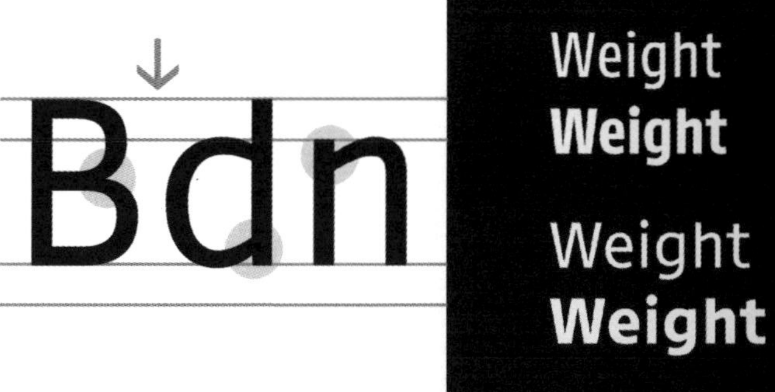

Lager x-height and less contrast inside the typeface but higher contrast between the weights

Screentype Ragedn
SCREENTYPE RAGEDN
Screentype Ragedn
Screentype ***Ragedn***

Real custom online typefaces made for *orf.at* by Ole Schäfer

What's New in Glyphs 2.0

RAINER ERICH SCHEICHELBAUER

Three and a half years after the initial release of Glyphs, the first major upgrade is out in the wild. It brings some significant changes, as well as a bucketload of new features, including support for webfonts, colorfonts, TrueType hinting and three-dimensional interpolation.

The most shining new feature of the new Glyphs is the ability to create and preview color fonts. You have the choice of three formats. Firstly, you can build a classic layer font, i.e. simply a few fonts that stack nicely on top of each other. You have been able to do that in Glyphs for a while, but version 2.0 provides some extra goodies that facilitate multi-layer work. In the Font Info, you can now define colors for each master with a custom parameter. When you activate the layers in Edit View, you can preview them in their colors right away. And you can even select and edit multiple layers at once with the new Select All Layers tool. For a font sample, you can download the open-source colorfont Sapperlot by Thomas Maier on *github.com / DrTypo*.

Secondly, you can build a Microsoft-style COLR / CPAL font. COLR (short for color) and CPAL (color palette) are two OpenType tables proposed by Microsoft for enabling multicolored glyphs. Currently, the tables are only supported in the latest versions of Internet Explorer, but technically, COLR / CPAL is very promising. Again, you define colors in Font Info, but this time in the form of a color palette, a collection of numbered colors. Then, to build such a font, you can add any number of additional layers, called *Color X*, where X is the index number of the color you defined. Again, Glyphs will let you preview your COLR / CPAL font, directly in Edit View, in the colors you defined.

Finally, it is also possible to add PNG or JPEG files in various resolutions to a glyph. If the glyph layers adhere to the specific naming scheme *iColor Y*, where Y stands for the image size in pixels, Glyphs will build an Apple-style *sbix* colorfont. Its images show on the Mac and iOS devices. You have seen the Apple Emojis before, I am sure.

Webfonts? You got it.

The next big thing in version 2.0 is webfonts. You can export WOFF and EOT files straight out of Glyphs. No more upload of your unreleased fonts to shady web services. Even the latest, better-compressed WOFF2 variant is supported. The WOFFs are supported in both their PostScript and TrueType variations. With these formats, you can cover all major web browsers of recent years. To add to that, you can have automatic subsetting, on the fly and per instance.

Speaking of TrueType, there is much better TTF support in Glyphs 2.0. For one thing, Werner Lemberg's *ttfautohint* is built into Glyphs. And you can define your own TT stems in Font Info. You can even add your own manual TrueType instructions with a new TT Tool. You do that on the PostScript outlines, and both overlap removal and TrueType conversion happen on the fly at export. The instructions are then smartly added onto the TT splines. The current implementation focusses on horizontal stems, so it is ideal for environments with subpixel rendering, such as DirectWrite in Microsoft Windows.

Non-Latin no problem

Many little features focused on non-Latin scripts have been added to Glyphs 2.0. To pick out just one example, Indic script support goes so far that many of the complex OpenType features are automated, including Devanagari i-Matra variations. It comes as no surprise that many of the recent Google-produced Devanagari fonts were created in Glyphs.

Interpolation unchained

The Multiple Masters implementation has been significantly revamped for version 2. Tim Ahrens, the German type designer and coder of Remix Tools fame, helped create support for the third axis. So now, you can have a customized third dimension in your font families.

Much wished for, Glyphs 2.0 also facilitates putting a large number of masters on a single axis. The UI supports up to five named masters on one axis, but you can actually add any number you wish.

Glyphs has been supporting glyph-based master alternation for quite a while with a technique called *Bracket Layers*. But in many situations, a simple intermediate master for a specific glyph is all you need. This can now be done with *Brace Layers*: additional layers are recognized as intermediate masters if they carry the two- or three-dimensional interpolation coordinates in their name, written between braces, hence the name. This makes it much easier to keep the font at two masters only, while adding precision for the glyphs that need it, most typically dense glyphs like the lowercase e. Thus, you can avoid a font-wide middle master, and you get to reap the added benefits of continuous kerning interpolation.

There is a dramatic new exploded view for Master compatibility. Compatibility detection now also respects Bracket and Brace Layer—and anchors. That makes it easier to keep your interpolation completely compatible. And to achieve master compatibility more conveniently, some menu commands now have an all-master option. For instance, if you hold down the Option key while opening the Paths menu, the *Correct Path Direction* command will turn into *Correct Path Direction for all Masters*.

Parts and Pieces

Okay, so we have individual interpolations on a glyph level, that is nice. But what about interpolation on a sub-glyph level? Say, you want to re-use the shoulder and stem of "a" lowercase "n" in your lowercase "h" and lowercase "m." You will need to make small optical adjustments to the paths every time. That is why you could not really use components for that. Up until now, you had to copy and paste the paths. This gave you maximum flexibility, but it was also inefficient, because when you changed the shoulder in the "n," you had to redo the changes in the "h" and the "m."

Well, no more. Glyphs 2.0 introduces smart components called *Parts* and *Pieces*. For this, you first define a so-called *Part*, a special glyph with a name that starts with an underscore, followed by the word "part" and an arbitrary dot suffix, e.g., *_part.shoulder*. A Part can have many extra layers, each of them containing an interpolation master, e.g., a layer with narrow version of the shoulder for the "m," and a layer with a deeper crotch for the "h." Now, if you right click in a Part, you can access Part settings, and define properties such as *shoulderWidth* and *crotchDepth*, and assign those properties to the various layers.

Once you have the Part set up, you can add Parts like components to your glyphs. When the Parts are inserted, we call them Pieces. Right-click on a Piece to access its Piece settings and interpolate it between its Part layers. Now adjust the width of the shoulder and depth of the crotch to your liking. And if you change the Part, all the Pieces will update automatically, according to their interpolation settings.

Parts and Pieces were developed with CJK radicals in mind. So, apart from *_part glyphs*, every CJK radical already counts as a Part. That makes the adjustments of radicals in bigger compounds much, much easier, and will help you keep your sanity if you go through the creation of 30,000 glyphs.

Colors everywhere: Glyphs 2.0 supports color font editing and export straight out of the box.

Corners and Caps

So, we can re-use and adjust shapes on a sub-glyph level. But let's dig a little deeper: what about a sub-shape level? What about partial paths that reappear often in a typeface? Think serifs, for instance. For slab serifs, you have already been able to pack the serif shape into a component, which you pasted on top of the outline. The problem was that its position was kind of free-floating, and you had to re-align the components over and over again. Besides, if you wanted the serif to flow smooth out of the stem, you could not use the component approach, because, again, you had to adjust the path individually in order to make the outline curve smoothly into the stem. And on diagonal stems, you were out of luck, because serif components would quickly become too short on one side of a slanted stem, and too wide on the other.

Enter Corners. Corners are open paths, which you can dynamically attach to a corner node in your glyph outlines. All you need for Corners to work are separate glyphs named *_corner* with a dot suffix, e.g., *_corner.leftSerif.* Inside these glyphs, you place an open path around the origin point, or alternatively, around an anchor called *origin*. Then, you select a node in a regular glyph, and add a Corner via the context menu. The serif is then fitted into the outline according to its path direction. It even works on slanted outlines; the connection to the stem stays smooth, while the serif itself stays straight. And you can even influence the width correction to the left and right, with an additional *left* or *right* anchor above the origin: the distance between anchor and origin determines the amount by which the width of the serif will be corrected.

Similar to Corners, Caps are open paths that can be fitted on two nodes instead of just one. Again, it requires a dot-suffixed glyph, this time starting with *_cap*. Caps are meant for spurs or head serifs. To apply a Cap to the outline, select two adjacent nodes and add a Cap via the context menu. It's that easy.

Many small improvements

Are we done yet? Far from it. As soon as you open the app, you will notice a bunch of little changes in the user interface. Corner nodes, for instance, now display as squares, whereas smooth nodes are still shown as circles, making differentiation easier. And now, you get to customize the colors in the app preferences. Handles are displayed slightly smaller than on-curve nodes, again, making it easier to keep the oversight in glyphs with a high density of nodes.

The gray boxes where Glyphs displays information about the current glyph, its metrics, options for the current selection, etc., have been redesigned with more intuitive symbols. And the glyph info is always visible, no matter what the selection is. Contextual info boxes are dynamically inserted to the side of the glyph info box whenever necessary.

The whole Palette has been moved into a sidebar that slides into the window from the right: much cleaner interface, and no more obstructing the Edit View. Speaking of which, the Transformations Palette has been reworked and outfitted with new functions. Now, all the options for the transform origin are always in view and quickly accessible. And three new buttons allow simple boolean path operations: combining, subtracting, and intersecting.

Metric Keys can now be applied on a per-layer basis if you use a double equal sign for the formula. So, while *=n+10* applies to all masters, *==n+10* only counts for the layer in question. Via the *Add Glyphs* dialog, whole Unicode ranges can be added as glyphs if you put a colon

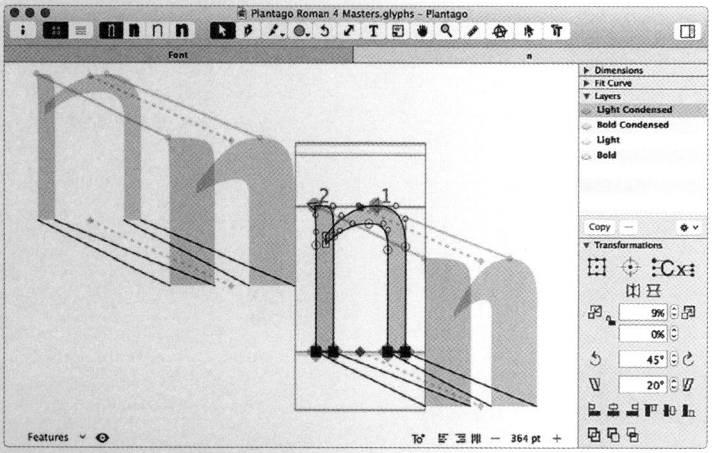

Baddaboom: The new exploded view makes finding and fixing incompatibilities a snap.

between two glyph names or characters. E.g., *uni0300:uni0330* will add all combining marks in that range that are still missing in the font. It will gracefully ignore already existing ones. And adding glyphs with a preceding underscore in their name will create them as non-exporting.

Get plugged in
Plugin management has become a real treat. The app preferences now host a section called *Add-ons* where all installed plugins are listed. A right click gives you the option to reveal the plugin file in Finder, which is useful if you want to remove it again. Glyphs now also checks for updates among the plugins, and will offer to take you to the respective website if a new version is available for download.

For plugin developers, it is a snap to add that functionality to their add-ons. The freely available, open-sourced software development kit for Glyphs already carries the necessary documentation and a heap of Python and Objective-C templates. Glyphs 2.0 sells for EUR 250 on *glyphsapp.com*, upgrades from previous versions cost half. Any licenses purchased since July 2014 already count as licenses for Glyphs 2.0. Discounts are available for students, school staff, and volume licenses.

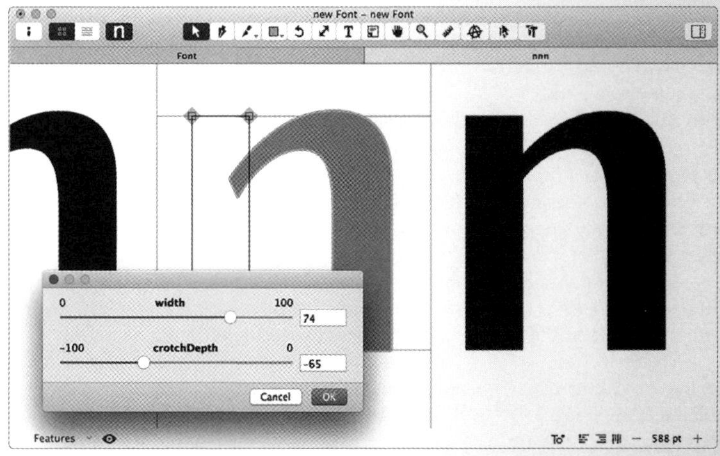

Piece by parametric piece: Insert glyph parts as piece components and interpolate them in place.

Swiss Type Design Now— The Centre of Excellence in Type and Typography at the Zurich University of the Arts

RUDOLF BARMETTLER

For almost 10 years, the ZHdK has offered two courses: CAS Type Design, a two-semester postgraduate course, as well as MAS Type Design, a four-semester master course. Both courses are part-time to accommodate working professionals. In these courses, text typefaces are developed to a high standard with a focus on legibility, aesthetics and technical quality for their practical application in print, on screen and for signage. The typefaces are designed, digitized, produced, tested and then finally optimized, during the courses. The students start their type design projects from scratch. The individual design concepts are usually based on visual innovations, interpretations of historical typefaces, experiments using combinations of styles, or even technical problem-solving creations. Type design was already included from 2000–2006 within the modules of the BA in Visual Communication.

The ZHdK is a prestigious university in Switzerland. Since 2007, it has been an amalgamation of various independent universities in the field of theatre, film, dance, music, cultural analysis and education, arts and media, and design. Since the summer of 2014, these universities moved to the so-called Toni-Campus, a former dairy factory. With a total of over 2,500 students, and 650 teaching staff members, we are among the largest universities of art and design in Europe.

The Design Department of the school has been in existence since 1875, and originally emerged out of the Arts and Crafts Movement. In 1916, Ernst Keller founded the Department of Graphic Design. One well-known type and graphic designer who studied in this Department was Walter Haettenschweiler (designer of the eponymous typeface), who was one of the publishers of *Lettera I–IV*.

At the beginning of the 1950s, Walter Käch and Alfred Willimann founded a type design course at our school. The most famous graduates are Hans Eduard Meier and notably Adrian Frutiger. Max Miedinger too was a student of the School of Applied Arts Zurich, as our Department of the Applied Arts was previously named. Other important typographers and type designers who were students at our school include Max Bill, Josef Müller-Brockmann, Emil Ruder and Armin Hofmann. Ruder and Hofmann brought international fame to the design school in Basel.

Postgraduate course CAS Type Design

Our program is concerned with the following aspects that require further explanation:

Our premise

In ancient times, various types of chisels and brushes, even stylus and reed, and later the quill, were used as tools. In the early modern times, alongside steel burins and engraving tools, different nibs, stencils and cutters were used. Designing type was a gestural process, which was acquired by practicing the writing and drawing of letterforms and by studying traditions. Some technical inventions of the 19th century, such as the pantograph, the typesetter and the typewriter, had a significant and lasting impact on letterforms. Bitmaps and outline fonts followed 100 years later. Today, type design is a matter of geometric constructs and numerical codes. Typeface development tools are omnipresent in the world of graphic design and are widely used. But even if new technologies potentially enable any designer to create their own fonts, most "users" seem to be lacking the requisite foundational skills for professional type design: skills like the ability to articulate, shape sensitivity, the ability to differentiate, methodological know-how of the design process as well as of implementation and production. Also, a good knowledge of technological and type history is extremely rare. Swiss type design enjoys a solid international reputation. Even if the designers often only receive commissions from abroad to undertake complex issues and jobs, their outstanding solutions have brought international prestige. Many of the world's best-selling sans serif typefaces from the past 40 years were drawn by former students of our school. The Swiss type design of the last 20 years has mostly emerged from trends in different local scenes and contexts. Alongside some outstanding examples of craftsmanship there has been a lot of tinkering and epigonism, some originating from some self-referential gimmicks, and yet many interesting designs are based on idealism. The pioneering spirit unfortunately disappeared early from the designer's environment, because the development of font families with several styles was not affordable without a commission. Only commissioned typefaces for regional or international companies and brands were sufficiently profitable to cover the cost of expensive creation and production work.

Fifteen years ago, my vision was to re-establish a center of excellence for type and typography at the Zurich University of the Arts. My goal was to create a specialized unit for research, experimentation and technical training in the field of type and typography. My motivation was not so much concerned with the attraction of something new but with how, through new insights, the range of type design, its formal and technical requirements, can be expanded and applied in real-world contexts. My goal was—in collaboration with my faculty colleagues—to bring professionals together and to promote dialogue about letterforms, to facilitate their exploitation and the exchange of ideas, the interaction of tradition with new opportunities and innovation in a laboratory-like environment. The first step towards this goal was to set up the CAS (Certificate of Advanced Studies) Type Design. Our part-time MAS (Master of Advanced Studies) Type Design / Typography was planned to unite and intensify our skills: to rethink and evolve type and typography in print, on screen and in the environment.

Our position

The well-known universities in the field of type design, the Royal Academy of Art in The Hague and the University of Reading in England, offer to some extent state-subsidized BA and MA degree courses. Unfortunately, our courses are not supported by the Swiss government. The

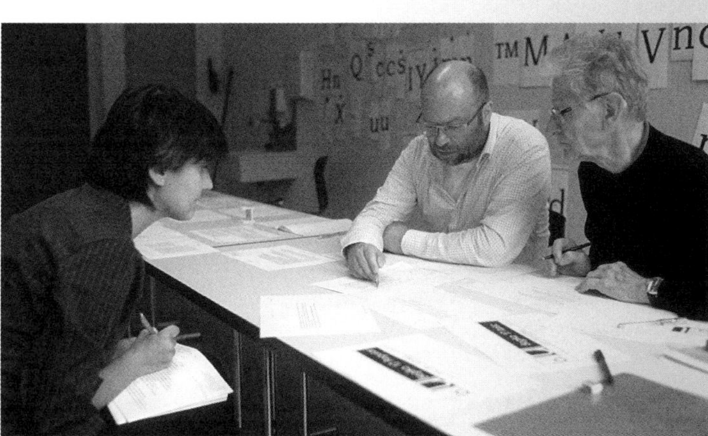

The final typefaces are reviewed together with Prof. Andre Baldinger (middle) and Prof. Hans-Jürg Hunziker (right). Almost always some final adjustments need to be made by the students, particularly with regard to the ductus or spacing.

courses are integrated in the further education program of the Zurich University of the Arts but the students bear the total cost.

Therefore, our courses are offered as a part-time postgraduate degree. They include 200 lessons of teaching and accompanied laboratory work and at least 340 hours of self-study in the form of project work at home. The CAS Type Design is awarded with a total of 20 ECTS.

From the beginning we sought to develop a distinctive profile—regardless of temporary font fashions and trends—which should enable our graduates to tackle later projects contextually and creatively in a most professional manner. Our focus is not to match the status quo of international type design; our priority is to create an environment that allows the creation and production of independent, new, legible and permanently usable fonts.

Our teaching goals

Our aim was, and still is, that our courses should enable the participants to acquire foundational skills. This means skills in creation, development and production that may be applicable in various fields such as visual communication, signage as well as in the media and in the cultural sector. Since most of our students have a background in visual communication they are familiar with the questions and problems of real-world situations. Our course is a specialized postgraduate degree program, in which traditional forms and ideas are examined and questioned. In addition, new forms are created and compared with existing ones. The skills to be acquired can be extended through training in both traditional and contemporary methods. The aim of the course is to enable the participant to design and produce font families, in accordance with the design brief, at a professional level. Basically, the objective to be achieved during the course depends particularly on the developmental skills of the student (previous experience, personal commitment, time management, enthusiasm and also persistence).

Who are our students?

Most of our students are educated in graphic design. Some have an apprenticeship in manual typesetting. All come with excellent professional skills in typography. Quite a few are independent entrepreneurs, some even head larger reputable companies. The class size is well defined: we never admit more than 12 to 14 participants. Thus, we are sure to have enough time to discuss all issues individually. 47 course participants have received a certificate in the field of type design since 2006. In 2012 and also this year we offer a summer school course.

Courses, instructors and their skills

Core program: Type Design Prof. Hans-Jürg Hunziker (Auxerre) and Prof. André Baldinger (Paris) have been the instructors of the core program Type Design since the beginning of the CAS Type Design. The two facilitate the versatility of the projects whilst respecting the different requirements of the students. The two professors advise the students in terms of working methods and perspectives. They assist in defining the goals, providing suggestions and comments, so that these can be realized.

Prof. Hans-Jürg Hunziker describes it as follows: "The course teaches the foundations. It is not concerned with propagating recipes, exemplars and models, but with developing independent working methods and with imparting a visual culture of type design. Specific issues are addressed by the diversity of projects and

The students' typefaces are rigorously reviewed in individual meetings with Prof. Hans Jürg (middle) and Prof. André Baldinger (right), who make suggestions for improvements and corrections.

through the sharing of experiences. This benefits all." In relation to the content of our course, he adds: "The project work consists of an interaction, which depends essentially on the work of the participant, his continued independent development of the typeface and his research of cultural and historical backgrounds." The theoretical and practical part is what we undertake together:

- Understanding the morphology
- The interaction of black and white
- Optical phenomena
- Design and production, by hand and digital
- Introduction to the font editor Glyphs
- The impact of technological developments on the letterform
- Learning to see, perceive and judge

Prof. Hans-Jürg Hunziker, with whom we have collaborated excellently for over 10 years, retired at the end of 2013. His successor, Anton Studer, is a young and promising type designer from Zurich. With Prof. André Baldinger he will be responsible for future student projects.

Foundational courses:

– Calligraphy

This important foundational course for designing letterforms is managed by Catherine Wolff, a designer, calligrapher, and lecturer from Chicago / Basel. She also teaches at the Basel School of Design. Her lessons are about the practice and understanding of basic shapes, rhythms, as well as the diversity of forms in movements and detail. The following four letterforms are the core topics:

- Majuscule skeleton (Majuscule)
- Roman majuscule (Roman square capitals)
- Humanist minuscule
- Cursive

The participants learn and practice the sensitivity and ability to differentiate character proportions, line thickness and the various manifestations of strokes.

– Knowledge, History and Theory of Type

The course Knowledge, History and Theory of Type, is given by the author of this article, Prof. Rudolf Barmettler, who teaches typography and type at the ZHdK and is the director of the postgraduate courses in this field. The focus is on typographic terminology and classification systems to enable professional discussions with and among the students. Prof. Rudolf Barmettler teaches this course according to the specific periods of Latin type history from the ancient Romans to the private presses in the late 19th century. In addition, Swiss type design in the 20th century is another topic that is addressed—a topic central to Barmettler's own research.

The online archive that he has created, *www.swisstypedesign.ch*, is now available as a reference tool for researchers. It provides detailed information about numerous typefaces that have been created by Swiss designers during the 20th century.

The Museum für Gestaltung Zürich (Design Museum of Zurich) is housed in the same building as our school. It is the largest design museum in Switzerland and has a huge graphics collection, which can also be consulted by the students for research purposes.

Further modules

– History of Typesetting and Printing Technology:

The key themes in this module are type foundries, font management, font formats and technology. This module also provides students

At regular intervals, the typeface designs are discussed in group meetings. The students benefit from viewing other projects and the feedback from their fellow students.

with a detailed insight into the various analogue and digital typesetting systems, printing processes and printing materials. It is concerned with the different materials and technology-related influences that primarily in the past have affected the image of the letterform. Bruno Margreth, the instructor of this additional module, is a former compositor and therefore has personal working knowledge of these materials and the technological transformations that have occurred in this field. He later studied visual design, and now works as an internationally successful book designer in Zurich and Berlin.

– The Law on Fonts and Typefaces
This supplementary module, the Law on Fonts and Typefaces, includes basic rules in the field of intellectual property rights, design, trademark and competition law and regulation in the use of fonts. The person responsible for this module is Prof. Dr. iur. Mischa Charles Senn, Professor of Communication and Intellectual Property and Director of the Centre for Cultural Law at the ZHdK.

Master Course: MAS Type Design / Typography
Since 2007, we also offer MAS Type Design leading to graduation in type design at master's level. This course is part-time. Its duration is four semesters, comprising 600 lessons and is awarded with a total of 60 ECTS. Besides the core program type design for Print, it includes two other topics: type design with a focus on signage and wayfinding, and type design for screen media. For this, the students develop case studies and create new approaches that are related to existing typefaces. The knowledge about design history and theory is taught in different theory modules. In contrast to CAS Type Design, in which the creation of a single typeface is expected, the students have to create and produce a type family, with additional weights and italics. They also write a master's thesis in the cultural sector of the fields of history or theory of type. We now also offer the module Introduction to non-Latin Type Design, which is headed by Prof. Dr. Ross. It allows the students an insight into non-Latin type forms and their development.

What is probably unique in our courses is the fact that all lecturers speak German, French and English. Therefore, we have students from the French-speaking area (Suisse Romande and France), and students who prefer to communicate in English, or who depend on it as a lingua franca.

Our particular approach
We place a high value on drawing, lettering and craftsmanship. The preparatory exercises are carried out with precision and perfection. The instructors make corrections that must be completed by the students. The criteria specific to our school is that the created fonts have to be produced to the industry standard and must contain a minimal character set of at least 260 characters. At the end of the two semesters, the final typefaces are reviewed by the instructors. Nearly always final adjustments need to be undertaken by the students. The typeface will then undergo another review or reviews, depending on the number of necessary iterations. This process may even continue for another five months until the certificate (CAS) is awarded to the student. To earn the certificate, the typeface must be completed with great attention to detail and with high technical proficiency. Our goal is to create legible typefaces for body texts not graphic fonts for ephemera.

Katharine Wolff, teacher of calligraphy and lettering, provides support in discovering the form and correct sequence of movements in a student's trial with a broad nib of humanistic minuscule

Guest lecturers
Every month, professionals, either local or from abroad, are invited to give a lecture. They provide a deeper insight into the fields of type design, theory and technology.

Up to now we have been pleased to host the following guest lecturers (in alphabetical order): Peter Biľak / Prof. Erik van Blokland / Matthieu Cortat / Lucas de Groot / Walter Haettenschweiler / Prof. Sibylle Hagmann / Akiem Helmling / Otmar Hoefer / Prof. Thomas Huot-Marchand / Prof. Robin Kinross / Jérôme Knebusch / Henrik Kubel / Jean Larcher (†) / Bruno Maag / Martin Majoor / Hans Eduard Meier (†) / Peter Rosenfeld / Prof. Dr. Fiona Ross / Georg Salden / Ole Schäfer / Volker Schnebel / Prof. Fred Smeijers / Jeremy Tankard / Prof. Dr. Gerard Unger

From time to time, we offer two-day workshops for the graduates of our courses: for example, an Introduction to the Font Editor Glyphs with Rainer Scheichelbauer, or an Introduction to Arabic Type Design with Prof. Dr. Fiona Ross.

Further information: *www.zhdk.ch/furthereducation*
Information in German and French is available on: *www.typetypo.ch*

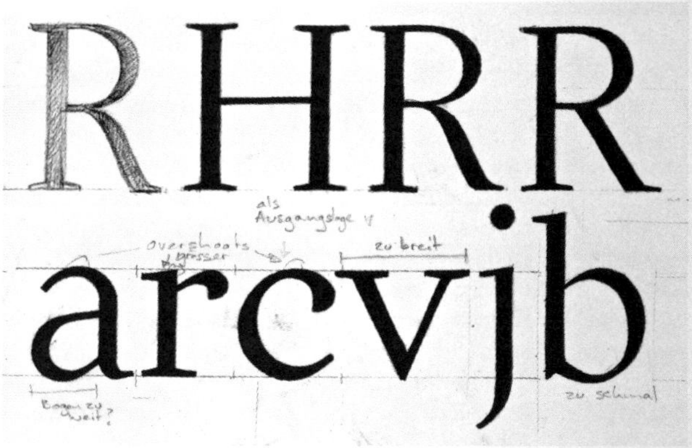

The students usually start their typeface projects with sketches in pencil or ink. Then the best forms are scanned and reworked in a font editor.

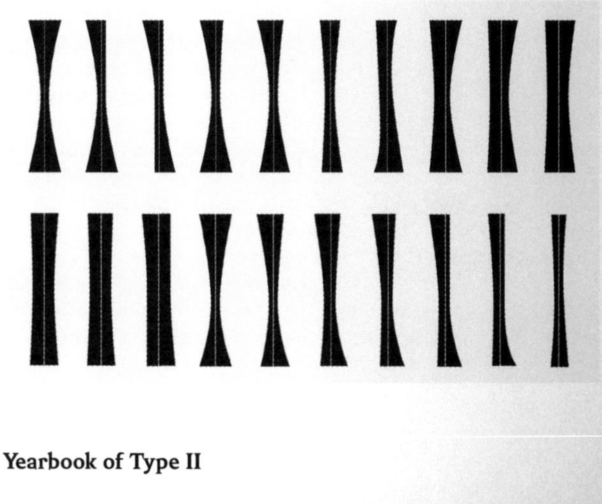

Often the students do some visual research to find the perfect form for their typeface project. This one is a study on the downstroke of an incised typeface.

Atelier National de Recherche Typographique

THOMAS HUOT-MARCHAND
ALICE SAVOIE

The Atelier National de Recherche Typographique (ANRT) was created in 1985 by the French Ministry of Culture and the Ministry of Economy and Finance, with the aim to "contribute to the development of type design and typography." Originally established at the Imprimerie Nationale (under the name of Atelier National de Création Typographique, 1985–1996), it was later transferred to the École Nationale Supérieure des Arts Décoratifs in Paris (1996–1999). Since 2000, the ANRT is based at the École Nationale Supérieure d'Art (National School of Art) in Nancy. Directed by Peter Keller from 1990 to 2006, it has trained about one hundred researchers and designers, contributing to the dissemination of French type design and typography, and to the structuring of typographic education in schools of art and design.

After a closure of six years, the ANRT reopened in October 2012 with a new course director, a new academic project and a new team.[1] In the meantime, a number of MA courses dedicated to type design and typography had flourished in Europe, reflecting the growing interest in this discipline. More importantly, French art schools had achieved that their DNSEP (Diplôme National Supérieur d'Expression Plastique) become a Master degree. Consequently, ANRT redefined its position in the field of French higher education to become a post-master course.

ANRT is now an established research unit within the Nancy School of Art. It welcomes new postgraduate students every year and brings together experts in the fields of type design and typography, with the aim to become one of the leading European centers for research and higher education in this area. The course develops a singular approach to typographic research, with a strong emphasis on connecting theoretical and practical work, as well as on developing long-term collaborations with world leading research laboratories in other areas, such as linguistics and computer sciences.

ANRT currently offers two kinds of curriculum: a taught "post-master" course, and PhD research programs in partnership with other institutions. The post-master course welcomes students for eighteen months, with the aim of developing a selfinitiated project dedicated to type or editorial design.[2] Some students might decide to pursue the research previously undertaken during their MA, while others choose to embark on an entirely new project. A strong connection between research and practice is required, and interdisciplinary projects are encouraged. Six students are recruited for each session and receive an allowance to support their research project. Students meet with the core teaching staff on a weekly basis and attend a range of seminars and workshops by guest lecturers throughout the year.

Recent projects developed at ANRT include: the design of a multiscript Tifinagh-Latin typeface family for road signage (Redouan Chetouan); the development of new tools and educational material for teaching schoolchildren how to read and write (Eloisa Perez); the creation of a typeface for the notation of Gregorian chant (Francis Ramel); and a theoretical research on the issue of consistency and aesthetics in typeface design, based on a study of nineteenth century British typefaces (Julián Moncada). These are only a few examples of the kind of projects that can be undertaken at ANRT, and we welcome a wide range of projects in the fields of typography and editorial design.

In some cases, students who wish to take their research further have the possibility to undertake a PhD in partnership with another research laboratory. Such research programs are necessarily more ambitious and must aim at providing an original contribution to research. They are co-supervised by ANRT and the partner institutions, and are carried out on the longer term, with PhD students typically working on their project for 36–48 months.

Developing interdisciplinary research
Interdisciplinary research is at the core of the new ANRT philosophy. As part of the Nancy Art School, we are involved in the dynamic ARTEM consortium[3], which brings together on one campus the ICN Business School, the Engineering School (École des Mines), and the Art School. Moreover, ANRT has been developing specific collaborations with a number of world leading research laboratories in the fields of linguistics and computer sciences such as ATILF (Analyse et Traitement Informatique de la Langue Française) and LORIA (Laboratoire lorrain de recherche en informatique et ses applications) as well as with internationally renowned institutions such as the Bibliothèque Nationale de France.

Two main lines of research are currently being developed, bringing together researchers, postgraduate students, teaching staff, and international guests with a specific expertise in the chosen fields. Some of the projects under way are described below.

Research *through* typography: designing typefaces to answer the specific needs of researchers
Several research communities make use of specific notation systems, thus requiring that dedicated typefaces (and, in some cases, dedicated layout engines) to be created to suit their particular needs. Since 1993 ATILF, a linguistic research lab based in Nancy (known for its *Trésors de la Langue Française* dictionary), is home to the Französisches Etymologisches Wörterbuch (FEW), an etymological dictionary of the Gallo-Romance languages. Its author, the Swiss philologist Walther Von Wartburg (1888–1971), brought together in this colossal treatise a detailed account of the origin, history and evolution of all words contained in the French lexicon, including dialects and Gallo-Romance languages such as Franco-provençal, Occitan and Walloon. The dictionary uses a specific phonetic alphabet and a complex syntax, which require the use of a dedicated typeface. The character set includes a few hundred glyphs, some of which combine up to three different diacritics with one base character.
To this day, no complete digital font exists that suits the need of the FEW, thus limiting its circulation. This has become particularly troublesome in recent years, as the entire content of the dictionary is currently being digitized in order to be made available online. To solve this issue, ANRT is currently working on developing a typeface family tailored to the needs of ATILF and its FEW. The project is also at the core of the PhD research carried out by Sarah Kremer at ATILF, who started out the project during her post-master course at ANRT and now benefits from a joint supervision from both institutions.

Another project currently under way is PIM (Project for Monetary Inscriptions), a research program carried out jointly by ANRT and the Numismatic Department of the Bibliothèque Nationale de France.[4] The aim of this project is to create a typeface that will include, in a unified style, all of the stylistic variants to be found ina collection of about 10 000 medieval coins and medals dating from the late antiquity to the early sixteenth century. As an example, nearly thirty different forms for the letter A have so far been catalogued, for a total of about 800 characters. Beyond the meaning of these inscriptions, the specific letter shapes used on the coins and medals carry valuable information for researchers regarding the period, the geographical location, and the techniques used to produce these artefacts. The design of a new typeface that will include

Eloisa Pérez: Apprentissage

all possible character shapes will greatly benefit curators at BnF and the wider research community in the field of numismatics, who will be able to catalogue and investigate these major collections in ways that were not previously possible.

Research for typography: working with computer scientists for the automatic reconstruction of document typography

The digitization of a printed document can be done in two ways: either by producing a static image of the text, which remains usually fairly faithful to the original, or through an OCR (Optical Character Recognition) process. The latter usually results in an editable and searchable text string, whose appearance tends to significantly differ from the original document. Generally speaking, the older the original document, the greater the difficulties encountered during its digitization and the OCR process. In contrast, an intermediate mode, which would preserve the typographic form of the original document while offering the dynamic capabilities of an OCR process, would enable the development of new levels of transcription. Such a process would combine the advantages of both the "image" and "text" modes, without their respective drawbacks. To tackle this technological challenge, ANRT teamed up with the LORIA computer science laboratory and the Engineering School in Nancy. Their joint research program, named "Re-Typograph," aims at automating a process for reconstructing typefaces "on the fly" based on photographs or scans of an original document, by using advanced image analysis and algorithmic reconstruction of letterforms. The process relies on various technologies, and is divided in several steps: the image of the original page is first automatically analyzed and segmented, and recurring components (such as all occurrences of the letter A) are identified and grouped into one ensemble. In a second step, an average letterform is deduced within each group based on all found occurrences of a letter. A series of algorithms enable the calculation of an average contour, as well as an average skeleton. A typeface can eventually be generated from this process; however, a number of solutions still remain to be found for automating issues such as letter spacing and baseline alignment. Such a project requires tackling some ambitious challenges, but as solutions are progressively being found, they reveal the several benefits to be drawn for digital humanities as well as for typeface design. This program benefits from the financial support of the French Ministry of Culture & Communication, and will be further developed in the coming years.

The examples above illustrate our approach to research, which favors a constant dialogue with other areas, while always placing design at the core of the process. Historical research is another component of the work we undertake in Nancy and that has not yet been addressed here.Among other projects, the ANRT archives, which document the work carried out by its alumnus between 1985 and 2006, are currently being digitized and catalogued. Their content is both significant and fascinating, since it documents a key period in the evolution of design processes and technologies. It also provides an insight into the working methods developed by prominent designers such as Franck Jalleau, Johanna and Peter Bil'ak, Andre Baldinger, and Alejandro Lo Celso, all ANRT alumni. The archives will soon be the subject of a thorough study and of a publication, and part of the 10,000 documents it contains will also be published online.[5]

Redouan Chetuan: Awal

1 The team includes André Baldinger, Roxane Jubert, Jérôme Knebusch, Charles Mazé, Philippe Millot, Émilie Rigaud, Alice Savoie (teaching staff) and Thomas Huot-Marchand (director).

2 The programme is open to graduates in visual communication and graphic design who have completed a master's degree or equivalent (Bac +5 in France), and to designers, architects, professionals, artists, academics and even engineers or teachers who possess an equivalent level of knowledge, regardless of their nationality. The main language is French, however one-to-one sessions can also be conducted in English. No age limit applies.

3 ARTEM stands for Art-TEchnology-Management.

4 Other partners for this project include the Institut de recherche sur les Archéomatériaux (IRAMAT) and the Centre d'Études Supérieures de Civilisation Médiévale (CESCM).

5 For more information: *www.anrt-nancy.fr*

1)

Sarah Kremer: FEW

1) Historical phonetic transcriptions used to typeset Romances languages

2) New typefaces especially designed for the FEW in use

3) New typefaces in use

2) Lt. TRANSIRE lebt weiter in siz. *trásiri* „eintreten" (schon 14. jh., RDR 2, 395), kal. apul. *trasire*, Matera *trasű́*, abruzz. *trasí*, neap. *trásərə*, Agnone *trasúye*, lomb. *strazí* „erstarren", sowie in ablt. wie neap. *trasonda* „vicolo, viottola" R 39, 471 (< -*eunda*), altumbr. *trasanna* „capanna" R 36, 249, apav. *tresenda* „durchgang" R 12, 20 (> it. *tregenda*), Brescia *tresánda* „viottola" KrJber 7, 126, vses. *tresenda* „fascia di terreno orizzontale", kors. *trasándu* „grosse menge" RLomb 49, 844. So lebt es als erbwort auch im gallorom. (oben I) und zwar in zwei bedeutungen. Die eine betrifft das erste spriessen der frisch angesähten getreidefelder im frühling (I 1). Diese bed. lebt ausschliesslich auf

3) (schon 14. jh., RDR 2, 395),
sire, Matera *trasű́*, abruzz.
trásərə, Agnone *trasúye*,
i „erstarren", sowie in ablt
sonda „vicolo, viottola" R31
da), altumbr. *trasanna* „cap
49, apav. *tresenda* „durchg

A little bit of everything — The making of FF Franziska

JAKOB RUNGE

This text reflects the initial design of FF Franziska, published in 2014, displayed on page 134 / 135.

The Design Process of a Text Face is Always the Same

Typefaces with serifs in Latin script haven't changed much since 15th century. After the transition from ancient calligraphers writing texts by hand to the production of texts using reusable typefaces, which began with the invention of movable type, our eyes had to be trained to read texts in a completely new way. Today, our eyes are still trained to read texts according to this standard. The American type designer Jonathan Hoefler (born in 1970) justifiably stated that "to some degree, any typeface has some historical elements.[1]" This is because in the 15th and 16th centuries in France and Italy, the typeface characters formed on lead type metal at that time are still in use today (Fig. 1). Some of the printer workers and punch-cutters during this time include Nicolas Jenson (1440–1480), Aldus Manutius (1450–1515) and Claude Garamond (1490–1561). To this day, their designed characters have only been altered minimally. It wasn't until two centuries later when the Dutchman Hendrik van den Keere (1540–1580) and William Caslon (1692–1766) from Great Britain designed new typefaces with a modern, but still similar style. The letter "A," however, still remained "A." Had the shape of the character been changed, it could have potentially hindered the illustrated text from being understood by the reader. Making a text more difficult to read is something that very few type designers would ever want to do, especially since the function of writing is for it to be read.

In short, typeface characters have always looked the same. Granted, there may be subtle, yet hardly noticeable variations or a more modern font design, but all of these typeface characters have remained within a strict construct. Jean François Porchez (born in 1964), who in 2002 designed the typeface "Sabon Next"— a more modern version of the "Sabon" typeface designed in 1967 by Jan Tschichold— stated that "in type design, you've done your best when people don't notice what you've done.[2]" In support of his statement, Porchez's typeface "Sabon Next" derives from a protected typeface called "Garamond" (1530 / 1602).[3]

The Design Process of Text Face is Always the Same, but Always Done Differently

It may seem unfortunate that historical developments have made type designers less needed in today's world, but these historical and continuing developments also paved their way. Over time, humans need things to evolve and change. In other words, in order for humans to redefine themselves as individuals, there needs to be a way for them to differentiate themselves between the past and the present. Lawyer and type designer Matthew Butterick (born in 1970) euphorically claimed that "solving problems is the lowest form of design. [Design] wants us to fill [unsolved problems] up, fill them with ideas, emotion and humor and warmth.[4]" These very emotions are exactly what enables us to visualize things in a new light – even when the function of the newly visualized design hasn't been changed. This is because "A" remains "A." This human drive to redefine the old and call it new—even though it may actually be restating the past—is what all humans do to keep art alive. This drive is what continues to make graphic design relevant in today's world.

Franziska's Construction: A Dynamically Static Design

Starting with the first text ever printed, typefaces imitated the character letters that were initially written by hand.[5] Even the humanistic roman typefaces designed during the Renaissance in the 15th and 16th centuries were based heavily on the idea that type comes from writing. When writing by hand, the quill or pen is held at a 20° angle. This automatically changed the letters' appearance and contrasting features, meaning that the characters could be written horizontally, vertically or asymmetrically (Fig. 2).[6] For Roman typefaces, however, it is the adaptation of the characters' asymmetry that differentiates them and makes them distinguishable.

During the 17th and 18th centuries, new printing and writing techniques were developed. Along with relief printing, whose prints appeared rougher in nature, fine intaglio printmaking techniques were established and calligraphy pens with broad nibs were introduced followed by those with pointed nibs. These developments made the various forms of text distinguishable. Contrast increased and the construction of the typeface class "Antiqua," or Roman typefaces, began to be developed more and more. Giambattista Bodoni (1740–1813) and Firmin Didot (1764–1863) were at the core of this development, designing roman typefaces during the Classical period (Fig. 3).[7]

The modern approach to classifying typefaces is based on these historical changes. For example, in Dutchman Gerrit Noordzij's (born in 1931) research, he focused on the differences in broad nib writing and pointed nib writing. By observing the form and shape of the writing styles, he was able to see how these writing styles were carried over to become typefaces without serifs, also called sans-serifs.[8]

The typeface Franziska has a design which, in its conceptional construction, is a unique composition blending the Renaissance and Classical script styles together. Although the typeface's finished design can be formally seen as a variation of the Roman type transitioning into the Baroque period, Franziska's construction follows the Renaissance script style while showing some resemblance to the Classical one. It almost seems as if the angled broad nibs outlined the characters and then pointed nibs traced over them, making the script thick. This can especially be seen with the letter "o." The letter's counter, or the space enclosed in the letter, follows the classical script style while, in comparison, the external space is slightly tilted (Fig. 4).[9]

Two additional character traits that Franziska has are its somewhat angular construction and exaggerated details. These traits give Franziska its unique character but are still easier to read in small point sizes. This way of designing typefaces was first done by the American type designer William Addison Dwiggins (1880–1956). In 1937, Dwiggins noticed how the soft facial features on marionettes became blurry the further one stood in the distance. However, from this distance, the facial features' exaggerated and ridged appearance also became soft again, just as it had appeared from up close.[10]

In other words, initially, Franziska's round serifs were teardrop shaped and ridged. The typeface's final design, however, was partly designed by the reader since the teardrop shape was perceived as being round again. Along with these details changing because of perception, as was the case with the ridged teardrops, the vertical serifs and the script's diagonals were bent slightly, as well. This gave the typeface a formal hybrid between soft, yet still ridged, and ridged, yet still soft (Fig. 5).

Franziska's Contrast: Slab and Serif

For a long time, from the 15th century to the mid-18th century, typeface designs were almost solely intended for book printing. They were, therefore, cut for text sizes and printed in these sizes, as well. It wasn't until the 19th century

Fig. 1: Adobe Jenson Pro, Bembo, Adobe Garamond, DTL Vanden Keere, Adobe Caslon, Akzidenz Grotesk.

Fig. 2: Natural angle and contrast in handwritten text.

during the industrial revolution when the typographical market began to grow considerably. Companies demanded for print workers to provide larger, bolder and more appealing texts for their advertising.[11]

For his typeface FF Tisa (2006), the Slovakian type designer Mitja Miklavčič (born in 1978) followed the concept of making typefaces with easy-to-read text sizes and interesting character traits which could be printed in larger point sizes. By combining the forms of contrast taken from Roman type and the slab serif, FF Tisa became an ideal serif typeface for digital media. To explain why this happened, Christoph Koeberlin (born in 1980), a font engineer for FontShop Berlin, said that the more elaborate the details are, the harder it is for the text to be optimized in small sizes and for low-resolution forms of media.

As a conceptual variational design of FF Tisa, Franziska follows a hybrid style taken from Roman type and slab serif. However, it does lean more towards the Antiqua typeface class and, in its differing font weights, has varying levels of contrast (Fig. 6). The difference in low-resolution line thickness gives FF Tisa her robust "slab serif" appearance but still has the preferred, easy-to-read contrast of Roman type.[12] Along with this contrast, the shape of Franziska's serifs also resembles a hybrid between Roman types and slab serifs. Whereas the Renaissance Roman types are known for their curved serifs, many people who use slab serifs prefer serifs that aren't curved. Although Franziska has serifs that are not curved, they do slightly curve at the stem (Fig. 7).

Franziska in Italics: Form Instead of Angles

The Italic text family plays a minor role in typography today and is clearly influenced by the upright Roman text family.[13] Nonetheless, Italics is sometimes used when text passages indicate that something is being emphasized. Initially, however, Italics formed its own typeface that developed from the Roman text family and was then transferred over into handwriting. With Italics being directly impacted by the smooth writing

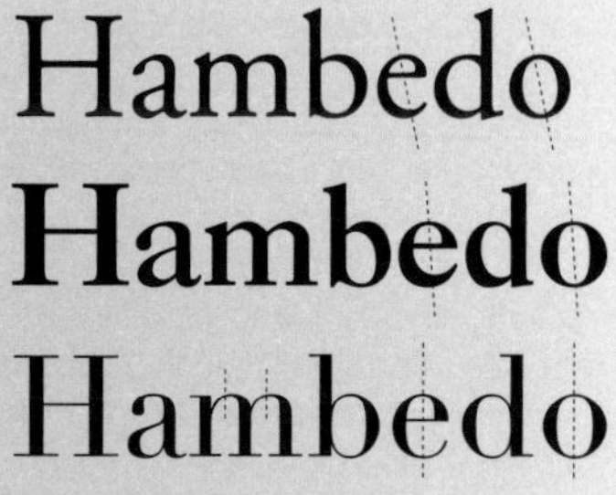

Hambedo
Hambedo
Hambedo

Fig. 3: Renaissance-Serif (Garamond), Transitional-Serif (Caslon) und Neo-Classical Serif (Didot).

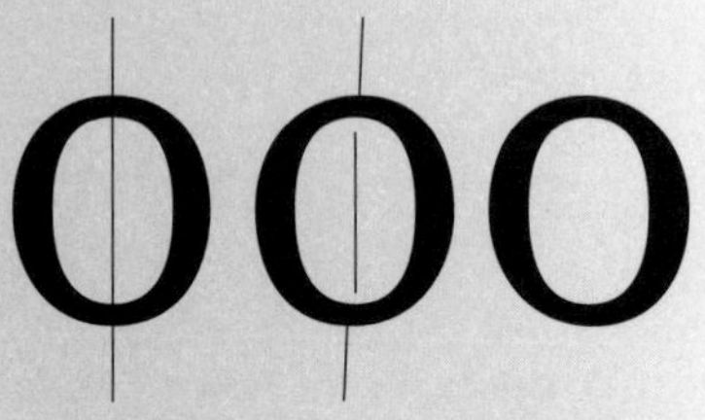

OOO

Fig. 4: Completely static shape, slanted outer shape and—for comparison—the mirrored outer shape.

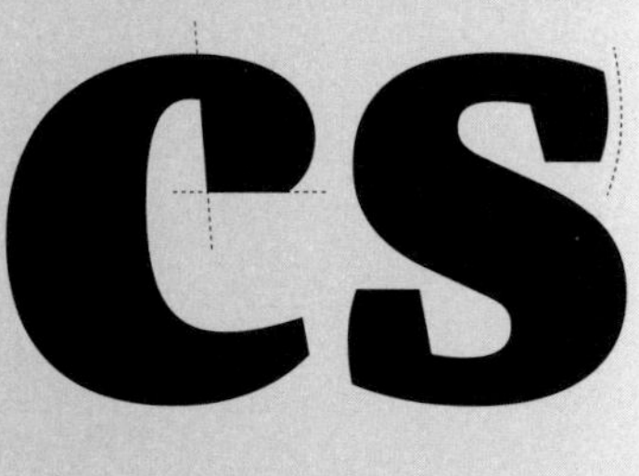

cs

Fig. 5: Edgy ball terminals and curved serifs.

Egypt Egypt
Egypt Egypt

Fig. 6: FF Tisa Pro in Regular and Extrabold weight plus Franziska in Book and Black weight.

rhythm of cursive, like in the handwritten manuscripts by ancient calligraphers, the word "cursive" gets its name from the Latin word currere, which could be translated as running. Traditionally in handwriting, many italic scripts are characterized by the unique styles and inclined angles seen in hand written calligraphy.

In Italics, Franziska shows both of the main aspects seen in cursive scripts: the angle and the form. Both of these characteristics are not seen when Franziska is written in Roman, or Regular. Franziska in italics offers a balance between a flowing and unique form and a visual relation to cursive. This is what allows the italic Franziska to function as an appropriate counterpart to its Roman design. While the first designs were a lot bolder, Franziska's final italic design went from 4 to 7.5 degrees. With its strong incline and upright form, this angle also gives the typeface its cursive-like character (Fig. 8).

For a long time, Capitalis Monumentalis, also known as square capitals, were the only capital letters used in cursive script, and they had a tendency to be confused with the lowercase letters in cursive. In order to make the difference between them more clearly, the Italic Franziska, in comparison its Roman design, used completely new forms of constructing digits and capital letters (Fig. 9). Ultimately, the Franziska typeface serves as a hybrid system since its Roman type design and italic design combine two different constructions in one optical text family.

Franziska's Font Weights: From Typeface to Text Family

Franziska already represents a small text family with its unique Italic design, Roman design and small capital letters. However, it is by Franziska's varying font weights that it becomes a multifaceted, typographical tool that can be used for a number of differing purposes.

Whereas lead typefaces had to be designed for each text size, texts today can be scaled continuously using desktop publishing. Almost every script designed for a computer typesetting challenges Franziska to function perfectly

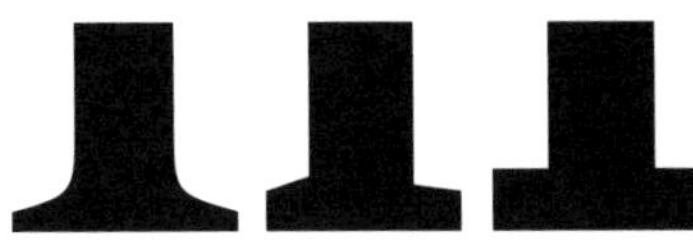

Fig. 7: Serifs of a Serif, Franziska and a Slab Serif.

laufen*laufen*
laufen*laufen*
laufen*laufen*
laufen*laufen*

Fig. 8: During its development, the inclination of the italic Franziska decreases more and more.

JeGupS§2
JeGupS§2

Fig. 9: Different construction in Roman and Italic.

compatible
compatible
compatible

Fig. 10: Antithesis

in both lowercase and capital letters. Therefore, this is an avoided hybrid. Despite this ambivalent outlook, the middle font weights are intended explicitly for continuous texts. Furthermore, the light and dark text values are used in large point sizes because, as typographer Reinhard Albers (born in 1954) so wonderfully explains, the font family's marginal figure, as well as the group's bold and light cuts offer a lot of capabilities.[14] In order for the "poles in the typographical refinement" to have varying capabilities within its own text family, Franziska's lightest sections lean towards a monolinear slab serif while the bold sections lean towards a Roman type that is rich in contrast. (Fig. 10)

Jan Gerner (born in 1982), also known as Yanone, explained the idea of the Trinity in three completely different typefaces in his Antithesis (2011): one regular typeface using serifs, one in Italics with digits and one in Bold without serifs (Fig. 11). The stark contrasts between these typefaces, however, are not compatible to each other. Each one is manually drawn and adapted to the font weight's character.

In order to make Franziska's design as useful as possible in its shift from slab serif to Roman type, each font weight's character is technically compatible.[15] In a clearly unusual fashion, Jérôme Knebusch (born in 1978) demonstrated in his typeface "Instant" (2005) that missing compatibility in a typeface can still support the individual font weight's character. When a text is to be given emphasis, it is done so by using angle (cursive) and weight (bold), which are both displayed on an axis pointed in reverse. In Italics, its thin, lively and handwritten appearance gradually becomes bolder and more static. There is no Bold Italic in this case (Fig. 12). From another standpoint, Franziska in Italics is in a system capable of interpolation: The thinnest sections in italics appear playful and lively while the font becomes softer and more compact with increasing font weight (Fig. 13).

Hybrid as a Method

Although the hybrid character of Franziska isn't obvious—possibly because it uses hybrid motives on so many levels that it appears to be an even patchwork—it illustrates the potential to create a new typeface using hybrid forms and capabilities. And that in times where everything has already been done before. In reference to the pros and cons discussed when designing new typefaces, Jan Middendorp stated "that alone is a legitimate function of type design: adding subtle new colors to the typographic palette."[16] In other words, if this is about leaving a mark in the world that everyone has already seen before, the combining of previous designs to create new ones may be a good way of going about it.

Ham Ham
Ham Ham

Fig. 11: Franziska Hair and Slab Serif (Archer) plus Franziska Black and Serif (ITC Galliard).

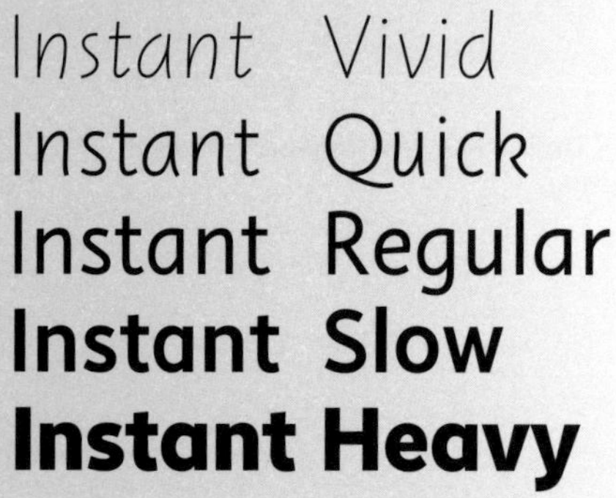

Instant Vivid
Instant Quick
Instant Regular
Instant Slow
Instant Heavy

Fig. 12: Instant

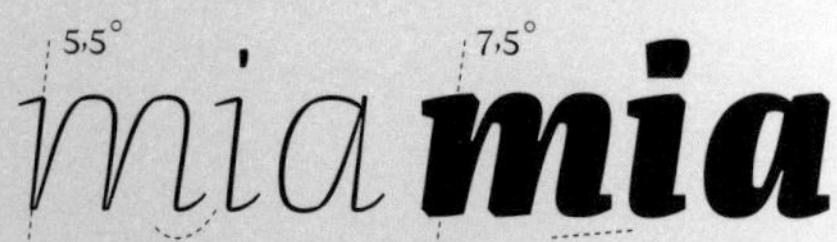

Fig. 13: Franziska Italic—Light and vivid, heavy and strudy

1 Hoefler, Jonathan in an interview with Ellen Lupton: *elupton.com/2010/07/hoefler-jonathan/* (13-02-01).

2 Shepter, Joe: Jean-Francois Porchez: *solutionpartners.adobe.com/ap/print/gallery/porchez/* (13-02-01).

3 The typeface Garamond was developed by Claude Garamond in 1530 for a size of 12pt to be used in hot metal setting and has been re-punch-cutted Jean Jannon in 1602. The digital transfer of this type family was done in many derivates, like the Stempel Garamond (1925) by Linotype, the ITC Garamond (1975) by Tony Stan or the Adobe Garamond (1992) by Robert Slimbach.

4 Butterick, Matthew: In his speech at TYPO Berlin Reversing the Tide of Declining Expectations, 2012: *typotalks.com/de/video/2012/05/19/matthew-Butterick-gegen-die-stromung-der-sinkenden-erwartungen* (13-02-01).

5 Cf. Middendorp, Jan: *Shaping Text*. BIS Publishers, Amsterdam, 2012, S. 76.

6 Cf. Frutiger, Adrian: *Der Mensch und seine Zeichen*. Marix Verlag, Wiesbaden, 2006, S. 88.

7 Cf. Bringhurst, Robert: *The Elements of Typographic Style*. Version 3.2, Hartley & Marks, Vancouver, 2008, S.12 f.

8 Cf. Noordzij, Gerrit: *The Stroke of The Pen*, Koninklijke Academie van Beeldende Kunsten, Den Haag, 1982.

9 A trick used by type designers like Fred Smeijers in his Quadraat (1992) or Peter Bil'ak in his Fedra Serif (2003); both arisen from the Dutch—very calligraphic based—style of designing type.

10 Cf. Beier, Sofie: *Reading Letters, designing for legibility*, BIS Publishers, Amsterdam, 2012, S. 92 f.

11 Cf. Cheng, Karen: *Designing Type*. German version, Verlag Hermann Schmidt Mainz, 2006, S. 14 f.

12 As uniting both, the Serif typefaces ans the Slab Serifs, Franziska was started under the heading "Slab & Serif"

13 The term "Serif" refers to the revival of Roman antiquity, and is also known as Roman. With its origin in Italy cursive type is described as Italic. After melting both models, today the term Roman is used for all fonts with serifs and a contrast in stroke, which in turn are designed as upright Roman or cursive/oblique Italic.

14 Albers, Reinhard: *Randfiguren*. Published in: *Slanted 16*, MAGMA Brand Design GmbH, Karlsruhe, 2012, S. 18 ff.

15 A font is compatible to an other when same characters are constructed with the same with the amount of anchor points and tangents. Virtually if the description of the shapes are managed with the same words.

16 Middendorp, Jan: *Shaping Text*. BIS Publishers, Amsterdam, 2012, 173.